Corporate Blogging FOR DUMMIES®

by Douglas Karr and Chantelle Flannery

WILEY

Wiley Publishing, Inc.

Corporate Blogging For Dummies®

Published by
Wiley Publishing, Inc.
111 River Street
Hoboken, NJ 07030-5774
www.wiley.com

WILEY

About the Authors

Douglas Karr has been working in the online industry for over 20 years. Douglas started in the newspaper industry, converting systems for use online, designing, and developing data warehouses, and automating marketing systems. He's worked with some of the largest media corporations in the world including Gannett, the *Toronto Globe and Mail*, and the *New York Times*.

Douglas relocated to Indianapolis seven years ago and has made a name for himself regionally with businesses looking to adopt technology and leverage it for marketing. Douglas worked with the Indianapolis Colts on the launch of Colts.net, the city of Indianapolis for their 2012 Super Bowl bid, and launched Smaller Indiana with co-founder Pat Coyle, the most successful socio-economic network in the state.

Douglas worked for ExactTarget for several years, growing their integration capabilities with clients and developing future visions of the application. ExactTarget has been named one of the top e-mail service providers on the planet. Douglas also developed the original concept for Compendium Blogware and as a shareholder remains active in the company's growth, support of its clients, and its ongoing vision.

In late 2009, Douglas launched DK New Media to assist Compendium and its clients with social media consulting and marketing automation. With Webtrends, ChaCha, and Walker Information as key clients, the company has grown. Douglas is now one of the most in-demand speakers on corporate blogging, social media, and search engine optimization in the country.

DK New Media assists large companies in the development and execution of online, search and social media marketing strategies to acquire measurable business results.

Douglas blogs daily at The Marketing Technology Blog (www.marketing techblog.com) that's continuously recognized as one of the top 100 blogs on the Internet.

Douglas is a single father of two — his son, William, a math and physics honors major at Indiana University Purdue University Indianapolis (IUPUI), and his talented and beautiful daughter, Katherine, who is still in high school. Douglas is also a United States Navy veteran of Desert Shield and Desert Storm.

For the past eight years, **Chantelle Flannery** has immersed herself in online marketing, working for small businesses, not-for-profits, and Fortune 500 companies. She currently works at a social media agency focusing on strategy, client relationships, and production management. Chantelle spent several years working at a SaaS organization managing blogging education, as well as gaining experience at a new media advertising agency developing and maintaining marketing plans.

Chantelle has focused on creating unique metrics for clients to measure and monitor ROI as it relates to corporate blogging. Her experience ranges from Web site creation to producing and directing short films. Chantelle has a passion for helping clients successfully execute their marketing initiatives and reach their target audience. To learn more about what Chantelle has to say, check out her blog at www.hertakeonmarketing.com.

Chantelle also helps to keep Douglas on track and out of trouble — for which he is eternally grateful.

The legal portions of *Corporate Blogging For Dummies* were written with the generous assistance of David Castor, partner and founder of Alerding Castor Hewitt. David provides counsel to entrepreneurs, venture capital firms, large businesses, and technology companies on licensing and computer law.

Authors' Acknowledgments

To properly acknowledge everyone on one page is nearly impossible but we're going to try.

For personal support, Douglas wishes to thank: William and Katherine Karr.

As a single father, finding quality time with my kids is already a challenge. During the duration of writing this book, family time was rare. Bill and Katie were not only forgiving, but cheered me on. I am truly blessed to have such incredible children. My parents, William and Carol Karr, and their parents, who inspired me to be an entrepreneur and find my own way in life. Brother (from another mother) Jason Carr and his wife, Chris, who would always take time to call or stop by to make sure I had my priorities in order. My best friend, Mike Moroz, and his wife, Wendy Russell, who called regularly from Vancouver and continued to cheer me on. My friends continue to amaze me with their selflessness and generosity.

Chantelle wishes to thank her husband, Nate Flannery.

For advice and friendship: Chris Baggott, Kyle Lacy, Lorraine Ball, Pat Coyle, David Castor, James Paden, Adam Small, Bill Dawson, Carla Ybarra-Dawson, Erik Deckers, Michael Reynolds, Jason Falls, Robby Slaughter, Jenni Edwards, Jeremy Dearringer, Kevin Bailey, Jascha Kaykas-Wolff, Justin Kristner, Matt Nettleton, Kristian Andersen, and Mark Ballard.

For the case studies, thanks to Webtrends, ChaCha, ExactTarget, Compendium, Tampa Bay and Company, Formstack, Roundpeg, Carhartt, Walker Information, Lifeline Data Centers, Alerding Castor Hewitt, Fairytale Brownies, Brandswag, Problogservice, Raidious Digital Content, MediaTile, Flexware Innovation, Tuitive, The Bean Cup Slingshot SEO, Lydia's Uniforms, Good Grape Blog, HH Gregg, Kristian Andersen and Associates, Bitwise Solutions, Paper-Lite, The Trustpointe, and Social Media Explorer.

Thanks to our clients (both DK New Media and Firebelly Marketing) and to our friends at Wiley for their patience while we worked through this book project.

Publisher's Acknowledgments

We're proud of this book; please send us your comments through our online registration form located at `http://dummies.custhelp.com`. For other comments, please contact our Customer Care Department within the U.S. at 877-762-2974, outside the U.S. at 317-572-3993, or fax 317-572-4002.

Some of the people who helped bring this book to market include the following:

Acquisitions and Editorial

Senior Project Editor: Christopher Morris
(Previous Edition: Jean Rogers)

Executive Editor: Amy Fandrei

Copy Editor: Brian Walls

Technical Editor: Bruce Castleman
(`www.blogbloke.com`)

Editorial Manager: Kevin Kirschner

Editorial Assistant: Amanda Graham

Sr. Editorial Assistant: Cherie Case

Cartoons: Rich Tennant
(`www.the5thwave.com`)

Composition Services

Project Coordinator: Sheree Montgomery

Layout and Graphics: Kelly Kijovsky

Proofreaders: Jessica Kramer,
Nancy L. Reinhardt

Indexer: Sherry Massey

Publishing and Editorial for Technology Dummies

    Richard Swadley, Vice President and Executive Group Publisher

    Andy Cummings, Vice President and Publisher

    Mary Bednarek, Executive Acquisitions Director

    Mary C. Corder, Editorial Director

Publishing for Consumer Dummies

    Diane Graves Steele, Vice President and Publisher

Composition Services

    Debbie Stailey, Director of Composition Services

Table of Contents

Introduction **1**

About This Book 1
Conventions Used in This Book 2
What You Don't Have to Read 2
Foolish Assumptions 2
How the Book is Organized 3
    Part I: Getting Started with Corporate Blogging 3
    Part II: Mapping Out and Implementing Your Corporate Blog 4
    Part III: Engaging Your Search Engine Optimization Strategy 4
    Part IV: Expanding Blog Posts and Promoting Content 4
    Part V: Measuring Success 4
    Part VI: The Part of Tens 5
Icons Used in This Book 5
Where to Go from Here 6

Part 1: Getting Started with Corporate Blogging 7

Chapter 1: Corporate Blogging from Soup to Nuts 9

Why Blogging Is Different than Your Web Site 10
    Understanding blogging as a communication tool 10
    Using blogging as a search engine marketing platform 12
    Recognizing blogging as an inbound lead strategy 12
Differentiating Corporate Blogging from Personal Blogging 13
    Putting a human voice on your marketing communications 14
    Speaking to your audiences 15
    Writing with a purpose to build a blog that sells 16
Defining Key Features of a Blog 16
    Basic user interface features of a blog 16
    Basic back-end features of a blog 18
    Expanding your blog's functionality 19
Recognizing the Benefits of Corporate Blogging 22
    Booking public speaking engagements 22
    Publishing opportunities online and offline 23
    Attracting leads through your blog 23
    Driving conversions online through blogging 23
Blogging: From Concept to Content to Conversion 24
    Establishing your strategy and goals 25
    Picking and training the blogging team 25
    Identifying platforms and resources 26
    Compiling search-engine-optimized content 27

Monitoring, measuring, and analyzing 28
Adjusting strategy or messaging 28

Chapter 2: Laying the Foundation for Blogging 31

Understanding What a Blog Can Do for Your Company 32
Defining a Blogging Strategy 35
Assemble your blogging team (and have backups) 37
Create a publication schedule 37
Determining Your Blog's Content 39
Putting your customers and employees first 40
Understanding industry expectations of corporate bloggers 40
Writing your company's blogging manifesto 43
Determining Who Owns Blogging 44
Letting leadership define the voice of your blog 44
Letting marketing define the voice of your blog 45
Understanding What to Publish on Your Corporate Blog 46

Chapter 3: Deciding On Your Blogging Goals .49

Setting Goals for Your Blogging Strategy 49
Defining the target audience for your blog 50
Estimating Your Return on Blogging Investment 52
Measuring conversions to improve your content 57
Reviewing objectives and measuring results 62
Identifying Marketing and Promotion Goals 63
Building authority in your industry 64
Search engine goals for keyword ranking 64
Setting Goals for Customer Relationship Management (CRM) 65
Using blogs to communicate with customers 66
Leveraging blogs for your organization's knowledge base 67
Sharing customer testimonials 67

Part II: Mapping Out and Implementing Your Corporate Blog 71

Chapter 4: Using a Domain That Matters for Your Corporate Blog . . .73

Integrating Your Corporate Identity into Your Blog 74
Bringing your brand and corporate identity
to your blog theme 76
Ensuring that your customers recognize your blog
as authentic 77
Personalizing your corporate blog with
portraits and biographies 79
Using Your Existing Search Engine Authority with Your Company
Domain 81
Controlling how a domain affects search engine authority 82
Using your existing authority to your advantage 84

Working to establish authority as fast as possible 84
Moving your blog and retaining authority.............................. 85
Selecting the Best Domain Structure for Your Organization 88
Understanding the pros and cons of subdomains...................... 89
Understanding the pros and cons of putting your blog
in a subfolder 90

Chapter 5: Choosing a Blogging Platform **91**
Determining Your Blogging Platform 91
Budget Considerations When Selecting Your Platform.................... 93
Building your blog on a solid infrastructure 94
Hiring a blog consultant to assist with your strategy 96
Choosing a Hosted, Self-Hosted, or SaaS Solution........................ 96
Advantages and disadvantages of hosted solutions 97
Advantages and disadvantages of self-hosted solutions 98
Advantages and disadvantages of SaaS solutions 100
Flexibility in Blog Templating Engines... 102
Balancing SEO and optimal design 104
Developing an attractive and readable blog theme 106
Enhancing Your Platform with Plug-Ins, Widgets, and Gadgets 108
Installing WordPress plug-ins and widgets on your
Hosted WordPress Blog 110
Selecting components that drive traffic to you, not away
from you 113
Testing components to measure performance........................ 115
Expanding Blogging Platforms Capabilities through Integration 117
Using a blogging platform's API 118
Automating and routing content through integration 119
Differentiating your feed from your blog with
integration tools 121

Chapter 6: Regarding Time, Resources, and Content **123**
Using External Content Resources 124
Winning back time with ghostbloggers and
professional content writers 124
Purchasing topical content to enhance your blog content........... 126
Hiring industry bloggers to write for your blog..................... 128
Owning Your Content.. 130
Exporting Content to Import It to Your Next Platform 131
Protecting Your Content... 132
Securing your corporate blog from hackers 133
Backing up your content regularly...................................... 133
Monitoring your blog to ensure it's up and running............... 133
Providing Legal Protection for Your Blog 134
What to do when your content is stolen............................... 134
Including all the required legal components......................... 135

Chapter 7: Working with Your Blogging Team **141**

Deciding Who Should Blog in Your Organization....................................141
Choosing the best bloggers...142
Recruiting bloggers: You'll be surprised at
who gets the results...143
Marketing with your bloggers 144
Setting expectations with your blogging team.................................145
Planning Your Content Strategy 146
Planning topics, owners, and timelines 147
Developing backup content strategies...147
Planning content for weekends and vacations 148
Developing an Education Program for Your Bloggers.............................151
Informing your bloggers of their responsibilities...........................153
Setting the vision for your bloggers 155
Balancing autonomy, individualism, and expectations 155
Monitoring Your Bloggers' Performance...156
Balancing content versus traffic and conversions 156
Using analytics to monitor specific bloggers 156
Dealing with poor blogging performance 159
Motivating and Rewarding Your Bloggers...159
Moving a blogger from behind the keyboard to
in front of the podium..160
Developing a performance-based rewards program
for your blog 160
Recognizing bloggers without breaking the bank 160

**Part III: Engaging Your Search Engine
Optimization Strategy** *163*

Chapter 8: Making the Most of Search Engines **165**

Understanding How Search Engines Find Your Content 166
Building your robots file to allow search engines permission.....168
Publishing a sitemap that directs search engines properly.........170
Setting content priorities in your sitemap.......................................171
Implementing canonical URLs in your post pages 173
Using Keywords Correctly...176
Using page components to emphasize important keywords.......176
Evaluating keyword competitiveness 179
Finding long-tail keywords that drive relevant traffic..................180
Researching keywords 180
Improving Your Blog's Keyword Content...185
Adding keywords to meta descriptions 185
Modifying existing posts to increase their
search engine ranking...186
Optimizing your content for local searches......................................186

Registering Your Blog with Search Engines 187
  Verifying your blog is located and indexed by search engines ...187
  Identifying problems in Webmasters and how to correct them....188
  Monitoring your ranking and how you are being found 190
Putting Your Business on Map Results for Regional Searches..............191
  Registering your business with local search on
    Google, Bing, and Yahoo! 193
  Adjusting your location on the map to ensure
    customers can find you...193
  Promoting your entry with customer reviews 194
  Using your entry to publish and offers 195

Chapter 9: Writing Content That Drives Search Engine Traffic.....197
Writing Post Titles That Make Searchers Click 198
  Avoiding link baiting...200
  Getting traffic from the search engine results page....................201
  Formatting page titles with post titles 204
  Using keywords effectively in page and post titles 206
  Repeating yourself and reusing material.....................................207
Using Keywords in Content to Get Indexed Properly
  in Search Results...209
  Using the correct balance of keywords and content 210
  Finding synonymous keywords and phrases...............................212
Driving Home the Message with Images and Diagrams.........................213
  Using alt tags effectively for image searches and
    keyword placement...215
  Using representative images for improved comprehension........216
  Effectively sizing and formatting images for your page...............216
Formatting Your Posts for Better Comprehension 220
  Considering the importance of whitespace.................................221
  Using bulleted and ordered lists...221
  Sizing paragraphs for easy scanning...221
Writing High Converting Content 222

**Part IV: Expanding Blog Posts and
Promoting Content.. 225**

Chapter 10: How to Blog without Writing 227
Spotlighting Other Experts with a Guest Blogging Program................227
  Finding industry bloggers to guest write on your blog...............229
  Trading posts with other blogs and requesting
    permission to guest blog..233
  Soliciting industry experts to reach their audience....................234
Promoting Your Customer's Voice for Maximum Impact 235
  Writing effective customer testimonial blog posts 235
  Automating customer testimonials directly into blog posts........237
  Promoting vendors and partners to build your authority 238

Keeping Your Content Alive with Comments 239
    Using comments as a measure of engagement 240
    Moderating comments to add value and avoid spam 240
    Deciding whether a third-party comment service
        is right for your blog 241
    Encouraging employees to comment 242
Incorporating a Multimedia Strategy to Add Personality 243
    Leveraging audio technologies for audible learners 243
    Incorporating video for increased engagement 245
    Hosting options for audio and video 247

Chapter 11: Marketing and Promoting Your Blog 251

Using RSS to Syndicate Content 252
    Syndicating content to your corporate home page 252
    Keeping static pages fresh with syndicated excerpts 253
    Aggregating RSS into server-side pages 254
Getting Engaged in the Blogosphere to Attract Attention 256
    Using a feed reader to organize and follow industry blogs 257
    Interacting with other blogs through guest posting
        and comments 258
    Respectful dissent to attract and build readership 259
    Responding effectively to negative criticism 259
Integrating Your Blog into Other Social Media to Expand Your
    Readership 260
    Using URL shorteners 261
    Syndicating your blog in Twitter 262
    Syndicating your blog in LinkedIn and Plaxo 264
    Integrating your blog into Facebook profiles and Fan Pages 265
Promoting Your Posts through Social Bookmarking 267
    Understanding social bookmarking and its impact
        on search and traffic 268
    Automated posting to social bookmarking 268
    Guerilla marketing and social bookmarking 269
Combining E-Mail and Blogging for Better Marketing 270
    Using advanced e-mail service features to automate content
        to e-mail 271
    How to automate RSS to e-mail with MailChimp 271
    How to automate RSS to e-mail with ExactTarget 272
    Driving e-mail readers to your blog 274
    Promoting e-mail subscriptions on your blog 275
    How to automate RSS to e-mail with FeedBurner 275

Part V: Measuring Success **277**

Chapter 12: Imagining Your Blog as a Sales Funnel **279**

Using Your Blog as a Sales Funnel..280
    Optimizing conversions from the search engine results page.....281
    Understanding rank and its effect on traffic................................282
    Using Google Webmasters to identify search engine
      placement for keywords...285
Measuring Engagement and Conversions on Your Blog 287
    Understanding bounce rate and its effect on your blog 288
    Measuring trends versus instances...289
    Comparing your analytics to industry results 292
    Differentiating traffic sources and business benefits....................294

Chapter 13: Directing Your Readers through Calls-to-Action **297**

Understanding Why You Need Calls-to-Action 297
Designing Calls-to-Action That Readers Will Click...............................298
    Finding images that draw attention to your call-to-action 300
    Keeping it simple; writing call-to-action content.......................300
Measuring Click-Through Rates on Calls-to-Action................................301
    Implementing onclick events and campaign codes for
      tracking...302
    Building goals in analytics 305
    Tracking and reporting calls-to-actions 307
Testing and Improving Your Calls-to-Action Click-Through Rate 308
    Understanding A/B testing versus multivariate testing................309
    Implementing simple A/B tests with your calls-to-action.............309
    Analyzing results and optimizing calls-to-action 310
    Targeting calls-to-action 310
Dynamically Displaying Calls-to-Action to Increase
  Click-Through Rates 312
    Increasing click-through rates with relevant calls-to-action........313
    Integrating third-party ad serving systems for your
      e-commerce blog..313
Understanding Where Readers Click on a Web Page............................314
    Laying out your blog's content to impact retention
      and conversion..314
    Implementing heat-maps to monitor where readers click 315
    Figuring out what elements are important...................................317

Chapter 14: Leading Your Readers through Landing Pages **319**

Designing a Landing Page That Closes the Conversion..........................320
    Designing the path from a call-to-action to a landing page..........320
    Checking out the elements of an effective landing page
      strategy..321
    Knowing your landing page goals and tactics..............................322
    Laying out your landing page..322

Narrowing the Focus with Your Landing Page's Content......................323
  Understanding how much information is enough 324
  Trading information for benefits to capture inbound
    marketing leads 325
Capturing the Right Amount of Info on Your Landing Page..................329
  Requesting the right amount of information.............................330
  Integrating your landing pages with your CRM 332
  Using third-party form solutions to capture information...........332

Chapter 15: Measuring Success with Analytics **337**
  Implementing an Analytics Solution That Works 338
  Translating Statistics to Improve Your Strategy 339
    Tracking visits and visitors 340
    Tracing site references and visitor traffic 341
    Measuring pageviews and bounce rates.................................343
    Evaluating overall performance..344
    Assessing visitors' language and platform needs.....................346
  Translating Traffic Sources to Opportunities 347
    Viewing traffic sources...348
    Calculating social media as a referral source 349
  Observing Trends and Opportunities in Reporting Data 351
  Setting Goals in Analytics to Measure Conversions................................353
    Capturing click events in Google Analytics 354
    Developing custom reports for conversion tracking 355
  Determining the Value of a Blog Post for Your Company 356
    Measuring lead-to-close ratios with sales................................357
    Measuring leads coming from your blog 358
    Measuring conversions from blog to landing pages 359
    Tying it all together — estimating the sales value of
      your blog and each post..360
  Monitoring Shortened Links with Third-Party Applications.................360
    Setting up backtweets to alert your company of mentions.........361
    Monitoring shortened links more effectively with bit.ly 361
  Measuring Your Feed's Consumption and Number of RSS
    Subscribers 362
    Setting up your blog and its feeds on FeedBurner 363
    Modifying your blog's theme to integrate FeedBurner.................364

Part VI: The Part of Tens..**365**

Chapter 16: Ten Ways to Promote Your Blog **367**
  Publishing Posts on Your Home Page...367
  Publishing Your Blog's Link in E-Mail Signatures....................368
  Promoting Your Blog in Business Cards......................................370

Publishing Posts to Twitter..370
Publishing Your Blog in Facebook 370
Publishing Your Blog in LinkedIn 372
Publishing Posts in Company Publications......................373
Promoting Your Blog in Other Blogs' Comments............373
Publishing and Distributing Your Corporate Blog in Print 374
Submitting Your Blog for Awards and Recognition 375

Chapter 17: Ten Ways to Grow Your Audience.................377
Buying Visitors with Pay-Per-Click...................................378
Paying for Blog Reviews...379
Commenting on Other Industry Blogs 381
Trading Posts and Guest-Blogging 381
Promoting Other Blogs 382
Driving Traffic from Social Media.....................................382
Link Baiting Traffic to Your Blog 383
Holding Promotions and Giveaways 385
Offering E-books, Whitepapers, and Case Studies 386
Syndicating Your Blog Everywhere....................................386
Integrating Word-of-Mouth Widgets in Your Blog.................388

Chapter 18: Ten Ways to Reignite Old Content.................389
Promoting Old Content in New Blog Posts.........................389
Promoting Old Content in Other Blogs' Comments...................391
Reviving Old Content with New Comments 391
Modifying Post Titles 392
Modifying Meta Descriptions 393
Modifying Content with Keyword Enhancements...................393
Removing Dates from Blog Posts 394
Submitting Excerpts to Social Networks 395
Tagging Content and Building Tag Clouds 395
Promoting Internal Search on Your Blog............................396

Index.. *397*

Introduction

*O*nce a hobby for writers on the Internet, blogging has evolved over the years into a mature strategy with incredible platforms that now support enterprise corporations. Blogging has every element needed to develop a great online presence. Blogging is an exceptional strategy for search engine optimization as well as a solid social media strategy for businesses to safely engage in.

Corporate blogging, however, requires a much different strategy than personal blogs or publication blogs. The objective for a corporate blog is to build a company's online authority by using search engines and by acquiring a positive reputation. Ultimately, this will lead to customer acquisition and improved retention.

Most corporate blogs fail. As Seth Godin states in his book, *Linchpin: Are You Indispensable?* (Portfolio, 2010), "most corporate blogs suck." If you don't want your corporate blog to fail, you'll need to develop a strategy before you ever publish your first blog post. You'll also need to stick by that strategy and build momentum over time. Your journey won't be easy, but it will be fruitful in the end.

Corporate blogging not only transforms your company's online presence, but it can also transform your company's culture and vision by providing your employees with the spotlight they deserve.

About This Book

Douglas Karr and Chantelle Flannery have developed strategies for, educated, and consulted with more than 200 companies throughout the country on their corporate blogging programs. They've worked with companies with a single employee to companies with thousands of employees throughout North America.

This book lays the foundation for a great corporate blogging strategy by ensuring that your company invests in the right platform, optimizes your blog to ensure it's found by search engines, educates you on keyword research, provides you with content strategies, and helps you to develop your sales funnel to turn visitors into customers.

In short, this book shows you how to leverage blogging in order to grow your business online and off.

In its entirety, this book can take you from the selection of a platform all the way to optimizing landing pages to increase conversions. You need not read every section. If you're an experienced blogger and already have a corporate blogging strategy underway, you can skip directly to the topics that are important to you.

Conventions Used in This Book

If the value of an attribute is in normal type, you enter it exactly as shown. If it's in italic, it's only a placeholder value, and you need to replace it with a real value. In the following example, you replace *myownimage* with the name of the image file you intend to use:

```
<IMG src="myownimage">
```

Whenever you see the URL for one of the top sites we've tracked down, it appears in a special typeface within the paragraph, like this: www.dummies.com. Or it may appear on a separate line, like this:

```
www.dummies.com
```

What You Don't Have to Read

The content of this book is written so that any section can be read without having to read the book all the way through. While we believe every ounce of this book will add value to your corporate blogging strategy, we recognize that you probably already have a pile of work to do and need to jump directly to the areas you need assistance with first.

Foolish Assumptions

You speak English; otherwise, you'll need to talk to the Dummies folks about translated versions of the book.

You're not a tech genius but you have basic computer skills, and you've operated a browser and experienced the Web before. You have a basic understanding of Web sites, marketing, and analytics, and an interest in blogging to drive leads from the Web into your company's sales funnel.

If you're the Chief Operating Officer of a large organization, this book helps you understand what an effective blogging strategy can provide your company. If you're an entrepreneur and a "do-it-yourselfer," this book gets down enough details enough for you to plan, select, deploy, measure, and improve your company blog all by yourself.

If you've already got a blog and are getting some lackluster results, this book will help you to optimize your blogging platform and develop a plan for improvement.

Other great Dummies books make great companions to *Corporate Blogging For Dummies*, including *TypePad For Dummies, WordPress For Dummies, Search Engine Optimization All-in-One For Dummies, Twitter Marketing For Dummies, Facebook Marketing For Dummies, Web Marketing For Dummies, Blogging For Dummies,* and *Social Media Marketing For Dummies.*

How the Book is Organized

Corporate Blogging For Dummies is organized so that you can quickly find, read, and understand the information you want. The book is also organized so that if you have some experience with blogging, or want to deepen your knowledge of a particular topic, you can skip around and focus on the chapters that interest you.

The chapters in this book are divided into parts to help you zero in, quickly and easily, on the information you're looking for.

Part 1: Getting Started with Corporate Blogging

Blogging has evolved from a hobby into a critical component that's being leveraged by the best and brightest companies in the world. From the largest companies to one person shops, blogging has become the centerpiece of building and leveraging online marketing to improve communications and drive business. Part I of the book describes all of the advantages of blogging, from search engines to social media, and helps you visualize how an effective corporate blogging strategy can be leveraged to improve your business.

Part II: Mapping Out and Implementing Your Corporate Blog

Most corporate blogs fail and are abandoned because companies didn't have the right platform, the appropriate resources, or set the right expectations on how their program would work. This part helps you to develop your strategy and implement a solid plan of attack to fully leverage blogging for business results.

Part III: Engaging Your Search Engine Optimization Strategy

As more and more businesses and consumers research online, the search engine has become the gateway to seeking information, finding solutions, and engaging with the businesses that are present. Blogging has all the elements of an effective search engine strategy — the ability to easily produce content.

An effective corporate blogging strategy produces recent, frequent, and rich content that can be easily found by search engines and presented to businesses and consumers when they are looking. In marketing, that's the right message at the right time. If your business isn't competing in search, you're losing a huge acquisition opportunity. This part helps you understand how search engines work, why blogging helps, how to optimize your blog, and how to target the right keywords to capture the attention of the right audience.

Part IV: Expanding Blog Posts and Promoting Content

LinkedIn, Twitter, Facebook, e-mail marketing, online video, word-of-mouth marketing . . . the job of the online marketer has become extremely demanding and complex. This part of the book shows you how to deploy a blog and fully leverage syndication to expand the footprint of your blog beyond your own domain. Automation, integration, and providing a path of engagement back on your blog is the most effective means of maximizing results while reducing your workload.

Part V: Measuring Success

Too often, companies don't have an effective strategy for measuring success. This part of the book provides you with all the information you need to fully leverage analytics as part of your corporate blogging strategy. Analytics not only provides you with the reporting necessary to measure an effective corporate blogging strategy, it also provides you all the behavioral data you need to improve your blogging and increase the return on investment over time. This part shows you how to measure and improve your strategy.

Part VI: The Part of Tens

A requirement for the *For Dummies* series is the Part of Tens — reference guides for you that break down some pretty complex stuff about corporate blogging in easy-to-digest sections.

This part of the book should be earmarked, written on, highlighted, and checked every week as you launch your corporate blogging strategy. These are simple and effective lists of ideas and techniques that will promote your blog, acquire new readers, and continue to improve overall business results. Your corporate blogging strategy doesn't stop at publishing content, this part helps you take it up a few notches!

Icons Used in This Book

The icons in the margins of this book point out items of special interest. Keep an eye out for them — they're important.

Psst! Listen, pal, we wouldn't tell just anybody about this, but here's a way to make things a bit easier or get a little bit more from the material.

Time to tiptoe on eggshells. Make one false step, and things can get pretty messy.

You don't really need to know this stuff, but we just like to show off sometimes. Humor us.

Well, of course, it's all memorable material. But these bits are ones you'll especially want to keep in mind.

Where to Go from Here

Do you remember the first time you picked up the phone at work or the first message you sent out with your company e-mail? Publishing your first blog post will be just as exciting. Over time, just as sending e-mail or answering the phone became natural and second nature, so will managing and writing for your blog.

Remember that you're not alone and that the online marketing landscape continues to change. During the writing of this book, the search engines continue to change their algorithms to find and present the best content on the Web, Twitter continues to enhance its offerings, Facebook has build out new widgets and integrations, and mobile devices continue to skyrocket in popularity.

This book helps you deploy and leverage a world-class blogging strategy. Your business will prosper, your clients will appreciate your transparency, and your employees will enjoy getting their voice and expertise out to the masses. Don't stop there, though. Follow industry blogs, attend conferences, and continue to educate yourself on what's coming next.

Douglas and Chantelle have set up a site, Corporate Blogging Tips (www.corporatebloggingtips.com), an e-mail newsletter, Twitter (@corpblogging), and Facebook pages to keep you up-to-date and answer any questions you might have.

Get started or improve your corporate blog. We expect big things from you and so does your organization — growing your business online and obtaining great search engine ranking is very important.

Let's blog!

Part I
Getting Started with Corporate Blogging

The 5th Wave   By Rich Tennant

"It's web-based, on-demand, and customizable. Still, I think I'm going to miss our old sales incentive methods."

In this part . . .

This part introduces corporate blogging and the value it provides your organization — from customer service to customer acquisition and sales to an overall Web presence.

Chapter 1 discusses corporate blogging in general terms, laying the foundation for the rest of the book and your team's blogging efforts. You discover the key factors that set corporate blogging apart from everyday corporate Web sites.

Chapter 2 shows you how to make sense of blogging for your organization — everything from who owns the program to what content to publish on your corporate blog. Most importantly, you find out about setting expectations with the blogging participants from the start to create accountability from the beginning.

Deciding your blogging goals is the focus of Chapter 3. All good marketing efforts start with goals for short and long term business results. After reading this chapter, you'll be able to successfully set measureable goals for marketing and promotions, public relations, and customer relationship management.

Chapter 1

Corporate Blogging from Soup to Nuts

In This Chapter

▶ Defining corporate blogging

▶ Delineating a corporate blog from a Web site or a personal blog

▶ Surveying the key features of a blog

▶ Understanding the benefits of a corporate blog

▶ Outlining the best ways to create a successful corporate blog

*W*hat is blogging? Blogging is the ability to publish articles via the Web, using platforms that are simple to use. These articles are published in descending order, providing the most recent articles first. Blogs make content easy to publish and easy to find. You read about the distinctive blog characteristics throughout this book.

As social media continues to rise in both popularity and demand, businesses are compelled to join this incredible marketing and communication movement. Blogging is the centerpiece of a great social media strategy because it can lead Internet traffic from various sources into your sales funnel.

Blogging isn't simply about garnering more online prospects, though. Blogging is a strategy that has enormous benefits to organizations well beyond prospecting. Blogging can help leaders communicate the vision of their company to employees, prospects, and shareholders. Blogging can provide a great knowledge base to support your customer service department. Blogging can also spotlight the talent in your organization, giving your company authority in your industry.

Why Blogging Is Different than Your Web Site

Your Web site is an essential part of your online marketing presence. Consumers expect certain standard conventions and user experiences from business Web sites: Web sites tend to be online marketing brochures, with standard pages for information about the company, products, and services.

If your Web site is your marketing brochure, then your blog is your public relations representative. It's the face and voice of your business beyond the marketing mumbo jumbo that's written into a product page. Your public relations representative is there to talk about the company, answer questions, and put some personality into your brand.

Your blog can be the face and voice of your company. Your blog also provides a fantastic medium to introduce talent from deep within your organization. The talent within your company is one of your biggest investments and the largest differentiator between you and your competitors.

More and more customers are demanding (and rewarding) companies who have a social media presence online. Blogging is a perfect platform for engagement; it's a safe place where your company can manage the conversation and leverage the medium to drive business. Your company can own the content, control the message, and respond effectively through a corporate blog.

Understanding blogging as a communication tool

Companies have several mediums at their disposal to communicate with their audience. A Web site is your well-produced brochure. E-mail is an opt-in communication that is timely or relevant. Forums that allow members to help other members are effective for companies to deploy. Twitter offers the opportunity to update followers 140 characters at a time.

There's nothing on the market quite like a blog, though. A blog allows your company to lead the conversation with a great blog post and manage the conversation that follows. That conversation can be found through search and syndicated throughout the Web for anyone to find and read.

Companies are using blogs to control their messages and responses rather than waiting for traditional media to portray their companies. Public companies are using blogs to communicate to shareholders. Large companies are using blogs to communicate the direction of the company to employees — from the CEO to the most junior hire.

Of course, the most popular use of blogs as a communication medium is to acquire inbound marketing leads and support clients. (Figure 1-1 shows HP Community, a collection of blogs from HP employees focused on their customers.)

Your customer service department answers calls and responds to e-mails on a daily basis. This is one-to-one communication and is most likely the most expensive form of communication your company enlists. Imagine if your customer service department, instead, wrote a blog post with a great response to each support question. Clients could help themselves online via an incredible knowledge base that's categorized, indexed, and easily searchable.

Figure 1-1:
HP leverages blogging to effectively communicate with the industry, the media, its employees, and avid customers.

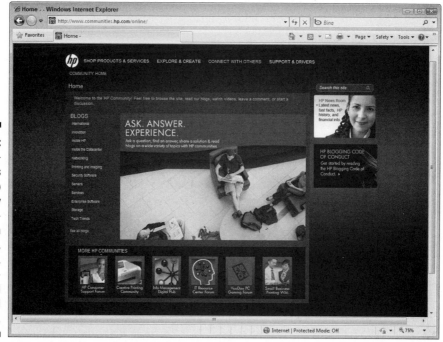

Using blogging as a search engine marketing platform

According to Nielsen, there are over 10 billion searches on search engines each month in the U. S. This number continues to grow, but that's about 33 searches per day per American! Google leads the search market with 66 percent of all searches. As the content on your blog grows, so does the *farm* of content that is harvested by search engines and the opportunity for your company to be found in those searches.

Consumers and businesses use search engines to research their next purchasing decision, so it's essential that your business be found if you wish to capitalize on this traffic. Optimizing Web sites in order to be found organically on search engines can be a costly (but still worthwhile) investment. Because your Web site is typically a set number of pages, each page must be carefully optimized and the number of keywords you're optimized for is limited.

Blogs, on the other hand, provide a means for businesses to write limitless quantities of content and target countless combinations of keywords. Each post that you publish is aggregated on category and tag pages and published as its own page, providing several ways for search engines to find and index the content. Publishing a single blog post per day, your blog can provide thousands of pages that attract search engine traffic found organically through countless numbers of searches for relevant keywords.

Search engines want to provide relevant content to search engine users, so they identify sites that are relevant, updated frequently, and are popular. Blogs have the ability to be relevant, can be updated frequently, and can gain major exposure and popularity. It's no coincidence that blogging has become an effective search engine strategy for businesses!

Recognizing blogging as an inbound lead strategy

Inbound marketing is a strategy that drives prospective customers to your business without you having to send resources out to contact them. That is, the prospective customer calls your business, contacts your business through contact forms or e-mails, or even completes a purchase online. Inbound marketing is an effective means of marketing because it drives prospects to you, which is cost effective and typically results in a very high conversion rate.

Conversions take time, though. Blogging often takes more time than a simple pay-per-click or e-mail marketing campaign because your blog needs time to build traffic, authority in its industry, and trust with its readers. Unlike a pay-per-click or e-mail campaign, though, a blog post doesn't have an expiration date. A great blog post can continue to acquire new customers long after it's written. As a result, the long-term return on investment on blogging is typically much higher than short-term campaigns.

Blogging is a marathon, not a sprint. The irony of corporate blogging is that many great corporate blogs are abandoned because companies fail to see results a month, two months, or six months into their blogging program. The company also doesn't take into consideration the other advantages of blogging and the accompanied savings.

Unless you decide to remove your blog, your content will never expire, it can continue to be found in search results and continue to drive customers. When you design your blogging strategy, be prepared for the long haul — possibly writing posts for the next year to see where it takes your company!

Do not to trade in your other marketing efforts for blogging. If you have a positive return on investment from other marketing strategies, continue them. Incorporating a blogging strategy in addition to those other strategies provides a comparison of which strategies produce the best leads at the lowest cost per lead.

Differentiating Corporate Blogging from Personal Blogging

As personal blogs gained momentum as trusted resources and a great search engine strategy, companies took notice and began adopting blogging as well. Early corporate blogs looked very much like their personal predecessors, except the great content of the original was replaced by marketing-speak. These corporate blogs did not perform well and most corporate blogging strategies were abandoned altogether.

It's important to recognize the difference between a corporate blog and a personal blog or other published blog, though. Personal blogs are often used to provide one's opinion or personal experience. Personal blogs can be controversial, not safe for the workplace, and aren't necessarily focused at building a blogger's reputation in an industry. A publication blog does tend to focus on an industry, but the goal is to garner large audiences so that advertising revenue through banner advertising, sponsorships and pay per click revenue increases.

Your corporate blog's purpose is to do neither.

Visitors to your corporate blog may not be interested in your personal posts and may even be offended at your opinions. Ensuring the articles written on your blog maintain the integrity of your corporate brand yet provide a glimpse at the people behind your brand is a careful balance that you want to keep close tabs on.

Traditional brand marketing is all about having pixels perfectly placed and messaging that is always positive and on target. Because blogs allow prospects and customers to openly voice their opinion (or complain) about your company, you open your company to scrutiny.

Fear of scrutiny stops many companies from entering the social media realm, but the benefits have been proven to far outweigh the risks. Your company's response to a negative issue is the very information that opens a reader's trust in your authenticity. Transparency has risks, but how you handle challenges publically will pay off.

Many companies have leveraged blogging through corporate crisis to actually grow their business and reputation rather than hiding in silence.

Consumers know that businesses aren't always perfect. Blogging provides an opportunity to show how the company works through that imperfection. Honesty and transparency are important to a corporate blogging strategy that quickly builds authority and a great reputation.

Putting a human voice on your marketing communications

People don't want to work with brands. People want to work with people.

Many company blogs fail because they don't provide a personal touch, publish posts that are relevant to the business and the visitor, or drive the conversions necessary to support the strategy. Your blog should accomplish all this, but it's a very careful balance.

Every blog post you publish on your corporate blog should provide value to your visitors and build your authority in the industry. However, a blog should avoid marketing spin or press release regurgitation. Plainly put, readers mistrust marketing content and are drawn to a human voice.

Humanize your blog further by sharing stories about how your company and its employees give back to the community. Spotlighting employees, their interests, and the groups they belong to connects with your readers. Share events and conferences your company will be attending and let readers know how to meet up for coffee.

Over time, you find the content that draws the most attention to your blog are controversial topics, topics that make your blog stand out in your industry, and blog posts that answer the questions that visitors are seeking. You might be surprised to find bloggers within your organization that have incredible writing talent and humor. They can attract attention and business, too.

Don't just put up a blog that showcases your Chief Executive Officer or some other executive. The bloggers who work closest to the clients provide the most value to a corporate blogging strategy. Your sales team will blog and acquire leads. Your leadership team will blog and get opportunities to write and to speak at industry events. Your customer service team will blog and answer questions for clients, which reduces customer service costs. Your public relations team will blog and get industry attention.

Speaking to your audiences

Many companies make the mistake of thinking their blog is simply reaching one audience. They ignore that readers are coming from all directions:

- ✔ **Prospects** find your blog from sites that are referring traffic or from search engines. Be sure each of your blog posts, even if written specifically about your product, is written so that someone unfamiliar with your product can still understand it.

- ✔ **Shareholders** read your blog to better understand your products, services, and vision.

- ✔ **Customers** read your blog to keep up on releases, enhancements, new products, issues, and anything else that impacts their use of your product or service.

- ✔ **Employees** read your blog to keep up on company information and to learn more about the direction the company is heading.

- ✔ **Industry professionals** read your blog, looking for news and information that your company brings to the industry as a whole.

- ✔ **Competitors** read your blog! Don't make the mistake of comparing or criticizing your competition if you can't stand up to scrutiny.

The more your content can relate to the audience, the stronger the message is for the visitor. Your bloggers should write as though every post was written for every audience to fully leverage the blog for maximum impact. Back up your blog posts with supporting data, and link to strong industry resources to deepen your audience's trust of your company.

Writing with a purpose to a blog that sells

As you continue to write content, over half of your audience will be first-time visitors who arrived at your blog through a relevant search. Over half your audience! Many companies don't think about this and forget there's an incredible opportunity to drive sales to your organization through your corporate blog.

You may get thousands of new prospects visiting your blog on a weekly basis, so it's critical that your blog is designed and optimized to drive sales. Every blog post should be written with a desire to sell to new clients.

Visitors to a personal blog or publication blog typically don't appreciate being sold in a blog post. Because your blog is represented as a corporate blog, visitors recognize that one of its purposes is to sell. Don't be shy about providing direction to your audience on how to make their next purchase from your company.

Defining Key Features of a Blog

Aside from publishing content in descending chronological order, some important blog features aren't found in other content management systems on the Web. The combination of these features makes blogging platforms highly desirable to businesses seeking to grow via the Web.

Basic user interface features of a blog

The majority of what visitors see on a blog is viewed on the publication, or front-end of a blog. Blogs typically consist of:

- A **header** throughout the pages. This might be a combination of a logo and navigation menu.
- A **body** that is page or blog post content.
- **Blog posts**, with a title, publication date, author, content, and commenting system.
- **Sidebars** where calls-to-action are provided for visitors to click and engage your company further. Sidebars may also contain a breakdown of categories that a visitor can jump to directly.

- ✔ A **footer** with copyright information, terms of service, or disclaimer information.
- ✔ A **really simple syndication (RSS) feed address** for visitors to subscribe to the blog through a feed reader.
- ✔ **Contact information** available via a publicized phone number, and physical location. Corporate blogs also have ways for readers to engage online, either through a contact form or published e-mail address.
- ✔ A **search field** to search the blog internally.

The purpose of these components is to effectively publish content that is easily digested by the reader and to provide additional navigation for those visitors who are seeking to engage further. (See Figure 1-2.)

Figure 1-2: Brian Solis's blog uses a standard layout with sidebar right.

Header   RSS feed   Search field

Body/blog post   Sidebar

Basic back-end features of a blog

The front-end of your blog may not look very different, if at all, from a typical Web site. The back-end, or administrative, capabilities are much different, though.

- ✔ An **editor** for the author to easily add, edit, or manage blog posts.
- ✔ An **administrative section** for managing users, categories, pages, and design of the blog. (See Figure 1-3.)

Newer content management systems (CMS) incorporate many of these features, too, but most blogging platforms have them by default.

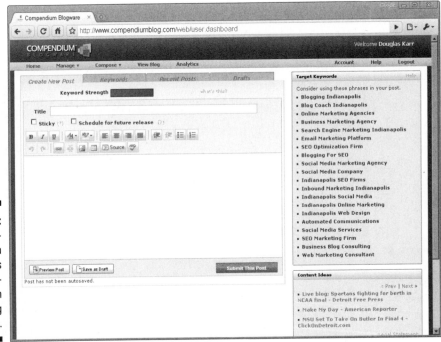

Figure 1-3: Compendium Blogware's user administration for blog authors.

Expanding your blog's functionality

Blogging platforms have evolved and you can find or even develop your own advanced features with the following:

✔ **Widgets:** Widgets can add additional features to your blog without the need for development or integration. Widgets typically are added by simply pasting a small chunk of code or dragging an unused feature into a sidebar element. (See Figure 1-4.)

Once installed, WordPress has a dozen or so available widgets, and you can add more by adding plug-ins for additional features and functionality. One of the available widgets is the Tag Cloud widget, which allows you to *tag* your posts with specific keywords. Tags can be visualized in a *tag cloud,* which displays the tags you write in a size proportional to the number of times you've written about that topic. (See Figure 1-5.)

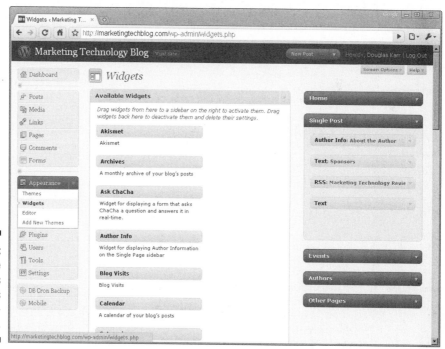

Figure 1-4: Viewing the WordPress Widgets Administration Page.

Tag cloud

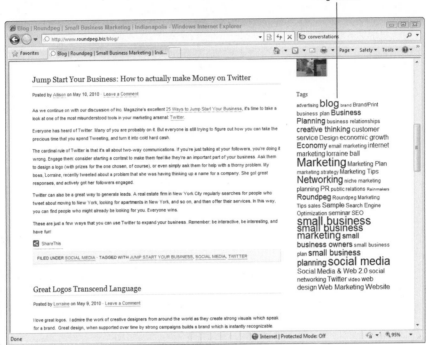

Figure 1-5:
The Tag Cloud in the Roundpeg. biz Blog sidebar.

To add a Tag Cloud widget to your WordPress blog, follow these steps:

1. **Log in to WordPress Administration.**

2. **Navigate to Appearance⇨Widgets.**

3. **Drag the Tag Cloud widget from the Available Plugins section into the sidebar where you want to view it.**

4. **Add a title for the Tag Cloud section.**

5. **Click Save.**

✔ **Plug-ins:** Plug-ins are developed third-party integrations that add additional features and functionality to blogs using the blogs' development platform or application programming interface (API). Platforms like WordPress have an extensive directory of thousands of plug-ins to expand your blog's functionality and integration.

Plug-ins can also enable new widgets. One great plug-in is the Related Posts plug-in, which displays links after each of your blog posts to contextually related blog posts. If your reader doesn't find what she needs, then the resulting related posts may offer the precise answer she's looking for. Providing alternative posts like this increases the number of page views per visitor and can reduce your *bounce rate* (the ratio of visitors who stay versus the ones who leave the page they arrive on).

To add the Related Posts plug-in to your WordPress blog, follow these steps:

1. **Log in to WordPress Administration.**

2. **Navigate to Plugins⇨Add New.**

3. **Click Install on the WordPress Related Posts plug-in.**

4. **Click Install Now.**

5. **Activate the plug-in.**

6. **Navigate to Appearance⇨Widgets.**

7. **Drag the WordPress Related Posts widget from the Available Plugins section into the sidebar where you want to view it.**

8. **Add a title for the WordPress Related Posts section.**

9. **Click Save.**

✔ **Application Programming Interface (API):** A series of development commands that allow for content to be imported, enhanced, integrated, or exported.

For example, if you want to solicit questions directly from your audience, you can integrate a service like ChaCha.me. ChaCha.me (`http://me.chacha.com`) allows businesses to set up a site to answer questions online, but it has a number of integrations to make publishing of that content to your blog very easy.

To add a Questions and Answers site with ChaCha.me to your WordPress blog, follow these steps:

1. **Add an account at ChaCha.me by clicking Sign Up.**

2. **Add a username that represents your company.**

   The username is used in the full Web address and advertised on your page.

3. **Add an e-mail address, password, and your business name.**

4. **Log in to your new account and navigate to Settings⇨Services.**

5. **Click WordPress and add your WordPress login and password.**

6. **Add your blog address with "/xmlrpc.php" at the end of it.**

   This location is where ChaCha.me posts your answers when you submit your response.

7. **Enter a blogid of 1 (or your blogid if you're using WordPress Multi-User).**

8. **Log in to WordPress Administration and navigate to Settings⇨ Writing.**

9. **Enable XML-RPC and then click Save Changes.**

   Your ChaCha.me account can now publish to your WordPress Blog.

> **10. (Optional) You can copy the ChaCha.me widget to your sidebar via the ChaCha plug-in or a Text Widget plug-in.**
>
> This allows users to post a question directly from your sidebar.

Recognizing the Benefits of Corporate Blogging

A successful corporate blogging strategy can have many benefits. Success in blogging can be measured in many different ways.

- ✔ If you're an e-commerce company, a blog can provide product information that leads to a direct sale from your blog post.

- ✔ If you're a technology consulting company, your blog may be a means of building authority or raising awareness of your staff's expertise so that you can be invited to speak at industry events to attract and acquire customers.

- ✔ If you're a public company, a blog may be a means of providing valuable information to stockholders so that you maintain a good public image, and in turn, attract more investment.

- ✔ If you're a real estate agent, your blog may provide invaluable information about the geographic region you serve, which will attract more buyers and sellers to your firm.

- ✔ If you're a large organization, you may wish to have multiple strategies. Webtrends is a Web analytics company in Portland, Oregon that deploys multiple blogs: leadership blogs specifically for their leadership team that speaks about company vision to employees and stockholders; customer service blogs that are specifically focused on assisting customers; and marketing blogs that promote upcoming events, partnerships, and integrations.

Booking public speaking engagements

Great content draws regular readers to your blog. After you've been blogging for a long period, your following becomes attractive to industry professionals who wish to promote their events and conferences on your site. Be sure to include your presentations and speeches from industry events on your blog so that other industry professionals know that you're available.

Speaking at industry events not only puts you in front of relevant prospects, it also drives traffic to your blog. When you become better known in the industry, that following grows. These opportunities (and the associated growth) can generate a lot of leads for your business.

Publishing opportunities online and offline

Each time your bloggers publish content, you add to a collection of content relevant to your business. These blog posts can support your products by publishing frequently asked questions (FAQs), developing a series of best practice guides, and repurposing the content in other publications — both online and offline.

When you're looking for content for whitepapers, case studies, e-books, industry articles, or e-mail newsletters, take the opportunity to get content from your blog and repurpose it. You've worked hard to build this impressive collection of content; don't be afraid to use it wherever possible.

Attracting leads through your blog

Regardless of whether the goal of your corporate blogging strategy is to attract leads, leads will come. Designing your blog with this in mind makes it easier for you to drive them into your sales funnel. Your blog should incorporate contact details, a contact form, your full mailing address, and calls-to-action (CTAs) for visitors to click and engage with your company.

Many companies start a corporate blog to increase authority or service their customers but neglect to provide a path for leads to engage with their company. Your blog should have multiple, clear methods for visitors to contact you or make a purchase directly (if possible).

Driving conversions online through blogging

The majority of visitors to your blog will be first-time visitors. While you continue to blog and appear in search engines, you may even find that that number exceeds 80 percent of all your visitors. Each of these visitors may be a relevant lead for your business, so it's essential that you provide multiple paths for them to convert.

To view visitor statistics in Google Analytics, follow these steps:

1. **Log in to Google Analytics.**

2. **Navigate to Visitors⇨New vs. Returning**

    The resulting report provides you with a comparison of new versus returning visitors for the period selected. (See Figure 1-6.)

Figure 1-6:
Viewing
visitor
statistics
in Google
Analytics.

Blogging conversions typically occur through a variety of calls-to-action that direct the user to a landing page where they can make a purchase or contact your sales team. Your blogging sales funnel starts with a search engine and referring traffic directing the visitors to your posts. After the visitors read your posts and wish to do business, they click a call-to-action that leads them to a landing page. The landing page allows the visitor to convert.

Designing your blog, your calls-to-action, your landing pages, and writing your content with this sales funnel in mind helps you increase conversions through your blog.

Blogging: From Concept to Content to Conversion

The first step of a successful blogging strategy is understanding what content is going to drive traffic to your blog from search engines and other referring Web sites. This is accomplished by identifying keywords that are relevant to your business, that have large search volumes, and by targeting other social mediums and blogs that could drive content to your business.

While you write your content, you want to syndicate and promote the content throughout your social networks — Twitter, Facebook, LinkedIn, and so on. You also want to connect and comment on other blogs of influence within your industry to try to drive traffic to your site.

Driving relevant traffic to your site should grow the number of leads, and ultimately, the number of conversions to your business.

Establishing your strategy and goals

The first step in establishing your blog may be simply to get relevant, compelling content published on a regular basis. The more content you write, the more opportunities visitors have to find you so don't start out slow. Be consistent in delivering great content and try to increase the volume over time.

When your blog begins to attract traffic, you want to track the number of people clicking through on your calls-to-action and, ultimately, the number of conversions acquired through your blog. When your posts, leads, and conversions acquire a certain consistency, you can begin to assess your blogging program and set goals. You should set goals for the number of articles published, the number of visitors, the number of calls-to-action that are clicked, the number of conversions, and the revenue associated with those conversions.

Within your analytics application, you also want to set up event tracking and conversion tracking to easily monitor how well your blog is performing in comparison to the goals that you set for it.

Picking and training the blogging team

Don't restrict your recruiting of bloggers to public relations professionals, marketers, or leaders within your organization. Sometimes, the seasoned professional writes some of the worst blog posts and sounds more like a faceless brand than a human being.

When you provide opportunities for blogging to your personnel, realize that not all your team will be excited about the opportunity to blog. You should avoid recruiting bloggers who aren't excited because lack of enthusiasm is clearly evident in writing. Instead, focus on employees that are closest to the customers and who are looking forward to writing on the blog. You'll be surprised at the talent your staff has!

Before writing, your staff should fully understand any legal issues, their responsibilities, and content that's not suitable for the blog. Have a meeting with the team and set expectations with them. You may want to incorporate a blogging solution that allows for blog posts to be manually approved and published by an administrator.

Your team should also understand the objectives of the blog, your rewards or incentives, keywords that you want them to focus on, industry blogs or sites they should be frequenting, and how to promote the blog (and the company) via social media sites.

If a blogger is having difficulty keeping up or is writing content that's flat and not driving visits, leads, or conversions, cut them loose! Your blog's success depends on the quality of the content, not just the quantity.

Identifying platforms and resources

The majority of blogging platforms have evolved from either personal blogs or publication blogs. It's imperative that you realize the difference between these blogs and a corporate blog. Each requires a different editorial process, publishing design, and measurement.

Most companies default to a free blogging platform and throw it on a cheap hosting platform. Free turns out to be not free when you need to hire search engine optimization consultants, graphic designers, and integration specialists to fully realize the opportunities that a corporate blog can provide.

Cheap hosting platforms work perfectly until your blog is recognized as a great source and a ton of visitors come to your blog. A couple dozen visitors can freeze a self-hosted blog on a cheap hosting platform. Unfortunately, most companies don't find out how bad their hosting or platform is until it's too late.

Newer hosting solutions allow for cloud-based server resources that grow with demand and dynamically add resources as needed. Your blog can bring in hundreds or thousands of leads — this isn't an area that you want to risk saving a few dollars on.

Corporate solutions like Compendium, WordPress VIP (see Figure 1-7), or TypePad Business have service level agreements and resources that can handle massive loads of unexpected traffic, 24-hour support, security enhancements, and regular backups. Additionally, Compendium provides client success management to monitor and help you improve your blogging results.

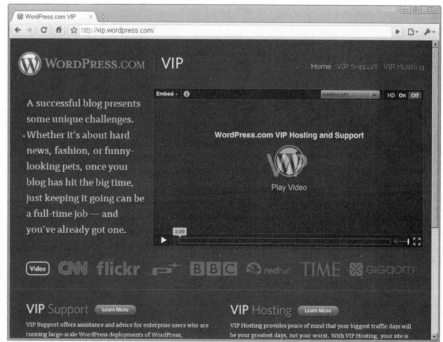

Figure 1-7:
WordPress
VIP service.

Compiling search-engine-optimized content

An *optimized platform* is a foundation that you must have when deploying a corporate blogging strategy that incorporates search traffic. Many compa-nies download and install free platforms as-is. The problem is that platforms like WordPress aren't fully optimized without the use of plug-ins to publish sitemaps and effective meta descriptions. You find details on optimizing your platform in Chapter 8.

After you optimize your platform, the next step is to design your theme using search engine optimization best practices. These incorporate the overall page structure, page titles, and headings on the pages.

Your theme construction or platform determines some of your search engine optimization, but your content will determine the rest. Keyword research is essential before writing your first blog post. *Keywords* are the terms used by searchers to find relevant content.

Using keywords in post titles, meta descriptions, subheadings, alternative image tags, bolded terms, and content presents your content to search engines in a manner that ensures it's indexed appropriately. When your content is indexed properly, it's much easier to find in the appropriate search results. This is also discussed in Chapter 8.

Monitoring, measuring, and analyzing

Understanding whether your blogging strategy is working is impossible unless you measure. Selecting the right analytics application is essential to monitoring and measuring your program's performance. Free analytics applications, such as Google Analytics, can accommodate your needs but have some limitations.

Google Analytics lacks any real-time measurement and has limitations in the event you exceed their maximum number of pageviews.

Enterprise analytics applications, such as Webtrends, have no limitations and have real-time analytics with campaigns, goals, and alerts. If you need finite measurement of your corporate blogging strategy, an enterprise analytics solution may be worth the investment.

Chapter 15 explores the metrics to analyze, monitor, and measure your blog and provides steps you can take to improve traffic and conversions.

Additionally, a convergence of social media monitoring and analytics is occurring in the analytics industry, so corporations can effectively measure the impact of social media on their inbound marketing strategies, including corporate blogging. Radian6 and Webtrends integration, for instance, offers off-site analytics monitoring for social media. (See Figure 1-8.)

Adjusting strategy or messaging

While you monitor your program, the content, the authors, and the sources of relevant traffic, you may also want to adjust your strategy. There's no secret program available that can turn your blog into a major revenue generator overnight (although a lot of blogs gladly try to sell you such a program).

Blogging requires time, energy, a strategy, and momentum. Blogging is a marathon, not a sprint. You want to make adjustments to your design, your keyword targeting, your content, your calls-to-action, your landing pages, and everything in between.

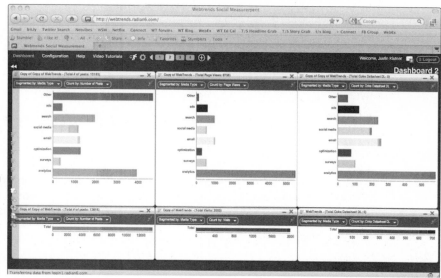

Figure 1-8:
Radian6 and
Webtrends
integration
analytics.

You might be asking why you would want to undertake such a strategy then. The reason is that every blog post you write adds another opportunity to acquire traffic and business with your blog. Unlike traditional marketing campaigns that start, run over a period of time, and then end, blogging grows and acquires leads every time you post.

As time goes on, your blog's return on investment will improve. Don't give up!

Chapter 2

Laying the Foundation for Blogging

. . . .

In This Chapter

▶ Defining corporate blogging strategies

▶ Determining your content and responding to criticism

▶ Understanding industry expectations

▶ Assessing your resources and defining ownership

▶ Planning your content

. . . .

*T*he vast opportunities of the Internet have changed consumer and business behavior when it comes to purchasing decisions. In the past, customers would contact sales personnel to find out more about your products or services.

These days, though, consumers and businesses use the Internet to thoroughly research their next purchasing decision in advance. By the time your Web visitor has made contact with you, he may know more about your company, products, and services than the person he connects with on the phone!

Consumers are seeking additional information so they can make the right choice. If your company wants to compete for that decision, they must deploy an effective strategy to have the information needed where the consumer expects it. A blog is the perfect platform for deploying this strategy!

An effective corporate blogging strategy, offers a number of benefits, including:

✔ It provides a voice for your company beyond your brand and marketing.

✔ It showcases your authority, knowledge, and experience in your industry, positioning you as a leader or expert.

✔ It provides content that attracts search engine traffic.

✔ It gives you a knowledge base of information in an easily organized and searchable online format, allowing your company to save on employee education and customer service calls.

✔ It is an effective inbound marketing strategy, providing a path for visitors to your site to convert into customers in a manner that's efficient and affordable.

Understanding What a Blog Can Do for Your Company

According to Nielsen, folks perform over 10 billion searches on search engines each month. This number continues to grow, and Google leads the market with 66% of all searches. On average, that's about 33 searches per day per American!

Organic search results are the results on a search engine results page (the page you reach after you submit your query) that show up naturally. Search engines analyze the content within the page and on referring pages, and then decide what terms to display in the search results and how to rank them. Paid results aren't displayed in this manner — they are simply bid on and the highest bids are displayed first.

Organic search results are the main column on the left side of the page. Paid or sponsored results sometimes surround the organic results to the top and to the right. (See Figure 2-1.)

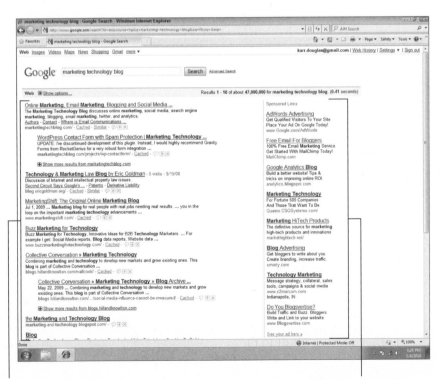

Figure 2-1: Organic versus paid search results on a search engine results page.

Organic search results

Paid search results

Consumers and businesses employ search engines to research purchasing decisions, so it's essential that your business be found if you wish to capitalize on this traffic.

Optimizing Web sites in order to be found organically on search engines can be a costly (but still worthwhile) investment. Blogs, on the other hand, provide a means for businesses to write limitless quantities of content.

Search engines want to provide relevant content to search engine users, so they identify sites that are relevant, updated frequently, and are popular. Blogs have the ability to be relevant, can be updated frequently, and can gain exposure and popularity.

That blogging has become an effective search engine strategy for businesses is no coincidence!

There's much evidence that people buy from people, not companies. People also buy emotionally — so if your marketing material contains nothing but complex acronyms, multi-syllable industry speak, and hard-to-understand marketing terms, a blog may provide the human touch that your prospective clients are seeking.

However, as a marketing strategy, blogging is a marathon, not a sprint. Most blogs are abandoned because companies fail to see results 1, 3, or even 6 months into their blogging program. If your business is new and you're putting a new blog on a new domain, it could take a few months for search engines to identify you as a viable source of information.

Compared to short-term marketing strategies, such as pay-per-click and e-mail marketing that produce immediate results, a blog seems a poor choice. Blogs are slow, methodical, long-term solutions. Because blogs produce authority, reputation, and content over time, results appear much later in the marketing cycle.

Typically, in a marketing campaign, you spend money, you obtain leads, and the return on investment (ROI) remains fairly constant over time. This is because once your campaign is over, the leads stop coming in.

With a blog, your content continues to work for you over time. Although the resources don't result in a positive return on investment initially, eventually, you see your ROI increase. (See Figure 2-2.)

Unless you stop writing, your blog never expires; it continues to appear in search results and drive customers. That's not to say you should stop spending on other strategies, though. If you have a positive return on your investment on other marketing strategies, you should continue them.

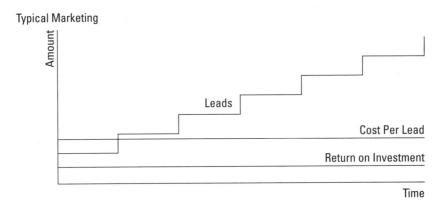

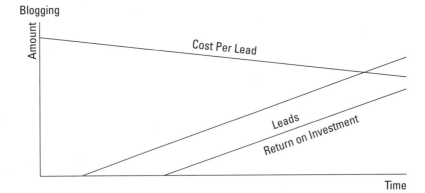

Figure 2-2:
Assessing
ROI on blog-
ging versus
typical
marketing
campaigns.

How can your organization benefit from blogging? Here are a few ideas:

- ✔ A blog can provide product information that leads to a direct sale from your blog post.

- ✔ A blog can build authority, raise awareness to your staff's expertise, or open avenues to speaking at industry events.

- ✔ A blog can provide valuable information to stockholders so that you maintain a good public image and attract more investment.

- ✔ A blog can provide invaluable information about the geographic region to attract more buyers and sellers to your firm.

- ✔ With multiple blogs, you can have multiple strategies. Webtrends, a Web analytics company in Portland, Oregon, has multiple blogs: a leadership blog for their leadership team that addresses the company's vision; customer service blogs that focus on assisting customers; and marketing blogs that promote upcoming events, partnerships, and integrations.

A blog has the opportunity to build sales and transform your business. A blog can provide many things, including the following:

- Company leadership can disseminate the corporation's vision so that employees are informed and understand how their responsibilities impact the bottom line.

- Blogging provides an open forum where employees can ask questions or provide feedback in an environment where they may feel more comfortable contributing.

- A blog can develop into a searchable, organized knowledge base. Blogging applications have built-in search mechanisms that make content easily findable.

- A blog can be used to confront crisis and keep customers informed without flooding your e-mail and phone systems.

- A blog can be used to promote upcoming events, to live-blog at events while they're happening, or to summarize events for those who couldn't be in attendance.

- A blog can be used to release new product information and company news to inform customers, the media, and industry professionals.

- A blog can help acquire new customers, retain current ones through improved communication, and upsell clients with new offerings.

- A blog can provide employees with the spotlight, encouraging them to promote their business and, ultimately, themselves. This can lead to improved employee satisfaction and improved productivity.

- A blog can drive business and build your company as a leader in its industry, without the costs or dependence on traditional media.

- A blog will provide your brand and company with a personality if you leverage the medium.

- A blog is a perfect platform for distributing video and making it easier to find in search engines. Some companies, such as Cantaloupe.TV, specialize in video blogging and hosting video for your blog.

- A blog can also be used to distribute audio.

By publishing information in text, voice, and video, you're reaching different audiences the way they wish to be reached.

Defining a Blogging Strategy

The first step of a successful blogging strategy is to understand the content that drives traffic to your blog from search engines and other referring Web sites.

As you begin to think about your blogging strategy, content will be your primary concern. Many companies embarking on a blogging strategy simply regurgitate the same information they've already published in their marketing and advertising. Your visitors are looking for something different. Your visitors are searching for answers, and they want those answers to be delivered from a real person.

To define your content objectives, you must first determine the questions that people might ask that would lead them to your business. The easiest means of doing this is to find out what sorts of problems your business solves for your clients. Ask your client what you've accomplished for them. The more your blog speaks to the problem(s) you're solving for customers, the more likely you are to attracting new customers.

Many companies use heavy jargon in their content — jargon that's lost on search engine users, or terms that target the wrong customers. Understanding the specific keywords and topics that lead the right customers to your business is critical if you wish to target and find the right visitors for your blog.

Walker Information is a company that consults with Fortune 500 companies on customer intelligence. Walker works through online content and sophisticated customer feedback to provide clients with strategies to improve their customer retention.

Some of Walker's most intensive work is in deciphering customer survey data. *Customer survey* is a common keyword that gets thousands of searches each month — but it's not a term that Walker is targeting because it won't attract the *right* audience. Over time, Walker experimented and identified *customer intelligence* as the term that better targets the companies they wish to do business with.

Understanding the topics that are going to attract the right visitors to your blog is essential. Writing about those topics frequently is key. The more focused your blog is on specific keywords, the easier it is for search engines to identify the topics your blog is writing about. Keywords are the common ties between the content you are writing and the terms that visitors are searching for.

There are a number of tools, free and paid, which can provide you with competitive research on keywords and content you should target in your corporate blogging strategy. You can find out more about this in Chapter 6.

Assemble your blogging team (and have backups)

Assembling a team of bloggers is the next step toward ensuring you're frequently delivering relevant content via your blog. Who should be on the team? Although you may be tempted to search your company for volunteers with English majors or master's degrees, this isn't always the best solution. You might be tempted to encourage *every* employee to blog.

Either of these choices could lead to challenges in building your blog's audience, however. Because the majority of Web readers digest information written at a sixth-grade level, an overly educated blogger may prevent your message from getting to the right audience. On the other hand, poor grammar or spelling could turn away valuable prospects.

Just as you decide the terms that connect visitors to your business, you should also think about the variety of the voices on your blog. Are your customers Chief Executive Officers or are they blue-collar maintenance personnel? You may find that your target audience is everything in between. As a result, don't limit the voices on your blog to any one group.

Providing your audience with a diverse selection of bloggers varies the voice and the content of your blog — and over time you'll begin to see which type of blogger attracts the most attention and business.

You may be surprised at who produces a great blog within your organization. Robert Scoble is a well-known blogger from Microsoft and Matt Cutts is a celebrated blogger from Google (see Figure 2-3); however, neither company realized each man's talent until his blog grew to great heights.

Chapter 6 provides more details about assembling your blogging team.

Create a publication schedule

The easiest way to manage your bloggers and ensure your blog is producing content is to set a schedule, manage it, and reward your bloggers when they keep to it! You may have some bloggers with more opportunities to post than others, so set expectations properly.

You might be asking, "How often should we blog?" In the online marketing world, a blogging platform is the equivalent of a race car. The faster you push the pedal, the better the chances of winning the race.

Figure 2-3:
Matt Cutts'
Gadgets,
Google, and
SEO blog.

That doesn't mean you should drive recklessly, though. Great content will attract new traffic, keep readers coming back, and ultimately, compel visitors to do business with your company. If they're already doing business, great content will generate more revenue from current clients as well.

The answer is to have a balance of both frequency and quality. The best way to determine this balance is to track readership and business generated. Thankfully, blogging does not require polished prose from the best of English students. A 150-word post that simply comments on industry news may be the perfect fit for your audience.

When you're writing a press release and you want to ensure you get 100 percent impact, your marketing team may spend hours to get it right. In that case, you have only one chance to get it right.

With a blog, you have as many chances as you like to get it right. In fact, you can continue writing similar messages to ensure readers get the correct idea. Don't get discouraged that the great blog posts you're publishing aren't being discovered and promoted all over the Web. It takes time to build authority and to capture the attention of others within your industry.

People don't spend a lot of time reading online. Visitors arrive at your blog looking for an answer and if they don't see what they're looking for, they vanish into the thick of the search engine in a matter of seconds.

Don't spend time organizing your thoughts and words too carefully, just get the message out to the audience in a timely manner. If you can write a great blog post once a week and some short tips the remaining days, you're going to succeed!

Spend 80 percent of your time writing one great post and 20 percent of your time producing some other relevant, quality content. To spend the necessary time to make every post hit a home run would be nice, but even the best bloggers don't.

Determining Your Blog's Content

Traditional brand marketing encourages being positive and staying on-message. However, because prospects and customers can openly voice their opinion (and complaints) about your company, blogs open your company to public scrutiny. Fear of negative criticism stops many companies from entering the social media realm, but the benefits far outweigh the risks. In fact, your company may find that a 4-star recommendation may lead to 5-star sales!

Companies should not write about some topics and content, however. Proprietary information, content that could violate privacy laws, and information that could put your company at risk with your competition are topics to avoid.

There are even topics you cannot write about. In the United States, financial regulations prevent companies from releasing marketing material that could mislead investors. And a number of privacy regulations, including the Healthcare Insurance Portability and Accountability Act, prevent those in the healthcare industry from blogging on specific topics. Chapter 6 offers more information about protecting your blog legally.

When in doubt, discuss what you can and can't blog about with a public relations professional. Be sure to clearly communicate that information with the other bloggers on your team. To be absolutely certain, allow your bloggers to submit posts but ensure that you have a knowledgeable administrator who moderates and approves the posts.

Putting your customers and employees first

Traditional marketing is all about getting attention. Traditional marketing is about directly marketing your products and services. Blogging isn't always about getting attention or marketing your products and services directly, but you can reap the benefits indirectly. By improving communication to your customers and employees, you increase productivity and reduce customer dissatisfaction.

Instead of focusing your blog on your company, focus on your customers. How are customers using your products? What advice can you provide customers that will help them succeed? What questions do you get in sales and support calls that you can share online?

Blogging allows you to put your customers in the spotlight. Rather than using your blog to say why your company's great, use it to speak about your customers. Your readers will be more compelled to do business with you when they understand the benefits to your customers.

Blogging also provides a spotlight for your employees. Blogging is a medium that your employees can use to promote the company while advancing their careers.

Jon Arnold, CEO of Tuitive Group, a Web usability and design firm, said that he's never hiring sales staff again. All the quality leads his firm obtained in the last year were acquired through social media or speaking with people at industry conferences. This year, he's made it part of his team's goals to incorporate blogging, other social media, and networking to drive leads.

Each year, universities and colleges produce graduates who feel empowered to make a difference. Traditional top-down organizations often struggle to keep young talent. Providing these young, entrepreneurial staff members a voice on a blog can improve their satisfaction and help you retain great talent.

Understanding industry expectations of corporate bloggers

Once you begin blogging, you'll benefit from some unwritten expectations of bloggers. In the first years of blogging, the term *blogosphere* was penned to describe the underlying network of blogs on the Internet. Although no formal rules exist for interacting with the blogosphere, you should still follow some code of behavior. These "unwritten rules" include the following:

> ✔ Don't spam.
>
> ✔ Support other bloggers.
>
> ✔ Give credit where it's due.

Don't spam

Blogging applications used to speak to one another through a feature called *trackbacks*. If a blogger mentioned one of your posts in his blog, the platform would "ping" your blog. The "ping" was simply a request that was made with the Web address of the post where the mention was made.

Trackbacks could be seen within the blog's administration panel so you could see who wrote about you (and vice versa). With the widespread adoption of blogs, trackback spam became prevalent. Spammers would send false trackbacks and clog your administrative panel with nasty links.

Now, feeds from search engines are common in your administrative panel, so you can still see who's writing about you, but the feeds are called *incoming links*. You can check your incoming links in WordPress by following these steps:

1. **Log into WordPress through your administration page; typically, your blog address plus /wp-admin.**

2. **Select Dashboard⇨Dashboard.**

3. **Find the Incoming Links section, as shown in Figure 2-4.**

   Sections can be dragged and dropped within WordPress, so you can drag them to a location that's easier to locate.

If you just started blogging, you may not have any mentions yet. Over time, you'll build authority and generate links from other sites.

A lot of blogs programmatically steal content and produce sites they hope will capture search engine traffic and subsequently advertising. These sites may show up in your Incoming Links section. Research the person who started the blog and contact them if you're not quite sure. Spammers won't answer e-mail.

Support other bloggers

Bloggers are a generous bunch! You write about them and they'll often reciprocate and write about you. This is fantastic because it generates backlinks and popularity — which means a better search engine ranking!

Become aware of other bloggers within your industry, comment on their blogs often, and mention them once in a while in a positive light. Sometimes it's fun to start a respectable debate online as well. Any publicity is good publicity when it comes to promoting your blog.

Incoming links

Figure 2-4:
Discovering
who has
written
about you
in your
Blogging
Administra-
tion.

Be cautious of speaking about other bloggers in a negative light. You never know when that blogger you insult may wind up on a panel of professionals who are evaluating your business. Proceed with caution, even when you vehemently disagree with another blogger.

Give credit where it's due

Be sure to always link to a blog that you reference within your posts. Mentioning or discussing another blog without actually linking to it is just plain bad manners and inconsiderate. If you're directly quoting, be sure to apply blockquotes with your text editor. (See Figure 2-5.)

In HTML, the `blockquote` tag is written like this:

```
<blockquote>Here is my quote from a <a href="http://where.com">blog</a></blockquote>
```

Always give credit where credit is due and never, ever, post someone else's content in its entirety without their permission.

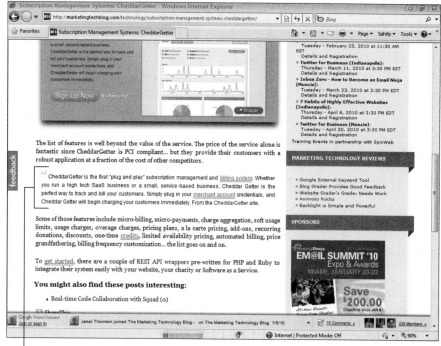

Figure 2-5:
Dressing up block quotes for easy identification.

Blockquote

Writing your company's blogging manifesto

A *manifesto* is written declaration of principles, policies, and objectives. In 2005, IBM decided to write blogging guidelines because blogging caught on in popularity. These guidelines, IBM's Social Computing Guidelines, are a great example of a blogging manifesto. (You can find them at www.ibm.com/blogs/zz/en/guidelines.html.)

Preparing your blogging team with some guidelines on blogging, social media, and the associated legalities will strengthen your corporate blogging strategy!

Determining Who Owns Blogging

Ultimately, it's up to the leadership within your organization to recognize who owns blogging and who is responsible for the management of the strategy and the results. Some pros and cons associated with ownership, though, must be discussed beforehand.

In large organizations, the group most likely to assume the ownership is the public relations department because they are often in charge of the long-term communication strategy of the organization and held accountable to ensure the right information is properly disseminated. However, other groups might make more sense for you.

Establishing an owner is important to ensure that content is being created and a community is starting to form. Your organization decides who will lead your corporate blogging strategy. In many companies, the voice of the corporate blog is defined by corporate leadership or marketing.

 Some companies have developed cross-departmental social media teams who collectively measure results, develop the strategy, and report directly to the leadership team. This ensures accountability from all departments on the strategy.

Letting leadership define the voice of your blog

Some companies believe their leader to be the voice of the organization, so they believe that leader is the natural choice of the blog. This has advantages and disadvantages.

The pros of leadership ownership:

- ✔ The vision of the company can be clearly communicated on the blog by the visionaries of the company. This ensures that there will be clarity to the message and no confusion.
- ✔ The voice of the blog comes with great authority. Seeing *President* or *CEO* next to a name may generate more attention and more authority.

The cons of leadership ownership:

- ✔ A top-down model may not capture the true voice of the organization, especially if it's a large enterprise. Insight from employees may be the greatest selling point your organization has.

- ✔ Often, visitors to your company blog are seeking an answer that impacts their decision to purchase your products or services. A CEO may not know the answer.

- ✔ Your employees don't feel empowered to help change the organization, lowering employee morale and, as a result, productivity. Not every employee needs to blog, but seeing your employees get a voice and spotlight through your company blog can increase the morale of everyone.

- ✔ Leaders within your organization already work long hours and don't have additional time to blog.

Letting marketing define the voice of your blog

Marketing departments are often identified as the owners of the corporate blogging strategy. Businesses, such as Compendium, hold the marketing group accountable for the blogging program, although, they don't interfere with it. They allow the employees to be heard, while motivating and encouraging them to blog well.

The pros of marketing ownership:

- ✔ Having a consistent message across all mediums and channels within your organization can simplify and optimize marketing efforts.

- ✔ Marketing often owns the content on your corporate Web site, so adding another medium is a natural fit.

- ✔ Marketing generates the content within your organization for the Web sites, other media, whitepapers, case studies, press releases, and e-mail marketing campaigns. Repurposing that content to the blog can be done with little effort.

- ✔ Marketing often has the resources for writing content while other departments have different goals and responsibilities.

The cons of marketing ownership:

- ✔ Your blog sounds like your marketing material. That's not what people are seeking when they read a blog.

- ✔ With bloggers throughout the organization, your marketing team feels compelled to "tweak" the message; therefore, losing its natural voice.

- ✔ Because bloggers throughout the organization don't report to marketing, the marketing team may have difficulties motivating employees or finding resources to ensure quality content is delivered.

Understanding What to Publish on Your Corporate Blog

You've developed your manifesto, gathered your team, set some goals for your blogging program. Your blogging platform is up and running and the team has been fully trained. You find yourself sitting at the keyboard, staring at the screen, and wondering what to write.

Your mind is blank.

Thinking that you may have to write a post every day for the next year is daunting. Two hundred posts that will grab attention and drive sales to your products and services. But it's not that difficult.

What was your last e-mail to a client? What were you explaining? What about the last sales prospect's questions? What questions does everyone keeps asking? Coming up with blog post ideas is easy. Part of your job every day is to answer questions, you just need to learn how to write the answers online. To start, open your Sent folder in your e-mail and read the responses you provided your staff, your prospects, or your clients.

Often, sales and support teams have to document prospect and client questions in a customer relationship management system. Adjusting the content and writing it into a nice, short blog post is a great way to repurpose information, save time, and place more value on the time spent answering those questions!

If you're not sure where to repurpose content from, look no further than the Sent folder in your e-mail client. Browse through the folder until you find an e-mail sent to a prospect or customer that answered a question they submitted. These are often perfect pieces of content to repurpose on your blog.

The adjustments necessary for optimizing the content for a blog post are pretty easy. Just follow these steps:

1. **Write a compelling a post title that contains the question and associated keywords that the blog post will answer.**

2. **Make edits to the blog post to take it from a message written to the recipient to a message written for any client or prospect who is visiting your blog.**

3. **Use keywords that visitors would use in search engines to get to your response. You'll want to use the exact phrases throughout your blog post.**

If you're still stuck, search Google for *200 Corporate Blog Post Ideas,* or you can use any of the following ideas:

- **Distribute company news through your corporate blog:** Humanize your blog by sharing stories about how your employees give back to the community. Share exciting news about expansions, or include new hires and new clients. Blog about upcoming events or how your clients can connect with you offline.

- **Work your public relations strategy into your blog:** Share your press releases through your blog with a personal note on the points you want to share. Press releases used to be the primary distribution method for getting news to the media. Now, you can ensure your company's news is heard by publishing it yourself. Think of your blog as your own self-publishing platform for your public relations team!

- **Integrate other marketing communications into your blog:** News that you're already communicating through other mediums, such as e-mail, newsletters, whitepapers, case studies, print publications — even speeches — can be converted to blog posts easily. Repurposing content and distributing it via a blog is a great investment of the time it takes to produce the content.

  For example, if you have a great PowerPoint presentation that was recently presented, write a blog post from each slide's material — that's potentially 30 posts!

Reinforcing the same information, but providing different perspectives is a great way of producing content that connects with your visitors. Not all visitors will connect on every post — so repurposing content and reinforcing the central themes in different ways will produce results.

Chapter 3

Deciding On Your Blogging Goals

In This Chapter

▶ Defining goals for your blog

▶ Calculating your return on investment

▶ Measuring the impact of your blog

*A*business grows by both increasing revenue and reducing expenses. Your corporate blogging strategy can help either, but you need to decide what your objectives are, how to determine goals for each objective, and how to measure the success of the objectives.

Setting goals may be difficult at first but over time, you'll observe trends in visits, pageviews, and conversions that you can monitor and predict, making goal-setting much easier.

Ultimately, your return on investment for blogging will not be found in the first month or even the first quarter. Each post that you publish may have the information necessary in it to produce revenue for your company, but that revenue may not come today, tomorrow, or next week. Blogging is a strategy that requires time and momentum.

Your blogging strategy may ultimately take months, even a year to realize results — but those results will only continue to grow while you continue to write content. This chapter helps you define your strategy by showing you how to determine your target audience, how to design objectives, and how to estimate your return on investment and evaluate results. Let's get started!

Setting Goals for Your Blogging Strategy

Understanding the business benefits of corporate blogging for your company is imperative. Your blog will have an impact on your company culture, your sales and marketing efforts, and your customer service and customer satisfaction.

Without a specific direction, it's hard to reach a destination. Setting goals and plotting the progress of reaching those goals is key to your blogging strategy's success.

In broad terms, the five goals for defining your blogging strategy are as follows:

- ✔ **Define a target audience:** Who are you trying to reach, where are they, and how are you going to effectively reach them?

- ✔ **Determine a blogging platform:** It's critical to select a platform that allows you to hit the ground running and to maximize your return on investment.

- ✔ **Estimate your blogging return on investment:** Determining how you're going to measure success, in dollars, provides your organization with a valuable yardstick. Start out with estimating the cost of the program — the cost of software, infrastructure, consulting, and content creation. Now compare that cost to your goals and the savings or additional revenue that your strategy will generate. Monitor your progress closely and expect that the return on investment will continue to increase over time.

- ✔ **Measure conversions:** Use analytics and a customer relationship manager to fully compare the volume of leads your company gets to the sales or *conversions*. This provides you with a baseline conversion rate. Over time, you can measure against that conversion rate and also monitor your cost and revenue per conversion.

- ✔ **Review objectives and evaluate results:** Set aside time each month to measure the impact of your programs, fine-tune your analytics to provide the necessary reporting, and review the results with both your team and your company's leadership.

Defining the target audience for your blog

The first step of determining goals is to determine the readership audience that you want to grow from your blog. Are you looking for clients, prospects, industry professionals, job candidates, or addressing your own employees?

Your new audience online is going to be found through search engines, in social media and other blogs, and within your own customer and prospect base. Integrating your blogging strategy with your other marketing efforts helps you grow your audience immediately, and other strategies help you add a following.

Targeting an audience through search engines is accomplished by identifying the keywords or phrases they use to look for the products and services that you can deliver. In Chapter 8, you'll find detailed information on how to do research and identify those keywords.

In Chapter 11, you'll find strategies and ways to target relevant audiences and market your blog to them.

Blogging is an efficient and effective communication platform. What you decide to communicate on that platform determines the audience to target.

Providing a single blog that incorporates all news and information for your company is effective, but multiple blogs can assist you in focusing on specific audiences. Are there secondary audiences you should be targeting? Additionally, some businesses have multiple blogs to target different strategies, such as the following:

- ✔ Leadership blog focused on the media, employees, and stockholders
- ✔ Marketing blog focused on innovation, product promotion, services, events, and acquisitions
- ✔ Customer service blog focused on clients to provide direction, work-arounds, fixes, and best practices and to communicate outages and issues
- ✔ Event-specific blogs to communicate event information and times
- ✔ Philanthropy blog to discuss the company's work within the community and its support of charitable initiatives
- ✔ Industry blog to focus on providing feedback and vision to other industry professionals
- ✔ Public relations blog to publish news releases and respond to public relations issues
- ✔ Partnership blog to promote partnerships with other companies and vendors
- ✔ Integration blog for distributing information, code, and updates about your software solutions' integration capabilities
- ✔ Frequently Asked Questions blog to provide answers to commonly asked questions from sales prospects and customers

Sun Microsystems, for example, has deployed more than 5,500 blogs and has more than 4,600 bloggers in their organization. (See Figure 3-1.) Blogging is part of the organization's life-blood. Blogging at Sun includes CEO and President Jonathan Schwartz writing (somewhat infrequently) to shareholders, employees, and the technical community.

Figure 3-1:
The impressive blog homepage at Sun Microsystems.

The blogs at Sun span every portion of the organization, including the Sun Security blog that communicates software vulnerabilities in real time and promotes Sun's certification, software, patches, upgrades, and toolkits in the sidebar. (See Figure 3-2.) This blog communicates issues directly to customers and promotes the openness and customer care that Sun provides system administrators.

Estimating Your Return on Blogging Investment

Return on investment (ROI) is the common name for the equation the industry uses to measure whether a strategy is worthwhile for a business to continue pursuing. Simply put, return on investment is the percent ratio of total revenue and total savings versus total expenses.

ROI = (total revenue+ total savings)/(total expenses) x 100

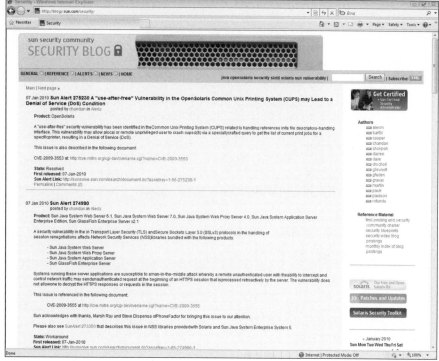

Figure 3-2:
Targeting customers and prospects in the sidebar on Sun's Security Blog.

Here's an example:

> Cost of blogging (software-as-a-service): $15,000
>
> Employee cost for writing daily posts over a year: $6,000
>
> Total cost: $21,000
>
> Savings in customer service: $12,000
>
> Revenue acquired through blog: $120,000
>
> ROI = ($120,000 + $12,000)/($21,000) x 100
>
> ROI = 629% Annually.

Determining the total revenue is simple — it's the revenue gained from the blog through direct purchases, leads that were acquired through the blog and closed, and leads acquired indirectly from the blog through speaking engagements and other blog-related referrals.

The total savings is evaluated by the reduction in human resources required to support call volumes and other support requests.

The total expenses for a blogging strategy may be the most complex to measure. Your expenses need to include the hourly human resource cost for content creation and support + infrastructure cost + software cost + design cost + optimization cost.

Evaluating cost per blogging lead

Understanding what your cost per lead is prior to starting is incredibly important so that you can fully understand whether blogging is reducing your cost per lead. Cost per lead should equal your marketing and sales costs divided by the total leads that are acquired.

A *cost per blogging lead* is the cost of your blogging program divided by the number of leads that are provided to your sales team for closing. Companies should never abandon advertising and marketing efforts that have a positive return on investment, but recognizing the cost per lead through each of the mediums they use will help them determine where to focus their effort.

As an example, many companies use paid search (pay per click) to acquire leads. You may pay upwards of $200 per lead through this advertising medium. Your blogging strategy might lower that cost per lead under $100 over time. If your blogging strategy is acquiring great leads at half the price, this will help you decide the effort you wish to put into each of your marketing mediums.

Over time, you'll find that you're attracting more and more leads so your cost per lead on a blog will eventually decline as long as your traffic and conversions are increasing.

Measuring the value of search traffic

Additionally, it may be worthwhile to measure the value of the traffic your blog acquires through organic search traffic by evaluating the same cost for that traffic via paid search. Organic search traffic is the traffic that your blog acquires by showing up naturally in search engine results. Paid search traffic is traffic that is acquired by bidding on keywords and having small advertisements placed on a search engine results page (SERP).

Google and other search engines freely distribute keyword data for advertisers to use to develop paid search campaigns. Each keyword is tracked for the number of searches per month, the competitiveness of the word as well as the average bid to win that word. Because so many companies participate in paid search, it's an accurate means of evaluating keywords and the associated traffic that those keywords produce.

This is accomplished by using a combination of Google AdWords and viewing your analytics traffic by search keyword.

Multiplying the value of the keyword (cost per click) by the number of visits you received from that keyword provides you with the value of that traffic.

As an example, if companies bid $0.50 per click for a keyword, that visit is worth $0.50 for a company. If you would like 10,000 visitors, you're going to spend $5,000 in your paid search campaign. With a targeted blogging strategy, if you rank well and acquire 10,000 visitors for a specific keyword via your blog, it may have cost you a fraction of the cost per visitor. Perhaps it was a single blog post that cost your company less than $100 in time to write and publish!

Understanding relative cost of the traffic you're acquiring via organic search can help you recognize the value of the overall program to generating traffic to your site without having to calculate and track the return on investment.

Just follow these steps to calculate your own:

1. **Using your analytics program, identify the keywords that drove traffic from search engines to your blog.**

    a. Log in to your analytics application.

    b. If your company uses an enterprise analytics application such as Webtrends, search for *Phrases* in the report search. The keyword information you're seeking is in the Most Recent Search Phrases (All) report. If you are utilizing Google Analytics, the report is available in Traffic Sources⇨Keywords.

    Figure 3-3 shows the number of visits from the term *marketing technology* is 23.

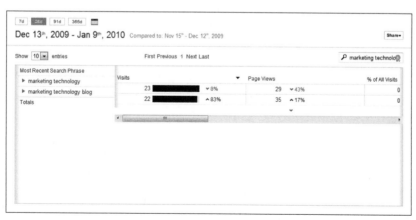

Figure 3-3: Viewing Webtrends' Most Recent Search Phrases (All) Report.

2. **Utilizing Google AdWords External Keyword Tool, look up the value of the keyword.**

   Figure 3-4 shows the estimated average cost per click (CPC) for *marketing technology* was $4.00.

3. **Multiply the quantity times the average cost per click.**

   23 visits per month × $4.00 = $92.00 per month or $1,104 annually.

4. **Repeat for each of the keyword terms that is driving traffic to your blog and get a grand total. This is the value of the search traffic that your blog is attracting.**

By using this technique, you'll be able to evaluate both your paid and organic search efforts. Paid search may be more expensive at times, but has advantages like being able to "turn up" your volume of inbound leads when you need to. Blogging is more of a long-term strategy and not always as predictable.

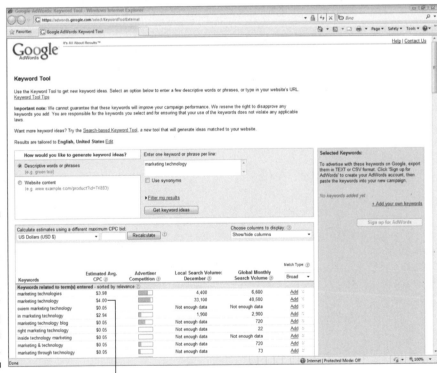

Figure 3-4:
Looking up a keyword phrase in Google AdWords' External Keyword Tool.

The CPC of "marketing technology"

Visits, pageviews, and conversions

What's the difference between a visit and a pageview? A *visit* is a unique person who has arrived at your site. A *pageview* is a single page viewed by a visitor. If five people visit your site and look at two pages each, that equates to five visits and ten pageviews, or an average of two pageviews per visitor.

A *conversion* is a step a visitor takes that brings them closer to becoming a client. Ultimately, a conversion is a prospect who becomes a customer, but along the path from prospect to customer, many independent conversions occur. A search engine user clicks a search result and converts to a visitor. A visitor registers for a Webinar and converts to a lead. A lead is called by your sales team and is converted to a customer.

As well, some companies have found it very advantageous to "own the search engine results page" on both paid and organic search. If your company is listed in organic and paid search results, there's a far greater chance of acquiring that visitor from the search engine.

When you can accurately identify which keywords are actually converting traffic for you, you can narrow your focus and content strategy, increasing your overall return on investment.

Measuring conversions to improve your content

When your blog begins to attract attention, you can see and measure how those visitors are getting to your blog, determine how effective each referring source is, and adjust your strategy accordingly.

Segmenting your traffic by source

Analytics applications segment your visitors four ways:

- **Direct traffic:** These are visitors that have bookmarked your blog in their browser or typed in your Web address (URL) and arrived directly.
- **Referring traffic:** This is traffic that comes to your blog from a link on another site.
- **Search engine traffic:** This is traffic that comes to your blog from a search engine.
- **Other traffic:** This is traffic that comes to your site from other programs like e-mail marketing newsletters.

Understanding the source of your visitors is the first opportunity to begin determining where you need to focus on traffic. Segmenting your traffic by source provides you with an understanding of the value of those sources. The following steps show you how to view traffic sources in Google Analytics:

1. **Log in to your Analytics account.**

2. **Select your account and site.**

3. **Choose Traffic Sources➪Overview from the left sidebar. (See Figure 3-5.)**

If you find that specific keywords draw the most business, focus your content in those areas and abandon keywords that don't attract any business. Keywords often change over time so be prepared to adjust accordingly. For example, fewer than 10 years ago, the world referred to the Internet as the *World Wide Web* or the *Web*, but now only rarely so. Try to keep up with changes like these.

Figure 3-5:
Viewing
Traffic
Sources
Overview
in Google
Analytics.

Tracking visitors with analytics and Google Webmasters

Many bloggers focus their strategy and attention on analytics only. Remember that analytics only measure the visitors that have actually clicked through and have landed on your blog. You may be showing up in many search results but not acquiring the traffic because visitors aren't compelled to click through.

Most blogs with an effective search engine strategy acquire over 50 percent of their traffic from search. If you'd like to monitor and improve the volume of visitors you're acquiring from search engines, you'll need to dig deeper into the way your blog is showing up in the search engines.

You can monitor your ranking and click-throughs using Google Webmasters, Bing Webmasters, and Yahoo! Site Explorer. All of the major search engines provide you with information on what content is being found in search results, where it's ranked, and how often searchers are clicking through on your results. As important as analytics is to measure your visitors' behavior on your blog, Webmasters is key to measuring your visitors' behavior in search engines.

Although the traffic you're getting from search engines is important, the traffic you're not getting may be more important. Google Webmasters provides you with keywords and how your pages rank. You may find that you rank very well for certain keywords, but you're not getting clicks for those search queries. Follow these steps to view your traffic click-throughs in Google Webmasters.

1. **Log in to your Webmasters account.**

2. **Select your site.**

3. **Choose Your Site on the Web➪Top Search Queries from the left sidebar.**

   The left column (see Figure 3-6) lists the searches that your site appeared in. The right side (see Figure 3-6) lists the search results that actually generated traffic to your site by visitors clicking them. Sort these in ascending order by clicking the Position link.

To increase that conversion rate, you may wish to write more compelling post titles and meta descriptions so that the viewable information in the search engine drives more click-throughs. If the keywords you're ranking high for (say, in the top three) aren't getting clicked, that's a sure sign you need to rework the content.

Figure 3-6:
Viewing
keyword
ranking
and click-
throughs
in Google
Web-
masters.

After visitors are on your site, it's much easier to track them with your Web analytics package. All analytics packages have conversion tracking and goal tracking that you can customize to properly track a purchase made from a visitor to your blog.

Adjusting your strategy to increase conversions

Tracking the referring sites and keywords that drive conversions allow you to adjust your strategy and push more content on keywords that drive the most traffic, or make changes on ones that are driving traffic but not conversions.

To increase conversions within your blog, you can deploy a number of tactics, including the following:

> ✓ **Link directly to the conversion source within your blog posts.** Many companies simply put a call to action in the sidebar of their blog and forget to actually promote from within the blog post. You may even want to add a line to your blog post with your phone number for prospects to call you directly.

> ✔ **Test and swap out your calls to action in your sidebar to figure out what works.** Improving your calls to action can have a huge impact on your conversion rates.
>
> ✔ **Simplify your landing page.** After visitors click a call to action, they are typically brought to a landing page. Landing pages sometimes have high abandonment rates if they have a form requesting too much information, have unnecessary navigation, or aren't written with compelling language.

Your blog posts are the best chance you have of driving traffic and conversions. Monitor your analytics and find out what's common with blog posts that are driving the most conversions and those that are not. Sometimes, it's the day of the week, sometimes the author, sometimes the post title, sometimes an image in the post or a conversion link. It could be any number of things that motivates a visitor to connect with you.

Many bloggers within the industry determine the success of their blogs by visitor *engagement* — meaning the number of comments visitors leave. However, you should always measure engagement as the effect your blog has on your business and the return on investment it generates. For business blogs, comments don't equate to dollars in any way, shape, or form, so don't gauge your blogging strategies success by the number of comments.

Corporate blogs often produce no comments at all. Even on a popular blog, very few readers will actually come forward and comment on a blog. Many times, the blog post content itself has to be highly charged to solicit a response — something you may not wish to risk on a corporate blog!

Don't be discouraged if you're not seeing huge growth or huge numbers! You may see other bloggers getting thousands or tens of thousands of visitors or subscribers each day. This is very important for blogs that publish content for advertising revenue.

Publishers need to have large numbers to attract advertisers. As a corporate blogger, your goal is not advertisers, your goal is revenue. A couple hundred visitors may be all your company needs to fully realize a positive return on investment. After you optimize for conversions, growing traffic is your next goal.

Don't make the mistake of focusing on the referring sources that provide you with the highest number of visits. Instead, focus on those sources that provide you with the highest number of actual conversions.

Reviewing objectives and measuring results

Just as with any marketing campaign, your blog's administrator should be reviewing analytics and measuring your program's performance on (at least) a weekly basis. Monitoring analytics to see the keywords that are driving the most conversions, the content that is driving the most traffic, how social media is driving traffic to your blog, and even which days of the week drive the most results helps you fine-tune your strategy.

On a monthly basis, evaluating how many leads you've acquired and the associated conversions and revenue per conversion helps you stay on track. On an annual basis, measuring your return on blogging investment, cost per lead, and comparing your blogging strategy to your other marketing efforts will help you plan your next budget. (For more on these evaluations and on analytics, see Chapter 15.)

These reviews also give an administrator an opportunity to praise or encourage staff members who have done well.

Jeremy Fairley, for example, is the head of Interactive Marketing at Tampa Bay & Company. Jeremy administers the Visit Tampa Bay blog (`http://blog.visittampabay.com`) and has a team of bloggers throughout the organization whose primary duties aren't blogging — they manage sponsorships, corporate relations, events, promotions, and consumer relations. Blogging is something Jeremy's team has to fill in between all their regular duties. It's working, though, and his team has been recognized as a leader in the travel industry, driving traffic and attention to Tampa as a great city for companies to hold their events.

Jeremy makes it a point every week to write an e-mail to his blogging team that highlights the highs and lows of their performance. (See Figure 3-7.) He publically praises those on his team who attracted a lot of attention with great content. He also loves to take playful jabs at his bloggers that haven't performed well. The motivational e-mail is just what the program needs to keep his bloggers having fun and ensuring they keep the great content coming.

Figure 3-7:
Keeping
your blog-
gers on
track.

Identifying Marketing and Promotion Goals

An integrated marketing strategy with a blog as part of a larger promotion strategy can maximize your results. Publishing your latest blog posts on your Web site can help with search engine optimization. Repurposing blog content in your e-mail newsletter can save your staff time. Additionally, promoting events through your blog can increase attendance.

Don't relegate your blog to a blogger that sits in the back room with no connection to the rest of the organization. Put your blog at the center of your communications strategy, and when you start a promotion ask, "How can we leverage the blog on this?"

Building authority in your industry

Authority is a word that's used to describe the level of expertise that a company, blog, or individual has in a given industry. Authority requires first that you are either educated or have a proven history of experience.

Even with education and experience you're not an authoritative figure, though. You must be acknowledged by other authoritative figures within the industry. The Internet provides a great platform for accumulating authority. The currency of authority on the Internet is measured with mentions and backlinks.

Writing a compelling industry blog that drives a lot of attention will drive your company's authority or the authority of employees within the company. That authority can open many doors, from speaking at industry events to writing a book.

Authority doesn't have to begin and end on your blog, either. Participating and adding valuable feedback to other industry blogs will garner attention from those bloggers. Stay involved in online industry networks, on Twitter, and on LinkedIn Groups. Be sure to get your company's name out there.

Search engine goals for keyword ranking

Search engines are honestly not that intelligent. Although the challenge of organizing billions of pages of content and displaying a search result is an incredible achievement, the quality of the results still stinks.

Think about how many times you've done a search and how many results you had to read through before getting the correct result. Think about how many times you had to search over and over with different word combinations. Search engines display multiple results and pages because you may not find what you're looking for in the first result.

Recognizing this as an issue, the search engine optimization industry has exploded in growth. *Search engine optimization* is the act of incorporating best practices across your site to ensure content is properly found and indexed properly by search engines. eMarketer reports that search engine optimization is an industry that will grow from $1.5 billion in 2008 to over $3.8 billion by 2013.

Search engine optimization is a necessary practice to ensure that your content is found where it should be by the target audience seeking it. Search engine optimization helps to overcome the severe lack of intelligence that search engines have.

At its core, a search engine "crawls" your site, identifies keywords, and makes an educated guess on the search keywords your site should show up for. They also account for the keywords employed when you're linked to from other authoritative sites, how long your site has been around, and any problems actually locating your content.

If you want to be found for specific keywords, you must use those keywords effectively in page titles, post titles, headings, content, and meta data. If you present the content appropriately to the search engine, there's a better possibility that your content will be found by the people you want it to be found by.

The key to being found in search engines is to answer a searcher's question — and to be found within the search engine results pages. Knowing the keywords to use that will drive traffic and sales is important, but don't forget to monitor how your pages are ranking for those keywords.

For more on improving your search engine ranking, see Part III.

Setting Goals for Customer Relationship Management (CRM)

Customer relationship management (CRM) has been the rallying cry of the last decade and it was going to change the world, making it much easier for us to automate and communicate with fewer resources. *Customer relationship management* systems are software platforms in which companies maintain a history of all contact with prospects and customers. By maintaining this information, a company can maintain effective communications and a full profile of each of their customers.

CRM helps companies better understand key metrics with regard to customers — such as retention, satisfaction, customer service, sales goals, and so on. CRM also helps companies better manage the relationship with the company, communicate with them automatically at key times, and provide employees with the information they need to better manage the clients.

CRM requires companies document and record all interactions with customers. Some companies spend more time configuring and entering data in their customer relationship management system than actually helping customers.

Blogging offers a platform for you to speak to all your customers at the same time and offer them a means to respond. If you want to improve your relationship with customers, managing an effective blogging strategy that responds to their needs and provides them with additional value may provide you a much better return on investment in the long run.

Using blogs to communicate with customers

Compared to pricing in the past, modern companies often sell products and services at a fraction of previous costs. Being able to produce much more with fewer resources, many companies have huge volumes of customers but lack the human resources to commit to great service because the price of the product or service simply doesn't allow for it.

Blogs are a one-to-many, permission-based medium. Blogs also have robust search and categorization methodologies that make the content easy to find. Combined with search engines, blogs are an incredible platform to publish just about everything your company wants to publish. With a blog you can do any of the following:

- ✔ Promote upcoming Webinars, conferences, and other events.
- ✔ Promote Webinars, conferences, and other events while they are happening.
- ✔ Provide a synopsis of Webinars, conferences, and other events. This is a great way of showing non-attendees what they missed so they will come to the next event.
- ✔ List promotions and specials. This is a great way to increase conversion rates, upsell current clients, and find new ones. Often, a great special is virally communicated from a blog through social media.
- ✔ Publish releases, changes, and updates. This keeps customers up-to-date on what's happening with your company.
- ✔ List partner and industry news so customers are informed of additional opportunities.
- ✔ Promote upsell opportunities or cross-sell opportunities. This can impact revenue directly and increase your average customer value.
- ✔ Publish customer support issues and workarounds. This reduces the volume of inbound calls to your service department.

Blogging can have a significant impact on cutting costs within your organization. Think about the last time you had to copy and paste a response to a customer about an issue that was previously raised. Through your e-mail or phone system, you may only be dealing with one client at a time. Through your blog, you may be able to prevent hundreds of phone calls by simply publishing common issues that used to take up time and resources.

Leveraging blogs for your organization's knowledge base

Providing a searchable, organized knowledge base not only helps your customers, it also helps your company! Employees can educate themselves just as easily as your customers can. This knowledge base should include the following:

- **Frequently Asked Questions about billing, the company, the products, the employees, the services, and the support.** These are perfect topics that will reduce the dependence on your customer service, accounting, and sales departments. Proactively promote your blog as *the* place for customers to seek and find the information they need.

- **Industry best practices.** Distributing this information via your blog educates clients on how to most effectively leverage your product or service.

- **A glossary.** Blog content is an easy place to define industry terms and vocabulary — make it an education source for clients, prospects, and employees.

If you have a very large array of products and solutions, you may even want to deploy multiple blogs. Providing your customers with a specific path to the information they are seeking is important.

Sharing customer testimonials

Perhaps the largest missed opportunity of corporate blogs is the opportunity to speak about the customer. Customers love sharing the spotlight and will promote your blog posts when you make mention of them. Customer testimonials are a powerful marketing message because it's not you speaking — it's your customers!

Corporate blogging platform Compendium built a feature, Web to Post, directly into their application so that customers could actually write their own blog posts and share their stories.

The system is used frequently on Carhartt's Tough Jobs blog (`http://blogs.carhartt.com/blog/tough-jobs`). Carhartt is a clothing manufacturer who makes tough, high-quality work clothing. Their customers are nuts about the product and proudly display their "Carhartts" where ever they go.

The Tough Jobs blog consists of direct submissions from customers, which include maintenance workers, fiberglass grinders, scrap metal operations workers, lumberjacks, monster truck crew chiefs, oil rig drillers, mechanics, and even some welders from the World Trade Center site in New York City.

Each shares their story of what they do for a living and why they love their Carhartts. This is an incredible strategy because Carhartt doesn't even have to write the content! Their customers are writing content that's being found through search engines and social media and turning that content into attracting new customers! (See Figure 3-8.)

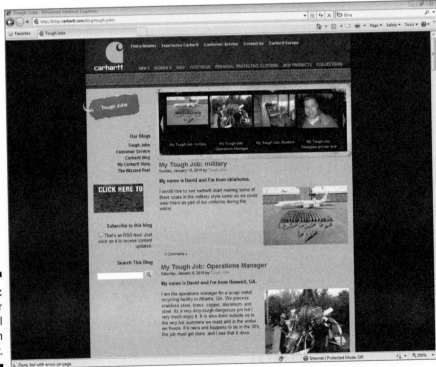

Figure 3-8:
Customer testimonial blogs from Carhartt.

If you don't have the means for customers to submit their testimonials directly, here are some tips for capturing them:

- Obtain permission from the customer to publish the testimonial.
- Tell the story behind the testimonial and be sure to include keywords.
- Use first names unless the person is widely known like President Barack Obama or Bill Gates.
- Write the story as if you were an observer or reporter and not actually working for the company. Refer to the company in the third person. This will put focus on the customer and not your company.
- Include some personal facts about the customer so they are humanized and not seen as some generic, made-up person.
- Include a photo of the customer. If it's a business, include a link to their site and include some information about their products and services.
- Include a call to action to offer the same products or services that the customer testimonial refers to. It may be as simple as a link to the product page.
- If a photo is worth a thousand words, a video is worth a million! Video testimonials are a fantastic way of conveying sincerity.

Having your customers speak and sell your product is the most powerful and effective means of growing your customer base. Make the collection and publishing of customer testimonials on your blog part of your blogging goals. Highlight these blogs in e-mails and promote them through social media.

Part II
Mapping Out and Implementing Your Corporate Blog

The 5th Wave   By Rich Tennant

"Our customer survey indicates 30% of our customers think our service is inconsistent, 40% would like a change in procedures, and 50% think it would be real cute if we all wore matching colored vests."

In this part . . .

This part is dedicated to helping you understand corporate blogging from a technical and logistical perspective. Chapter 4 introduces the domain structure of your blog, providing you with the information you need to make an informed decision about your blog's setup.

Chapter 5 takes you through the different blogging platform options, giving you information about what key factors should be used to evaluate and select the right platform for you. Explore all of the options before making a decision to ensure that you choose the best fit for your organization.

Although selecting the correct platform for your needs is necessary, your blog's success is determined by the results from the effort put into it. Chapter 6 helps you identify who should be on your blogging team and what type of content they should write. Ghost blogging and legal protection of your blog content is covered, too.

Chapter 7 builds your strategy for selecting, educating, and motivating your blogging team. All organizations should read this chapter no matter how much blogging experience they have.

Chapter 4

Using a Domain That Matters for Your Corporate Blog

In This Chapter

▶ Putting the company's best foot forward online

▶ Adding search capabilities to a corporate blog

▶ Fitting an online domain to your company's needs

▶ Placing your blog to best advantage

*Y*ou may have just written a blog entry that will set your industry on its ear or get the masses clamoring for your product. But if the company Web site is so clunky or boring that nobody manages to find your blog, then nobody can see what a fascinating, informative, valuable resource it is for your company, right? Well, the old marketing maxim that "you don't get a second chance to make a first impression" is more relevant than ever when you're trying to make contact on Internet time. Hordes of Web-surfing visitors may land on your company Web site — but how many stay long enough to become customers, or even regulars? How many just glance at your site and zip away to somewhere else? An inviting, attractive site may capture your visitors' attention just long enough to give your blog a chance to start building relationships. An ugly or dull site may repel all those visitors in the blink of an eye. It's worth asking two questions: (1) How will your blog fit into the company Web site, and (2) can your company really *afford* ho-hum Web design?

This chapter is about giving your corporate blog its best shot at reaching your business audience. Here you can find a perspective that may help you change some in-house minds about the importance of a dynamic Web presence. You get pointers on helping to jazz up the company Web site, integrating your company's look, brand, and mission into your blog, and positioning your blog to best advantage within the company's online domain.

Integrating Your Corporate Identity into Your Blog

As companies are pressured to become more social by their customers and prospects, the line is blurring between the corporate brand and the personal brand. Brand management has always been a critical component of marketing, but ordinary brand management never allowed for consumers to have insight into the actual people behind the brand.

In the early days of corporate blogging, there was a wide gap between marketing and blogging. In fact, many company's marketing departments felt threatened by the transparency that a blog provided. Now that companies have been blogging for a decade, companies with a tight integration between the blog and the marketing have been able to successfully capture attention on the Web, to engage readers, and to route them directly into the company's sales funnel.

Corporate blogs are no longer outside of the company's domain; they are now being integrated directly into an overall Web presence. This convergence has made it easier to measure, manage, and implement inbound marketing strategies between the blog and the company. Your Web site is still a critical component, providing all the data, facts, figures, and other expected information — but your blog has become the *voice* of the company. To maximize the benefits of a corporate blog, investing in a comprehensive, integrated strategy with your other marketing efforts will maximize your return on investment.

As chairman and founder of the Online Marketing Summit (http://online marketingsummit.com/), Aaron Kahlow has a practiced eye for what does and doesn't work to get a company's message out. He often remarks that most businesses spend more money on decorating the company lounge than they do on sprucing up the company Web presence. Of course, when you think about it, most visitors these days drop in via the Web — and many will form a first impression of your company when they arrive at its Web site. Sure, putting an Italian leather couch in the real-world waiting room is impressive — gee, nobody seems to question the Return on Couch Investment (ROCI) — but you can bet that most of the online visitors will never see or touch it.

This neglect of the Web presence is strange, considering how little it can cost a company to incorporate good design ideas into presenting its message (*and its corporate image*) online. A minimum investment of $3,000, for example, can get a company a professional design through *crowdsourcing* — essentially connecting with Web designers online: Companies and individuals post design requests, and then artists from all over the world submit ideas. The process allows you to fine-tune the design, and you only pay after you make a selection. Two of the more popular sites are CrowdSPRING (`www.crowd spring.com`) and 99designs (`www.99designs.com`).

If you're a larger company, hiring a professional design firm or agency could cost you $50,000 — and be well worth the price tag, depending on the situation. A talented designer can often work miracles. A great design firm can make a small company look like a Fortune 500 corporation — and sometimes that's all it takes to get the revenue flowing. Whichever route you take, don't skimp on your design.

Balancing your personal expertise and your corporate brand isn't difficult, sometimes it can be accomplished simply by allowing an author page that displays a friendly portrait and biography. If you already have a team responsible for your online presence, that team should ultimately decide on the look and feel. Blog administrators or bloggers, though, should fight to ensure that *people* are the focus of the design and not products or services.

Who's responsible for paying the bill can differ greatly! If the purpose of your blog is to acquire leads, typically, the team that's responsible for acquiring those leads would also be responsible for funding and monitoring the progress of your corporate blog. If the purpose is to reduce customer service calls, the customer support team may be responsible for the investment. If the purpose is simply to build authority in your industry to get the spotlight more, it's typical that the marketing team covers the costs. In any case, be sure to justify the investment by reviewing the purpose of the blog with the decision-makers. Many companies severely underestimate the power of great design, but design matters — the proof is all over the Web. One example is National Savings & Investments. In 2002, NS&I spent two million pounds on a rebranding effort, and the result was a sales increase of forty-four million pounds in just eight weeks! Your blog may not see those kinds of results, but an investment in the design of your blog can significantly impact its performance.

You should know that crowdsourcing has some pretty stiff opposition from many professional designers who are opposed to producing designs without the guarantee of getting paid. The professionals, after all, have worked hard to hone their craft and point out that their portfolio should be the deciding factor on whether they're hired. "Spec" work is the official term for supplying samples at no cost, and many designers believe it's pure evil. So, if you decide to use a crowdsourcing service, you may want to keep it hush-hush.

Bringing your brand and corporate identity to your blog theme

The overall layout and graphical designs behind a blog are typically referred to as a *theme*. Most blogging software allows you to install add-ons, plug-ins, or other packages that have no impact on the content of the site and leave all the changing up to you (which is as it should be). Be sure to ask about whether your blogging software has this feature — it makes updating your blog's design or rebranding easy!

Your blog's theme doesn't have to be a perfect match for the company's corporate look and feel — but it should reflect your purpose clearly. So, from time to time, refer to your original goals for your blog — make sure its look and feel match the goals. Is it too sedate when you're trying to be friendly? Too frivolous when you're trying to build credibility? Often a corporate blogging goal is to create engagement and show the true personality of the organization — which is (ideally, at least) expressed in its branding. If this is the case, then your approach to the blog should reflect what the branding is saying to the customer. If what you want to say is, "We're trustworthy," that will affect not only the look and feel of the design theme, but also the tone of the writing and presentation. Ditto if you're saying, "We're a fun place!" Either way, what the brand represents should feel authentic and personal to the readers of your blog.

When your blog's theme does match the corporate brand, it conveys consistency and authority. Walker Information, for example, is an international customer intelligence company. Walker has built an incredible organization, and does its best to ensure that the branding is consistent across their Web site (www.walkerinfo.com) and their blog (http://blog.walkerinfo.com). Figures 4-1 and 4-2 give you a look at how they do it.

When you compare Walker's blog with its Web site, it's easy to see that both come from the same company. Note, however, that the blog provides a focus on the company's internal talent and how they lead the industry and help customers. The Web site focuses on results, products, and features.

A quick look under the hood shows that Walker's Web site and blog are on two totally different content management systems — but the brand and identity expressed is identical. (See Figure 4-2.) It's a neat trick. Here's where robust content management systems with fully customizable theming (software that supports cascading style sheets [CSS] and editing of template files) come in — they allow your company to match your look and feel with precision! All the popular blogging platforms offer this customization, including WordPress, TypePad, Expression Engine, Compendium, Blogger, and many more.

Figure 4-1:
Walker
Informa-
tion's Web
site and
brand.

Ensuring that your customers recognize your blog as authentic

Okay, what (in practical terms) does it mean for a business to be "authentic" these days? Well, people still prize good service and the feeling that their needs matter — those desires can't be met by stale information, robotic dullness, or an aloof attitude. So one highly effective way to show that your blog is authentic is to combine consistent branding with attention to detail — in effect, showing that real people from your organization are writing the content. Then you're sending an inviting message — "Somebody here cares enough to tell you what you want to know." After all, when prospects arrive at the company blog, they're looking for answers. Before they decide to do business with your company, they'd like insight into the talent of the people who work there. A blog provides a unique experience that breaks down the barriers of the brand and allows the consumer to read (and even converse with) the company, person to person.

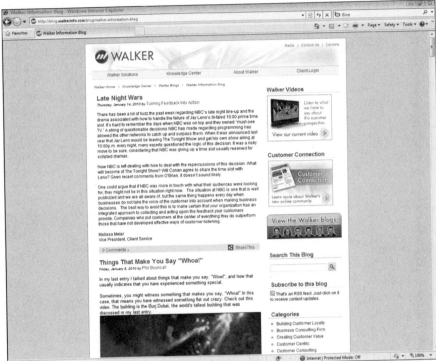

Figure 4-2:
Walker Information's blog shows clear consistency with the company Web site.

Some companies have decided that the expense of integrating and designing their corporate blog is too difficult. Instead, these companies host their blogs on subdomains of free blogging engines. This means the domain is totally different from the corporate site, the design is inconsistent, and because the corporate site doesn't actively promote it — visitors to the blog wonder whether or not it's actually part of the company! There are hundreds of thousands of blogs out there — many of them spam sites hosted on these free platforms — so your blog simply gets disregarded because it can't be trusted. That's counterproductive to the entire purpose of blogging: building trust!

Trust is ultimately what businesses and consumers are purchasing when they decide to do business with your company. Here's a striking example: Doug Theis, Vice President of Business Development for Lifeline Data Centers (www.lifelinedatacenters.com), likes to say that people hire his company so they don't get fired. In this case, he's talking about fending off the effects of disasters that can take down a business.

Lifeline Data Centers houses tens of millions of dollars in hardware for companies throughout the country. Their facilities have custom cooling, fire suppression, redundant power, and 24/7 security and maintenance. Hospitals and other organizations depend on Lifeline to keep their infrastructure running through power outages — even an F4 tornado. When the Information Technology team at an organization decides to move into Doug's facilities, they are putting their jobs in his hands.

Doug's blog is a reflection of this responsibility. Doug blogs about industry certifications, power systems, requirements, outages, best practices, challenges, and changes throughout the industry. Although Doug is often blogging to clients directly, he's also picked up readers over the last few years who are drawn in by the information — so he's grown an impressive clientele. This hasn't happened by accident, by cutting costs, or by writing flawless requests for proposals. Lifeline Data Centers continues to grow as the Midwest's largest Data Center provider because people trust the staff at Lifeline. And Doug is the public face of the company, so his blog has to reflect and cultivate that trust.

Doug networks extensively and is often seen at many regional events, including running a local network organization called Techmakers (whose parent company is Rainmakers). People instantly recognize Doug because he is trustworthy and always available via the blog, at events, and by e-mail.

To take full advantage of blogging as a strategy, put your people out in front of your brand — especially those who are good at developing trust and following through.

Personalizing your corporate blog with portraits and biographies

If putting your people first is a key strategy, then it's only logical that providing a photograph and biography is essential. Most blogging platforms have author biography sections, and plug-ins or sticky post options to display them.

A *sticky post* is a blog post that always sticks to the top of the blog. When new posts are added, the sticky post remains. Sticky posts are perfect for displaying the profile of your blogger.

Law firm Alerding Castor Hewitt displays a photo and biography of each of its attorneys on their blog through sticky posts (http://blog.alerding castor.com/blog/alerding-castor). Alerding Castor specializes in new business startups. Instead of piling on the jargon of business law, they actually become partners with many of their client companies — to help them become bigger companies.

That personalized touch was something that can't be fully described on a Web site but is easily identified in a corporate blog. The attorneys at Alerding Castor Hewitt may blog about privacy litigation, business politics, how to treat employees, or even the local art scene and everything in between. (See Figure 4-3.)

What Alerding Castor Hewitt has effectively accomplished through the blog is the removal of the stodgy, boring, sometimes frightening business of startup law and played directly to their audience — the entrepreneur.

For your profile, you will want to include your job title, responsibilities, qualifications, and even your outside interests. As the world dives deeper into social media and social networking, it's a great idea to share your Twitter, Facebook, and LinkedIn pages and links.

Figure 4-3: Implementing an inviting portrait and profile by using sticky posts.

Using Your Existing Search Engine Authority with Your Company Domain

Just as a driver's license number holds a lot of meaning to your personal history, your domain holds your *traffic* history on the Internet. Search engines place a lot of value on the history of the domain, what topics people searched it for in the past, whether the domain was ever used to produce spammy or questionable content, and how popular the domain is (measured in links back to the site).

Domainers are people or companies who find expiring domains and buy them for later sale or profit. Many domainers figure out the history on a domain and purchase them simply because they have a great history with a lot of backlinks. This allows them to launch a new blog and immediately get a decent ranking with the search engines.

Some companies are tempted simply to use a free online blogging service to host their corporate blog. They select a subdomain at a provider like Blogger, TypePad, or WordPress — creating a blog at a Web address that looks like this: `http://mycompany.wordpress.com`. Sorry, but this is a huge mistake: The company has handed over all of search engine authority to the core domain! (To see more about why that's a serious no-no, flip to the section called "Controlling how a domain affects search engine authority," later in this chapter. ***Hint:*** Somebody just lost control of something valuable.) If you are using a free online blogging service, don't use a provider subdomain — set up an alias. Each of these services allow you to set up what's called a *canonical name record* (CNAME) that allows you to point your domain or point a subdomain to the service. If you decide to go this route, ask about — and use — the CNAME option. For corporate purposes, it's an absolute necessity!

For example, if your company decides to set up a blog at Blogger.com, you might host the blog at `mycompany.blogger.com`. Any search engine authority that you build up, all the subsequent links, and all your rankings, then, are basically in the property of blogger.com — they don't belong to your company. If blogger.com decides to close down, or if you decide to move to another platform, you lose all your search engine visibility and authority. By hosting the blog on your own company domain, you can freely move between software-as-a-service blogging solutions or even host the blog on your own server because the search engines have built up reputation and authority on *your* domain, not blogger.com!

A canonical name record (CNAME), is a record within your domain registration service that you can add that will point a domain or subdomain that you own to another server. Canonical name records make it convenient since you can still own the authority but have the flexibility of moving to any hosted blogging provider.

If, for example, you're hosting your blog at Compendium, you'll add a record with your domain registrar to point your blog (example: `blog.yourcompany domain.com`) to `compendiumblog.com`. This is invisible to visitors. As a person types in `blog.yourcompanydomain.com`, they are brought directly to your blog — which is simply hosted and managed by Compendium.

Controlling how a domain affects search engine authority

Search engine authority is the history of your site that's maintained by search engines. It's analogous to credit ratings: With a high credit score, you're able to get credit easier, and with a high authority, you'll be able to get better ranking on search engines. Google measure authority with its pagerank score. *Pagerank* is a number between 0 and 10, where 10 means you had outstanding authority.

Starting a blog on a new domain— or on a totally separate domain — can be a very slow climb because the domains lack any authority. It could be six months or more before you're starting to see any significant quantities of search engine traffic coming your way.

Search engines are slow to pay immediate attention to a new domain because there are so many companies out there launching thousands of domains and blogs to try and garner search engine ranking without any quality content. Some companies buy up thousands of domain names and throw hundreds of pages of content up overnight to simply try to build links back to another site or get some search engine traction for some keywords they hope to sell goods on. Don't be tempted to take this route if you hope to build credibility with your readers and truly help your business.

There's another factor as well: The actual words in your blog's domain could have an impact on its authority. There are three ways to select a domain:

✔ To identify your corporate brand. These are domains that are specific to the brand like `dknewmedia.com`, `compendium.com`, `pointbrake.com`, `xemion.com`.

✔ To identify what your company actually does. These are practical domain names, and speak more to what your company does like `corporatebloggingtips.com`, `marketingtechblog.com`, `digital homeinfo.com`, `hertakeonmarketing.com`. Notice that the brand name isn't included in these but they have combination of words that describe what they do.

✔ A combination of the two. These companies use keywords in their brand or combine the brand with a keyword. Examples are `blendtec.com`, `smallboxweb.com`, and `slingshotseo.com`.

With a strong brand on a domain with a lot of history, adding a blog and getting search engine traffic is practically expected — especially if your site is already getting some search engine traffic.

Without history, it's difficult to gain momentum with search engines. In this case, if you don't have a highly remarkable brand and you're open to it, you may want to try using a practical domain name instead. By ensuring that your domain has relevant keywords in it, you are providing a relevant destination. In search engine results, you will sometimes find that the domain that has keywords within it rises above other results.

Fairytale Brownies, for example, is a national brand that strategically purchased the practical domain name for the keyword *brownies.* Their blog can be found at `http://blog.brownies.com`. (See Figure 4-4.)

Figure 4-4:
Fairytale
Brownies
uses a
keyword-
rich domain
name.

Using your existing authority to your advantage

If you have an existing domain with authority, be sure to use it by building your blog on a subdomain or subdirectory. Some businesses decide to build their blogs on new domains. Unless you're confident that you can attract a lot of attention on a new blog on an external domain, take advantage of your existing domain. Your domain already has history and is (most likely) trusted.

There are plenty of geeks in back rooms out in the Internet that would love to argue the point about using an existing company domain. If you feel compelled to argue, putting your resources into writing a few more blog posts will proba-bly benefit your company much more than wasting the energy on an argument that's virtually impossible to prove a result for.

Subdomains do afford other opportunities for inbound marketing efforts. By pushing different efforts to different subdomains (such as `email.your companydomain.com`, `landingpages.yourcompanydomain.com`, `blog. yourcompanydomain.com`, `sales.yourcompanydomain.com`, `support. yourcompanydomain.com`), it's much easier to maintain multiple profiles in your analytics program. If you simply had these pages and strategies mixed in subfolders or subpages across a single domain, trying to analyze each strategy and how visitors are arriving, behaving, and converting can be a huge challenge.

Subdomains can be more convenient for establishing different analytics pro-files and accurately measuring your traffic to the blog alone. You might want to take advantage of this characteristic if it fits the needs of your blog and your company.

Working to establish authority as fast as possible

When your blog is ready for you to write that first blog post, imagine some-one just provided you with the keys to an incredibly powerful race car. Many companies ask, "How many blog posts should I write?" That's a lot like asking "How slow can I go and still win the race?" You've got a state-of-the-art con-tent engine and if you want to win, you must hit the gas when the green flag comes out and continue to push it as hard as you can!

A business blog with entries written once a week has about 50 posts by the end of the year. That's 50 chances to win search and win some customers.

A business blog that publishes a post a day has over 250 posts by the end of the year. If a blog has 5 times more content — assuming, of course, that the stuff is worth reading — it has 5 times more opportunities to capture search-engine traffic!

Your blogging platform is going to allow you to publish as often as you'd like. So, if you have a lot to say about your business and can make it a thundering good read, take advantage of this incredible content engine and go win the race!

Be sure to use keywords that are going to attract search engine traffic within your blog posts. Always write quality, compelling content. Many businesses make the more-is-better mistake, and seldom see results because poor content (that is, say, too redundant, too obscure, too superficial, or too complex) leads to little or no business. Writing quality content will drive conversions.

Link your content from your Web site to your blog and your blog to your Web site. Associating new content with content that has already been indexed and ranked by search engines by association makes it easier for the search engines to find.

Chapter 8 shows you how to find out more information about the ways search engines find your content.

Moving your blog and retaining authority

Many companies start with a free subdomain and are actually surprised when their blog grows in popularity. They decide to move the blog and are aghast when they're not getting any traffic where they moved it. That's because the search engines recognize all the authority at the provider's domain.

If you decide to ever move your blog from one service to another, there are a number of steps you must take to ensure that nothing disrupts search-engine traffic. Remember, a new blog platform may have a new Web-address structure — which could cause incredible problems when someone clicks an old address! It can also result in the search engines dropping your ranking for specific pages because the links back to the pages that guaranteed your popularity no longer exist.

To move your blog from one service to another *and* retain your search-engine authority, just follow these steps:

1. **Export your old blog content and then Import that content into your new blogging platform. (See Figures 4-5 and 4-6.)**

   Most major blogging platforms have a universal export feature. Even if you have to do this manually, however, get it done; it's better than starting with no content at all.

Figure 4-5:
Exporting
your blog
content
from
WordPress
for use with
another
blogging
platform.

2. **Write redirects from the old blog post Web addresses to the new blog post URLs. Some platforms have redirection modules or plug-ins to make this easier.**

   Each time a request is made for a Web page, a code is sent to the requesting service. You've probably noticed this when you've seen "Page Not Found" errors associated with the number 404. *404* is the code that is actually sent to the requesting service. Users typically don't see these codes passed back and forth — that's the job of browsers and Web servers. A normal Web page produces a code of *200*.

   A *301* code tells the requester that the page has been moved. This technique ensures that users who click a search-engine result will still land on the content they were looking for. It also notifies the search engines that the page has moved. You will still lose some momentum in your search rankings, but at least you're not losing it all. Be sure to deploy 301 redirects on any pages that are being redirected.

Figure 4-6:
Importing your blog content from another blogging platform into WordPress.

Although you may want to employ the assistance of an expert to create your redirect, you can do it yourself in a number of different ways, including the following:

- You can write directly to an `.htaccess` file if your blog is deployed in a Unix or Linux hosting environment.

- You can add the redirects in Internet Information Services (IIS) if your blog is hosted in a Microsoft environment.

- You can deploy the use of a plug-in. If you're using WordPress, John Godley's Redirection Plug-in allows you to manage redirects with an easy-to-use management interface.

- You can also program the redirects directly in the code of the old page to point to the new page. In PHP, this looks like:

```
<?php header("Location: http://newdomain.com/newpage",
        TRUE, 301); ?>
```

Some content management systems also accomplish this for you. Squarespace is a popular content management system and blogging platform that allows you to import your blog and it ensures that all of your old content URLs will still work properly!

3. **Write a redirect from the old blog RSS feed to the new blog RSS feed.**

   An RSS feed is nothing more than a Web page that's formatted differently (instead of HTML, it uses XML so that it can be read easier by applications and programming languages). Just as you wrote a 301 redirect for your pages, you'll also want to write one for your blog's RSS feed. I recommend using a feed analytics application such as FeedBurner so you can update the feed without interruption in the future. Read more about setting up your blog on Feedburner in Chapter 15.

4. **Switch your CNAME record to point to the new service or server.**

   If you're moving domains or subdomains, it's still possible to redirect to the new blog address. You will lose some of your ranking when you transfer the subdomains but you may be able to bounce back quickly.

   Changing domains altogether can have a drastic impact — avoid it at all costs.

5. **Test many of your old blog posts' Web addresses and ensure they forward properly to your new blog address.**

6. **Monitor Google Webmasters, Bing Webmasters, and Yahoo! Site Explorer for pages that are not found — and correct them. Don't bother checking every day, though — it will take a week or two before you'll see problems.**

7. **Republish your Sitemap and resubmit each time you correct items.**

   This is accomplished by logging into Google Webmasters, selecting Site configuration⇨Sitemaps, checking your sitemap, and clicking Resubmit.

If you're changing your domain or subdomain, the biggest loss you're going to take are on sites like Technorati, which require that you register your new blog address. They don't have a means of updating your actual address.

Moving your blog is painful and will hurt your momentum, regardless of how hard you tried to keep all the pieces moving. This is why selecting a great domain and an outstanding platform is such a critical *early* decision.

Selecting the Best Domain Structure for Your Organization

A *subdomain* refers to the portion of text in your Web address before your actual domain name. Typically, the default of the Web has been to use the main "www" as a Web site. As the Web has evolved, subdomains are used to designate other sections of the domain.

Companies use subdomains for shopping, mail, support, video, and, of course, blogging. Subdomains are convenient for many companies because they can point a subdomain to another server much more easily than they can point a subdirectory to the same location.

The taxonomy of a Web address appears like this:

```
http://subdomain.domain.com/subdirectory
```

You can have multiple subdomains and subdirectories as well, of course. You might be wondering which is better — hosting your blog in a subdomain or in a subdirectory. There are some advantages and disadvantages to each approach, but ultimately there appears to be little difference in ranking between them.

Understanding the pros and cons of subdomains

In some ways, search engines treat subdomains like a separate domain altogether. For example, in search engine results pages you will often find a company with multiple subdomains gets additional results while a company with a single domain only gets one. There are other advantages as well, such as the following:

- ✔ Real estate matters, even online — maybe *especially* online. By having both a domain and subdomain showing up on search engines, you can cover more area in the Search Engine Results Page (SERP). Search engines are adjusting accordingly, filtering subdomains, and only showing a single relevant result.

- ✔ Consumers are tuning into blogs to make purchasing decisions more and more, so prominently using a blog subdomain makes it clear to them that your company is trying to achieve a relationship with them as customers. Blogging denotes honesty and trust — and that's what you want search engine users to see.

- ✔ Putting your blog on a subdomain can be a distinctive advantageous to differentiate your company's polished, slick, glitzy marketing from its inviting "voice."

- ✔ Organizing subdomains used to be difficult — but by now it's pretty mainstream in hosting administration panels.

- ✔ Using subdomains opens you up to taking advantage of existing third-party software as service applications that may be best suited to do the job. Delegating your e-mail subdomain to an e-mail service provider, for example, is a great way to monitor and maintain your e-mail reputation.

- ✔ A subdomain can be pointed anywhere, internally or externally, giving you a lot more flexibility in moving your blog between providers or changing your Web site's content management system, and so on, without having much impact on the blog's content.

✔ A subdomain can be set up independently within Webmasters' accounts and analytics accounts, providing you with discrete search engine monitoring and measurement on your blog strategy alone.

✔ Blogging platforms often have their own software for generating sitemaps. Keeping your sitemap independent of the blog — in effect, parking it on a subdomain — ensures that your blog is getting crawled properly and won't require you to manage multiple sitemaps throughout a single domain (which can be a major headache).

✔ Subdomains will allow your company mobility if you ever decide to switch blogging platforms or set up your own servers and do it yourself. Pointing a subdomain is much easier than configuring subdirectory redirects. Most blogging platforms do not offer anything but canonical name (CNAME) records to manage this situation.

✔ Most importantly, using a subdomain allows you to control, monitor, and adjust your corporate blogging strategy separately from your other marketing initiatives.

Understanding the pros and cons of putting your blog in a subfolder

Okay, you have an absolutely killer blog, decked out in the company livery, ready to bring in new friends from all over the Web. Where do you *put* it on the Web? Much of what you read out on the Web simply compares subdomains to subfolders, but says nothing about the advantages and disadvantages of each when you're singling out a corporate blogging strategy.

Matt Cutts of Google has some interesting feedback on this question, and promotes the use of a subdirectory, largely because or the complexities involved in configuring a subdomain.

"The single largest advantage of a subfolder is that it's simple to set up," he says. "If your company is setting up your own blogging software, it's often very simple to just place it in a subdomain and be up and running. This doesn't require any domain name changes and the blog will directly inherit search engine authority of the domain."

When you're blogging for business and tracking conversions, the advantages of a subdomain become a bit clearer. Although subdomains will allow your blog to assume some of the search engine authority of your parent domain, you will be provided all the advantages of communicating with search engines, monitoring, and analytics.

Chapter 5

Choosing a Blogging Platform

In This Chapter

▶ Determining a budget for implementation

▶ Choosing a platform that fits your company

▶ Assessing blogging platforms

*N*ot all blogging platforms are created equal — and that's great for your organization! If you have competent internal resources with the time and expertise to implement it, a variety of blogging platforms are available for your team to download for free, purchase, or integrate with. If you're a large enterprise without the resources, fantastic Software as a Service (SaaS) vendors can will host and manage the blog — including the infrastructure, backups and software for you. If you're a one-person shop, you still have options.

Blogging platforms come in all shapes and sizes, across all Web technology platforms, and with a variety of costs, from open source with no licensing fees up to enterprise software that can cost more than $100,000 (US). And you'll find everything in between.

Determining Your Blogging Platform

Determining the right blogging solution for your company is critical, but your choice is dependent upon your internal resources, your internal expertise, and your ultimate goals. If your company has the IT resources, search engine optimization experience, analytics expertise, content writers, and online marketing experience for driving inbound marketing strategies, a simple platform like WordPress can be an outstanding platform to deploy.

If your IT team is restrictive and difficult to work with, you don't have internal expertise, and you really need a coach and professionals to help you build a successful program, then investing in a professional software-as–a-service solution like Compendium may be your best option. Choose wisely!

There are hundreds of blogging platforms on the market to choose from, but several stand out:

- **Blogger:** Used by personal and publication blogs.
- **Compendium:** Specifically developed for corporate blogs.
- **Expression Engine:** Used for personal, publication, and corporate bloggers.
- **Movable Type, TypePad, Vox:** Used for personal and publication blogs.
- **TypePad Business:** Used for professional publication and corporate blogs.
- **Wordpress.com, WordPress, and WordPress Multi-User:** Used for personal, publication, and corporate blogs.
- **WordPress VIP:** Hosted solution for professional publication and corporate blogs.

Make the right choice by taking the time up front to assess the pros and cons of each blogging platform.

Perhaps the most widely adopted blogging platform is WordPress. WordPress offers several versions of their content management system and has an entire ecosystem of developed integrations, themes, and plug-ins. WordPress can be expanded for use with forums (bbPress) and even social networks (BuddyPress). The basic versions of WordPress are as follows:

- **WordPress.com:** A fairly restrictive, hosted solution. This version is simple to use, but users are very restricted in the customization of their platform. Many plug-ins and themes cannot be used with WordPress.com.
- **WordPress VIP:** A version of WordPress that is a full software-as-a-service hosted solution that is supported and monitored by WordPress and is targeted towards large scale implementations. Companies like CNN, the BBC, and TimeWarner use WordPress VIP.
- **WordPress.org:** The most commonly used version. The software is free to use for commercial use and runs on Linux with an Apache Web server using PHP and MySQL (LAMP). This version allows you to operate a single blog on a hosting platform of your choosing. You are free to customize your blog however you see fit. If you want to fully leverage the platform, though, you'll want to hire a professional to get you off the ground, a designer to build out your theme, and possibly even a search expert to fully optimize the platform.
- **WordPress Multi-User (MU):** A version of WordPress that allows you to run unlimited numbers of blogs within the same installed instance.

✔ **WordPress MU powers edublogs (`http://edublogs.org`):** A system of more than 400,000 blogs for students and educators. WordPress MU could be selected for large organizations that wish to offer their own platform where users can simply sign up and begin blogging or for industry organizations who wish to manage blogs throughout multiple companies.

However, you don't have to be an educator to use WordPress MU. JC Hart is an apartment management firm in the Midwest that operates over a dozen different apartment communities. JC Hart implemented WordPress MU, providing each community with its own blog, but also distributing centralized news throughout all the communities.

Again, although this is "free" software, it's pretty complex stuff. You'll be best served by hiring a professional firm with extensive experience in optimizing the platform and ensuring its stability and performance.

The Compendium Blogging platform (`www.compendium.com`) is new on the blogging platform block but ingeniously combines all the features of a single corporate blog and rolls user blogs and keyword-centric blogs into one enterprise platform. This allows the company to have a comprehensive blog with all the latest posts, users to have their own unique blogs, and keyword-centric blogs that focus on micro-target search engine users.

Budget Considerations When Selecting Your Platform

Selecting a blogging platform that your company can grow with is an important decision, so you don't want to simply jump to a quick conclusion because of the popularity of a platform or the price. Too many companies jump into free, open source solutions, only to find that they can't properly implement, maintain, scale, or integrate with them.

Too many companies, at this point, are mesmerized by the notion of *free* software. Blogging is not *free*. Your company is going to invest a lot of hours of employee time to build your content. A single blog post per day can cost your company more than $5,000 in human resources yearly. That time spent on blogging might be time that was budgeted for your employees' primary responsibilities as well. Making a hasty or ill-advised decision based on the cost of the platform will not only cost your company lost time and resources — it will also cost you in lost revenue as your competitors pass you by.

Therefore, you must bring in a solution that's easy to implement and use, can grow with your organization's goals — and most of all, provides you with a return on investment (ROI). You want to make the right decision early.

Building your blog on a solid infrastructure

At its simplest, a blogging platform doesn't require a lot of resources. Written content is stored in a database, and when someone visits the site, that content is extracted from the database and displayed. Simple. As companies continue to integrate and add tools to their blog, though, the blogging platform begins to do much more work, including, at times, any of the following:

- ✔ Handling, at times, waves of traffic produced by mentions on other blogs or social media sites. Your blog may be able to handle a hundred visitors easy, but can it handle tens of thousands when you need it most?
- ✔ Performing scheduled publishing tasks.
- ✔ Integrating comments with external spam systems.
- ✔ Integrating third-party plug-in, widgets, and integrations.
- ✔ Publishing sitemaps and communicating with search engines effectively.
- ✔ Capturing analytics and information.
- ✔ Categorizing and tagging content and retrieving that content.
- ✔ Automatically syndicating that content to countless other platforms.

As you continue to integrate, automate, and enhance your blog — and your blog continues to acquire new readers, it can require much more resources than the average hosting platform can supply. And the average company doesn't realize this until it's too late.

Say that you're tempted to purchase a $5-per-month hosting package with the most popular hosting company. You purchase the hosting platform, go for the infamous one-click install, and your blog is up and running. You blog with the platform for a few months and feel great about the decision you made. It was effortless!

Then it happens. . . .

Guy Kawasaki or Seth Godin or Jason Calacanis or Michael Arrington or perhaps a *BusinessWeek* editor reads one of your posts and thinks your product may be the greatest thing since sliced bread. They comment on Twitter about your latest blog post, and then the world comes crashing down on you.

Gee, your hosting platform ran fantastic when you had only a few dozen visitors per day. However, on the day that Guy, Seth, Jason, or *BusinessWeek* readers decide to click the link to your blog, they get nothing but a blank page. Your blog is dead — argh! — because your $5 hosting package can't handle it. And that single day could have turned your business around, but you risked it all to save a few hundred bucks a year.

There is a trail of tears across the Internet from bloggers who missed their big day because they didn't have a platform that could keep up, or they didn't have a platform that even backed up their data on a regular basis, or they used a platform that got hacked because they weren't installing patches and upgrades when the alerts hit their dashboard.

A corporate blogging platform like Compendium offers redundancy, backups, monitoring, and can dynamically add server resources instantaneously if your blog's performance begins to suffer. They also use Amazon EC2 services, a platform that caches resources geographically so a visitor from Tokyo or New York won't see a major difference in your blog's performance. Using a high-end platform like Compendium can help you concentrate on blogging and executing your corporate blogging strategy instead of worrying whether your blog is down!

If you wish to host your blog yourself, newer *cloud* services offer inexpensive alternatives. The Marketing Technology Blog is hosted on a combination of MediaTemple and Amazon Web services. Amazon S3 serves all the images while MediaTemple serves WordPress and the database runs on another service — all for under one-hundred dollars per month. (Amazon pricing is dynamic based on how much bandwidth you're consuming).

Even pairing up Amazon S3 with a five-dollar-a-month hosting account can significantly increase your blog's performance. Caching plug-ins can help as well. Caching plug-ins publish pages in a file and refer to that file directly instead of making a database query for the content.

If you are going to host the blog with internal resources, be sure to accommodate for growth of one-thousand times and even ten-thousand times the traffic. Don't risk your business on a cheap solution that won't be there when you need it most.

Recent additions to Google's algorithms take the amount of time it takes for your pages to load into consideration when ranking your content. Most of Google's recommendations are to keep your pages serving in under five seconds. You can monitor your site's page speed in Google Webmasters⇨Labs⇨Site performance. Google has a number of tips and even browser plug-ins that assist you in analyzing your page speed and troubleshooting issues that are slowing your site down.

Hiring a blog consultant to assist with your strategy

If you're not sure what to implement, hire a blogging consultant with experience in implementing corporate blogging solutions. If the consultant begins talking about the free platform he uses without ever asking you about your resources, goals, infrastructure, cost per lead, marketing budget, and so on . . . finish your coffee quickly and show him the door.

A corporate blogging consultant isn't the same as a blogging consultant, a social media consultant, or an IT consultant. Corporate blogging consultants can take in your resources, goals, and research and develop a blogging strategy around them.

Blogging consultants can vary in cost from twenty-five dollars an hour to launch your blog up to tens of thousands of dollars to implement a complete blogging strategy for your company. As with any consultant, it's important that you understand the impact that a consultant will have on your business results.

Choosing a Hosted, Self-Hosted, or SaaS Solution

The first decision you need to make is which type of hosting solution your business will use:

✔ **A hosted solution:** You manage a blog on the blogging platform itself.

✔ **A self-hosted solution:** You install and manage the blog on your own servers or hosting platform.

✔ **An SaaS solution:** *Software as a Service (SaaS)* refers to a new model of purchasing software where you purchase it as a service. That is, you don't have any rights or access to the core application code, but you purchase usage of the application. Typically, annual licensing fees and scaled cost models are associated with SaaS. In recent years, this has become a very popular way of purchasing software.

Advantages and disadvantages of hosted solutions

Hosted software solutions, such as Blogger (www.blogger.com), TypePad (www.typepad.com; nonbusiness), and WordPress (www.wordpress.org; hosted solution), provide basic blogging that's simple to set up and easy to use. Typically, getting your blog up and running on a hosted solution takes only a few minutes. (See Figure 5-1.)

However, because hosted solutions are often housed on shared server farms, there are limitations on how you can use the software, whether you can integrate with it, and strict licensing conditions.

Often times, a hosted solution may actually have a Terms of Service limitation that denies users the right to reclaim its own content in the event the service is no longer available, provides no guarantee of up-time, and sometimes retains rights on users' content for their own purposes.

Figure 5-1:
Blogger is an example of a hosted solution for personal blogs.

Hosted solutions are typically best for nontechnical, personal blogs of individuals. Few hosted solutions allow you to use your own domain name without incurring an additional fee. If the domain on which you're writing your blog isn't owned by your company, you're providing someone else with the content and authority you worked hard to attain.

In sum, then, hosted solutions aren't suited for hosting business blogs. For a corporate blog, steer clear of this solution.

Advantages and disadvantages of self-hosted solutions

Self-hosted solutions are the most popular solutions for corporate blogging. (See Figure 5-2.) Companies that host on specific technologies such as ASP. NET can find a blogging solution (like Subtext) that's natively designed for their servers.

If your company already has the server space and bandwidth available, adding a blog may not add to the expense at all. If you are starting from scratch, you may spend a few thousand dollars on a server, hundreds of dollars per month in rack space at a datacenter, and hundreds of dollars per month for bandwidth. You may also want to pay more for backup plans, monitoring, and deployment services. Consult your IT management team or a data center representative for additional details and costs.

One big advantage of using a self-hosted solution is that it can typically be integrated directly into your Web site's content management system (CMS), customer relationship management (CRM) solution, and e-mail marketing platform. If your company has full rights to the source code or is using an open source solution, self-hosted solutions allow you to develop some incredibly complex and usable solutions for capturing data, processing content, and reusing content for other publications.

On the other hand, disadvantages of self-hosted solutions include the following:

✔ Many self-hosted solutions were developed without the average user in mind. As a result, some of the interfaces are horrid, and the user experience can be very poor. You might have to hire developers who are familiar with the platform to ensure you have a usable system.

Placing software that's been developed by other parties on your own servers comes with a certain degree of risk. In recent times, open source platforms have been a popular target of hackers.

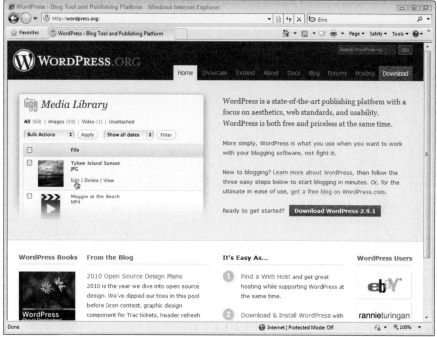

Figure 5-2:
WordPress.
org is a
self-hosted
solution.

✔ Many necessary components of a business blog are third-party integration packages for typical self-hosted solutions. Adding third-party plug-
ins is a great way to expand the versatility of your blog, but plug-ins that
aren't well written can add a lot of resources to your server — or worse,
leave security gaps that typical maintenance upgrades won't help to
block.

✔ Self-hosted platforms often come in an all-in-one package but can't take
advantage of high-performing infrastructures, such as cloud hosting,
Web acceleration, redundant databases, caching, load sharing, and so
on. Companies that built enterprise blogs on free or self-hosted solutions have often had to invest hundreds of thousands of dollars to
upgrade to a system that's reliable and performs well.

✔ Self-hosted platforms with plug-ins can have software upgrades that are
required on a daily basis, resulting in a lot of unforeseen maintenance
that might not be anticipated. Thankfully, many of the latest blogging platforms — like WordPress — have upgrade alerts and can be
upgraded at the click of a mouse.

✔ Self-hosted platforms aren't optimized for search engines and can
require a number of enhancements to the blog themes as well as third-
party plug-ins to get up to par. Within the setup of the blog, simple

settings can weigh heavily on your blog's ability to be found in search engines. Without an experienced blogging optimization expert, this is difficult to identify and correct.

✔ Designs of your blogging theme must be accomplished not only to be aesthetically pleasing and to match your corporate brand, but they must also be optimized for search engines. The typical theme designer doesn't realize the effect that they will have on search engine optimization (SEO). Applying a poorly designed theme that looks fantastic can spell disaster for your program.

✔ Many blogging platforms come with little or no documentation on how to use them. This dearth of information might be okay when your blogger is a techy geek, but the average employee could face a very steep learning curve.

✔ Blogging well requires additional insight and training on how to effectively use keywords, write compelling content, use white space effectively, write post titles that generate clicks, and write posts that will drive more sales. Blogging software doesn't provide any of this direction.

✔ Blogging applications lack any analytics to provide feedback on how the blog is actually performing. Initiating a blogging strategy and understanding what tools need integrated, how to analyze the results, and implement new strategies for growth is information that doesn't come with the software.

✔ When you host your blogging solution, you're responsible for how well it performs, what your up-time is, how fast your pages load, how you're backed up, and so on. If your blog goes down after you release the big news on the company that's going to drive a lot of traffic, who are you going to call?

Self-hosting is the most common method for implementing a corporate blogging strategy nowadays because until recently, no other options were available. Many companies absolutely underestimate the cost and resources needed to maintain a corporate blog. Free is not free.

Advantages and disadvantages of SaaS solutions

The new method on the block is the SaaS solution. (See an example, Compendium, in Figure 5-3.) Just as companies like Salesforce (www.salesforce.com) revolutionized the CRM and ExactTarget (www.exacttarget.com) revolutionized e-mail, with SaaService solutions, blogging platforms are now being adopted in the SaaS model.

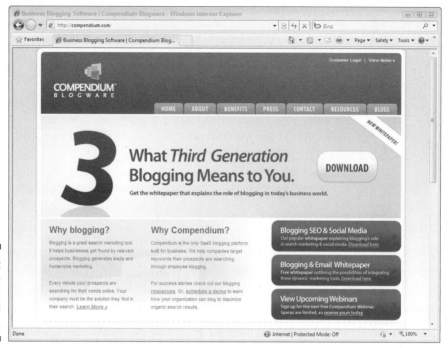

Figure 5-3:
Compendium is a SaaS solution.

SaaS solutions are hosted solutions that companies subscribe to and use via a Web browser. SaaS advantages include that your company does not have to install or maintain software or worry about infrastructure costs. SaaS companies monitor their software and security, ensure system performance, and regularly upgrade their software with features and fixes. Additionally, many SaaS providers also include professional training and services when needed (sometimes at an additional cost). Companies have moved to SaaS solutions because they require minimal startup investment and internal IT resources.

Businesses like Rubbermaid, Coca-Cola, General Electric, and Forrester — and even publishing giants like the *Los Angeles Times*, ABC News, and *USA Today* — have chosen the SaaS model using services like TypePad Business (www.typepad.com/business).

The advantages of using a company like TypePad or Compendium are many, including the following:

✔ Businesses have access to superior infrastructures, security, and monitoring that they could not likely invest in if they were self hosted.

✔ Some companies like Compendium provide additional services, like *cloud bursting*. This service allows your blog to dynamically add resources on the fly when they're needed to ensure that your blog is up and running when it's needed most— when hundreds of thousands of visitors head your way!

✔ SaaS solutions typically offer Service Level Agreements (SLA) that guarantee up-time, monitoring, and backups.

✔ Your blogging team can focus on the blogging strategy and not the blogging platform.

✔ Using these systems typically comes with account management, support, coaching, and training.

✔ SaaS providers rapidly develop new features and integrations as demanded by their clients and the competitive marketplace. Your company will continue to benefit from these updates with no additional costs or maintenance issues to implement.

✔ Blogging companies like Compendium often solicit the expertise of others in the industry to help them prioritize features and ensure that clients get maximum results.

The ultimate advantage a company has when using a SaaS solution is that the ROI will determine whether you continue to use its platform. If you don't get results, you're not going to use it. This is huge pressure for SaaS companies to ensure that they get the results you demand.

On the other hand, SaaS blogging platforms have at least one disadvantage. Because the platform is shared, there's typically little or no opportunity for modification of the core platform.

Many SaaS providers overcome this with a robust application programming interface (API), which allows your company to develop whatever solutions you require on top of the platform.

Flexibility in Blog Templating Engines

As technology has advanced, so have blog templating engines. Early blogging platforms had simple customization components, which allowed for simple things like changing a header or a background color. Newer platforms allow designers and administrators to fully customize the look and feel of the blog and even integrate it with external platforms.

Technologies like Cascading Style Sheets (CSS) have been incorporated and allow a user to publish content in one page but define how it looks in another file altogether. This means that two blogs running the identical content can look totally different from one another. For more information on CSS, check out *CSS Web Design For Dummies.*

Using a template, your company can integrate forms with a third-party tool like Formstack, or integrate e-mail subscriptions with a tool like MailChimp. Perhaps you want to integrate social media commenting using a tool like JS-Kit Echo: all are possibilities because you can make edits directly to the blogs' template. Using CSS also allows a blog to look different depending on whether you're printing the page, viewing it on a mobile device, viewing it on an iPhone, or accessing the actual content through other devices (for those users who employ accessibility aids).

Modern text editors allow writers to go crazy with their content. If you don't want your bloggers throwing in different fonts, enlarging and reducing fonts, or changing spacing and colors, you should be able to control all your content by using CSS and having your bloggers write only plain text.

However, CSS can't handle everything. Exceptions include adding subheadings, bolded words, images, and links. These are editing techniques you might want to train your bloggers on. Ask them to avoid any additional editing so that you can ensure your blog is consistent and readable.

If your blogging platform doesn't provide you access directly to the template, but instead has a simple interface that only asks you to define the header image, the footer image, and some pages, you're not using a blogging package that provides the customization that you might need.

Some blogging applications will claim to offer "highly customizable templates" where CSS can be employed, but that doesn't necessarily mean you can customize every element of the template. The easiest way to ensure that you're adopting a CSS-compliant platform with a robust templating engine is to get that guarantee in writing.

If you view your page content and see that everything resides in tables rather than an XHTML CSS-driven solution that allows elements such as divs, you might wish to walk away from the solution altogether. (Check out *CSS For Dummies* for more information.) Tables were used in the early days of HTML editing to control page layouts, but CSS allows much more flexibility. Not only are table-driven systems difficult to customize, they are also difficult to optimize for search engines. A templating engine that has table-driven content needs its engine rewritten to move components around the page. A templating engine that has CSS-driven content simply requires an edit to the attached stylesheet.

Balancing SEO and optimal design

A great design for your blog can lead to increased conversion rates by providing the reader with a perception of professionalism. However, your company can pay up to $50,000 for a custom-designed theme for your blog.

You'd probably guess that if you paid $25,000 for a custom design, the theme would be optimized for search — and you'd be wrong. Most theme developers don't realize the effect that their beautiful design has on SEO.

Search engines recognize HTML components, so the use of specific HTML tags as well as the layout of your overall page can have a significant impact on your blog's optimization.

Search engines view the importance of those HTML components on a page to evaluate the importance of the words used in those components. Aside from your domain name, here are the elements ranked from most important to least:

✔ **Home page title tag:** Your home page title tag provides the words that you wish to associate with your domain to the search engines. The home page title tag looks like this:

```
<title>A few keywords | My blog name</title>
```

✔ **Page title tags:** Each blog post has its own title tags. The title tag should start with the keyword-rich blog post title and optionally end with your blog name. The page title tag looks like this:

```
<title>Keywords in my Post Title | My blog name</title>
```

If at all possible, keywords should be used in the first words of your post title rather than the last.

✔ **Heading tags:** HTML uses heading and subheading tags. The most important is the H1 tag, followed by H2, H3, and so on. After H3, there's little focus from search engines. Your blog's name should always be held in an H1 tag. Best practice dictates following your H1 tag with an H2 for your blog post title and then using H3 for subheadings within your post. A heading tag looks like this:

```
<h1>Blog Name</h1>
    <h2>Keywords in Post Title</h2>
        <h3>Keywords in Subheading</h3>
        <h3>Keywords in Subheading</h3>
        <h3>Keywords in Subheading</h3>
```

Your theme designer should avoid the common mistake of using high-level headings in the sidebar headings. If you use an H2 tag for sidebar headings and an H3 tag for your blog content, you're effectively telling search engines that the information in your sidebar headings is more important than your post titles!

✔ **Content in the top of the page:** Content at the top of your page is more important than content at the bottom. This doesn't have anything to do with how the page looks — it's how the page is designed. Here are two pages that can look exactly the same:

```
<body>
    <div id="sidebar">
        My sidebar content
    </div>
    <div id="content">
        My blog posts
    </div>
</body>
```

and

```
<body>
    <div id="content">
        My blog posts
    </div>
    <div id="sidebar">
        My sidebar content
    </div>
</body>
```

Whether your sidebar is on the left when you view your blog doesn't matter to a search engine. The search engine doesn't *look* at your page: It reads the HTML in the page source. Your page design should ensure that your content is higher than any sidebar content. This is another common mistake made by designers.

There is a tool for everything on the Internet these days! If you don't wish to learn HTML but want to see how your page might look to a search engine, you can use SEO Browser `www.seo-browser.com`. (See Figure 5-4.)

Follow these steps to find out how your page is viewed by a search engine:

1. **Copy the Web address of a typical blog post page from your blog.**

   Much of your site's search engine traffic comes directly from single post pages, so don't test just your blog's home page.

2. **Enter your Web address in the Address field at `www.seo-browser.com`.**

3. **Click Parse URL.**

4. **Review your results.**

   As you review your page, note whether the headings are sized according to their importance on the page. Also check whether the content on the top of your page is shown at the top of this page with any sidebar content below.

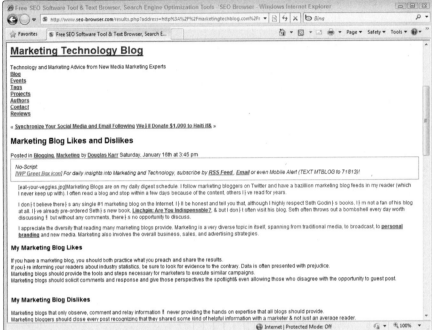

Figure 5-4:
Viewing a
blog post
page in
the SEO
Browser.

If the layout of the content doesn't appear logical or if all the font sizes appear the same, your designer might not have incorporated headings and subheadings properly. And if your sidebar content is listed first, be sure to ask the designer to swap the HTML and adjust the CSS to correct the issue.

Developing an attractive and readable blog theme

Fact: People don't read blogs or Web pages. No, don't shut this book and run away in disgust! People don't *read* blogs — but they do *scan* them. You can deploy a number of techniques with your Web theme to make your content more digestible to the human eye, including the following:

✔ **Don't use a dark background with light text.** Use dark text on a white background so that visitors can read your content with much less effort. Black can look cool on the background on your page, but don't use it for your actual post content. Keep your content background light and contrast the font significantly darker.

✔ **Don't use tiny fonts.** We live in a world of giant screens that support very high resolutions, and advanced users will have a difficult time reading your tiny fonts. Even on a normal screen, you're making a visitor work harder to digest your content.

✔ **Use a theme width that matches your audience.** Use analytics to get a breakdown of screen resolutions. For example, if you select a layout with a width of 1,024 pixels (px) and more than 95 percent of your readers have screen resolutions larger than that, you're fine.

Here's how to view your screen resolution breakdown in Google Analytics:

1. **Log in to your Google Analytics account.**

2. **Navigate to Visitors⇨Browser Capabilities⇨Screen Resolutions.**

3. **At the base of the report, select the maximum amount of rows to view all resolutions and the breakdown of resolutions. (See Figure 5-5.)**

4. **(Optional) To make analyzing this information easier, choose Export⇨CSV for Excel and view the data within Excel.**

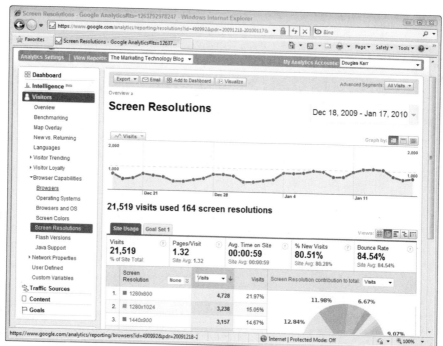

Figure 5-5:
View a breakdown of screen resolutions in Google Analytics.

✔ **Incorporate mobile CSS and themes to optimize reading on PDAs, iPods, iPhones, Android Phones and other mobile devices.** If you're using WordPress, Crowd Favorite has developed a theme-and-plug-in combination, WordPress Mobile Edition, which displays your content perfectly for each device.

✔ **Use white space effectively throughout your theme.** *White space* is the area of padding between objects. When elements like images, text, borders, and so on are too close together, it makes reading difficult. Adjusting your template to provide additional room around objects will make it easier to comprehend. Use significant amounts of space (from 10px to 20px) between components and also above and below headings. Also use a line height large enough that you don't cross lines as you read from left to right.

✔ **Go longer rather than shrinking content, reducing white space, or going wider.** Don't try to keep content within the height of the screen. Visitors won't mind scrolling, but they will mind a site that's difficult to read.

✔ **Use serif fonts.** Serif fonts (like the type used in this sentence) increase the speed at which people can read content. Don't be afraid to use a serif font in your blog's theme to make it easier to read the post content. Georgia is a serif font that's common across operating systems. Avoid using Arial and Comic Sans, both common sans serif fonts.

Enhancing Your Platform with Plug-Ins, Widgets, and Gadgets

Don't want to do all the work yourself? A number of different technologies can enhance your blog for you. Plug-ins, widgets, and gadgets are all technologies that make new features, integrations, and enhancements easy to package and distribute. So what exactly are plug-ins, widgets, and gadgets? This is where it might get confusing with all the overlap between the three.

Yahoo! purchased a company called Konfabulator that had developed a desktop application for Windows to display small applications — *widgets* — on your desktop. An example might be a weather widget where you get weather information displayed directly on your desktop without opening an application. Of course, now Windows offers applications very similar to the Yahoo! widget technology, but Windows calls them *gadgets*.

Google gadgets are a bit different. These gadgets are intended only for Google pages, but because you can use Google to build mini-applications and distribute them, you can find gadgets more or less everywhere. All this is similar to an iPhone with its applications, which you can search for, download, and install, and that are developed in their own proprietary language.

In addition, Adobe launched *AIR,* a technology to build applications or widgets easily for Windows and Mac.

A nice feature of all these technologies is that they're typically independent of whatever operating system you're running (aside from Microsoft Windows gadgets). See Figure 5-6.

Confused yet?

Blogging applications liked the approach and developed their own methodology for developing sidebar widgets. Developers could now develop a simple widget that's installed through a plug-in and then can be dragged and dropped in the widget interface of the blogging platform.

Plug-ins, widgets, gadgets, or even custom integration are fantastic ways of enhancing your customer experience, including Related Posts plug-ins that provide recommendations for further reading. This helps keep visitors on your site longer, reduce bounce rates, and increase the opportunity for conversion.

You can find some very robust plug-ins for other purposes as well, such as the Webtrends analytics plug-in that allows you to view your analytics directly within the WordPress dashboard. (See Figure 5-7.)

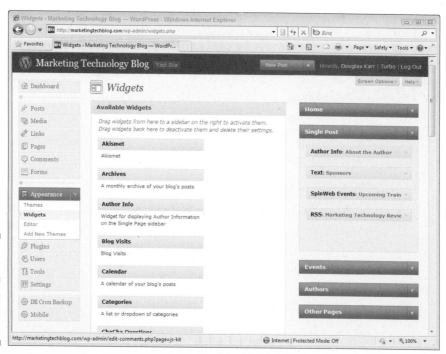

Figure 5-6:
Viewing
a list of
sidebar
widgets in
WordPress.

Figure 5-7:
Viewing a
Webtrends
analytics in
WordPress
with the
Webtrends
plug-in.

Installing WordPress plug-ins and widgets on your Hosted WordPress Blog

WordPress provides a unique statistics package that shows you how many visitors your blog is getting as well as what they're reading. This can be helpful for you to target your content to what's most popular as well as monitor the number of visitors you're getting to your blog. Follow these steps to install this plug-in:

1. **Navigate to Plugins⊸Add New.**

2. **Search for WordPress.com Stats. (See Figure 5-8.)**

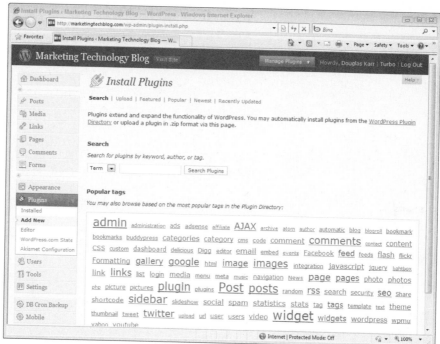

Figure 5-8:
Viewing
the search
screen in
WordPress
Plugins.

3. **Click Install.**

   A window pops up that provides additional details about the installation, including the number of downloads, the versions it works on, and its ratings. You can also view the instructions and screenshots and find out additional information.

4. **Click Install Now.**

   The plug-in is installed but not yet activated.

5. **Click Activate Plugin to make the plug-in live.**

6. **You might be required to register for WordPress.com and obtain an API key for the plug-in. If so, follow the instructions and enter that information.**

   After the plug-in is installed correctly, you can see analytics information in your WordPress dashboard. (See Figure 5-9.)

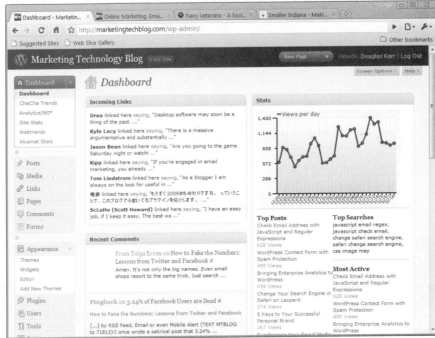

Figure 5-9:
Viewing analytics in the WordPress dashboard.

Then, after a plug-in is activated that enables a widget, you also need to add that widget to your sidebar. All you need to do is follow these steps:

1. **Navigate to Appearance⇨Widgets.**

   The page is broken down into Available Widgets, Inactive Widgets, and your sidebar. Depending on the complexity of your theme, you might even have more than one sidebar to add widgets to.

   If you don't see any sidebars listed, your blog theme might not support them. This is a rip-off! Go see that developer and tell him to add them.

2. **Drag an available widget to the sidebar within the location you wish to add it.**

   The widget opens and asks for any additional information you need to enter. (See Figure 5-10.)

3. **Enter the requested information.**

4. **Click Save to publish the widget.**

   To remove a widget, simply drag it back to the Available Widget section.

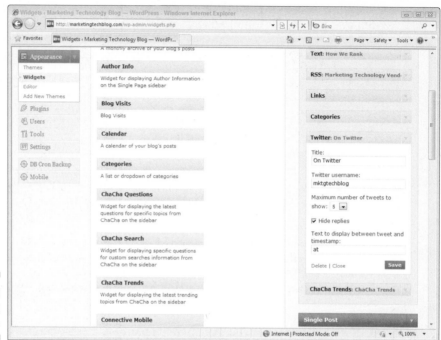

Figure 5-10:
Customizing
a widget.

You can also load a widget without enabling any plug-in if the widget developer developed the widget with JavaScript or Flash. These widgets are easily identified because they are surrounded by `embed`, `object`, or `script` tags. You can select a text or an HTML widget from the Available Widgets, drag it to your sidebar, and it will open. Enter your title and paste the code in the body of the widget.

Resist the temptation to get a bit plug-in and widget crazy after you see how easy it is to add new features to your blog. Be mindful of the line between cool and distracting. Your blog's objective is to build authority, attract new visitors, and close business — not to show the world how many widgets you can stick in your sidebar.

Selecting components that drive traffic to you, not away from you

Your theme, content, sidebar widgets, and every other element of your blog should be focused on driving leads to your company. Many companies add widgets that have little or nothing to do with their strategy, like local weather or news widgets, or worse, widgets that promote other social sites on given topics. These widgets can be a distraction or even drive visitors away from your corporate blog.

Other widgets can help in establishing authority; for instance, if your blog is ranked or awarded within your industry. Other widgets may be social media widgets that relay your latest Twitter or Facebook updates. These may entice a visitor to follow you and do business with you later.

To decide, think about whether it will drive traffic to your business or away from your business. Many publishing Web sites have dozens of widgets, advertisements, and other noise on their blog. That's okay because their objective is to increase advertising revenue, not a direct purchase from their company.

But don't mistake your own corporate blog for a publishing blog. The objectives are very different. As an example, Kyle Lacy, marketing authority and author of *Twitter Marketing For Dummies,* has a personal blog (`www.kyle lacy.com`) that drives business to his company, Brandswag. Kyle's blog is carefully designed to accomplish five objectives (see Figure 5-11):

- ✓ **Increasing sales:** The Buy My Book photo in the header is a great call to action to drive book sales.

- ✓ **Defining Kyle as an authority:** A photo of Kyle with a Contact link above his head helps make more recognizable his authority in the social media space and provides a means of reaching him.

- ✓ **Providing ways for visitors to return:** Social media requires trust, and often a visitor has to return multiple times before making a purchasing decision, so Kyle promotes his e-mail newsletter and his feeds for visitors to subscribe to.

- ✓ **Increasing offers to appear as a speaker:** Kyle speaks on the subject of Twitter Marketing a lot so he's provided a call to action in his sidebar to request a speaking engagement.

- ✓ **Directing traffic to Brandswag:** Kyle provides a call to action to his company so that visitors can find out additional information.

As you scroll down Kyle's sidebar, there's a ton of additional information, but all of it provides readers with a sense of authority as they read his blog. Kyle was careful in the design to include only those components that drive his goals and keep visitors.

Figure 5-11:
A blog layout for a social media author and consultant.

Bottom line: If you have a corporate blog and provide an industry news widget, for example, you might end up driving away traffic from your blog and to the other Web sites that are syndicated in the widget. Unfortunately, Google Analytics doesn't provide any detail on links that are driving traffic out of your blog.

Webtrends (www.webtrends.com) has an Offsite Links custom report that you can add to your profile that will supply this information. Another is the small analytics application, Clicky (http://getclicky.com/5416). See Figure 5-12. Clicky isn't an analytics application built for enterprise corporations, but being able to view outbound links is a great feature to keep an eye on. You can develop similar reports in enterprise analytics applications.

Testing components to measure performance

Plug-ins and widgets can also be resource intensive, slowing your page load times and overloading your server. Page-load times have a direct correlation to visitors' site experience, and many visitors will leave if a page fails to load within a couple of seconds. Keep your blog lean, mean, and on target for your objective.

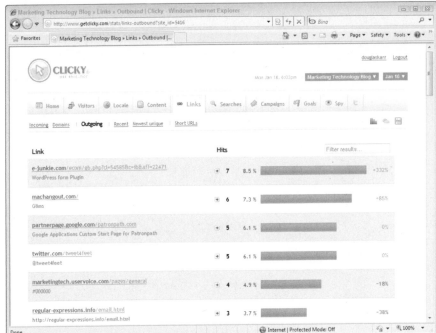

Figure 5-12:
Watch out
for links that
drive traffic
away from
your blog.

Measure how well your blog performs before and after you publish a widget or install a plug-in.

Many widgets use a technology called Asynchronous JavaScript and XML (AJAX). Widgets that use AJAX typically load content after your page is opened and won't slow you down. This is a great way of managing performance and still providing some additional value.

Measure your blog's load times with a monitoring tool like pingdom (www.pingdom.com) before and after your plug-in is loaded. Test it several times throughout the day under different load conditions (peak and off-peak times). Review the data to look for a change in the overall performance.

Don't rely on local testing applications or your own browser to see how your site is performing. Your browser will typically load objects on the page locally so that pages will load faster the next time you return. This is called *caching*. As well, in a corporate environment, you might have an Internet connection that leads directly to your servers . . . your visitors don't have that.

Monitoring tools like pingdom will test your page from noncached resources around the globe. pingdom also has services you can set up to alert you if your blog is down or if pages are taking an excessive time to load.

Expanding Blogging Platforms Capabilities through Integration

As your company gets accustomed to blogging, there are also incredible opportunities to integrate other services through your blog. You can integrate your newsletter sign-up; push content from your e-mails to your blog or vice versa; and integrate shopping carts, registration systems, calendars, Webinars, and even live streaming video.

For just one example, Cantaloupe (`www.cantaloupe.com`), a video production company, offers a compelling video-management product called Backlight. Backlight's VideoHere feature allows you to embed a video directly into your blog's text editor at the click of a button. As well, Backlight enables you to add links to your video timeline — perfect for driving sales. (See Figure 5-13.)

Understanding the capabilities of your blogging platform will open a lot of doors to new opportunities to communicate effectively with your audience. Take advantage of them.

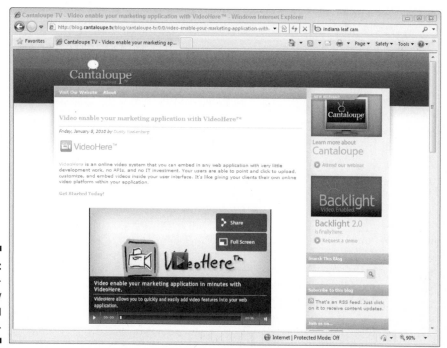

Figure 5-13: Embed videos directly in a blog post.

Using a blogging platform's API

Most blogs have an application programming interface (API) that allows you to embed content or add additional processes to your blog through third-party services. An *API* is an interface created by a software program that enables other software applications to interact directly with it. An API, then, is essentially a gateway for direct interaction from one set of data to another. Because it allows you to transfer data from one location to another to build a more complete picture though data sharing or collection, this is a powerful tool, one that allows you to share and display data in a format that serves your needs. One robust example is the WordPress API, which enables you to program your self-hosted WordPress blog externally through the use of plug-ins.

One example of such a plug-in is a Text Messaging plug-in developed for Connective Mobile for crime alerts, emergency notifications, concert notifications, or even simple restaurant specials. (See Figure 5-14.) Connective Mobile (`www.connectivemobile.com`) has a text group feature that companies can purchase for companies to opt in to text alerts. The Connective Mobile integration connects the Mobile account to WordPress so that each time you publish a new post, an alert goes out to all of your mobile subscribers. This feature is great for universities and colleges; in the case of a security incident, the school can simply publish the alert via WordPress, and all the subscribers are notified.

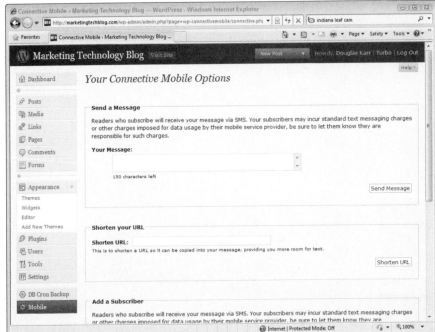

Figure 5-14: Using your blog as an alert platform with text messaging.

MailChimp (www.mailchimp.com) is an e-mail service provider (ESP) that has integrated heavily with WordPress. MailChimp has an RSS to E-mail feature that allows you to effortlessly publish your blog directly to a daily e-mail that goes out to a mailing list within MailChimp. No fuss, no muss — you don't even have to click Send! MailChimp has taken it a step further and developed a Google Analytics, MailChimp, and WordPress integration — Analytics360 — that breaks down your blog performance, your e-mail performance, and the effect of each on the other. (See Figure 5-15.)

These plug-ins are great, but be careful. Many plug-ins offer third-party integrations whose authors have bypassed key security controls within the framework of the application programming interface. This could put your company at great risk.

Automating and routing content through integration

Syndication has been around before the Internet. Mass media producers in television, newspapers, and radio have syndicated content for many years. Syndicated content is content that one media outlet owns but other media outlets can use, either for free or at a cost. Blogging supports syndication as well, through a key feature, called really simple syndication (RSS).

Figure 5-15: MailChimp Analytics360 integrates MailChimp and Google Analytics statistics.

RSS is a way to publish your content in a standardized way so that it can be syndicated to other locations. Sometimes syndication is not that easy to use, though. Most applications have the tools necessary to syndicate content from a blog into the application simply by inserting the Web address to the feed. However, if you're developing an integration, feeds can be a little bit more difficult to work with. A feed has several components and there are a few different standards to work with. You'll want to consult a developer when it's time to do some heavy lifting!

The power of RSS is its ability to automate and route your corporate blog content to multiple platforms/locations, such as Web sites, corporate social platforms (Ning), social sites (Twitter or Facebook), or other industry blogs that wish to syndicate your content.

RSS is an inherent feature of blogging. Each time you publish your content, a mirrored version of that content is available via a "feed" address. Your feed address is a specific URL that other people or applications use to access your content.

Generally, feeds are most commonly used through *feed readers,* which allow you to centrally read blogs without having to visit them. All you have to do is subscribe. To subscribe to a feed using Google Reader (www.google.com/reader), just follow these steps:

1. **Login to Google Reader.**

2. **Click the Add a Subscription button.**

3. **Enter the name of the other blog you wish to subscribe to.**

   Google Reader visits the blog and identifies the feed URL automatically.

   You should now have a message saying that you have subscribed to your blog.

   You will now see the actual blog posts in the reading pane. You can scroll through and read the posts. Google Reader automatically keeps track of what you read. (See Figure 5-16.)

Set up folders within Google Reader and find blogs by searching for blogs on Technorati, PostRank, or BlogCatalog. All these sites have an extensive directory of blogs, and they keep track of the popularity of each. You'll also want to add your blogs to them after you get started.

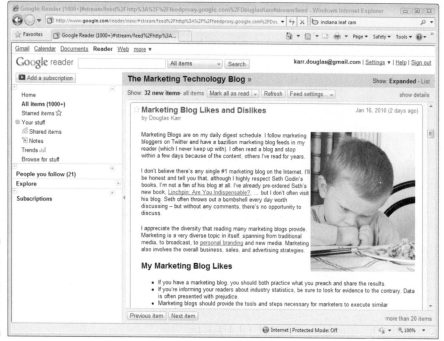

Figure 5-16:
Read feed
content
in Google
Reader.

Differentiating your feed from your blog with integration tools

As they strive to drive conversions, many blogging platforms and companies ignore their feed subscribers. Because your feed subscribers read your content as often as you publish it, they may be the best prospect list you have. Don't forget to market to this group as well.

Although your blog design integrates sticky posts and calls to action, your feed is clean of all blog design components. Be sure to customize your feed with a call to action directly in the feed. If you're using WordPress, this can be accomplished with the PostPost plug-in.

Figure 5-17 shows three additional customizations:

✔ **Author Plugin**

    http://marketingtechblog.com/projects

This plug-in displays a photo of the author and his user profile information.

✔ **PostPost Plugin**

```
http://marketingtechblog.com/projects
```

This plug-in allows you to post custom HTML at the base of the feed: in this case, a Thanks for Subscribing and a link to download an e-book.

✔ **Related or Most Commented Posts**

```
http://fairyfish.com/2008/03/21/wordpress-related-
                 posts-plugin
```

This plug-in allows visitors to find relevant topics or topics that received a lot of attention. This can lead readers back to your blog, where you can convert them.

The last way to differentiate your feed is to always include images in your blog posts. As subscribers quickly scan their feeds on a daily or weekly basis, having a great image in your blog post will make your blog stand out.

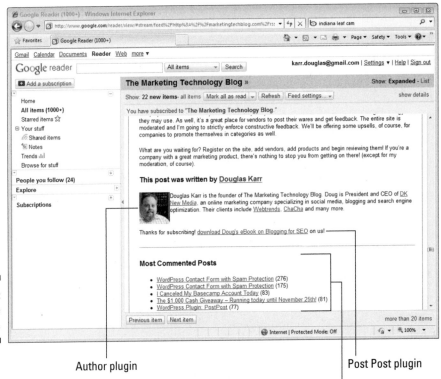

Figure 5-17:
Customize
your feed.

Author plugin

Post Post plugin

Most Commented Posts

Chapter 6

Regarding Time, Resources, and Content

In This Chapter

▶ Finding resources to blog

▶ Evaluating external resources for content

▶ Protecting your content

▶ Adding the necessary legal statements and disclaimers

*L*ike with many organizations, a key concern when it comes to launching a corporate blogging strategy is, "How am I possibly going to add this to my plate?" In hard economic times, marketing departments are typically the first to have staff cuts and are always figuring out how to do more with less. Blogging is a marathon, though — not a sprint — that requires many resources to produce the content, administer the program, and analyze the results.

Blogging does take time, but you can minimize the demands on your organization by finding nontraditional sources of fresh content or by reusing content. Rather than wondering how *you* might find time to write every day, recruiting a team of 10 bloggers can produce enough content so that you have to write only once per week!

Purchasing content, although one way to fill pages, has been controversial because the appeal of blogging is the humanity and transparency it provides. Just like the President of the United States has a speech writer, though, you can find quality content providers to speak well for your company. And guest bloggers can provide new perspectives as well as an additional layer of authority to your blog. Even better still is finding customers and industry leaders!

Of course, before you publish a word of content, remember to take the necessary precautions to protect your company from using or distributing content that could cause problems. The section, "Providing Legal Protection for Your Blog," later in this chapter, discusses your blog and legal issues in greater detail.

Using External Content Resources

One of the first actions any bad marketer takes is to try and manipulate the medium. In the early days, marketers discovered the hard way. Politicians hired third-party companies, sometimes offshore, to develop their blogging platforms and even seed them with positive comments. When their efforts were discovered, it ruined their credibility online and turned a great opportunity into a terrible public relations incident.

Taking a medium whose core strategic advantage is transparency, built on trust, and manipulating it like this will surely get you in trouble. Don't be tempted to do it. That said, many critics of blogging disparage the hiring of third-party content writers and believe they're in violation of some cardinal law as well. (There are no cardinal laws, by the way.)

As the demand for quality digital content is rising, so is the very lucrative business of supplying companies with that content. Here are three kinds of external content providers:

- ✔ *Ghostblogging* is the most common method. A blogger writes on behalf of an individual and authors the blog posts with the name of the individual.

- ✔ *Supplemental blogging* is purchasing content written by other bloggers to supplement the blog: for example, an article about how to keep your home safe while you're on vacation, posted on an insurance or a real estate blog.

- ✔ *Third-party blogging* occurs when the source of the blog posts is actually transparent, and the people providing the content are named. These may be paid engagements or simply guest-blogging opportunities offered to industry leaders.

We discuss each of these cases more fully in the following sections.

Winning back time with ghostbloggers and professional content writers

Ghostblogging isn't a dirty word, nor is it a dirty profession: It's an incredible profession, in fact. A great ghostblogger investigates a source and accurately writes the posts on the company's or company leader's behalf. Attorneys, for example, often use ghostblogging because of the high return on investment (ROI) in search engine acquisition from blogging and because they are often too busy to find time to blog themselves.

problogservice (`http://problogservice.com`) is a company that ghost-writes for many professionals, including attorneys. (See Figure 6-1.) problog-service calls or visits its clients on a weekly basis, asking lots of questions, compiling a list of ideas for content, and then writing that content on behalf of the client. The client ultimately decides whether the posts will be published, but over time, problogservice will often gain enough confidence with the client to write and publish without moderation.

Companies like problogservice write the words of the client for the client. Just like the President of the United States has his own speech writers, so do the clients that use these services. That doesn't mean that the content is any less transparent or sincere. In fact, it usually ensures better results because firms like this understand the importance of search engine traffic, transparency, and humanity.

You might be surprised that the blog you're reading of a well-known Internet guru isn't actually written by them at all — but by a ghostblogger!

How can you go about selecting a ghostblogger? The following list provides some tips:

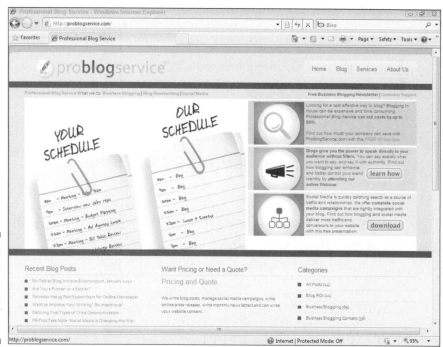

Figure 6-1:
You can use a ghost-writing service for businesses.

✔ Find a ghostblogger who is experienced with your industry and its jargon. Most ghostbloggers promote themselves on the Web. Doing a search by city and the term *ghostblogging* should provide many results. Review his work online and speak to his clients.

✔ Find a ghostblogger who is experienced in writing for search engine optimization. Calling the first few search results may be a great tactic — since these writers are obviously getting the right search results!

✔ Find a ghostblogger who understands your corporate culture and the level of education you're wishing to target.

✔ Find a ghostblogger with writing credentials. Writing well is important, even in an informal medium such as a blog. Be sure your ghostblogger has the formal education, they spell correctly, and their writing is grammatically sound.

✔ Decide ahead of time whether you wish to disclose that you're using a ghostblogger. There is always the possibility of a ghostblogger being discovered — is that something you're comfortable with?

✔ Set budget expectations in accordance with the frequency of the writing as well as the size of the blog posts.

✔ Many ghostblogging organizations have some serious credentials when it comes to public relations and crisis management. If you require consulting in addition to content, be sure your ghostblogger understands the expectations of their turnaround time and assistance he'll be providing.

✔ Most of all, find someone whose writing accurately reflects the professionalism and tone that you wish to provide.

Purchasing topical content to enhance your blog content

Almost all industries can seed their content with other content to enhance their readers' experience. Services like Raidious Digital Content Services (http://raidious.com) have sprouted up to reach this demand. Raidious isn't a gang of writers; rather, it's an organization structured like a traditional newspaper. Raidious has writers and journalists, editors, and publishers who ensure content is original, relevant, and of the highest quality. (See Figure 6-2.)

Services like Raidious can work on-demand, providing a number of articles on a given topic for a specific period of time, or they can fulfill content writing schedules just like ghostbloggers.

Figure 6-2:
You can use
a content
services
provider for
profession-
ally written
content for
businesses.

Here are some ideas for buying blog content from other sources:

- If you're a technology company, purchasing content about products, services, or technology can be a boon to your blog.

- If your blog promotes security services, purchasing content about home defense, self-defense, crime statistics, and other relevant information can make your blog invaluable to prospects.

- If your blog is a real estate blog, purchasing content about neighbor- hoods, school districts, local news, and real estate trends can get your blog found for relevant terms.

Your company will need to do a cost-benefit analysis on whether supple- menting your content is worthwhile. An easy way to calculate the value of the content is to divide the total revenue per year acquired by your blog by the number of blog posts.

Many companies with higher return on blogging investment find that a blog post may be worth $200 (US) or more. In these cases, paying $50 per blog post is a great investment.

Hiring industry bloggers to write for your blog

Using tools like PostRank (www.postrank.com) or Technorati (http://technorati.com) can help you track down the top bloggers or influential blogs on specific topics. (See Figure 6-3.) If these folks are industry bloggers who don't work for competitors but can provide authority with your blog, you may invite them to guest blog on your blog.

Most bloggers will appreciate the opportunity to reach a new audience and build a relationship with your organization. Most will blog at no cost and will even promote the post, providing some new traffic to your blog. Additionally, there is benefit to them as well since they can link back to their blog. This is known as *backlinking* and helps sites gain search engine authority.

Some bloggers put themselves out for loan as well. If you're paying a blogger to blog for you from time to time, you might want that blogger to state that you are a client: that is, the blogger isn't simply doing it out of the goodness of his heart. In fact, new Federal Trade Commission (FTC) laws may require it. There's still a lot of confusion as to how and when bloggers must disclose compensation, please refer to FTC guidelines (www.ftc.gov/opa/2009/10/endortest.shtm).

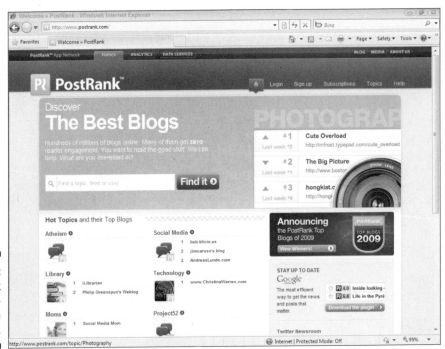

Figure 6-3:
PostRank helps discover the best blogs.

The distinction between someone blogging for compensation and someone ghostblogging is a thin line. One blogs on your behalf, writing your words but crafting it with their talent. A guest blogger or a paid blogger is writing his own words and putting his reputation on the line for your company.

If you're interested in getting content this way, you'll need to first track down top bloggers with tools like Technorati. The following steps show you how:

1. **Click Blogs in the Technorati search field (at the top of the window).**

2. **Click the magnifying glass icon to execute the search.**

   The resulting list provides you with a list of blogs in descending order of "authority." (See Figure 6-4.) In this context, *authority* is a proprietary number applied by Technorati that takes into consideration a blog's popularity.

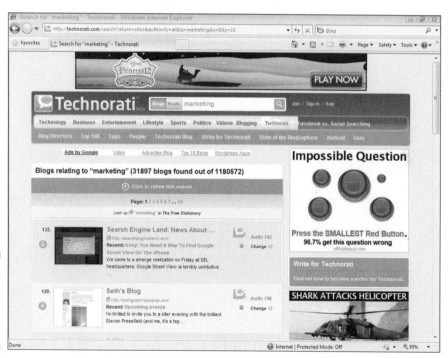

Figure 6-4: Finding marketing blogs on Technorati.

Owning Your Content

Many companies jump onboard blogging and social media platforms that provide them an audience but don't provide them ownership over the content they publish there. At issue is that your blogging platform might actually have Terms of Services that enable it to own your content. Through ownership, your blogging platform might be able to use your content to market its brand, or it might even be able to sell it altogether. For personal bloggers, this might not be of importance. However, for a company, it's important that you own the content that you've invested so much in. If you do not legally own the content that you've published on another site, the company who owns the platform can sell your content, republish it, or utilize it for their own benefit.

Verify the terms of service associated with all platforms you wish to use to identify whether or not you own your content and have the right to leave with it. Consult legal counsel if there's any doubt. Also ensure there is a way to export your content in the event you do leave.

The other problem with putting your blog on another domain that you don't own is that you cannot control what happens to your content. If the business that owns that domain decides to move the service, shut down the domain, or even simply remove your access, you could lose all of your content, all of your search engine authority, and the subsequent traffic and business you were acquiring through it.

Always, always, always publish your blog on a domain name that you control through a domain registrar. Blogging will provide your domain with search engine authority over time. If you're blogging on someone else's domain, regardless of how powerful they are, you're simply giving them the authority that you should have.

In 2009, JournalSpace was sabotaged and their client data lost. Some bloggers lost 6 years worth of data. The lack of a backup strategy, and their clients' dependence on their domain, left their customers high and dry with all content lost. This is a risk that you do not want to take with your corporate blog. Ensure you're blog is on a domain that you control, that your content is backed up regularly, and can be accessed when and if you need it.

Owning your domain allows you to host your blog yourself, or host it with a Software as a Service (SaaS) provider. This means that you can move it whenever and wherever you'd like and keep the authority that you've worked so hard to attain.

As well, if the provider ever goes belly-up, you can launch your next blog at the same exact address with another service or internally with no issues. Regardless of where you decide to blog, ensure that the provider's standard contract allows you to extract your content in a standard format that you can import into your next platform.

Exporting Content to Import It to Your Next Platform

Exporting content from your old blog to import into your next can be a bit tricky, especially if you wish to maintain integrity with the links you have out there. You don't want someone clicking on a link in a search engine results page (SERP) and landing on a `Page Not Found` (also known as a *404 error*).

If you migrate your content to different Web addresses, you will lose search engine authority. Don't be surprised if your ranking drops significantly and search engine traffic drops off. If you move from one domain to another, you will lose most of your authority.

The best way to migrate your content to a new blogging platform is by following these steps:

1. **Export your old blog content and import it into your new blogging platform.**

   Many platforms (such as WordPress; see Figure 6-5) have features that help you do this. Even if you have to do this manually (by copying and pasting the content), that's better than starting with no content at all.

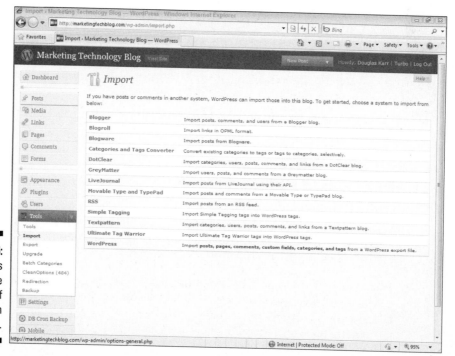

Figure 6-5: WordPress has a wide variety of built-in import tools.

2. **Write 301 redirects from the old blog post addresses to the new blog post URLs. Refer to Chapter 4 for additional information.**

   Some platforms have redirection modules or plug-ins to make this task easier.

3. **Write a redirect from the old blog's really simple syndication (RSS) feed to the new blog feed. Refer to Chapter 4 for additional information.**

   We recommend using FeedBurner (`http://www.feedburner.com`) for this step so that you can update the feed without interruption in the future. (We do wish, though, that someone would come out with an alternative to FeedBurner. It's terrible).

   If you're moving domains or subdomains, it's still possible to redirect to the new blog address. If your blog is hosted using Apache's Web server, you can write a redirect using an `.htaccess` file. Refer to Apache documentation on writing redirects using `.htaccess` files at `apache.org`.

   If you're changing your domain or subdomain, the biggest loss you're going to take are on sites like Technorati, which require that you register your new blog address. Unfortunately, Technorati doesn't have a means of updating your address. We've noticed that clients lose some of their ranking when moving subdomains although they can sometimes bounce back quickly. However, changing domains altogether can have a drastic impact. Try to avoid this at all costs.

4. **Test many of your old blog URLs to ensure that they forward properly.**

5. **Monitor Google Webmaster (`www.google.com/webmasters`), Bing Webmasters (`www.bing.com/webmaster`), and Yahoo! Site Explorer (`http://siteexplorer.search.yahoo.com`) for pages that are not found and correct them.**

   Don't bother checking every day. It will take a week or two before you'll see problems.

6. **Republish your sitemap and resubmit each time you correct items.**

Protecting Your Content

Content theft and hacking are becoming commonplace because content has become such a valuable commodity on the Web. Sites called *splogs*, which republish your syndicated content without your permission and benefit from the results in both search authority and advertising revenue, are on the rise.

The first means of protecting yourself is to ensure that your blog has the necessary legal statements to notify those interested that your content can't be used without your permission. Refer to the section, "Providing Legal Protection for Your Blog," later in this chapter, for detailed information.

Securing your corporate blog from hackers

As corporations dive into blogging and blogging software is not adequately maintained, more and more companies are finding their blogs hacked. If you host your own blog, you need to monitor the blog for any intrusions as well as keep the blog maintained. Open source blogging platforms like WordPress often publish security patches immediately, but most companies don't have monitoring services to ensure implementation.

If you're hosting your blog with a service provider, ensure that the service provider has intrusion detection and find out what its security prevention methods are.

Backing up your content regularly

Believe it or not, most hosting and blogging packages don't back up your data by default. This means in the event that your blog is hacked, the service has a system-wide failure, or you accidentally delete content, you have no way to get that content back.

Ensure that you or your service provider has offsite backups and can be readily available to restore content in the event of an outage. Some platforms, such as Blogger, require you to manually back up the data. Other platforms, such as WordPress, have backup plug-ins. If your blog is hosted on your own servers or a hosting package elsewhere, you may simply wish to back up the database and files through a solution or service they provide.

Monitoring your blog to ensure it's up and running

There are many services for ensuring your blog is up and running and that it's performing well. The monitoring program from pingdom (www.pingdom.com) tests your blog from different parts of the world, and will actually e-mail or text message you if your blog isn't available. Webmetrics, Uptrends, and Panopta are additional services for monitoring outages, performance, and uptime.

Like with your blog, you should also ensure your feed is also available. You can point a service like Pingdom to your feed address to ensure it's up as well.

Many administrators set up alerts that to test that a Web page actually displays. Because blogging systems generate content queried from a database, your blog could be down but alerts never go off. Alert systems have additional steps you can take to ensure that your site is completely available, including checking for specific text within the content of the page.

Providing Legal Protection for Your Blog

If your company has ever gotten into legal trouble, you realize how much it can cost to protect yourself, even when you've done nothing wrong. Your blog is an extension of your company and requires all the benefits and protections of the law as well.

There are three key concerns when it comes to protecting your blog:

- ✔ Ensure that your bloggers understand the legalities and ramifications of blogging as well as what they can or cannot say on the corporate blog.
- ✔ Protect your company from legal attacks from others.
- ✔ Ensure that you're protecting your intellectual property and know what to do if it's infringed upon.

Copyright infringement occurs when someone uses your content, text or images, without asking your permission or providing you credit. You must have copyright statements on your site to notify readers of your expectations of use of your content.

What to do when your content is stolen

Setting up Google Alerts for mentions of your domain is a good idea. Each time your domain is mentioned, Google Alerts can send you an e-mail alert to let you know that you've been mentioned. Because blog posts publish with internal links, this is a simple way to identify whether or not someone has stolen your content and published it on their site. This is a tactic used by spammers and aggregation sites to build content and gain advertising revenue using tools like AdSense.

When you've identified a domain that has stolen and republished your content, take immediate action. At times, tracing down the culprits who stole your content can lead to dead ends. At minimum, you should

✔ **Use a Whois service to look up the domain owner.** All major domain registration companies (dotster.com, google.com, whois.net) offer a Whois service that allows you to search for the owner of a domain. If the domain owner is available by e-mail, send him a notice and request that he immediately remove the content in question. If there is no e-mail address, a physical address is legally required for the registered owner. Send him written notice. Requesting an attorney's assistance is recommended.

If you can't reach the owner, contact the Web host or Internet service provider listed in the Whois record.

✔ **Contact business partners listed on the site in question to try to reach the person.** Advertisers and affiliate organizations have strict terms that do not allow for stolen content. Notify them of the site in question and be sure to provide evidence of the stolen content.

✔ **Notify each of the search engines of the stolen content.** There is always the chance that a search engine may believe you are the root cause of the content being misused, and your search engine authority could thus be at risk.

Including all the required legal components

Your corporate blog should have four specific legal elements:

✔ A disclaimer
✔ A privacy statement
✔ A copyright statement
✔ A Terms of Service statement

These are discussed more fully in the following sections.

Writing your blog's disclaimer

Many law and law-related articles are available regarding Web site disclaimers. Blog sites, however, are different than most Web sites. Blogs often have more of an interactive feeling and advice-giving component than standard Web sites often provide. Blog sites are more closely comparable to popular social media sites than traditional company Web sites.

Most company blogs provide a level of advice to the reader regarding areas of the blog writers' expertise. Thus, disclaimers need to address issues of opinion versus fact. Also, reader comments and comment responses provide a conversational function of the site that serves to provide direct advice on particular subjects. This can give rise to claims by readers that the advice was directed toward them, which becomes more aligned with traditional professional consulting rather than broad publication.

Blog disclaimers are usually short and appear on the bottom of each page of the blog site. The disclaimer terms are also included in the more comprehensive Terms of Use section of the blog, discussed in more detail later in the chapter.

The disclaimer should approach a few key points.

✔ All blog posts are purely of the opinions and personal views of the authors and are not supported or endorsed by the authors' employer.

✔ The post should not be relied upon and may contain inaccuracies or mistakes, and the reader should seek professional advice on any subject matter addressed.

✔ Any comments or comment responses are the opinion of their authors.

Depending on the sensitive nature of the blog itself, the disclaimer might approach the following points:

✔ Content contained in posts may change over time; links may be dated; the content may not be valid.

✔ The author's opinions are not intended to malign any religion, ethnic group, club, organization, company, or individual.

✔ Links from the blog site can change, and the end of a link might not be the intended link of the author.

✔ Content on the blog site (such as videos, photos, PowerPoint or other presentations, or documents) are believed to be covered under Fair Use.

✔ Content is drafted in and intended for a specific language (say, English).

✔ If your company has a copyright or privacy policy, include a link to each policy.

If your blog posts include paid endorsements from third parties, you have to disclose that. In October 2009, the FTC issued its Guides Concerning the Use of Endorsements and Testimonials in Advertising (www.ftc.gov/opa/2009/10/endortest.shtm), and those rules went into effect on December 1, 2009.

The key to these rules is that a blogger must clearly and conspicuously disclose any paid endorsement in blog posts. The rules provide several examples of what is or isn't a paid endorsement. In one example, a student operates a private blog site where he reviews video games. A game company provides the student with a free copy of a video game and asks him to write a review. The fact that he was given a free video game with the direction of writing the review is considered by the FTC to be a paid endorsement, which must be clearly and conspicuously disclosed in the site.

For some sites that regularly endorse certain products or companies, adding the endorsement disclaimer to the general disclaimer might make sense. Otherwise, if the endorsement is being made in only one or a few posts, include the endorsement disclaimer in each individual post itself.

What you need to know about privacy

Privacy law, a fast-emerging area of law, is one of the hottest legal subjects in international Internet law as well as a large concern for bloggers. To complicate things, every country approaches privacy issues very differently. Some countries, like the United States, approach personal data as generally public information unless the data is of a protected class that requires heightened protection. Other countries, such as those of the European Union (EU), treat personally identifiable data as private and belonging to the individual. In those countries, certain privacy protections must be provided in the blog site.

In the United States, the general rule is that for information related to children, health, or finances, details should be avoided. Some of the federal laws protecting these types of information include

- **Children's Online Privacy Protection Act (COPPA):** COPPA applies to any online collection of personal information by *minors* (younger than 13 years of age) in the United States. Many blog sites contain in their disclaimer that the site is not intended for children 13 years of age and younger and that individuals between 13 and 18 must obtain parental consent before accessing the site.

- **Health Insurance Portability and Accountability Act (HIPAA):** Title II of HIPAA provides protections related to health care information of individuals. HIPAA is intended for health care providers and insurance companies. Blog sites from these companies must adhere to the strict requirements of this act.

- **Financial Services Modernization Act, also known as Graham-Leach-Bliley Act (GLBA):** GLBA applies to financial, securities, and insurance companies, and protects financial information of individuals. Like HIPAA, GLBA provides strict rules related to the treatment of this type of information.

If your blog site is related to health care or the financial or insurance services fields, consult with an attorney. For children's information, you are safe to just avoid it. If your site is intended for children, COPPA requires certain disclaimers and consent provisions for parents. Again, consult with an attorney on the specific requirements.

If your blog site collects data from individuals in other countries, certain countries require you to provide adequate security protections and opt-out options for users. The EU, for example, enacted its privacy directive in 1998. In response, the U.S. Department of Commerce negotiated a Safe Harbor framework, which allows U.S. companies to comply with the EU directive provisions. For more information, see www.export.gov/safeharbor.

Many blog sites contain privacy statements to address how the site owner will collect, store, and use information obtained from users. That said, most blog site owners avoid requesting or collecting any personal information about its users (except possibly on comments, where users opt-in to providing information).

The key for any privacy policy is disclosure. Disclose if you will be collecting any personal data. Disclose how you intend to use, or not use, the data collected. Disclose the types of other information that may be collected.

Understanding Creative Commons and Copyrights

Creative Commons (www.creativecommons.org) is a nonprofit organization that provides anyone a standard means of granting copyright permissions to their creative work.

With a Creative Commons license, you can keep your copyright but allow others to copy and distribute your work provided they give you credit — and they agree to the conditions you specify.

Writing your blog's Terms of Service

Terms of Service and Terms of Use are interchangeable phrases that shield the blog from the audience. The analogy could be drawn that if the disclaimer and privacy statements are the shield for the blogger and the company owning the blog site, the Terms of Use are the dagger. The Terms of Use provide rules by which any user of the blog site will abide and what remedies the site owner may have against any user who breaches the Terms of Use.

Terms of Use are often quite detailed and are usually a link from the bottom of each blog site page. Key areas to address in your Terms of Use include the following:

✔ A user has a limited license to access the site and use content for limited purposes. To be granted the license, the user has to meet certain eligibility bars. Often eligibility will refer to age and intended use of the content.

✔ Information on the site is copyrighted by the site owner and subject to copyright laws.

✔ Restate the disclaimer terms in the Terms of Use. You may also include standard warranty disclaimers if you're endorsing products or services on in your blog posts.

✔ If the site requires or has the option for registration, offer directions on how to register.

✔ Provide a link to the privacy statement.

✔ Provide details on user conduct. This is possibly the most important part of the Terms of Use. This relates more to blog sites that offer open comments and dialog fields, but certain terms will apply to all users. For example, state that users may not

- Use the site to abuse, harass, threaten, impersonate, or intimidate other users.

- Contribute any content that is infringing, libelous, defamatory, obscene, pornographic, abusive, or offensive or that you know to be false, misleading, or untrue.

- Contribute any content that violates any law or right of any third party or use the site for any illegal or unauthorized purpose.

- Create or submit unwanted e-mail (spam) to any other user or any URL.

- Use the site to support multilevel marketing schemes or off-topic content.

- With the exception of feeds, use any robot, spider, scraper, or other automated means to access the site for any purpose without the blog site owner's express written permission.

- Take any action that imposes an unreasonable or disproportionately large load on the blog site infrastructure.

- Bypass any measures used to prevent or restrict access to the site.

- State that you can remove any content or deactivate any user account at any time.

- Provide a user content section that states that the user is granting a perpetual license to the site owner for any content provided by the user on the site.

- Issue a blanket indemnity by the user against you for any violation of your Terms of Use by the user which causes harm or damage to a third party.

- Provide company contact information and copyright policy information if the company has one in place.

Chapter 7

Working with Your Blogging Team

In This Chapter
▶ Building a balanced blogging team
▶ Communicating your blogging strategy with your team
▶ Rewarding results with your blogging team

*R*eaching your blogging goals is possible only if your bloggers work as a team and execute your blogging strategy well. Imagine your blogging team as a football team with coaches, trainers, offense, defense . . . and maybe even some cheerleaders!

Most companies don't have the resources to fully man a team dedicated solely to blogging, so you'll have to negotiate with employees' time. As well, because blogging isn't a primary duty of your employees, you'll need to train and motivate them.

There's no trophy waiting for your company when they blog well, but over time, you will see that you're building authority in your industry, acquiring leads, retaining customers, and genuinely seeing a large impact. You need persistence, a great strategy, and a lot of time, though — especially if you're starting from scratch.

Deciding Who Should Blog in Your Organization

Many companies tend to want their internal leadership to write their blogs. Leaders within your organization are more often likely to promote the company externally, network with other professionals, speak publicly, or even write for periodicals. As such, leaders are fantastic candidates for your blog — a natural fit.

However, because companies are interested in the capability of blogs to put a face to their logo and brand, more often, they look to customer service–oriented individuals within the organization to blog. By doing a little digging, companies often discover internal writing talent they didn't even realize existed.

Choosing the best bloggers

If your company has hired the best talent, built the best products, and you know it, it's time to put your talent in the spotlight. Companies often ignore gifted employees; the irony is that allowing them to shine improves employee commitment and confidence, leading to improved customer retention. Corporate blogging allows companies to showcase their leaders' talents, as well as allow those gifted employees to shine. The audience of your blog suggests who your bloggers should be, including any of the following:

- **Leadership:** Providing information to stockholders and employees is best done by leaders within your organization. Your president or CEO need not be the actual writer, though. You can have a third-person blog that speaks to the overall strategy of the organization by quoting the leadership.

- **Sales and marketing:** Providing inbound marketing leads to your organization can be best achieved by allowing your marketing and sales staffs to blog. Your marketing department understands how to leverage your product in the industry. And your sales staff knows the questions prospects commonly ask — and the answers they're looking for.

  Marketing departments make great administrators and moderators for your program as well. Press releases, product whitepapers, downloads, upgrades, events, Webinars, and even company philanthropic work should be communicated through the blog. Key to incorporating this content on the blog, though, is rewriting the message to ensure it's both personalized and compelling for your audience.

- **Public relations:** There aren't many people better capable of effectively using blogging than public relations professionals. Public relations professionals have long practiced the art of communicating and measuring the impact of media marketing in the marketplace. A blog is a fantastic medium for your public relations and marketing personnel to deploy news and information about your company, products, and services. Blogs are also incredibly powerful crisis management tools as well; your public relations (PR) team can communicate directly to the audience rather than being filtered, edited, or ignored by traditional media.

- **Customer service:** Providing customer service and a knowledge base of frequently asked questions can be accomplished by your customer service and account management teams. To help achieve buy-in, stress that

improved communication through a blog will ultimately reduce their
workload by providing an invaluable knowledge base to customers.

✔ **Human resources:** Seeking human resources for your organization can
be done effectively through a blog. Because blogs are timely and search
engine–friendly, posting a job position on a blog is fantastic. Word will
travel quickly through your readers, and you'll be amazed at the qualified candidates you can acquire. As well, your human resource team can
blog about the culture of the organization, ensuring that those seeking
jobs with your organization already realize how they may fit.

✔ **Just about anyone:** Providing a human face to your company can be
accomplished through letting anyone within your corporation write
about the customers they serve, the industry they serve in, or the product they're selling.

Blogging should be fun for the whole team! If your team doesn't get excited
about the work they do each day, and they don't care about shouting about it
from the tallest mountains, then you may have the wrong team!

Recruiting bloggers: You'll be surprised at who gets the results

Imagine providing one of your Tier 1 customer service representatives with a
blog, only to find that his writing style is snarky and fun, and provides clients
with a chuckle each time they read the blog. What a fantastic way for your
organization to find and retain customers!

Writing is a talent that some people have and some people don't. Some find
it torturous to sit at a keyboard and publish a blog post. They fret about the
message and the language used. Their palms get sweaty, and they get a stom-
achache just thinking about it. Don't make these folks blog.

Still, you can find other opportunities for folks like this to support the blog.
Maybe the nonwriterly types are more than happy to take photos of events
or even narrate a video or two. This is content that your corporate blog can
use to increase the value of the strategy.

Here are some tips on creating the best blogging team you can:

✔ **Recruit bloggers from throughout your organization and set expectations with them up front that your blog is a performance-based strategy.** If they don't perform, it need not affect their compensation or job
requirements, but they could be replaced.

✔ **Don't drag your feet firing a bloggers from the team.** Bad content can really turn off readers and do more damage than good. Having said that, let a blogger gain enough experience over time to produce consistent results. Every blogger will make a few errors out of the gate. The great thing about a blog is that the next post will bury the last.

✔ **Recruit a lot of bloggers.** Of course, you want to produce quality content as quickly as possible, but you also want a wide variety of writers who speak with different points of view to attract different readers and audiences. Your blogging audience will be attracted to specific bloggers and topics.

Your best bloggers might not be the most obvious bloggers.

Marketing with your bloggers

Aligning your blogs, your bloggers, and your content will ensure that you're getting the right message to the right audience. Don't be tempted to limit your blogging strategy to your marketing team alone. Marketers already control the messaging of the Web site, the press releases, the marketing material, Webinars, and most other external communications.

If you're a marketer, you might not want to read this next sentence. The secret of blogs is that often, they don't contain the typical marketing terminology that a marketer loves to write. Sorry marketers!

Okay, not *all* marketers. Megan Glover, Marketing Director at Compendium, understands how to write for the blog versus writing for Web sites, case studies, and whitepapers. On the Compendium Web site, Megan writes, "Business blogging is a vital search marketing tool that's helping drive online demand and convert new business."

On the other hand, on a different blog post, Megan writes, "If my performance was measured on blog comments and RSS . . . I'd be fired." Instead, she states that her performance is best measured in leads and closed business.

That's a great example of two messages that are very similar but have different tones, audiences, and expectations. Megan and her marketing team (Meghan Peters and Mikey Mioduski) understand the technology they're using and the audiences they're targeting. They develop content strategies, design blogs, and landing pages to affect their targets, and they always are on top of who needs to be writing the next blog post.

Setting expectations with your blogging team

Many companies hit the ground running when they launch their blogging strategy. They set up some blogging software, send out logins, and tell their team to start typing. Although this approach isn't uncommon, it might not be the best way for your company to dip its toes into social media.

Setting up-front expectations with your blogging team is a great way to launch your blogging strategy. No, you don't need to drive everyone crazy by making them read this book and testing them on every chapter (although that sounds like a great idea!). Simply spending an hour or two with your team and going over some basics will help you avoid some obstacles on the way. Some ideas for this discussion include the following:

- ✔ **Discuss all the legal issues.** Your employees need to understand the liabilities of the company for slander, bad behavior in the social media space, invasions of privacy, and copyright infringement. If you're a public company or a healthcare company, very specific limitations exist as to what you can say, when you can say it, and where! Even if you already have counsel on staff, it's recommended to bring in a firm or attorney who specializes with respect to businesses, blogging, and social media. The legal issues associated with online content are changing on almost a daily basis.

- ✔ **Review the goals of your blogging strategy.** If your goal is search engine optimization (SEO), review the keywords and strategy that you're going to target. Encourage your employees to own and promote their content to get the word out. If the goal is authority, be sure to let your subject matter experts know that you want them to be leaders within the industry. If the goal is customer service, brainstorm on what the most useful topics will be to write about.

- ✔ **Set expectations on your bloggers' roles within the overall strategy, how often they will be required to post, and what rewards are associated with it.** Avoid negative reinforcement when it comes to blogging. An unhappy blogger can have a negative impact on your strategy.

- ✔ **Review the applications involved and the technologies involved, and demonstrate the best ways to use the tools you have.** If you're deploying additional SEO plug-ins for WordPress (for example, the All in One SEO Pack plug-in), teach the team how to use it. If you're using a system like Compendium, teach the team how to monitor the keyword strength meter to write optimal content.

After your team is clear on these issues, roll out a schedule to review and reward bloggers for their performance. If you're having difficulty motivating your team, be sure to share the results of their actions and the impact on the company. Your bloggers need to recognize the impact of their work as well as be rewarded for it.

This discussion should be the first in a series of regular strategy meetings. Here are some tips for holding great strategy meetings in the future:

- ✔ **Send out invitations and an agenda prior to each meeting.**

- ✔ **Review the action items from the previous meeting as well as the goals and metrics.**

- ✔ **Develop an action plan of who is required to blog, what they are going to blog about, and when the blog posts are required by.**

- ✔ **Distribute rewards and have fun.** The marketing team at Compendium hands out personalized rewards to the top three bloggers each month and three dunce caps to the folks who blogged least. It's innocent fun (and no one wishes to wear the dunce cap at the meeting).

Planning Your Content Strategy

Blogs provide recent, frequent, and relevant content to your audience, so it's essential to have content relevant to your goals and audience.

As your blog begins to convert traffic into customers, you'll want to grow readership of the blog to also grow the number of visitors who convert from readers to customers. Writing great content helps, but your best chance of growing traffic is to acquire attention from search engines.

Writing a blog post per week gives you 52 posts with which you can attract traffic within a year. Make sure that each blog post targets a few keyword combinations. Do some simple math — assembling a great blogging team to write two posts a day can mean more than 500 blog posts in the same year — more than 10 times the opportunity to attract traffic.

Blogging is a momentum-based strategy; when you post regularly, you continue to grow traffic. If you stop or pause, however, you'll lose some of that momentum and will have to work hard to get back the audience you lost. This is why planning and execution is so important with a blogging strategy.

Readers get used to the pace at which your blog publishes new posts. That is, your followers will begin to sense how periodically you're posting new content. If you're posting more than once a day, often, people will visit more than once a day. Don't disappoint them! Have plenty of content queued up and ready to publish for those days that your team is swamped and doesn't have time to blog.

Planning topics, owners, and timelines

In its simplest form, a blog is a publishing platform. Just like you would develop an editorial calendar to publish content, you should do the same with your blog. *Who, what,* and *when* are the key action items for planning.

- ✔ **Who:** Who will be writing the blog post or posts?
- ✔ **What:** What will they be writing about? What are the keywords to concentrate on? What are your goals? Will you be writing about specific products, services, and events?
- ✔ **When:** When will they be writing? How often?

Get agreement from your team and put your action plan in writing. Hold your team accountable by keeping score of who is succeeding and who is not keeping their blogging responsibilities. Problematic bloggers who don't find time will probably continue to plague you; unless their content is outstanding, you might want to replace them with someone who will execute.

Align your overall blogging calendar with your company goals. As you plan out your next year at work, your blog should reflect that strategy as well. Product releases, sales, events, and other known opportunities should all be written into your blogging calendar.

Assign the right bloggers to their topics of authority. It's okay to have some overlap, but explain to the blogger the benefit of his expertise as well as the long-term goal associated with having that person blog.

 Publish your calendar internally and meet with your team regularly to motivate, reward, and monitor how your blogging strategy is progressing. Share progress with your team members so they know they're making a difference.

Developing backup content strategies

Every company works through periods where resources are scarce. These are times when your blogging is at great risk. Blogging is a momentum strategy: The content must be written regularly for you to see results growing. Preparing for these periods with no resources is essential.

Every company has a ton of content lying around overlooked for publication on a blog. These are the times to push them:

- ✔ **PowerPoint presentations:** Each slide in a PowerPoint presentation can make a great blog post. Gathering a sales presentation and writing a paragraph or two with each slide can get you 10 posts or more!

- ✔ **Speeches:** If your company has recorded speeches, posting them to your blog is a great strategy, and it takes but a few minutes.

- ✔ **Whitepapers:** Writing a blog post with an overview of a whitepaper is a great method for capturing lead data and getting a post out quickly.

- ✔ **Customer testimonials:** The voice of your customer is the most powerful voice you can put on your blog. Resurrect old customer testimonials and share them on your blog. If you can add some additional detail and even a picture of your customer (you can settle on a logo), that's a powerful blog post that didn't take much time.

- ✔ **Industry news:** As your blog becomes more popular in the industry, sharing industry news is an effective way of writing relevant content that's applicable to your audience with minimal resources.

- ✔ **Guest bloggers:** Having a handful of industry professionals who can write posts for you will expose your blog to a larger audience and can fill in gaps when you lack the resources to post.

Having backup content strategies is essential when you develop your blogging strategy. Be sure to have backup content ready to publish or backup bloggers who can write when you need them most.

Planning content for weekends and vacations

Businesses that serve other businesses tend to see a drop in traffic over weekends and during typical vacation periods and holidays. On the other hand, consumer sites sometimes see a traffic increase on hours and days outside typical office hours. Take advantage of other companies not publishing content and continue to schedule or publish posts on weekends and holidays.

The majority of business blogs drop all writing on these days. However, this is an opportunity for your company to get some great traffic. Although traffic might be down during these periods, the lack of any competitive articles can be a boon to your blog's readership.

All modern blogging platforms have means of scheduling blog posts for future publishing dates and times. This allows your team to write posts during the week but schedule their publishing on the weekend. Take advantage of scheduled blog posts and post content throughout.

If your company participates in external events on weekends or holidays, that's great content for providing the human side of your organization. For the most visibility, write the content in advance so it's published in the morning of the day. If you're one of the many businesses that donate gifts during the holiday season, be sure to blog about the success of the program — and even let folks know how they can help, too.

Scheduling posts can be accomplished by employees who are on vacation as well. A short note — with some content — letting your readers know that you're out of the office shows how sincere you are to your customers.

Don't forget to communicate your holiday hours of operation to readers. This will set expectations with sales prospects as to when they can expect a response to their requests. As well, you can supply emergency contact information for those customers who need assistance while your office is closed.

The following steps show you how to schedule a blog post using WordPress:

1. **Click the Edit link in the Publish pane next to the words Publish Immediately. (See Figure 7-1.)**
2. **Enter the date and time you wish to publish the post.**
3. **When your post is ready, click Publish.**

    The post will not be visible until the date and time selected has passed.

Here's how to schedule a blog post with Compendium:

1. **Select the Schedule for Future Release check box on the Create New Post tab. (See Figure 7-2.)**
2. **Enter the date and time you wish to publish the post.**
3. **When your post is ready, click Submit this Post.**

    The post will not be visible until your administrator has approved the post and the date and time selected is passed.

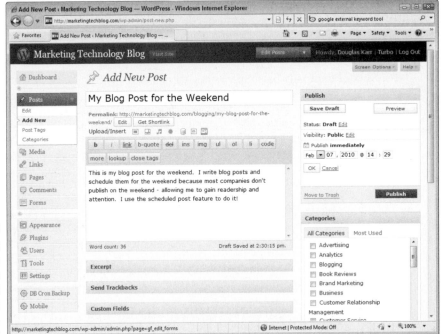

Figure 7-1:
Schedule a
WordPress
blog post
to publish
later.

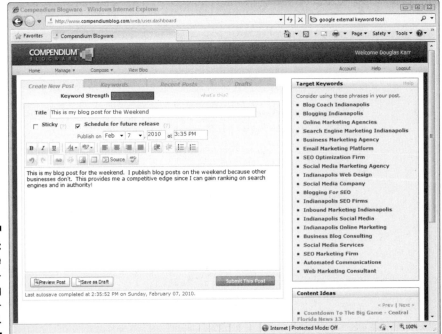

Figure 7-2:
Schedule
a Compen-
dium blog
post to pub-
lish later.

Developing an Education Program for Your Bloggers

Search engine optimization, keywords, whitespace, image usage, writing post titles, analytics, Webmaster data, ranking . . . there are thousands of tips and tricks that bloggers can use to improve their blog's visibility. As a result, your company might wish to enlist trainers and professionals to improve your blogging program. Do some research by utilizing search engines for local search engine optimization training, or content writing for search engines. An afternoon of training can make a substantial impact in the quality of the content your bloggers are producing.

If you don't find local resources, companies like Compendium offer free Webinars on corporate blogging, search engine optimization, and inbound marketing strategies. Also check out Corporate Blogging Tips (www.corporatebloggingtips.com) for events, Webinars, e-mail newsletters, and other ways to get the latest tips on corporate blogging.

If your company doesn't have the resources to train internally, you might also wish to have your bloggers attend regional and national events on blogging, social media, and SEO. The popularity of these topics has extended their reach to virtually every city.

Nationally, a number of conferences are available, including the following:

- ✔ **Blog World & New Media Expo** (www.blogworldexpo.com) is held each fall in Las Vegas.
- ✔ **South by Southwest** (www.sxsw.com) is a music, film, and interactive media conference held in Austin, Texas each spring.
- ✔ **SOBCon** (www.sobevent.com) is a social media conference held each year in Chicago.
- ✔ **Web 2.0 Summit** (www.web2summit.com) is held each winter in San Francisco.
- ✔ **WordCamp** (central.wordcamp.org) is a conference specific to WordPress and is held regionally throughout the world.

Of course, you can also follow a number of blogs that are consistently trying to educate bloggers on improving their writing and overall marketing strategies.

- ✔ **Marketing Technology Blog** (www.marketingtechblog.com): This blog provides practical marketing advice across all marketing technologies with corporate blogging being a category.

- **Social Media Explorer** (www.socialmediaexplorer.com): Jason Falls' blog targets marketers who wish to leverage social media to improve business results, including corporate blogging.

- **copyblogger** (www.copyblogger.com): Brian Clark's blog is one the best on producing content that gets business results.

- **ProBlogger** (www.problogger.com): Darren Rowse founded ProBlogger to help bloggers add income streams to their blogs. This blog targets publishing blogs but has tons of advice to incorporate into corporate blogs as well.

- **BlogBloke** (www.blogbloke.com): As long as blogging has been around, BlogBloke's been providing bloggers with useful tips on blogging and social media.

Your team can also review presentations that have recently been held on blogging and social media technologies from SlideShare (www.slideshare.net), a site where professionals share their presentations online. (See Figure 7-3.)

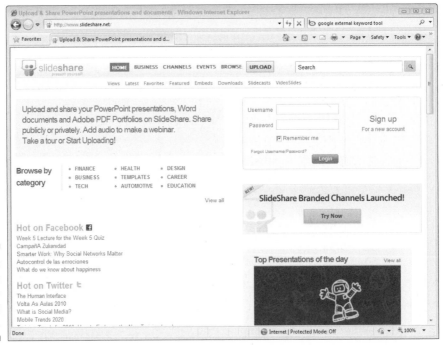

Figure 7-3:
Viewing presentations on SlideShare.

Informing your bloggers of their responsibilities

With many companies, your bloggers need to understand what information they cannot publish as much as what they can. Public companies are bound by federal communications regulations, healthcare companies are bound by privacy regulations, and your company may have intellectual property that is always hands-off when it comes to blogging.

Having your public relations team and your company's legal representatives speak to your bloggers is essential before they ever begin writing their first post. Your bloggers must realize they are responsible and will be held accountable for what they publish online. Just like your company has expectations for an employee when they attend a public event, your company must set expectations for the blog.

The benefits to the blogger are fantastic. By empowering the employee to blog and represent your company, you're making them indispensible to your organization and letting the rest of the world know it.

When your company publishes any information to the Internet, you must protect your company in a number of ways, including the necessary privacy statements, disclaimers, and Terms of Service. Those are notifications to readers, but there are also legalities that your bloggers must be aware of.

The Federal Trade Commission (www.ftc.gov/opa/2009/10/endortest. shtm) works for consumers to "prevent fraudulent, deceptive, and unfair business practices and to provide information to help spot, stop, and avoid them." Ensuring that your blog is clearly identified as a corporate blog is essential. Your bloggers should always identify themselves as representatives of your company and also always keep in mind that their goal is to inform — and, ultimately — sell products and services.

Your blog must protect the privacy of individuals within your organization or customers within your client-base. If you work in the healthcare industry, there are specific requirements on patients' rights and accountability. You can find these requirements at www.hhs.gov/ocr/privacy.

Within the content provided, your bloggers must understand copyright law as well as infringement and permissions boundaries when referencing other sites and images, or quoting content. Corporate blogging is "for commercial use," and your company is liable to pay penalties and fines for infringing on other sites' copyrights.

Your company needs to communicate intellectual property rules and how much information the bloggers can divulge on technology, products, services, competitive advantages, and the vision of your company. For companies with these concerns, employee guidelines will typically cover social media as well.

Developing blogging policies for your team

Writing a full-blown manual on blogging policies might not be the best way to motivate blogging as a strategy within your organization. Most major corporations have guidelines for blogging that are concise and offer additional resources for questions or concerns.

One example of a great blogging policy is the one from Yahoo! and Jeremy Zawodney, which you can find here: http://govsocmed.pbworks.com/f/yahoo-blog-guidelines.pdf.

Writing employee guidelines for social media

Employee guidelines extend beyond the blog into the entire realm of social media (if your company is using them), including Twitter, Facebook, LinkedIn, and other social networking platforms. What are the best guidelines for these platforms? Try these:

- ✔ Be transparent about the company or organization you work for. You should always disclaim any vested interests you have.

- ✔ Never represent yourself or the organization your work for in a false or misleading way. All statements must be true and not misleading; all claims must be substantiated.

- ✔ Post meaningful, respectful comments — no spam or offensive remarks.

- ✔ Ask permission to publish or report on conversations that are meant to be private or internal

- ✔ Don't violate your organization's privacy, confidentiality, or legal guidelines for external commercial speech.

- ✔ Stick to your area of expertise, but feel free to provide your own individual perspective on non-confidential activities at your organization.

- ✔ When disagreeing with others' opinions, keep it appropriate and polite.

- ✔ If you must write about the competition, make sure you behave diplomatically, have the facts straight, and have the appropriate permissions.

- ✔ Never comment on anything related to legal matters, litigation, or any parties your organization may be in litigation with.

Providing transparency while protecting intellectual property

When your bloggers doubt whether to write about a specific topic that may be intellectual property (IP) that should not be released, provide them a contact within the organization to validate first.

Intellectual property comprises data, information, plans, or strategies that a company owns that is typically protected and not released to the general public. There may be aspects of your company that you don't want the general public — or worse, the competition — to be aware of. Ensure that these off-limit topics are communicated clearly to your bloggers.

Setting the vision for your bloggers

The best way to motivate employees is to identify measurable goals that lead to a long-term goal. Sometimes, the long-term goal is big and audacious. Helping bloggers to understand the ultimate goal of the blog is key. A sample vision statement for your bloggers might be

> The [company] blog will be the number one resource for information and best practices regarding [industry]. Our blog will lead to speaking engagements for our employees with subject matter expertise and further our ability to acquire leads through the Internet by 400% as well as doubling our conversion rate to 16% while lowering our cost per lead to $35.

Your vision should be a combination of big (number 1 resource) and measurable goals that your team can monitor each month and celebrate when met.

Balancing autonomy, individualism, and expectations

Many companies enlist a copyeditor to make significant edits to employees' blog posts prior to publishing. Although silly grammatical and spelling errors should be avoided at all costs, rewriting the voice of an employee can demotivate your bloggers as well as remove the personality of the blogger from the post.

Good copy editors are great allies in ensuring that your voice is heard and your blogging goals are achieved. They will ensure that the content is well-written, compelling, and portrays the blogger and company how they wish. As a test, your company may wish to have a copy editor editing alternative posts on your blog. Measure the impact of the blog posts that were edited versus those that were not — it may be well worth the investment to hire or subcontract a copy editor for your corporate blog.

As important as grammar and spelling is, a blog's transparency and humanity may outweigh the rules of English. Be sure to provide your bloggers with autonomy, the freedom to write "outside the box," and let them add their own personalities. You'll find that diversity in the message and the team leads to diversity in your audience — attracting attention and business from all over.

Monitoring Your Bloggers' Performance

A blogger's performance isn't simply measured by the number of posts they write each week. It's also measured in the number of visitors, and ultimately, the amount of business generated by the blog.

Balancing content versus traffic and conversions

Your blog is a content farm, sprouting seeds of content that will eventually blossom into business. You might be tempted to sacrifice quality over quantity with your blog — opting into a greater volume of long-tail keyword terms and traffic rather than writing compelling content that sells.

Corporate blogs that sacrifice quality for quantity also sacrifice sales from relevant, qualified buyers. If an enterprise prospect views your blog and believes it to be nothing short of a content farm for search engine acquisition, you can lose their respect and their sale — before they ever contacted your sales team.

Don't choose between more content and less quality. More content with better quality will result in greater sales.

Using analytics to monitor specific bloggers

Analytics packages weren't designed to track authors, but they can accept additional data elements that are published on a page or added manually in the tracking code that you paste within your blogging template.

Enterprise analytics platforms like Webtrends allow you to track additional variables in a page, but Google Analytics is a bit more finicky.

To track multiple WordPress authors with Google Analytics, do the following:

1. **Add an additional profile to an existing domain in Google Analytics and call it Authors. (See Figure 7-4.)**

   This profile will specifically track authors.

2. **Add an Include Filter to the new Author Profile by choosing Analytics Settings➪Profile Settings➪Filters Applied to Profile➪Add Filter. (See Figure 7-5.)**

   This ensures that only the views applicable to an author will be captured in this profile. Name the filter Authors and follow the example in Figure 7-10 to include traffic to subdirectories that begin with "/by-author/". This filter added to the Authors profile ensures that all the analytics data can be segmented by author name.

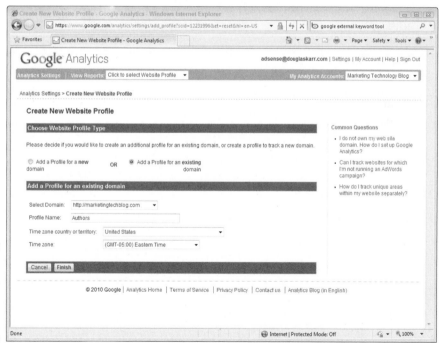

Figure 7-4:
Track authors in Google Analytics.

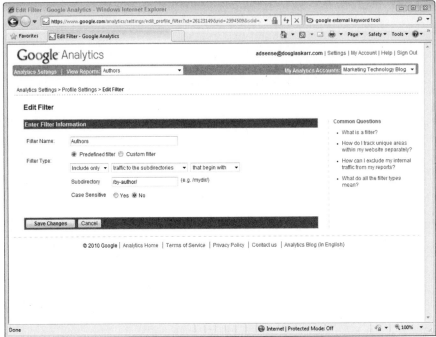

Figure 7-5:
Add a sub-
directory
filter to
include
authors.

3. **Close the Authors profile that you just updated and return to your original blog profile in Google. Add an exclusion filter for the same directory on the profile by choosing Analytics Settings⇨Profile Settings⇨ Filters Applied to Profile⇨Add Filter.**

   This ensures the author tracking doesn't happen in the primary profile. That would cause pageview data to be increased and bounce data to become inaccurate.

4. **Beneath your current Google Analytics script in your footer, add the following code underneath the trackPageview:**

```php
<?php if (have_posts()) : while (have_posts()) : the_post(); ?>
var authorTracker = _gat._getTracker("UA-XXXXXX-X");
authorTracker._trackPageview("/by-author/<? echo the_author(); ?>");
<?php endwhile; else: ?>
<?php endif; ?>
```

5. **Be sure to replace the *UA-XXXXXX-X* in the code above with your account number that's in your page's Google Analytics script.**

Now when you want to verify the performance of your bloggers, you can simply monitor this profile. You can monitor the number of visitors, pageviews, top posts, and bounce rates associated with each of your bloggers. This is also a great way of deeming which bloggers deserve rewards and credit associated with your blog.

If you'd like to take it up a notch, add some goals and conversions so you can actually track revenue by blogger.

Dealing with poor blogging performance

Blogging is a forgiving strategy. You can write a post that stinks one week and then a fantastic post the next day and all will be forgiven. That said, a blog post that's sub-par can cause interested prospects to leave and not return. Consistently blogging poorly will cause a decline in readership, popularity, and ultimately, business.

Keeping an eye on your bloggers and ensuring they maintain a high level of quality along with the quantity of posts they write is essential. Here are a few problems to keep an eye out for:

- ✔ **Poor quality content:** Work on methods for improving keywords, compelling post titles, use of media, use of bullet points, and recommending actions for readers to take inside of the content.

- ✔ **Lack of content:** Provide a content creation calendar with content ideas to encourage additional blogging.

- ✔ **Low search engine traffic:** Help your blogger utilize keywords effectively; write great post titles and compelling meta descriptions that searchers will want to click through on.

- ✔ **Low conversions:** Educate bloggers that they need to provide a path to engagement in their posts that invites readers to engage with the company by contacting them, downloading a whitepaper, registering for a Webinar, attending an event, or even simply e-mailing them.

- ✔ **Low time on site or high bounce rates:** Review Chapter 9 with your bloggers on writing content that is readable.

Motivating and Rewarding Your Bloggers

You don't have to give your bloggers payouts to ensure your team is motivated and blogging well. Employee motivation can take several forms other than monetary gifts. Providing your blogger with some attention within or outside of the company, providing gifts, and letting them travel and represent the company are potential options.

Moving a blogger from behind the keyboard to in front of the podium

Conferences are typically a great venue for driving leads into your company. Your bloggers will be acquiring authority and might get offers to speak at regional and national industry events. Take advantage of these events to leverage your bloggers' talent to acquire additional business.

Many bloggers are comfortable behind the keyboard but not in front of the podium. Be sure that your blogger is comfortable with public speaking before you volunteer her for that next international conference. Providing a few lessons with a speech coach can be a great investment for your blogger and your company.

Developing a performance-based rewards program for your blog

Review these three main metrics when evaluating performance rewards:

- **Content creation:** The frequency and quantity of quality blog posts your bloggers are producing.
- **Conversation:** The ability of your blogger to gain notoriety, build a following, and ultimately build authority within your industry. Reward your bloggers when their posts are picked up and noticed by professionals in the blogosphere.
- **Conversion:** Measuring the flow of traffic and the call to action conversions that take place off a specific blogger's content is often the most valuable measurement to the organization.

Depending on what your organization's goals are for the corporate blogging program, the performance rewards should be tied to these goals. If it's about being found in search, then perhaps quantity of content is the most important thing for you. If creating credibility and becoming an industry leader is your goal, then conversation is the most important to you.

Recognizing bloggers without breaking the bank

You don't have to spend tons of cash to get your bloggers engaged and creating content. Identify what your bloggers would like to attain through blogging for the organization and try to provide it when goals are reached.

Tying blogging to revenue is a key strategy for blogging so that you can also provide some monetary reward. It need not be money, knick-knacks and gifts can go a long way. Providing small incentives such as company branded items, a traveling blogging trophy, and giving time off (or special privileges, such as an extra day of casual dress) goes a long way.

Meghan Manning, Marketing Manager for Compendium, has had custom ties, mugs, stickers, and mouse pads created with the blogger's photograph or company logo. During monthly company meetings, Meghan distributes the prizes to the best bloggers. Meghan also hands out three dunce caps to the bloggers who performed the worst, and who must wear the hats throughout the company meeting.

The culture that Meghan, and her director, Meghan Glover, have developed for the company is both fun and competitive — but most of all it drives blog posts, views, and conversions.

Often times, you'll find your team in a blogging *slump* where no one is creating new content. At times like these, spontaneous blogging contests are a fantastic means of lifting everyone's spirits and getting the team back on track. Gift cards for a night out or a few prizes for first, second, and third prize can get a ton of great content out quickly.

Team contests also work well. Ordering lunch if everyone on the team posts by a specific date/time is a great way to motivate everyone and create some peer pressure for the team to commit. If everyone is rushed and busy, bringing in donuts for a blogging breakfast may give everyone an opportunity to blog . . . just don't forget to moderate posts written in a sugar rush.

Part III
Engaging Your Search Engine Optimization Strategy

The 5th Wave   By Rich Tennant

"So, you want to work for the best browser company in the world? Well, let me get you a job application. Let's see...where are they? Shoot! I can never find anything around here!"

In this part . . .

Search engine traffic can dramatically impact the success of your corporate blogging strategy. This part is dedicated to understanding search engines and how you can improve your results on the search engine results page.

Chapter 8 introduces how search engines find and rank your corporate blog. You also see how using keywords correctly helps you appear in relevant searches.

Chapter 9 builds the keyword foundation to help you with advanced keyword integration techniques. These techniques help you with search engines and guiding visitors to conversion.

Chapter 8

Making the Most of Search Engines

In This Chapter

▶ Analyzing keywords

▶ Reviewing how search engines find your content

▶ Using keywords and content to attract search engines

▶ Registering with search engines

▶ Leveraging search engines to increase traffic and conversions

Search engines have changed the way the Internet is navigated. According to recent statistics, 90 percent of Internet sessions start with or include a search. Search engines are constantly adjusting their algorithms to push the most relevant content to the top of the search engine results pages (SERPs) to keep users happy and coming back.

As the world's most popular search engine, Google and its algorithms changed the search engine world forever, allowing Google to dominate the search engine market. Google's methodologies incorporate the following criteria:

- **Popularity:** The more links from relevant, authoritative domains back to your page and domain the more your pages and domains gain in ranking for the relevant keywords and phrases.

- **Relevance:** The more relevant your content is to the keywords or phrases searched, the better the chances of your site being found for those keywords or phrases.

- **Recency:** The more recent your content is to the keywords or phrases searched, the better the chances of your site being found for those keywords or phrases.

- **Frequency:** The more frequently your content mentions the keywords and phrases, the better the chances of your site being found for those keywords or phrases.

Blogs allow you to write relevant, recent, and frequent content that searchers are looking for. This is what differentiates a blog from a static Web site as the ideal method of gaining search engine traffic. Blogs have back-end technology that allows them to communicate with search engines and with each other.

In this chapter, we provide you with the tools and tips you need to ensure you are optimizing your content and platform to fully leverage search engines as a source of relevant traffic.

Understanding How Search Engines Find Your Content

In the early days of search, programmatic crawlers would find a link to your site and then consume your page content trying to identify what the page was about and what results it should be categorized (indexed) for. These crawlers simply found your home page and then crawled through your site using the internal navigation. This is why many early Web sites included a visible sitemap that held all the links to the pages within. Many of the first search engines used meta data to properly index the page. *Meta data* is information that is not viewable in a Web page but provides additional information to programs and applications that require it.

Meta tagging, or the use of embedded keywords and other important info in meta data, was once an effective way of getting your pages indexed, but then authors figured out that they could garner a lot of traffic by inserting irrelevant but popular meta tags. As a result, search engines directed users to pages they weren't looking for. Because of this, search engines began to largely ignore meta tags as a key component of indexing a page.

In the present day, search engines take a much more thorough approach. For blogs, this approach usually involves the following steps (see Figure 8-1):

1. When you publish your blog on a blogging platform your sitemap file is published with the updates. A *sitemap* is a file that contains the paths of pages within your Web site, their importance, how frequently they're updated, and the time they were last updated. They provide search engines with a map to find and index the updated content.

2. Once updated, your blog contacts the search engines by using a process called a *ping,* which basically pushes your sitemap address to the search engine.

3. The search engine queues the request, recognizing that there has been a change to the site. Blogs that consistently change content are indexed more often than those that do not.

4. Once identified, search engines check for a `robots.txt` file in the root (base) of the Web site with a *bot.* Short for *robots,* bots are simply programs or applications that run repetitive processes across the Internet. Search engine bots are the processes that connect to your site and capture the necessary information for crawling and indexing the site.

   Your `robots.txt` file is a gateway and permissions file for the search engine. If the robots file doesn't exist, the search engine defaults that it has permission to crawl the site and begins crawling the site manually by bouncing from link to link. If the robots file does exist, the search engine identifies which directories to ignore and which to include, and tries to locate the sitemap.

   An extensible markup language (XML) sitemap is the most efficient means of providing a search engine with a roadmap of the content you want it to crawl, how important those pages are, how frequently they are updated, and when they were last updated.

   Without a sitemap, the search engine is left to determine the hierarchy and importance of the site on its own by crawling from link to link. With a sitemap, you can better direct the search engine to your pages and ensure your content is properly indexed.

5. As the bots view your pages, they first check for a meta robots tag to see if the page should be indexed. Search engines use a combination of page structure, hierarchy, HTML elements, keyword densities, and synonymous keyword terms to properly identify how the page should be indexed.

   Keyword density is the ratio of keywords to other words within your content. *Keyword stuffing* is a method by which page authors overpopulate a page with keywords to artificially get it indexed for those terms. If a search engine determines that the page is "stuffed," that page can be buried in the bottom of search results.

6. Search results are updated within the search engine.

Understanding this process is important because it allows bloggers to incorporate pinging, robots files, sitemaps, page structure, and keyword usage into their corporate blogging strategy. The following sections provide you with the necessary information to understand how to create, implement, and leverage these tools.

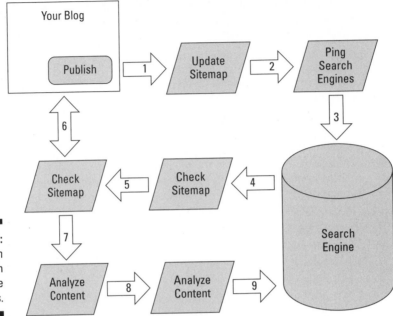

Building your robots file to allow search engines permission

The Web Robots Pages (`www.robotstxt.org`) fully explain the ways `robots.txt` files prevent or allow search engines to crawl your site. The process for generating a `robots.txt` file is quite simple. To write and install a `robots.txt` file for your blog, follow these steps:

1. **Open a plain text editor like Notepad.**

2. **In the first line, define which bots or search engines (described here by the term *user-agent*) you want to provide permission to. Typically, this is set to give permissions to any bots or search engines. To do this, insert an asterisk, which is a sort of wildcard symbol, as follows:**

   ```
   User-agent: *
   ```

3. **If there are directories that you don't wish the search engines to index, such as administrative directories, download directories, or feed paths, indicate them using the word *Disallow* and a line for each exclusion, as follows:**

   ```
   Disallow: */feed/
   Disallow: /download/
   Disallow: /tag/
   ```

If you're running a WordPress blog, you can exclude all default administrative directories with the path /wp-, as follows:

```
Disallow: /wp-
```

4. **Add a line to identify where your blog's sitemap file is located.**

   Typically, the XML sitemap file is located in the root (base) of the Web directory, as follows:

   ```
   Sitemap: http://www.yourblog.com/sitemap.xml
   ```

5. **Using an FTP application, upload the file to the base of your Web site in the root directory.**

   You should be able to navigate directly to the file by simply putting the path in a browser, like this:

   ```
   http://www.yourblog.com/robots.txt
   ```

A finished example of a robots.txt file is shown in Figure 8-2.

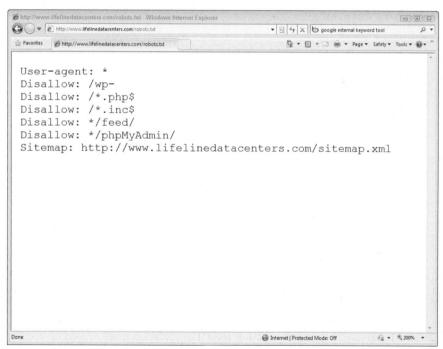

Figure 8-2:
Example of a robots.txt file.

Publishing a sitemap that directs search engines properly

Many content management systems, including blogs, offer sitemaps; at first sitemaps were viewable HTML pages that allowed the visitor to navigate the site and find what they were looking for. Over time, HTML sitemaps have become less and less common because they were difficult to keep updated and rarely used by visitors. Most sites don't incorporate HTML-based sitemaps anymore.

Content management systems, including blogging platforms, have adopted XML-based sitemaps. XML-based sitemaps are extremely useful for search engines because they can be accessed programmatically by search engines. The search engines agreed to a Sitemap protocol (www.sitemaps.org) for XML-based sitemaps.

XML-based sitemaps incorporate a site's hierarchy, a listing of all the pages within that site, how important the page is, how often the search engine should return, and when each page was last updated. www.sitemaps.org.

As you might guess, building a sitemap manually can be quite an undertaking. The best blogging platforms have sitemaps built in without any need for the administrator to do anything.

The following list describes some different blogging platforms and the way they implement sitemaps:

- ✔ **Compendium Blogware's corporate blogging platform (www. compendium.com):** This platform has automated sitemapping that's optimized to direct search engines through their keyword-optimized blogs. This is done automatically with no need for you to request or implement the sitemapping.

- ✔ **TypePad (www.typepad.com/business):** This platform has an option to enable sitemaps. Go to Weblogs⇨Configure⇨Publicity and select Yes under Google Sitemaps.

- ✔ **WordPress (www.wordpress.org):** The self-hosted version of WordPress has quite a few XML sitemap plug-ins, the most popular being Google XML Sitemaps by Arne Brachhold (www.arnebrachhold. de). To install this plug-in, follow these steps:

    1. **Log in to WordPress as an administrator.**

    2. **Choose Plugins⇨Add New.**

    3. **Search for XML Sitemap.**

4. **Navigate to the Google XML Sitemaps plug-in by Arne Brachhold and click Install.**

5. **You may need to enter your FTP login information for the plug-in at this point.**

6. **Choose Plugins⇨Installed and activate the plug-in.**

7. **Choose Settings⇨XML Sitemap to set content priorities. For some advice on these settings, look at the next section, "Setting content priorities in your sitemap."**

Setting content priorities in your sitemap

Sitemap generation systems often have advanced settings that allow you to optimize your sitemap to let the search engines know which content is most important or to specify which content actually should be included in the sitemap.

This is an essential step with some blogging platforms like WordPress, which tend to publish the same content several different ways (in feeds, author paths, tag paths, archive paths, category paths, and so on).

Optimizing your `robots.txt` file and sitemap to omit extraneous paths and promote the direct paths improves the way search engines index your site.

To update the settings for the WordPress XML sitemap:

1. **Select (enable) the Write a Normal XML File check box.**

   This is the most common file that's consumed by search engines and should always be included.

2. **Select (enable) the Write a Gzipped File check box.**

   Although this file has a less common file type, it is a compressed version of the sitemap that's quicker for some sitemaps to download and read. It won't hurt you to include it.

3. **Select (enable) the Rebuild Sitemap If You Change the Content of Your Blog check box.**

   This is an essential setting. Each time you edit your site, the sitemap will be reproduced.

4. **Test rebuilding your sitemap by clicking the Rebuild Manual link.**

   If the page times out, you may need to increase the memory limit setting. My blog has over 2,000 blog posts and it required me to increase the memory to 28M.

5. **Select (enable) the Build the Sitemap in a Background Process check box.**

   If you don't enable this, each time you write a blog post and publish it, it will take you longer and longer to commit the post.

6. **Review the options to increase the priority based on the comment count in the Post Priority section.**

   I find increasing priority this way does not work well. Comments may be an indication of how controversial or welcoming your post is to feedback but not necessarily an indicator of how much business a post will attract. I recommend that you check the Do Not Use Automatic Priority Calculation check box.

7. **Select Automatic Detection and simply name your file `sitemap.xml`.**

   Naming the file something else or locating it in a different location could cause issues when search engines are seeking to find your sitemap.

8. **In your Sitemap Content, include the home page, posts, and static pages, but don't include the others.**

   Adding additional paths provides unnecessary duplication of your content with the search engine (more on that later with canonical URLs).

9. **In the Change Frequencies area, set the home page and posts to Always. Also, set static pages according to how frequently you update the pages of your blog. Set the other options to Never.**

   This ensures the bots are checking your home page and posts consistently, but are not working on pages that aren't changing or are unnecessary.

10. **In Priorities, set the posts to 1.0 and your home and static pages next (0.9, 0.8). The rest of the pages can be set to 0.1.**

    Priority ranges from 0 (lowest) to 1 (highest). These settings ensure that your blog posts have the highest priority within your sitemap — something you definitely want!

11. **Click Update Options to complete the changes. (See Figure 8-3.)**

For additional research on the sitemaps protocol, visit `http://sitemaps.org`.

Google Webmasters ensure that your sitemap is published and written properly. To verify your sitemap is published and being accessed by Google, follow these steps:

1. **Log in to Google Webmaster Tools at `www.google.com/webmasters`.**

2. **Choose Site Configuration⇨Sitemaps.**

3. **Click Submit a Sitemap and enter the location of your new sitemap.**

   Typically, this location is `http://www.google.com/webmasters`.

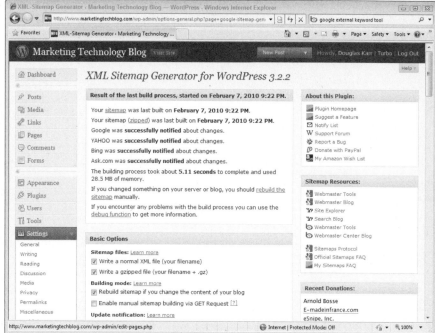

Figure 8-3:
After you publish your sitemap, you will see that the sitemap was properly published and the search engines were successfully notified.

4. **After your sitemap is submitted, check back after a day or so and verify that the status is checked and the URLs Submitted column has an approximate count of your blog posts and pages within your blog.**

5. **If there are any errors, troubleshoot using the information provided.**

Figure 8-4 shows an example of a properly submitted sitemap.

Implementing canonical URLs in your post pages

There is a lot of confusion on the Internet and within the search engine community regarding duplicate content. Google publically warned against *duplicate content,* which they defined as any two Web addresses that have the identical content within the pages. Many people believed this to mean that they could never have content published in two pages of the same Web site, or else their site would be penalized by Google and no longer found in search engines. Some blogging platforms have been openly criticized because they publish virtually every piece of content multiple times at different Web addresses.

Figure 8-4:
Example of
a properly
submitted
sitemap
in Google
Webmaster
Tools.

However, Google Webmaster Central explains the issue and goes on to state:

"In the rare cases in which Google perceives that duplicate content may be shown with intent to manipulate our rankings and deceive our users, we'll also make appropriate adjustments in the indexing and ranking of the sites involved. As a result, the ranking of the site may suffer, or the site might be removed entirely from the Google index, in which case it will no longer appear in search results."

Google has attempted to educate people that Google recognizes that modern content management systems, blogs, and forums naturally produce duplicate content and that this is not deceptive. Google Webmasters has even published posts on their own blog calling it the Duplicate Content penalty myth.

Blogs have a ton of duplicate content. Within a single WordPress blog post, for example, several different Web addresses display identical content: the home page, the post page, the author page, the archive year page, the archive month page, the archive date page, the tag page, the category pages, and the feed.

Blogs and other content management systems organize content in different paths and hierarchies so that readers can find it easier. Google refers to the real issue at Webmaster Central:

"In some cases, content is deliberately duplicated across domains in an attempt to manipulate search engine rankings or win more traffic. Deceptive practices like this can result in a poor user experience, when a visitor sees substantially the same content repeated within a set of search results."

There is a disadvantage to having identical content published on different Web addresses within your blog, however.

Google uses the number of links to your site to determine its ranking. You may have many backlinks to your blog post, but many of them may take different paths to the same content. To avoid this, Google, Bing, and Yahoo! have adopted the *canonical URL*. The canonical URL is a method of encoding each of the pages with a single path, meaning that these engines are capable of picking the best URL among several choices.

Google, Bing, and Yahoo! may have adopted the canonical URL, but that doesn't mean all blogging platforms are using it. Blogging platforms like Compendium Blogware automatically use canonical URLs because they leverage content through a multitude of keyword-optimized paths. WordPress has several canonical URL plug-ins, the plug-in authored by Joost De Valk (`http://yoast.com/-`) works well, and an All in One SEO Pack by Semper Fi Designs offers canonical URLs as an optional component.

To install the canonical URL plug-in for WordPress, follow these steps:

1. **Log in to WordPress as an administrator.**

2. **Choose Plugins⇨Add New.**

3. **Search for *canonical* within the WordPress Plugin Search field.**

4. **Navigate to the canonical URL plug-in by Joost de Valk or the All in One SEO Pack plug-in and then click Install. Joose de Valk's plug-in publishes the canonical element directly in each page header. The All in One SEO Pack is a comprehensive SEO plug-in that allows you to edit page titles, meta descriptions, and many other options to tweak your blog, of which one feature is canonical URL implementation.**

5. **You may need to enter your FTP login information because the plug-in will be installed at this point.**

6. **Choose Plugins⇨Installed and activate the plug-in.**

7. **If you install the All in One SEO Pack plug-in, choose Settings⇨All in One SEO and then select Canonical URLs to enable them and enable the plug-in.**

Using Keywords Correctly

Keywords are the currency of search engines. Search engines really don't do a great job at answering questions, but they do analyze content and categorize content for keywords with a high probability. For your blog to attract search engines, you must use keywords effectively.

To ensure your pages are found for specific searches, you must effectively use keywords, phrases, or synonymous terms. Even more important, though, is how you use those keywords within your pages.

Using page components to emphasize important keywords

Search engines view HTML page components in a hierarchy and the content from top down as it gauges the importance of the keywords on the page. (See Figure 8-5.) It's not easy to view your own pages from the perspective of a search engine, but here are a few tips:

- **Domain name:** Your domain name can have an impact on your search engine ranking. Blogs typically rank well for a keyword if that keyword is in the domain name.

- **Page title:** The page title tag is the top element. Using keywords as part of your page title tag can help place your blog appropriately in relevant search results.

- **Heading tags:** These often-underused tags are very important components. Search engine optimization sites, such as SEOmoz, have found that h1, h2, and h3 are the most effective tags in that order. Be sure to include an h1 tag at the top of your page Within the heading tags, use keywords. Again, the first words are the most important. A great method to use is to publish your blog title in an h1 tag on your home page.

- **Meta keywords:** Meta keywords have largely been abandoned by search engines as a resource for indexing page content. Using keywords in your keyword meta tag won't do your page any harm.

- **Meta descriptions:** Meta descriptions are not visible to the user but are an HTML component that's visible and used by search engines. Using keywords in your meta descriptions can place your content well.

- **Post slugs:** Post slugs are the text associated with your blog post within the Web address or Uniform Resource Locator (URL). Most blogging platforms generate this automatically based on your post title.

✔ **Post titles:** Post titles formatted as h1 and h2 subheadings with keywords are an effective element. Review the code within your theme and in the location of the post title, verify that they are wrapped in an h1 or h2 tag. Many designers use span or div tags without realizing that the heading tags are an important page element for search engines.

✔ **Subheadings:** Subheadings within your content should incorporate the use of h3 tags. Avoid using h1, h2, and h3 tags in your sidebar elements. If you use them, search engines may think your sidebar has more important content than your post.

✔ **Boldface terms:** Using the <strong> html tag around keywords within your content is very effective. Underlined or italic words may also have an impact.

✔ **Image alt and description tags:** Many bloggers upload fantastic images but neglect to take the opportunity to include keyword phrases that are specific to the image and the post. Leaving the alt or description tags empty when you insert an image is a lost opportunity.

✔ **Internal links:** These are links within your posts that point to other pages and posts within your blog. Internal links provide readers with opportunities to dig deeper into your blog. They also provide an opportunity to insert keywords in the title tags of the anchor tag, like this one:

```
<a href="http://mylinks.com/mypost.com" title="great
          keywords">more keywords</a>
```

Too many people use terms like *read more* or *click here* when they could be inserting some relevant keywords.

✔ **First words of your content.** Using keywords and synonymous terms within your content is important. Placing keywords in the first couple sentences can improve how your page is indexed, especially if your pages don't have meta descriptions.

✔ **Content placement in HTML:** If you view the source of your HTML, is your content at the top of the page? Many theme designers mistakenly insert the HTML for sidebars above the HTML for the content. Using CSS, a designer can place content first. Be sure this is how your theme is developed; otherwise, the search engine may believe your sidebar content is more important than your actual blog posts and page content.

✔ **Repetition:** Repetition is key with keywords. Don't use a keyword only once. Instead, find out where you can naturally add the keywords throughout your content in different combinations. Be sure to incorporate synonymous terms if it doesn't make sense to use the exact phrase.

If you really want to see how a search engine views your blog, you can use SEO Browser (www.seo-browser.com) to find out. Refer to Chapter 5 for more details.

Page title   Domain name   Bold terms

Figure 8-5:
Elements
on the page
with their
associated
keyword
importance.

Post title

Image Alt tags

Search engine optimization experts argue a lot about the impact and weight of page elements and their overall impact on optimizing a page. The goal of the preceding list is to provide you with a comprehensive list of elements that can be optimized on your blog. By covering all, you are not finding alternative key-words and phrases that will drive traffic.

Finding the appropriate keywords is key to getting your site indexed for keywords and phrases that people are searching for. Before modifying your site, then, it's useful to determine the keywords your site is already getting indexed for. Within your site's analytics, you should be able to find keywords and phrases that you are already being found for. Ensure those keywords and phrases match what users would search for when trying to find your business, products, or services.

Combinations of keywords that have search volumes that your site may already be ranking for are great keywords to start with. If your site isn't being found for any keywords yet, developing a list of keywords that have both search volume and low competitiveness is a great place to start.

As you decide upon specific keywords to use in your blog to attract traffic, you must be mindful of the competitiveness of those keywords. At its root, *keyword competitiveness* is the number of other domains trying to rank well for the keywords that you're trying to compete in.

Evaluating keyword competitiveness

Keyword competitiveness is an important element to monitor. If you find a keyword that's highly relevant to your company's products or services, you should evaluate its competitiveness. To rank high for a keyword, you must be more *popular* than other blogs on the Web. Popularity with search engines is achieved through links to your blog. A highly competitive keyword takes you much more effort to rank well on.

Google's keyword tools were developed for you to research and develop strategies for pay-per-click marketing, not organic search strategies. However, the competitiveness of pay-per-click aligns well with the competitiveness of organic search engine results. Competitiveness is determined by the volume of people bidding on a keyword. If you have a high number of people bidding on a keyword, chances are that you have a lot of sites competing for that organic search ranking as well.

Keyword competitiveness is easily measured by monitoring the cost per click (CPC) in pay per click (PPC) keyword analysis. If companies are willing to pay more for traffic via paid search engine advertising, you can be assured that the organic competitiveness for those keywords is high as well. You can also use the Google AdWords Keyword Tool; just enter a term to see its competitiveness.

Evaluating keyword competitiveness can be a science in and of itself. Keyword competivetiveness is driven by many more factors than simply the average search volumes. Some keywords can have seasonality (say, *valentines gifts*), and competitiveness is ultimately determined by the search engine results. If your competition has acquired targeted *backlinks* (links with keywords in the anchor tag) and has high search engine authority, you're going to have to work hard to gain on them.

You need to write blog posts that have an enormous impact in your industry and are linked to by the most authoritative sites on the Web. Sites that rank well on competitive keywords have a long history and high volumes of backlinks specifying those keywords, making it virtually impossible to unseat them. Major corporations with deep pockets spend a lot of money to ensure their content is distributed and promoted throughout the Web and build large volumes of backlinks.

As a result, your company might want to target keyword combinations that are still highly relevant but don't have as much competition. Lower competitiveness will equate to smaller search volumes. Gaining some visitors from relevant, low-volume keywords — known as *long-tail keywords* — is better than getting no traffic from terms that you won't rank on.

Finding long-tail keywords that drive relevant traffic

Long-tail keywords are typically combinations of three or more words that have search volumes less than 500 per month. If, for example, you were trying to get traffic on the topic *corporate blogging,* using the Google AdWords Keyword Tool, you'll find other keyword combinations with lower volumes that are still relevant. For example

- ✔ *Corporate communications blog* gets 48 searches per month on average.
- ✔ *Corporate blogging best practices* gets 36 searches per month on average.

Pursuing these long-tail keywords is a great way of acquiring search engine traffic. Many long-tail keywords have little or no competition, so you can write about those topics and typically begin getting relevant traffic immediately.

If acquiring search engine traffic is essential to your corporate blogging strategy, investing in additional keyword tools is essential. SEOmoz (`www.seomoz.org`) is an organization for SEO professionals. Aside from guidance, SEOmoz has a number of tools developed to assist with search engine optimization, including several keyword tools.

Researching keywords

You can perform keyword research in several different ways, including the following:

- ✔ **Using Webmasters or Site Explorer**: Each of the search engines provide comprehensive information on the keywords and ranking that your blog is found for. Google Webmasters and Yahoo! Site Explorer provide the pages and related keywords that your blog is indexing for. (See Figure 8-6.) Later in this chapter, you find out how to set up your blog for these services.

- ✔ **Using your analytics:** Within your analytics package, you can also find the keywords that are driving traffic to your blog through search engines. (See Figure 8-7.) Although Google Webmasters provide all search results, your analytics package only shows the keywords that search engine users actually clicked through to get to your blog.

Figure 8-6:
Viewing top search queries by keyword to your blog in Google Webmasters.

Evaluate the results of your analytics. You want to downplay irrelevant posts and pages by modifying the content so the irrelevant terms are not used in page titles, post titles, or within the content. It's essential that your blog be targeted for keywords you're trying to gain search engine traffic on if you wish to have a successful inbound search engine marketing strategy.

To view the keywords that direct visitors to your blog in Google Analytics, follow these steps:

1. **Log in to your Google Analytics account**

2. **Select your account from the Accounts list.**

3. **Select View Report for the profile you wish to view.**

4. **Select Traffic Sources from the primary navigation menu on the left sidebar.**

5. **Select Traffic Sources⇨Keywords.**

   The resulting report (see Figure 8-7) provides you with a list of the keywords and the volume of traffic you are receiving from each keyword.

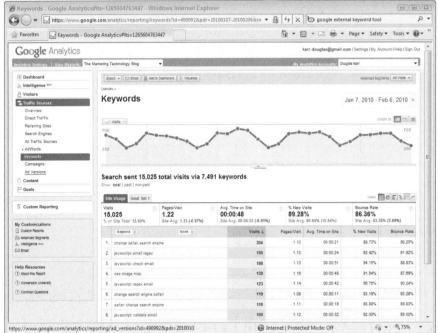

Figure 8-7:
Viewing top search queries by keyword to your blog in Google Analytics.

To view the keywords in Webtrends, follow these steps:

1. **Log in to your Webtrends account.**

2. **Select the profile of your blog.**

3. **Search for *"Search Phrases"* in the reports list field on the page.**

4. **Select the Most Recent Search Phrases (Organic) report.**

   Webtrends provides you with the search engines and the countries that the searches were made from. (See Figure 8-8.)

✔ **Using Google's Keyword Tool:** Google has a few keyword analysis tools. The Google Search-based keyword tool evaluates your site along with words and phrases you may wish to target. Google provides you with keywords related to the site as well as keywords related to the search words and phrases you add. The Search-based keyword tool is fairly limited but provides the monthly volume of searches as well as the competitiveness of those terms.

To view keywords with the Google Search-based keyword tool, follow these steps:

1. **Navigate to Google's Keyword Tool (`www.google.com/sktool`).**

2. **(Optional) Log in to your Google AdWords account to integrate AdWords details if your business is doing pay-per-click marketing.**

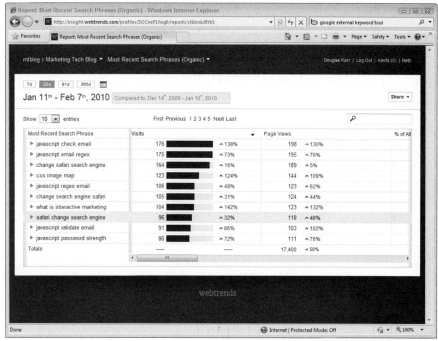

Figure 8-8:
Viewing
keywords
within
Webtrends.

3. **Enter your blog URL in the Website field.**

4. **Enter words and phrases applicable to your business, products, or services.**

5. **Click Find Keywords to get a comprehensive list of related keywords and their competition.**

Additionally, you can do research with Google AdWords Keyword Tool. This tool does not incorporate your domain in the results but can be used to evaluate keywords and phrases as well.

The AdWords Keyword tool provides a more comprehensive look at the keywords your blog might attract and can offer much more detailed information based specifically on the keywords or your domain.

To view keywords with the Google AdWords keyword tool, follow these steps:

1. **Navigate to Google's External Keyword Tool (`https://adwords.google.com/select/KeywordToolExternal`).**

2. **Enter descriptive words or phrases within the keyword field; be sure to only enter one phrase per line.**

3. **Enter the CAPTCHA (the distorted text you're asked to retype) and click Get Keyword Ideas to get a comprehensive list of related keywords and their competition.**

   You can also select Web site content from the left navigation and review keyword options that Google believes are relevant to your site.

✔ **Using third party tools:** You can find many other third-party keyword tools that can be used for research, including the following:

   • Wordtracker (www.wordtracker.com) is an online research tool that provides rich keyword data, related keywords, competitive data, and allows you to manage your keywords in lists and projects for campaign tracking.

   • SEO Book (www.seobook.com) has a keyword suggestion tool that's fast and easy to use. It uses data from Wordtracker.

   • Keyword Spy (www.keywordspy.com)offers keyword research tools, competitive intelligence, searches by search engine, domains, and keyword.

   • SEMRush (www.semrush.com) is an online research tool that tracks the top 40 million search terms. SEMRush is an outstanding tool to identify keywords that you're ranking for that you may have been unaware of. As well, you can identify competitive data.

   • Keyword Discovery (www.keyworddiscovery.com) is an online tool that compiles keyword search statistics from all the major search engines. It also offers spelling mistake research, seasonal search trends, and has tools to identify how keywords are used on your domain.

   • Raven Tools (http://raven-seo-tools.com) is a comprehensive tracking application for keywords, linking, social media, and design analysis and has Google Analytics integration.

   • Wordze (www.wordze.com) is an online tool for search trends, keyword research, ranking, and competitive insight.

✔ **Using trending topics:** Google also supplies some fantastic tools to see trends with keywords and phrases, like the Google Search-based keyword tool and Google Trends. Often, keywords change over time. As an example, the concept formally known as *SMS marketing* is now typically searched for using the terms *text marketing* or *mobile marketing*.

Google Trends can also be taken advantage of to produce content that will garner more attention. Many Internet marketers purposefully use trending topics as *link bait* — that is, they use terms that are controversial and trending high in search to attract high volumes of search traffic. This may get your site some additional hits, but you'll find that the irrelevance of the traffic will result in huge bounce rates and no conversions.

Improving Your Blog's Keyword Content

Writing posts that use page components effectively gets your pages properly indexed and found in relevant search results. Review the list of keywords that you wish to target as a source of inspiration for what to post about.

One method for writing great posts is to first write the post naturally. Be sure your blog post is informative, compelling, and pithy. After reading your post, ask yourself, "Would I want to do business with this company after reading this post?" You may even want to solicit engagement directly in the post.

After the post is fully written, go back and view the post for opportunities to insert relevant keywords in the post title and content. Try to insert three to four keywords in your content. Start with the post title, then subheadings and content, and even the meta descriptions, if your blog allows it. Applications like Compendium actually have a keyword strength indicator that provides you with feedback on whether or not you've used keywords that your business has targeted.

Writing for search engines can actually damage the conversion rates of your blog and, subsequently, lose relevant prospects. It's important that you use keywords effectively — they should never be noticeable. Write naturally!

Adding keywords to meta descriptions

If your blog allows you to update meta descriptions, be sure to use keywords in your posts' meta descriptions. The best way to update your meta descriptions in WordPress is by using the All in One SEO Pack plug-in, as follows:

1. **Ensure the All in One SEO Pack plug-in is installed and enabled on your WordPress blog.**

   For more on this, see the section, "Implementing canonical URLs in your post pages," earlier in this chapter.

2. **On your Post Edit page, scroll down to the All in One SEO Pack section.**

3. **If the section is closed, click the arrow on the right side of the section to expand it.**

4. **Evaluate your post title. If it sounds compelling and has keywords, don't make any edits to it.**

5. **Enter a description.**

   Write a compelling description with keywords that will motivate search engine users to click through to your post.

6. **Enter keywords if you'd like; there's a negligible impact on customizing the meta keyword data.**

Modifying existing posts to increase their search engine ranking

In reviewing your blog's ranking for specific keywords, keep in mind that unless you're in the top results, you won't be attracting much traffic. As you review your ranking, find posts that are ranked in fourth place or deeper and optimize them to improve their ranking. Optimization occurs a number of ways, including the following:

✔ **Backlinking:** If you have another site or blog, the best way of increasing your page's placement for specific keywords is to link to that content and use the exact keyword phrase in the anchor or title text of the link.

✔ **Deep linking:** As you're writing new content, link back to the page you wish to rank better using the exact keyword phrase in the anchor or title text of the link.

✔ **Adding comments:** A comment on a blog post changes the modification date and the content of the post and gets it re-indexed. Re-indexing with a newer date may be all you need to increase the ranking of that content.

✔ **Changing the post title:** If the post title doesn't include the keywords that it's ranked well for, change the post title to reflect those keywords. Do not change the URL, though — that generates a Not-Found error.

✔ **Modifying the meta description:** If you have the ability to alter a meta description tag for the page or post, modify it and use keywords once or twice in the beginning of the description.

✔ **Adding subheadings:** Insert subheadings with the keyword or phrase into the content.

✔ **Applying boldface:** If you didn't already, use `<strong>` tags to bold the terms within the post.

✔ **Modifying content:** Modifying the content to include the exact keyword or phrase toward the beginning of the content and repeating the keywords throughout the content can be effective.

✔ **Adding synonymous terms:** Inserting terms that are synonymous with the exact search term can be effective.

Don't overdo it! Stuffing keywords and modifying all these things at once could look artificial and actually drop your ranking. You still want your content to look natural so that it draws traffic and, ultimately, business!

Optimizing your content for local searches

Local search, or *geographic searches*, are searches that incorporate a geographic term in with the actual search. A local search might have an area code, zip code, city, or neighborhood combined with a keyword term. Local search has continued double-digit growth for the last few years. Google, Bing, and Yahoo! have integrated mapping and geographic searches directly within its search results. As the quality of local search results continues to rise, the volume of geographic searches continues to rise. Comcast saw 79 percent growth in local searches in a single year.

If your business is regional (most are, even if you don't want to admit it), using geographic terms in your content can help you appear on long-tail keyword searches that include geographic terms such as states, cities, zip codes, area codes, school districts, street names, and so on.

You can also aim for local map search results. For more on this, and for details on how to register your business with local searches, see "Putting Your Business on Search Engine Map Results for Regional Searches," later in this chapter.

Registering Your Blog with Search Engines

Your analytics package only provides you with details of how many visitors actually opened one of your site's pages, not details of how your site is represented in search engines. Because you didn't have people arrive at your site doesn't mean that you are not showing up in search results.

To monitor your appearance on search engines, you must register your blog with the applicable search engine's Webmaster tool. Google and Bing offer Webmasters, Yahoo! offers a Site Explorer tool. Details on registering your blogs follow this section.

There's a ton of information available through a search engine's Webmaster tools, including what links people are clicking, where you're found in search results, problems with your site, evaluation of your site's speed, and so on. New tools continue to be added. Take advantage of these free tools to tune up your blog.

Verifying your blog is located and indexed by search engines

The easiest method to verify whether or not your blog is located by search engines is to do a site search on the search engine. This can be accomplished on Google, Bing, and Yahoo! by entering `site:www.yourblog.com`. (On Ask, you can simply enter your domain name.)

If there are results in each of the searches, you know that your site is indexed in each. If there are no results, you can manually add each of your sites, as follows:

- ✔ Google (`www.google.com/addurl/?continue=/addurl`): Enter your blog's Web address, and a short description of your blog using keywords. Enter the verification letters that Google requests and click Add URL.

- ✔ Bing (`www.bing.com/docs/submit.aspx`): Type the characters from the picture, enter your domain name, and click Submit URL.

- ✔ Yahoo! (`https://siteexplorer.search.yahoo.com/submit`): Select Submit a Website or Webpage, type the Web address of your blog in the field, and click Submit URL.

- ✔ Ask (`http://submissions.ask.com/ping?http://myblog.com/sitemap.xml`): Substitute the path to your sitemap.xml, enter it in your browser, and click Go.

Because your site is found in a search result does not mean that each of your pages is being properly indexed, timely indexed, or that you are being found in all results that your content is relevant for. To do a more in-depth analysis, the top search engines all provide tools to Webmasters for analysis, such as the following:

- ✔ Google Webmasters (`www.google.com/webmasters`)
- ✔ Bing Webmaster Central (`www.bing.com/webmaster`)
- ✔ Yahoo! Site Explorer (`http://siteexplorer.search.yahoo.com`)

Register your site with each of these services and add your blog to each.

Identifying problems in Webmasters and how to correct them

To maximize the authority of your blog, you want to keep your blog ticking like a well-oiled machine. Using sitemaps, pinging search engines, using good page construction, and frequently writing relevant content are keys to optimizing your blog for search engines.

However, issues can damage your blog's ongoing reputation, such as the following:

✔ **Links that are not found:** If you're moving your blog posts from one address to another on a WordPress blog, a 301 redirect plug-in will help you remap your old Web addresses to new ones. This will result in no 404 errors (page not found) and your visitors can still reach your site from a search engine without interruption.

✔ **Pages timing out:** If your site's pages are timing out, you can optimize your site's performance a number of ways:

- Move to a new host or server with better, faster resources. Avoid free or cheap hosts. Chances are that they'll pile your blog onto a server that's already extremely busy. Purchasing a dedicated server can be expensive, but well worth it because performance has been proven to have an impact on visitors sticking around.

- Clean up the number of widgets, gadgets, and plug-ins that may be causing your site to load slower. Plug-in developers are often amateur developers who don't realize the significant impact their code has on site performance. Not only will these slow your site down, they're often a distraction from what you really want — a visitor to convert to a customer.

- Move your images and files to another subdomain or service. A browser requests one file at a time from a specific subdomain. If you host your images and your site at www.*yourdomain.com*, each file is retrieved one at a time. If you host your files on a subdomain — for example, images.*yourdomain.com*— your pages will load much faster.

- Incorporate Amazon S3, EC2, Akamai, or other content management services that will load your sites' resources much quicker. These services range in affordability but are extremely helpful in improving your page download times. Services like EC2 and Akamai cache components (such as images) regionally; so, regardless of where your server is located, all visitors can download the content quickly.

Don't underestimate page speed and site performance and their impact on business. Recently, Google said that it's actually testing page load times as a factor in its ranking algorithm. Be sure to get slow pages and pages that are timing out corrected.

✔ **Pages that are unreachable:** If you don't have a means of redirecting a dead address on your blog, don't ever delete a published post. You're better off adding additional information in the post. If, for example, you violated another site's copyright and had to remove content, make an edit to the post removing the content, apologize for the indiscretion, and point to the third party's Web site.

Changing content may impact your search engine ranking and how visitors react but removing the post will generate a 404 (page not found) error and will definitely result in users bouncing.

✔ **Your blog is not in any search results:** If Webmasters displays data that your blog is being indexed, but you are not receiving any traffic via search engines, there's a chance that your blog was buried by Google because they thought you were trying to deceive them to gain ranking. Keyword stuffing, duplicate content across domains, or content that's full of spam-ridden links (including your comments) may be to blame here. In short, correct the issues and request consideration at www. google.com/webmasters/tools/reconsideration.

Rand Fiskin, has an outstanding article on SEOmoz on what to do in the rare event that you were penalized by Google at www.seomoz.org/blog/how-to-handle-a-google-penalty-and-an-example-from-the-field-of-real-estate.

Monitoring your ranking and how you are being found

Too many businesses launch Web sites and blogs and neglect to ensure that search engines actually know the sites exist. Your site or blog could cost your company thousands of dollars in design and execution — don't waste that investment on a site that no one can find.

Unfortunately, Google doesn't provide a simple way for Webmasters to monitor whether their blog's rank is improving. Webmasters supplies snapshots from week to week, though. Each week you can download the results and compare the keywords. You can keep track of changes in a spreadsheet, such as Excel. To do so, just follow these steps:

1. **Copy the previous week's keywords and rankings in an Excel Spreadsheet (name it Previous).**

2. **Add a new sheet and copy the current week's keywords and rankings (name it Current).**

3. **Insert a column in the Current worksheet.**

4. **In cell A2, add the following formula:**

   ```
   =VLOOKUP(B2,previous!B:C,2,TRUE)-C2
   ```

5. **Copy the formula down to the bottom of the data.**

   The first column will show you how your site has gained or lost in keyword rankings. If you moved –1, you moved up one position.

Additionally, you can use a third-party service, such as Authority Labs (`www.authoritylabs.com`), to monitor your ranking by keywords over time. Observing your ranking and how you are changing is key to gaining search engine traffic. (See Figure 8-9.)

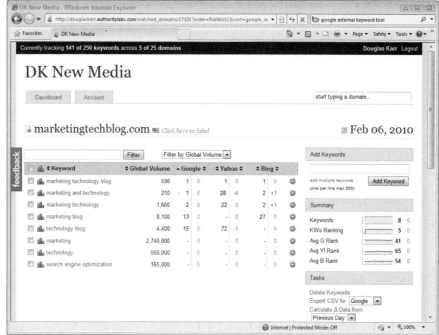

Figure 8-9: Viewing rank changes in Authority Labs.

A number one ranking on a given search engine results page typically garners more than 50 percent of all the traffic and the longest on-page time of any of the results. Keep pushing to get your pages in the number one slot.

Don't pay attention to all the SEO snake-oil salesmen that boast about getting sites to Page 1 of search results. Page 1 results aren't typically too challenging unless you're attempting to get ranked for a highly competitive keyword. True SEO professionals will always try to get you that lucrative top result on Page 1.

Putting Your Business on Map Results for Regional Searches

The majority of businesses, even those who serve national and international clients, are found locally. With the advent of Yahoo! and Google Maps, geography has become an important strategy for geographically located businesses. (See Figure 8-10.) Whether you have a single location or locations all over the world, it's important that you leverage your geographic location to increase your visibility in search.

Search engines have incorporated their mapping searches directly in the search engine results page (SERP) when a geographic keyword is added to the search. And these searches are getting more popular. In the last year, ComScore has indicated that local search is up 76 percent. Make sure you're doing whatever you can to be found regionally — including getting on local search maps.

There's no automated means of ensuring that your blog is identified geographically, although KML is now being accepted by search engines as part of the Sitemap protocol at sitemaps.org. KML is a standard extensible markup language (XML) file that is used across multiple geographic information system platforms for identifying point locations and paths. Using a tool, such as Address Fix (`www.addressfix.com`), Webmasters can identify their geographic location from a street address and download a KML file or KML tags to include in their site.

Figure 8-10:
Viewing a Bing search engine results page with map.

Geographic search is expanding in popularity with the use of mobile devices and location-based searches and services. Don't underestimate the power of geographic search when optimizing your blog and your content. If you're a regional business or you service regional customers, acquiring a presence for regional terms will get you business. Tools such as geographic meta tags, KML files, or geographic micro formats (`http://microformats.org/wiki/geo`) have not been widely adopted by search engines to date. Be prepared by adopting these methods for identifying your geographic-based business today.

In the meantime, be sure to insert your company's address in the footer of your blog. As you write content, insert regional terms as often as possible, including states or provinces, counties, cities, neighborhoods, area codes, postal or zip codes, school districts, churches, and other landmarks. As searchers are looking for local resources, they often combine regional terms with keywords. By using regional terms, you have a better chance of being found!

Registering your business with local search on Google, Bing, and Yahoo!

Each of the search engines has a free process for adding your business to their geographic search data:

- ✔ Google (`www.google.com/local/add`)
- ✔ Bing (`https://ssl.bing.com/listings/ListingCenter.aspx`)
- ✔ Yahoo! (`http://listings.local.yahoo.com`)

Each of the services allows you to upload information to your listing and even to manually locate your business by dragging and dropping a marker. Verification can be done by an automated phone process or by having a verification postcard mailed to the business. Google will even publish links to your site and blog on your Google Page.

Adjusting your location on the map to ensure customers can find you

When you register with local search, be sure to verify the actual location of your business marker on the map. Address cleansing and geocoding often gets your business close, but the ability to drag and drop the marker at your exact location ensures that those people who are mapping directions to your business find you.

Geocoding is the process of taking a standard mailing address and mapping it to a latitude and longitude. Typically, the process begins with cleaning the address programmatically and then calculating the approximate location by using address information combined with geographic data.

As a result, oftentimes a business address is displayed incorrectly on the map. The business centers realize this and actually allow you to drag and drop your marker to the precise location of your business. Verify your marker's location by zooming in all the way and switching to an aerial view. You should be able to identify the building you are in and drop the pin directly on it. Be sure to save your profile once completed. (See Figure 8-11.)

Promoting your entry with customer reviews

Your entry allows you to include ratings and reviews. Truth be told, a lot of competitors will use the opportunity to write negative reviews about your company. Stay ahead of them by soliciting your customers to write a review about you.

Figure 8-11:
Viewing your Google Local Business Center entry.

A great way of doing this is to hold a raffle for any of your customers who write a review and give away something substantial. You can get quite a few reviews by holding a contest like this once in a while. Positive ratings are quite visible in search results, so you want to maintain your profile.

Using your entry to publish and offers

Providing an offer on your Google page may drive a lot of traffic to your site, your blog, and your business. Don't underestimate the power of a simple coupon or discount offer to attract new customers.

To add a coupon, click the Coupons tab of Google Local Business Center and follow the instructions. See Figure 8-12.

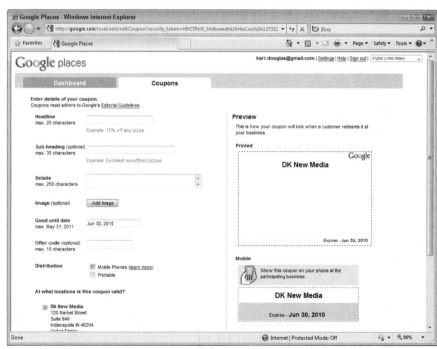

Figure 8-12:
Adding a
coupon
in Google
Local
Business
Center.

Chapter 9

Writing Content That Drives Search Engine Traffic

In This Chapter

▶ Attracting Web traffic from search engines

▶ Writing compelling content that drives search engine traffic

▶ Adding images and diagrams to convey meaning

▶ Using formatting and whitespace effectively

▶ Measuring the effectiveness of your search engine strategy

*T*he majority of companies use analytics packages to evaluate their blogging strategy and make changes. As search engines and social media become more popular, much of your blogs' activity begins off your site and beyond the reach of your analytics solution.

Search engine traffic is a key example of an offsite strategy that can dramatically affect the success of your blogging strategy. Bloggers who pay close attention to search can obtain more than one-half of all traffic from search engines. That's a fantastic acquisition opportunity for your company — and one that cannot be ignored.

Regarding search engine optimization (SEO), some naysayers liken optimization to *gaming the system*. Not only is this not true in theory, but the search engines continue to provide feedback and assistance to site owners to ensure their content is optimized properly. The better your blog is optimized, the more accurate the search results. This improves the quality of the search engines, their users' experiences, and ultimately gets the right searcher to your blog. The three critical "P's" of marketing are product, pricing, and placement. SEO improves two of those three P's, ensuring that your pages are placed properly and found by those who are searching for products and services that you offer.

When searchers view your entry on a search engine results page, they haven't arrived at your blog yet. If your site isn't on the search engine results page, how would a prospect even know that your site or blog exists? Companies sometimes spend thousands of dollars on their Web presence, but never see the fruits of their labor because new visitors aren't able to find the site in search engines. Coupling your design efforts with search engine optimization ensures that people will find and visit your site or blog.

Writing Post Titles That Make Searchers Click

If you're not already a blogger or a writer, most of your experience in writing has likely come from writing for school or at work and reading books, periodicals, or online venues. You've been trained your entire life to write titles that are a synopsis of the information within the chapter, book report, or article.

Writing for the Web is different primarily because most people actually don't read on the Internet. Rather, they browse and scan, searching for answers. Very few people open a Web page and devour every last word unless it's written by a very remarkable writer.

So, writing a great post title is important because it's how you hook a reader. Writing a great post title should accomplish three objectives:

- ✓ **It should summarize the blog post and set expectations with the reader that the blog post is relevant to their search.**

- ✓ **It should motivate the searcher to click through to your post.** There might be more relevant results written by much more authoritative sources. If your post title is compelling enough, though, searchers will click your entry on the search engine results page more than the others.

- ✓ **It should have relevant keywords to ensure that the post is properly indexed.** If it's a long-tail search, you might even find your article in the first position if no one else uses keywords effectively in their post titles. Chapter 7 provides information on keyword research and long-tail strategies.

Ten sure-fire headline formulas that work

Headlines are powerful and often underestimated. Selecting a post title that captures peoples' attention can drive tons of traffic through search engines and social media. Headlines are the most important element of your blog post and the first element to pay attention to. These formulas are courtesy of Copyblogger founder Brian Clark.

1. Who Else Wants [blank]?

Starting a headline with "Who Else Wants . . ." is a classic social-proof strategy that implies an already existing consensus desire. Although this approach is overused in the Internet marketing arena, it still works like gangbusters for other subject matter. Example: *Who Else Wants a Great Blog Template Design?*

2. The Secret of [blank]

This formula is used quite a bit — because it works. Share insider knowledge and translate it into a benefit for the reader. Example: *The Secret of Successful Podcasting*

3. Here Is a Method That Is Helping [blank] to [blank]

Simply identify your target audience and the benefit you can provide them, and fill in the blanks. Example: *Here Is a Method That Is Helping Bloggers Write Better Post Titles*

4. Little Known Ways to [blank]

Use a more intriguing (and less common) way of accomplishing the same thing as *The Secret of [blank]* headline. Example: *Little Known Ways to Save on Your Heating Bill*

5. Get Rid of [problem] Once and For All

This classic formula identifies either a painful problem or an unfulfilled desire that the reader wants to remedy. Example: *Get Rid of That Carpet Stain Once and For All*

6. Here's a Quick Way to [solve a problem]

People love quick and easy when it comes to solving a nagging problem. Example: *Here's a Quick Way to Back Up Your Hard Drive*

7. Now You Can Have [something desirable] [great circumstance]

This is the classic "have your cake and eat it, too" headline — and who doesn't like that? Example: *Now You Can Quit Your Job and Make Even More Money*

8. [Do something] like [world-class example]

Gatorade milked this one fully with the "Be Like Mike" campaign featuring Michael Jordan in the early 1990s. Example: *Blog Like an A-Lister*

9. Have a [or] Build a [blank] You Can Be Proud Of

Appeal to vanity, dissatisfaction, or shame. Enough said. Example: *Build a Blog Network You Can Be Proud Of*

10. What Everybody Ought to Know about [blank]

Big curiosity draw with this type of headline, and it acts almost as a challenge to readers to go ahead and see whether they're missing something. Example: *What Everybody Ought to Know about Writing Great Headlines*

Avoiding link baiting

Some bloggers abuse post titles and use a technique called *link baiting*. Link baiters identify trending search keywords using Google Trends or Twitter Trends. (See Figure 9-1.) Trending search keywords are those rising in popularity and typically denote an event or topic that's spreading like wildfire through the Internet.

Take the Google trending topic of the 2010 Olympics, as shown in Figure 9-1. To bait traffic, you might write a series of blog posts about how your product or service is like the Olympics. Even though your product has nothing to do with the Olympics, you might add post titles that include *Olympics* to draw the attention of searchers and bait them into clicking your link.

Although this might prove to be a successful short-term strategy for gaining search engine traffic, you will hurt the long-term strategies that impact revenue because you'll be seen as a search engine spammer and lose credibility. Visitors will arrive and bounce because they didn't find the information they were looking for.

Figure 9-1: A view of trending topics on Google Trends.

Getting traffic from the search engine results page

As prospective customers find your blog posts, their activity won't be much different than everyone else's. They will do a search for a given keyword, scan the search engine results page (SERP), and click the result they believe is most applicable. In a given month, a search can be repeated tens or hundreds of thousands of times, but you might not get a single visitor if your post title isn't written well.

Figure 9-2 shows an example of an SERP on the Microsoft search engine, Bing, for the term *headline titles*. The results page includes sponsored search results, also known as pay per click (PPC), on the right of the page. Relevant searches are on the left, and organic results are in the center of the page.

On this page, the first result appears to be a bland article on titles and headlines. The next has something to do with job titles. The third result might even be an error. Although the other titles are accurate, they don't have the impact of the fourth result, the copyblogger entry, "How to Write Headlines That Work." Following the three points I discuss in the earlier section, "Writing Post Titles That Make Searchers Click," the post title is concise and compelling and sets expectations, makes the search engine user want to click through, and uses the relevant keywords (in this case, *headline*).

Figure 9-2:
Compelling
post titles
in a Bing
SERP.

Try another search engine. Take a look at the Google search engine results page for *headline titles* to see that copyblogger owns the top two results on that page. (See Figure 9-3.) These post titles (such as "10 Sure-Fire Headline Formulas That Work") are structured a bit differently, but they're still worded well, and they'll still capture the attention of any search engine user.

Traditional journalists write titles a few words long that allow a reader to scan a large newspaper section and find topics of interest. Unfortunately, journalists often continue to use this style of headline on the Internet, garnering no attention at all. An Internet reader's behavior is much different than that of a newspaper reader.

A typical journalist might have written the blog post title, "Blog Provides Headline Writing Tips." Would you click that, or would you click "10 Sure-Fire Headline Formulas That Work"? I thought so! Broken down, the copyblogger post title sets the following expectations:

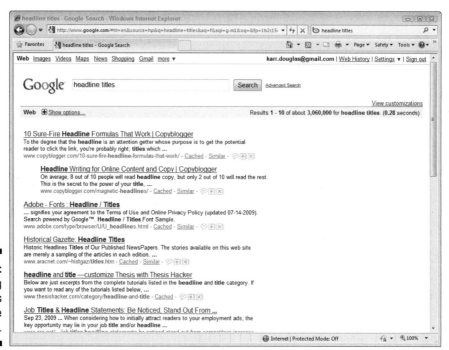

Figure 9-3: Compelling post titles in a Google SERP.

✔ **There is a list of ten formulas.** Lists are an incredibly powerful tack because they set absolute expectations on what the reader will find on the resulting page. People appreciate checklists and intelligently narrowing down a ton of information into a few bullet points.

✔ **The tips are "sure-fire."** This list isn't a theory, nor does it leave room for any doubt. These are *sure-fire* tips, meaning that they have been proven and tested. The wording is proactive and confident.

As you write your blog post titles, be keenly aware of how they will look to a search engines. Search engines typically cut off a post title in a SERP at 60 characters, so you must be succinct and creative. A blog post title, for example, "Acme Web Solutions Announces Partnership with World-renowned Professor of Analytical Studies from Harvard Business Schools to Release New Formulas for Ground-breaking Online Marketing Return on Investment Calculations" exceeds 200 characters!

Search engine users are only going to see "Acme Web Solutions Announces Partnership with World-renowned." A better post title might be, "Ground-breaking ROI Formulas under Development with Harvard." If that's not enough, use your meta description tag to provide additional information (see Chapter 8).

Search engines will highlight keywords that match the search term used, so your post title will stand out from the rest if you use keywords within the post title. People tend to scan left to right and top down on a search engine results page, so try to keep keywords at the beginning of the post title.

Clicks on a search engine results page follow the same pattern, the top left entry gets the most clicks and the amount of clicks significantly reduces as your ranking drops down the page. In Figure 9-4, click patterns follow the pattern overlaid on the search results page. This is why ranking high for keywords is important so use them effectively in the beginning of your post titles.

And just because you go ahead and publish a post, that doesn't mean you can't change it! Too many bloggers ignore the fantastic content already written, thinking that it's in the past and forgotten. There are no rules to editing old post titles. Repurposing is an incredibly effective means of harnessing search engine traffic.

To find blog posts that rank on page two or deeper in a search engine result, use a tool like SEMRush (www.semrush.com). SEMRush lists all your pages and where they rank on search engines. Identifying a post that's on a second page and reworking the post title to include keywords and make it more compelling can get that same post to the first page and sometimes even in the top search result.

Figure 9-4:
Where people click on a SERP.

Formatting page titles with post titles

The majority of blogging platforms treat a blog post title as a page title. Technically, they are different elements. The title is an HTML title tag and the post title is typically an HTML heading tag. Differentiating page titles and post titles really squeezes every ounce of optimization from your blog posts and templates — and, even so, might not result in a significant improvement in ranking.

In your blog theme's design, page titles and blog posts titles are distinctly different but often published exactly the same by the blogging platform. Search engines don't treat these two elements equally, however. For them, a page title is much more important than a blog post title.

Where can you find these elements? A page title is located in the title tags of your template code and is viewed in the browser page tab or window title (not within the page content itself). In the example in Figure 9-5, the page title is

```
<title>Inbound B2B Marketing Strategies and Blogging</title>
```

However, the post title is

```
<h2>B2B Blogging - Webtrends Engage 2010</h2>
```

The page title accompanies the search engine result page and will register high for the relevance of keywords for that page. The post title will also register well, though, because it's in an H2 tag. This method is one way that bloggers can target a specific title for the search result but another on the page.

Sometimes, the ideal blog post title doesn't have keywords, so by using this technique, you can insert relevant keywords in the page title without changing your blog post's title. And this allows you to target a variety of words — in this case B2B, Marketing Strategies, Inbound Marketing, B2B Blogging, B2B Marketing, Inbound B2B Marketing, and so on.

This method is accomplished by installing the All in One SEO plug-in from WordPress:

```
http://wordpress.org/extend/plugins/all-in-one-seo-pack
```

Other platforms might not offer this option.

Figure 9-5:
A single page template where the blog post and the page title differ.

Using keywords effectively in page and post titles

If search engine traffic is a strategy that you're pursuing, adding keywords and compelling titles in your page and post titles is where you want to focus the most attention.

From a search engine point of view, here are the two key characteristics of a page title:

- **The length of the title:** Search engines currently display only the first 60 characters of a page title. There has been some testing of longer page titles spotted on Google, but it's better to concentrate on the lowest common denominator in this example. Keep your titles within 60 characters.

  Because you're limited to 60 characters, try to avoid words that have little search engine weight — words like *the, is, are,* and so on. WordPress plug-ins, such as the All in One SEO Pack, provide you with the length of your page title. Other WordPress plug-ins, such as SEO Post Link, automatically remove unnecessary words and reduce the size of the title (see `http://www.maxblogpress.com/plugins/spl`).

- **Keywords at the beginning of the title**: Keywords at the beginning of the title are more important than those at the end of the title. Try to start all your titles with the keyword. If you're having a difficult time, try using a blog post with the keyword as the first term in the title:

  ```
  Inbound Marketing: How Blogging could double your
              qualified leads online.
  ```

One exception to this is the implementation of questions as post titles. Many search engine users don't simply type keywords into their search engine: They type entire questions! If you're answering a common question, you can attract a lot of long-tail traffic by naming your blog post with the exact question. Examples include any of the following:

- How can I improve search traffic?
- Where is the best restaurant to get cheesecake?
- What is the best brand of organic dog food?
- When should a company implement social media strategies?
- How do I protect my blog from getting sued?

A common theme mistake that designers make is to have their blog title preceding their post title. You'll see page titles that are formatted like this:

```
My Blog's Name - My Blog Post Title
```

Search engines will have no problem differentiating your blog's title from your domain and home page because it typically recurs on every page of your blog. To maximize the effect of your blog post titles but still include your blog's name, simply reverse the two in your theme, as in the following. (***Hint:*** Using a pipe symbol is a common way of differentiating the two from a reader and from the search engine user.)

```
My Blog Post Title | My Blog's Name
```

To format your page title in WordPress, follow these steps:

1. **Login to your WordPress Administration panel.**

2. **Navigate to Appearance⇨Editor.**

3. **In the right sidebar, click Header or `header.php` to open the header file.**

4. **Click Ctrl+S to open your browser's search field and then enter** <title>.

5. **When you find your title tag in your theme, change the following line (see Figure 9-6):**

   ```
   <title><?php bloginfo('name'); ?> <?php if ( is_single() )
           { ?> &raquo; Blog Archive <?php } ?> <?php wp_title(); ?></
           title>
   ```

   to

   ```
   <title><?php wp_title(); ?></title>
   ```

6. **Keywords are important at the beginning of the title, so modify your blog's name to appear at the end**

   ```
   <title><?php wp_title(); ?> | <?php bloginfo('name'); ?></title>
   ```

If you are using Blogger to publish your corporate blog, you can modify the title tag using these instructions from BlogBloke: http://www.blogbloke. com/successful-blog-seo.

Repeating yourself and reusing material

While reading through this book, you're probably wondering where in the world you're going to come up with all your content. If your company is going to target two blog posts per day, that's 500 blog posts (250 business days x two posts). What if you have only a single product?

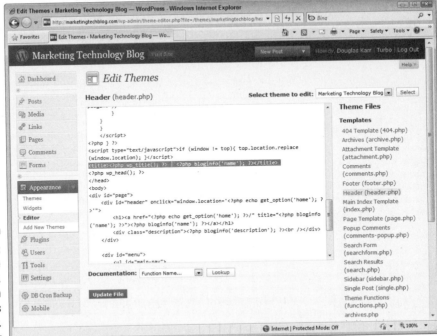

Figure 9-6:
Edit the
header.
php in
WordPress
Admin.

How in the world can you come up with 500 blog posts?

You're in luck. Not only is it okay to repeatedly speak about the same topics, but you should absolutely plan on writing about the same topics repeatedly.

Here are 14 ways to write about the same topic:

Concept	*Example*
Introduction to the Product	An Introduction to Blogging
Ten Benefits of Using the Product	Ten Benefits of Blogging
How to Use the Product	How to Blog Effectively
What Is the Product?	What Is WordPress?
Product Best Practices	Top Plug-ins to Install on WordPress
Product Advice	The Fastest Hosting Companies for WordPress
Product Events	WordCamp Los Angeles Is Next Month
Product Comparison	WordPress versus TypePad
Product News	WordPress Hits One Million Downloads

Concept	Example
Product Testimonials	Matt Cutts Loves Blogger
Product Opinion	Why Compendium Is the Best Corporate Blogging Platform
Product Humor	How I Learned to Back Up My Blog the Hard Way
Product Data	Blogging Platform Performance Statistics
Product Share	Top Blogging Platform by Market Share

When you listen to your customers and prospects, what are the questions they're looking to have answered? These are the questions and keywords that you will want to target for acquiring search engine traffic.

Using Keywords in Content to Get Indexed Properly in Search Results

In Chapter 8, I show you details on how search engines find your blog and index your content. Specifically, using keywords effectively helps your content to be indexed properly.

If your company has a wide range of products and services that equate to thousands of or more keywords, you might want to build multiple blogs on separate subdomains, or even domains, to help concentrate the keywords you're discussing.

Unless you have amazing search engine authority — meaning that you have a huge following, tens of thousands of links to your site, and millions of readers — you may have a difficult time targeting a wide variety of keywords. Targeting your content as narrowly as possible should educate the search engines on what your blog's content is quickly and effectively.

One example is if you do three types of promotion: traditional public relations, broadcast, and Web. Rather than speak about all of them on a single blog, maybe start three blogs: one for public relations, one for broadcast, and one for online marketing.

You can still promote each blog across one another in a sidebar or through your home page, but concentrating the majority of content on specific keywords will help you rank more effectively for the terms you're targeting. It will help you to ultimately target your calls-to-action and landing pages as well.

Finally, it will be much easier to track the success of each of your programs with analytics as well. To track multiple subdomains in a single Google Analytics account, follow these steps:

1. **Open your theme editor to the footer with your Google Analytics script.**

2. **Below the `var pagetracker` line and after the semicolon, add the following line of code, replacing *example.com* with your domain:**

   ```
   pageTracker._setDomainName(".example.com");
   ```

3. **Log in to Google Analytics, navigate to your blog's profile, and then click Edit in the Action column.**

4. **In the Filters Applied to Profile section, click Add Filter.**

5. **Select Apply New Filter for Profile.**

6. **Enter Subdomain as the Filter Name.**

7. **Select Custom Filter as the Filter Type.**

8. **Select the Advanced radio button.**

9. **For Field A -> Extract A, select Hostname from the Field drop-down list and then enter (.*) in the Value field.**

10. **For Field B -> Extract B, select Request URl from the Field drop-down list and then enter (.*) in the Value field.**

11. **For Output To -> Constructor, select Request URl from the Field drop-down list and then enter /$A1$B1 as the constructor.**

    Within that profile, you can now segment and organize the Analytics data. (See Figure 9-7.)

Using the correct balance of keywords and content

If you stuff keywords into every blog post, you're actually putting your blog at risk of being buried in the search engine results. This is called *keyword stuffing*. Aside from blatantly repeating keywords in your content, you can also be dropped from a search engine's results if you're adding keywords in hidden text, or stuffing keywords in `title` tags and `alt` attributes.

And keyword stuffing doesn't just put your blog at risk of being penalized by search engines. It's going to drive readers away, your blog will lose credibility, and you'll ultimately lose the opportunity to close business with your corporate blog.

Figure 9-7:
Advanced
filter setup
in Google
Analytics
for tracking
multiple
subdomains.

Too many corporate blogs that concentrate on search engine traffic win the battle (ranking in search engines) but ultimately lose the war (converting traffic into customers). Don't be tempted to stuff keywords.

Instead, write compelling, natural content that will attract readers and convert them. A common SEO practice for using keywords is to first write your post, and then see where keywords will naturally fit.

To write a keyword-rich blog post, follow these steps:

1. **Write three or four paragraphs of two to three sentences, each on a topic associated with your product or service.**

2. **Write a compelling post title.**

3. **Research keywords that people are searching for. See Chapter 8 for information and tools to help you find the right keywords.**

4. **Rewrite the post title with the keywords, trying to place them first.**

5. **Rewrite the first and second sentence of the opening paragraph and use a keyword naturally in the paragraph.**

6. **Review each subsequent paragraph and look for opportunities to insert a keyword.**

7. **Read your post title and blog post and ensure that it sounds natural, without too many keywords repeated.**

The primary goal of your blog is to drive business. That means that every blog post should be written with a purpose. If that purpose is to close a sale, make sure you have a call-to-action: for example, *Fill out our registration form, Contact me, Download our whitepaper, Register for our event,* and so on. If that purpose is to drive authority, ensure that the blog is noteworthy.

Optimizing your post should not affect the effectiveness of the content in making customers out of visitors! Review the content and carefully place keywords where they will make sense to a reader. A crawler will understand the keywords that are being targeted.

Finding synonymous keywords and phrases

As you insert keywords, keep in mind that you need not use the same expression over and over again. Search engines help you in this by associating keywords to blogs through synonymous terms.

As an example, if one of the keywords you're targeting is *cheap,* you don't need to blog about cheap per se, which can have a negative connotation. Words like *wholesale, inexpensive,* and *discount* are common synonyms with less negative connotations. These terms will also ensure your content is indexed properly and found.

If you're having trouble identifying synonymous keyword terms, try these tips:

✔ **Related search terms are provided by search engines.** In Google, scroll to the bottom or to the SERP to find related search terms. In Bing, the related searches are listed in the left sidebar. (See Figure 9-8.)

✔ **Review your analytics if you're already getting traffic on keywords.** Often, your analytics (in Google Analytics, navigate to Traffic Sources⇨ Keywords) will provide combinations and synonymous terms.

✔ **Using an application like SpyFu (www.spyfu.com) or SEMRush (www.semrush.com).** With these applications, you can do competitive analysis and find the common keywords between you and your competition. Or you can review your competition's keywords altogether.

Related searches

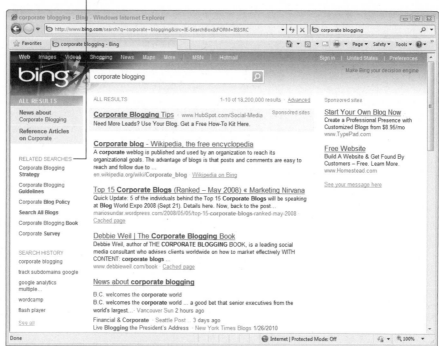

Figure 9-8:
Viewing
related
searches for
corporate
blogging in
Bing.

Keywords that drive traffic are important, but keywords that drive business
are more important. Take the example of Brozzini Pizzeria, a New York–style
pizzeria in Indianapolis. If Brozzini's blog ranks #1 for *New York style pizza,* it's
not going to do his business any good. However, if he ranks for *Indianapolis*
New York-style pizza, he will get a ton of relevant business. (See Figure 9-9.)

Driving Home the Message
with Images and Diagrams

You made it all the way to this chapter, and now you're going to get some
news that may be shocking — people who visit your blog don't read. Okay,
they *do* read a little bit . . . barely. There's a reason why they call Web surfing
applications *browsers.*

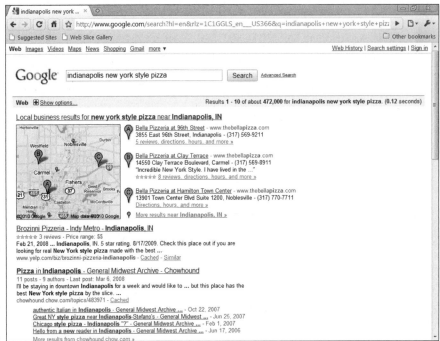

Figure 9-9:
Garner relevant search results for keywords.

As I mention earlier, the average visitor to your site will scan the content to see whether he can find what he wants. Most visitors will take in what they can and then immediately bounce. That's disconcerting, but you can do things to help them stay, including the following:

- **Use photos, images, diagrams, and other visuals that represent your message well.** Even when we read, our minds are a complex system that remembers images, not words. By supplying an image, you're making it easier for your content to be consumed and understood, thus encouraging the visitor to remain.

- **Use videos.** If pictures are worth a thousand words, videos are worth millions. Take advantage of inexpensive video equipment and video hosting services to produce videos as periodic blog posts.

- **Use effective whitespace.** Claude Debussy commented on music and the "space between the notes." Just as important as the words on your blog are the spaces between them. Ensure that the font you use is easily readable, spacing is used, bulleted and numbered lists are used often, keywords are bolded, and your posts are enhanced with images and video to help to improve cognition. Short, punchy paragraphs, subtitles, indenting, bold, and italic all help break up the monotony of the document and make it easier to scan. The upcoming section, "Considering the importance of whitespace," discusses using whitespace effectively.

The next few sections discuss these in greater detail.

Using alt tags effectively for image searches and keyword placement

Hypertext Markup Language (HTML) is the programming language of the Web. An HTML `alt` tag contains alternate text associated with a Web page graphic that displays when an Internet user hovers the mouse on the graphic. Every image or embedded object can have alternative text. `Alt` tags make the Web more accessible, specifically for the blind who use software applications (called screen readers) that read the text aloud. When an image is found in the content, the screen reader reads the alternative text — the `alt` tag.

`Alt` tags are used in several scenarios, such as the following:

✔ Alternative text comes in handy when you have a slow connection to the Web and don't want to wait for an image to download.

✔ Alternative text is often used by mobile devices and mobile browsers. For example, each time you open a Web page with a BlackBerry device, the images aren't downloaded but display with a border and the alternative text. You may then request to download the images.

✔ Alternative text is used by screen readers for visitors who have visual disabilities.

For these reasons, alternative text should be entered to describe the images or objects that you embed.

```
<img src="/image-directory/myimage.jpg" alt="alternative
          text describing image" title="title of the
          image" desc="There's even an element to put a
          very long description of an image or object" />
```

As with your content, this is a fantastic opportunity to insert keywords. Although alternative text is typical, title and description elements can accompany an image, too. Depending on how advanced your editing tools are in your blogging platform, you can enter one or all of these fields.

Don't ignore the opportunity to use a keyword within a title, alternative text, or description field that describes the image or object.

Search engines also have image search methodologies and people are often looking for photos of products, companies, logos, diagrams, and charts. By providing the images that searchers are looking for, you may find that your blog is growing in both search authority and readership because of the quality of your images.

Using representative images for improved comprehension

Your blog's visitors read words but remember images. Because of this, keep the following tips in mind:

✔ Use photos, images, diagrams, and other visuals that represent your message well. Even when we read, our minds are a complex system that remembers images, not words. By supplying an image, you make it easier to consume your content and be understood, which encourages a visitor to remain.

✔ If pictures are worth a thousand words, videos are worth millions. Take advantage of inexpensive video equipment and video hosting services to periodically produce videos as blog posts.

✔ Ensure your font is easily readable, spacing is used, bulleted and numbered lists are used, keywords are bolded, and your posts are enhanced with images and video. All these help to improve cognition.

Effectively sizing and formatting images for your page

When you find images to display in your blogs, you want to size and locate them properly in the post for maximum impact. Ensure that your images are saved in a high quality format. The PNG format is universal, allows for transparent sections, is compressed as much as possible, and maintains image quality. It's a great format for online viewing.

You may want to insert a small image, such as a logo, wherever it makes sense. If it's an image that displays data or a chart, resize the image to the maximum width of your blog's content column. If you're not sure how large that is, it's fairly easy to discover.

To determine your blog content area's width using Firefox, follow these steps:

1. **Navigate to Tools⇨Add-ons.**

2. **Select Get Add-ons.**

3. **Type** Measure **in the search field.**

4. **Locate the MeasureIt Add-on and select Add to Firefox.**

5. **Select Install Now.**

6. **Restart Firefox.**

7. **Navigate to your blog.**

8. **In the status bar on the lower left, click the ruler icon.**

9. **Drag the mouse across your content area. (See Figure 9-10.)**

10. **Record the width so you remember how to size your images.**

Your images should be resized appropriately to match your theme and to differentiate your blog posts that are read from the feed in an RSS reader. Resizing and aligning your images maintains the *aesthetics* — that is, the look and feel, of your blog.

If you align an image left or right, divide your content width into thirds or two halves. (See Figure 9-11.) This grid styling is not just all the rage on the Internet, it also keeps pages looking clean and neat. When all your images are proportional to your theme's layout, your blog will maintain a professional look and feel.

Figure 9-10:
Calculating
the appro-
priate width
for images
within your
blog post.

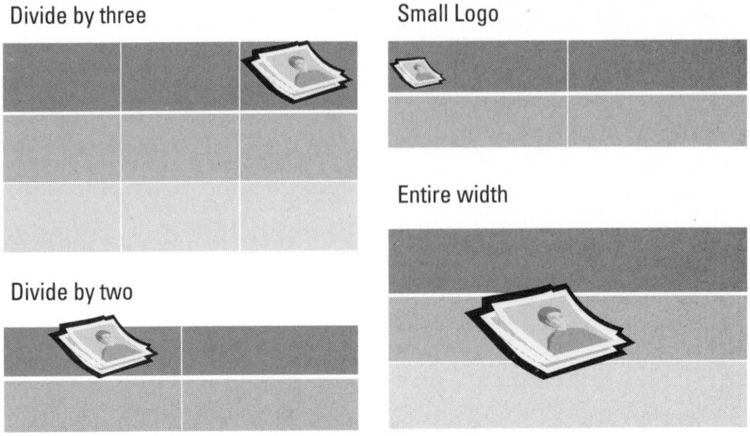

Divide by three

Small Logo

Entire width

Figure 9-11:
Effective
layouts with
images
within in
your blog
post.

Divide by two

Business buyers and consumers want to ensure they're buying from a reputable source, so keeping your theme and your blog post layouts looking professional does have a return on investment. It only takes a few minutes to properly prepare a post that can turn into revenue.

Here are some quick tips for properly formatting images:

✔ **Width and height:** Make sure that the ratio proportions are locked to ensure the image resizes proportionally. Note that images are resized to a lower resolution to speed load times.

To resize an image using Paint, follow these steps:

1. **Navigate to Start➪All Programs➪Accessories➪Paint.**

2. **Open the image you wish to resize. Click the document icon on the left of your tabs and select Open.**

3. **Click the Home tab.**

4. **Click the Image➪Resize icon.**

   The Resize and Skew window appears. (See Figure 9-12.)

5. **In the window, change the Resize By field to Pixels by selecting that option.**

6. **Be sure Maintain Aspect Ratio is checked.**

   This adjusts the height or width to make sure your image maintains its proportions and doesn't become skewed.

7. **Enter the width in the Horizontal field.**

Figure 9-12:
Resizing
your image
with Paint.

Depending on the quality of the image and the layout you developed, make the width the entire width, half the width, or one-third the width of your blog post).

8. Click OK.

9. Save the image after it's sized for your blog.

✔ **Padding:** Padding is the amount of space you wish to maintain around an object. If you insert an image and don't set any padding, the image may display directly next to your text, making it difficult to read. In your theme, you should be able to add padding to maintain space between your image and your text.

A typical method used is to add two classes to your theme's stylesheet, one for each alignment.

```
img.alignleft {
    text-align: left;
    padding-right: 8px;
    padding-bottom: 5px;
}
img.alignright {
    text-align: right;
    padding-left: 8px;
    padding-bottom: 5px;
}
```

Now, when you insert your image, you simply need to ensure the class, like this:

```
<img src="/directory/image.png" class="alignleft"
        alt="This is an image aligned left" />
```

✔ **Align:** Adjust the image in relation to the text to ensure that it's easier for blog readers to follow the content of the post and to catch their eyes.

✔ **Description:** This isn't really a formatting field. This is a field for search engines. Make sure to label the image with a description that's relevant to the image and the content in your post. If relevant, include a keyword-rich phrase.

Finding free quality images to use on your blog can be a challenge. Many choices for stock photography are available online, though. Here is a list of several sites that I have used. Check them out, try them out, and find out what works best for you.

✔ **Flickr:** www.flickr.com

✔ **morgueFile:** www.morguefile.com

✔ **Stock.XCHNG:** www.sxc.hu

✔ **Dreamstime:** www.dreamstime.com

✔ **FreeFoto.com:** www.freefoto.com

✔ **PicApp:** www.picapp.com

A good rule is to make sure you check the copyright restrictions and provide attribution. And because every organization handles image guidelines differently, make sure you contact your blog admin for specific guidelines.

Google Images search can also be used. From the Google home page, click the Images link in the top-left corner. Click the Advanced Image Search link that follows the Search button and then choose Labeled for Commercial Reuse from the Usage Rights drop-down menu.

Make sure you check the copyright restrictions and provide attribution. A typical fine for reusing an image can exceed $1,000! Even Google's licensing search isn't foolproof. Google doesn't take any responsibility if you choose an image you think you can use for commercial reuse and you actually cannot.

Additionally, if you find an image available for commercial reuse but that image is actually displayed in violation, too, your company is still liable.

Formatting Your Posts for Better Comprehension

When readers scan pages, they read from the top left to bottom right and focus mainly on the beginning of paragraphs. Therefore, when you write, you want to ensure that you have powerful content in the areas that visitors pay the most attention to.

Here are four things you can do to improve your formatting:

- **Keep your paragraphs short and leave space between them.** Make sure you leave space — *whitespace* — around your images.

- **Use numbered and ordered lists often.** Such lists stand out and are simple to digest.

- **Keep your posts pithy**. Try to keep to the point. Talk about a single point in each post and keep your explanations brief and concise. Your posts should be enough to explain your point but never longer. If you have multiple points, use multiple posts.

- **Emphasize important elements of the post.** Use bold, italic, and high-lights. Bolded text stands out for search engines as well.

Considering the importance of whitespace

Make sure you leave space around your images and paragraphs. This is called *whitespace* and is more important than people realize. Visitors who are scanning your site will tend to skip over large chunks of text that have no dif-ferentiation. If text runs into borders or images, it's more difficult for the eye to discern and comprehend the information.

Using bulleted and ordered lists

Lists are easy to digest and scan vertically on the page. Your visitors will skim over paragraphs, but an ordered list or bulleted list will be easier for them to digest. Try to use lists as much as possible. Be sure to leave whitespace around the list and between each list item.

Highlight a keyword or two within each of your list items. This will make it even easier to scan.

Sizing paragraphs for easy scanning

In high school English class you learn to open your paragraph with a sen-tence that introduces the topic, followed by three to five sentences of detail and a concluding sentence that sums it up. Forget what you learned in high school and jump directly to the concluding sentence.

Unless you're selling books with detailed prose that you want to provide examples of on your blog, you need to keep your paragraphs as short and pithy as you possibly can so that visitors get directly to the point.

Writing High Converting Content

Your objective when writing content is to build authority, gain trust, and ultimately, get business. Several techniques for writing content converts traffic into business.

Do your visitors understand the reward of engaging with your company? It's not enough to simply talk about your company, your products or services; you must relate the content directly to the readers' benefits. How are they rewarded for purchasing, for signing up, for downloading, and for engaging?

Reward-driven blog posts often use customer testimonials. Customer testimonials provide your blog post an additional level of trust and authority because you provide distinct examples of others who have been rewarded. Don't underestimate the power of a customer testimonial. Ask your customers for them often.

The most important technique, of course, is to ensure that every blog post is written with a blatantly obvious path for the reader to engage with you further. Don't rely on only calls-to-action or banner advertising on your theme — some people aren't actually reading your blog at your site! Closing each blog post with an invitation for the reader to engage with you, including how they can do so, is a great method for increasing conversion rates.

Actionable engagement terms for your blog posts include:

> "If you'd like to discuss this further . . ."
>
> "We've got a Webinar on this coming up, here's how to register."
>
> "Click here to add this product to your shopping cart."
>
> "If you'd like to donate now, here's an online form."
>
> "Check out our product page."
>
> "This is just an overview, be sure to check out our demo."

Each term, of course, should be written with an anchor tag that will allow the reader to click it and land where you'd like them to.

Additionally, don't try to pack too much information into a blog post. Blogs have categories, searches, tags, and related content suggestions to provide additional insight to your visitor. Keep each blog post limited to a single idea. One post, one topic — that should be your rule.

If you find yourself writing a long post that covers a collection of topics that are related, break them up. It's okay to post multipart blog posts that encourage the reader to come back and visit your "Five Part Series on . . ."

After you complete your blog post or review someone else's, ask yourself, "What was the question?" If the question is clear, you've got a good blog post. Now make sure that you answer the question! You may not want to give away proprietary or competitive information in your answer but tell your readers how to engage you to get it. Answer the question they are asking.

Part IV
Expanding Blog Posts and Promoting Content

In this part . . .

Writing content is part of a corporate blogging program — finding, promoting and engaging other influential bloggers and their audiences helps you accelerate the growth of your blog's authority, grow your readership, and build business results.

How to blog without writing is the focus of Chapter 10, equipping you with tools and tactics that allow you to maximize your blog content while minimizing your time writing.

Chapter 11 shows step-by-step instructions for promoting your blog and engaging the blogosphere. You find out about the benefits of syndicating your content with RSS, integrating your blog into social media to expand relationships, and promoting your blog via social bookmarking.

Chapter 10

How to Blog without Writing

In This Chapter

▶ Expanding your audience with guest bloggers

▶ Using customer testimonials to build your authority

▶ Adding life with customer comments

▶ Incorporating multimedia technologies

*B*logging is about setting expectations and delivering on them. To capture the audience attention, you must regularly publish relevant content. And to capture search engine attention, you must frequently publish.

After months of blogging, you'll begin to see sustained growth in the number of readers, the number of people referring to you, and the number of visitors from search engines. If you stop or even pause for a week or two, though, you'll find that your stats will drop — much faster than you gained them.

That's why blogging is a long-term strategy and one of momentum. The advantage of blogging is that after a month of blogging, you continue to grow your audience beyond that month. After a year of blogging, you'll have a substantial audience. Year two builds on the foundation of year one, year three on year two, and on and on.

As you continue to blog, your audience grows, your ability to be found grows, your authority grows, and your sales will grow as well. If you're tempted to take a break, don't! Instead, harness other content, bloggers, and resources to supplement your content so your blog will continue to grow.

Spotlighting Other Experts with a Guest Blogging Program

Guest blogging is a great tactic for sustaining momentum, getting great content, and growing your blog. First, though, you have to find good guest bloggers. With more than hundreds of millions of blogs out there, finding bloggers isn't difficult, but narrowing down the choices to just those bloggers who can make an impact can be difficult.

Many companies don't want to use guest bloggers because many of the bloggers in the industry might work for competition. However, if you do your research, you'll find a ton of bloggers with very high authority who have no allegiance to a specific company, product, or service. Also, finding a blogger who provides industry insight instead of simply promoting your blog is a fantastic means of proving your transparency and honesty to your audience.

Slingshot SEO (www.slingshotseo.com; see Figure 10-1) is a company well known for its ability to analyze search engine algorithms and to get its customers ranked in number one positions throughout the Internet. The Slingshot SEO statisticians and experts are uncanny in their ability to decipher changes in search algorithms in almost real-time. How do they do it? Many people would like to know. However, these experts don't blog.

Slingshot SEO is so good at what it does that much of its clientele comes from word of mouth and by other search engine optimization (SEO) experts finding out who was beating them. My blog, The Marketing Technology Blog, tries to keep up on search engine information, so getting the inside scoop from experts like Jeremy Dearringer or Kevin Bailey (co-founders of Slingshot SEO), is the Holy Grail.

Figure 10-1:
A guest post from an industry expert.

Jeremy admits that he doesn't like blogging, though. We invited him to blog at The Marketing Technology Blog, but he didn't have time and didn't want to. After we saw Jeremy give a presentation on the quality of inbound links and their impact on rankings, we sent him an e-mail asking him to address the issue. Jeremy quickly responded and wrote ten link temptations to avoid. The administrator of The Marketing Technology Blog replied, thanked him, and asked permission to use the e-mail as a blog post. Jeremy enthusiastically agreed, and the post was published.

The content of this post was fantastic, and it was well received by the readers of The Marketing Technology Blog. It didn't stop there, though. Jeremy was also very proud of the post and distributed it to experts around the search engine industry.

The readership of the blog increased by hundreds of new visitors in a single day, not simply because of the content but because of the exposure to additional audiences through the blog. Each of your guest bloggers will bring their own audiences to your blog. Some of those visitors will stay. And some of those visitors will turn into customers.

Finding industry bloggers to guest write on your blog

Here are a few places where you can find the leading bloggers in your industry:

- ✔ **Google Blog Search:** Google has a robust blog search that will return blogs with high authority for specific searches that you can follow and use to contact the blogger. You can select Blogs from the options at Google or visit Google Blog Search directly at `http://blogsearch.google.com`. (See Figure 10-2.)

  Although this search provides the most relevant blog *posts* for a specific topic, it might not always provide the most authoritative bloggers. It will provide you with other blogs that rank well on specific topics, though. It's also a great way to discover other blogs that speak to the topics relevant to your company. Google Blog Search also offers a feed so you can subscribe to keywords that you're interested in to get the latest blog posts being published out on the Internet.

Blogs

Figure 10-2:
Use Blog
Search to
return blogs
with high
authority.

✔ **PostRank:** PostRank (www.postrank.com) has skyrocketed in popularity and has become a popular resource for tracking your blog's influence, discovering other industry blogs, and connecting with other bloggers. (See Figure 10-3.) PostRank doesn't just track your blog's rank: It also uses a proprietary algorithm that monitors your blog's influence by category and keyword by tracking conversations that mention your blog.

✔ **BlogCatalog:** BlogCatalog (www.blogcatalog.com) is a kind of social network specifically aimed at finding and following blogs and bloggers. It's a community for discussing, sharing, and browsing blogs. (See Figure 10-4.) BlogCatalog doesn't have a ranking mechanism for capturing the most influential bloggers, but it will provide you with a network of active bloggers.

✔ **BlogRank:** BlogRank (www.invesp.com/blog-rank) is a great tool that identifies and ranks top blogs by a series of variables, including the number of feed subscribers, the rankings from Compete (a site that profiles domains and profiles visitors) and from Alexa (a site that ranks and tracks domains), Yahoo!'s now-defunct back-linking counts, and Google PageRank. The combination is provided a score and ranked accordingly. (See Figure 10-5.)

Figure 10-3:
Use
PostRank to
track your
blog's
influence.

Figure 10-4:
Use
BlogCatalog
to see
active
blogger
networks.

Figure 10-5:
Use
BlogRank
to view top
blog ranks.

✔ **Technorati:** Technorati (`http://technorati.com`), which has been around for quite a while, used to be the premiere resource for tracking blogs. Although it's no longer the best tracker, it's improved its quality, ranking, and site organization, and is still a great resource. Be sure to click the Blog button on the search bar to search for blogs rather than posts on a given topic. (See Figure 10-6.)

Hundreds of blog cataloguing and directory sites promise to get you more visitors and grow your traffic. Beware that the majority of these sites are actually developed to build their own traffic and authority rather than yours. If you find a site that requires you to post an external link or a linked image that points back to its site, let it go. You can fill your sidebar up with a ton of these links and never get a visitor — and the only thing you're doing is promoting that site.

As you're seeking these bloggers, you'll find that other bloggers and Web sites will also be targeting you. Don't be tempted into link-swapping unless the site linking to you has outstanding authority and recognition and you truly wish to put your reputation on the line by promoting it as well.

After you find a blog or blogger that you'd like to target, drop a nice note via that blog/blogger's contact form or look for an e-mail address for you to write them.

Figure 10-6:
Use
Technorati
to track
blogs.

And when you write the blogger, be honest! Let him know that you have a corporate blog for which you're trying to gain exposure and that you'd love for him to write a guest post on a specific topic. Bloggers will often take the opportunity to post on other blogs because it exposes them to new audiences. Don't ask the blogger to review your product or service, though, because the last thing most bloggers want to do is promote a product or service with which they have no affiliation. As you get to know one another, your prospective guest blogger might take interest in your company and what you're selling, but let him do that at his pace, not yours. Get pushy, and you're going to lose him.

Trading posts with other blogs and requesting permission to guest blog

Guest posting on industry blogs and trading posts with other relevant blogs is a great way of expanding your blog's reach. If you can write an effective post on another blog with authority and a large following in your industry, you will lead those readers back to your blog.

Having an authoritative blogger write a post on your blog provides valuable content for your readers (that you didn't have to write). As well, guest bloggers tend to promote their posts to their network. It's a win-win for both blogs.

Contact the blog and provide samples of your posts. Offer to provide a high-quality post on a relevant topic when you contact them. Entice them to write by offering the opportunity for them to write on your blog as well. Be sure to provide content that's neutral in nature — not sales or advertising information. The last thing another blog is going to do is allow you to spam their audience!

Soliciting industry experts to reach their audience

Unlike casual bloggers, industry experts are in a unique position to seek content about new companies, products, and services. They will often be very receptive to writing fresh content, but you have to find them. You can use some of the techniques discussed earlier to target bloggers, or you can work through public relations firms and e-mail list providers.

Over recent years, public relations firms like Vocus (www.vocus.com; see Figure 10-7) have accumulated substantial e-mail lists of bloggers. They often send out blanket, unsolicited e-mails to the lists with information on the companies they're trying to promote. This might sound like spam, but they do offer links for unsubscribing. Most of these e-mails offer free books or products, trials, interviewing the CEO, and other goodies, though. Good bloggers often take advantage of these!

Figure 10-7:
PR firms
often have
robust
e-mail lists.

Be sure to step very lightly when intruding on bloggers' inboxes, though. Don't buy a list and them dump e-mails: Validate that your offering is relevant to each blogger on the list and what they write about from day to day. No one likes spam, and bloggers are no different. If you practice this for long, you might find yourself on a list of PR firms who spam bloggers. You can easily find yourself in a position of defending your brand rather than promoting it online.

If one thing drives the blogosphere crazy, it's the scent of someone being insincere or lying altogether. Don't make the mistake of trying to manipulate your audience. After all, you're outnumbered by a few hundred million out there. Recovering your company or your brand can prove impossible if you're caught red-handed. Don't do it.

Promoting Your Customer's Voice for Maximum Impact

Visitors to a corporate blog recognize that the writer has an agenda. They want to dig deep and find the good and the bad with your company. They'll confront you on statistics, question your positioning, and keep you honest.

One of the most effective voices that you can put on your blog is your customer's voice. Customer testimonials are a fantastic means of adding credibility to your content and providing first-hand posts that have impact to your audience. Visitors who might not believe you are much more likely to believe a customer.

Writing effective customer testimonial blog posts

Customer testimonial posts can be written entirely by the customer, of course, but you can also add the customer's voice by promoting quotes from customer posts, interviews with customers, or even e-mails from customers. Don't be tempted to hand-pick the quotes or tweak the messaging in your favor, however. Visitors can smell a fake five-star rating a mile away.

Visitors want transparency and want to read the four-star rating. They want to understand what roadblocks or slips customers had and how you recovered from them. No one expects perfection anymore. This is key to why many corporate blogs succeed, and why others fail. "*Mea culpa*" blog posts attract a lot of attention — and a lot of customers!

For each customer testimonial blog post, you should do the following:

✔ **Obtain the customer's permission to post.** Be sure to show the customer the actual post you'll be publishing.

✔ **If possible, include an actual photo of the customer (the person, not the company).** Customers appreciate the spotlight, too!

✔ **Include a link to the customer's site or a way for visitors to get in touch with them.** This way, your visitors can assure themselves that it's an authentic testimonial.

✔ **Use quotes around actual customer statements.** In HTML, use the `blockquote` element, as in this example:

```
<blockquote>DK New Media was ahead of time, under budget, and delivered a
        superior product!</blockquote>
```

Block quotes can be highly customized by using Cascading Style Sheets (CSS). You can find some examples at `http://css-tricks.com/examples/Blockquotes` — see Figure 10-8. Colored backgrounds, indentations, specific fonts, and wrapping the block quotes in images will bring a lot of attention to the voice of your customers.

Figure 10-8:
View styled
block
quotes at
CSS Tricks.

Automating customer testimonials directly into blog posts

Customer testimonials need not be difficult to manage or create. Modern blogging systems typically have features that allow people to generate content and push that content directly to your company blog. Within Compendium Blogware, this is called Web to Post, a form that you can publish on an internal page on the blog where readers are free to submit their own blog posts and even add a few images. After the post is submitted, the administrator is notified and can immediately approve or decline the post for publishing on the blog.

Lydia's Uniforms is an e-commerce site for purchasing nursing scrubs online. To attract search engine traffic and provide a human touch to their site, Lydia's maintains a blog with nursing news and information that gets a lot of traffic — and sales. Lydia's supplements the blog content with customer stories, likening the posts to reality television for nurses.

Customers can write their story, enter their contact information, and even upload an image of themselves in beautiful scrubs that they probably purchased from the site. (See Figure 10-9.)

Figure 10-9: Customers can post testimonials.

To add a WordPress form to post to a blog, follow these steps:

1. Purchase Gravity Forms plug-in from `www.gravityforms.com`, licenses are very affordable at $39 for a single site, or $99 for multiple sites.

2. Upload the plug-in to your `wp-plugins` directory.

3. Login to WordPress and navigate to Admin⇨Plugins⇨Installed.

4. Click the Inactive link.

5. Click Activate on the Gravity Forms plug-in.

6. When prompted to add a key you received when purchasing the plug-in, enter the key. Choose Admin⇨Forms⇨Settings in the Support License Key field.

7. Choose Forms⇨New Form.

8. In the Add Fields sidebar, select Post Fields and then click Title, Body, Image, and Category.

9. Select Advanced Fields, and then click Name and E-mail.

10. Complete setting up the form and any notifications you wish to receive.

11. Navigate to Pages⇨Add New.

    Within your text editor, you see a Form icon.

12. Click the icon and select the form you'd like to embed.

13. Publish the new page to your site. (See Figure 10-10.)

Compendium's Web To Post and Gravity Forms post mechanism operate internal to your blog. Blogging platforms also have methods to post content that is published external to the blog. The majority of blogging platforms have an application programming interface (API) that allows you to publish content from third-party resources. WordPress has an extensible markup language remote procedure call mechanism (XML-RPC) that allows you to use third-party blogging software like Windows Live Writer or publish from other publication sites. Using the API, you can automatically publish links that you bookmark in Del.icio.us, photos you upload to Flickr, or questions and answers you've responded to in ChaCha.me.

Promoting vendors and partners to build your authority

Just as customers appreciate the spotlight and provide your blog with authenticity, so do blog posts written by vendors and partners. Your company doesn't work alone, and you're probably dependent upon a few vendors or specific suppliers to ensure you deliver on your promises.

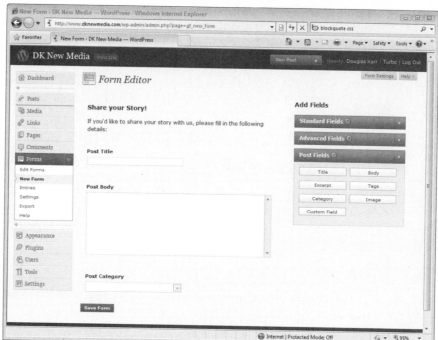

Figure 10-10:
Installing a Gravity Forms post form.

Request guest blog posts from time to time from your vendors. They'll look out for you because they depend on your company's success as well! Make sure that the blog posts aren't too pushy on sales or too stiff with marketing jargon. If you have a tough time getting good content, simply interview the client in person or via e-mail — although you should always ask permission before posting this material.

Be sure to provide a link to their company. In this case, an image in the post with a photo of the representative is okay. If it's a well-known brand, you might want to include an image of the brand as well.

Keeping Your Content Alive with Comments

People often forget about the posts they've published and continue to look forward to new content to get the business they need. Although fresh content is necessary, don't forget that you've invested in past blog posts — and there are ways of reviving it.

Adding a simple comment to a page, for instance, updates the page's content. That update often triggers the search engines to come back and revisit and re-index the page anew. Respond to comments on your blog within new comments and keep the ball rolling.

There doesn't appear to be evidence that merely having a lot of comments draws additional search engine attention, but blog posts with a lot of comments tend to weigh high in search engine rankings, so it clearly can't hurt.

Using comments as a measure of engagement

In the early days of blogging, bloggers didn't have strong tools to measure success. Because they weren't actually selling anything and they were simply publishing content, they often measured comments as an indicator of visitor engagement.

This is not the same with business blogs. Although comments might be triggered by controversial blog posts, they aren't relevant to sales. One of 100 or 1 of 1,000 visitors will comment on a blog post, and they're typically not the type of visitor who is going to buy from you.

Visitors comment on blog posts to complain, add their message to the conversation, or get attention. Many times, you'll find that comments to your blog are generated by industry professionals. These folks aren't going to purchase from you, but they could have an impact on sales in the long run.

In other words, don't use comments as an indicator of your blog's engagement or success. As a corporate blog, your blog should ultimately be measured in acquisition and retention numbers, which probably don't have any correlation with comments.

Moderating comments to add value and avoid spam

Comments should always be moderated. Unmoderated comments produce horrendous amounts of spam on your blog and reduce its impact. Comments should enhance and add value to the conversation you've started.

Here are a few ways to protect yourself from comment spam:

✔ **Incorporate a comment spam-blocking technology, such as Akismet or TypePad AntiSpam.** These companies maintain databases of addresses, commentors, and comments that have been reported as spam and they are automatically blocked from being published on your blog.

- *Akismet:* `http://akismet.com`
- *TypePad AntiSpam:* `http://antispam.typepad.com`

✔ **Incorporate a challenge question or CAPTCHA-type form.** *CAPTCHA forms* are those distorted words or phrases you see all over the Web. Where these are present, you must type in the distorted phrase verbatim to prove that you're a human and not an automated service. This stops automated scripting systems from posting comments to your blog.

✔ **Moderate all comments and check your spam folders daily.** Sometimes Akismet or TypePad erroneously pushes a genuine comment to spam.

✔ **Incorporate e-mail verification.** Only some blogs offer this service, but because spammers often use bad e-mail addresses, this is a great way to block bad comments.

Some blogs have taken it a step further, requiring commentors to register with the blog. Taking steps this drastic could reduce your comments to nothing and make your site look like it's simply an empty blog built to spam search engines. Remember that comments aren't just good for enhancing the conversation: They're often good for search.

The easiest means of staying on top of incoming comments is to turn on comment notification so your administrator is immediately aware of comments and can approve and respond to them. In WordPress, this can be enabled in Settings⇨Discussion. Enable the Before a Comment Appears an Administrator Must Always Approve the Comment option. Commenting system JS-Kit Echo also enables you to approve commentors indefinitely.

Negative comments are often deleted by companies, but this isn't always wise. After all, negative comments can become opportunities to respond and defend your brand. Of course, negative comments that are simply false shouldn't be published, but be sure to always warn the person who wrote it first. By e-mailing the commentor directly and letting his know that his comment isn't suitable for publishing, you'll be able to defend the action later if he decides to go public with it.

Deciding whether a third-party comment service is right for your blog

Third-party comment services like Echo, Disqus, and IntenseDebate have taken comment systems to another level. (See Figure 10-11.) Although they maintain your comment database and keep it up-to-date, these synchronized systems also help to promote your blog by collecting comments from social media sites and publishing to social media sites.

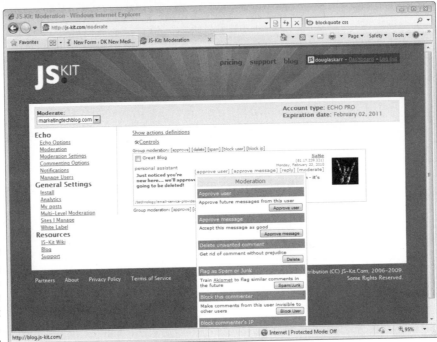

Figure 10-11:
Use third-
party
comment
moderation.

Third-party commenting systems operate from a site outside of your blog and then simply display the comments within your blog. If the third-party commenting system does not save the comments to your blog's database, then you could lose all comments if you decide to leave the commenting service or if they go out of business. Comments are valuable user generated content (UGC). When selecting a third-party comment service, be sure that the service synchronizes comments between your blog and theirs. If they don't synchronize and they go out of business, you're going to lose a lot of content.

Encouraging employees to comment

Writing the first comment is often the most difficult, so encourage your employees to subscribe to your blogs and add to the conversation. Reward employees who take the time to respond to comments. Comments can provide additional detail that thwarts customer service calls as well.

Keep an eye on employee comments, and you also might just find your next blogger in your organization. People tend to move up the ladder in social media, and critics often turn into creators. Take advantage and solicit great comments from employees with invitations to write more.

Incorporating a Multimedia Strategy to Add Personality

If a picture is worth a thousand words, a video must be worth millions. The majority of blogs are written, but the irony is that users of the Web don't actually read much. Visitors to your blog will skim more than they read: headlines, subheadings, and bolded print to obtain the information they want. A combination of whitespace and text will improve reader cognition, but there's more to a blog than text.

The world of the Web is pretty text-rich. Visitors don't remember words, though, and very few people have photographic memories where they remember what they read. Most people easily process and remember images, though. Associating your content with strong imagery will help visitors understand and retain the message that you've written.

The three types of learning are

- ✔ **Visual:** Remembering what you see
- ✔ **Audible:** Remembering what you hear
- ✔ **Kinesthetic:** Remembering what you interact with

As you develop the content strategy for your blog, it's imperative that you incorporate all three strategies into it. Many bloggers believe that writing alone covers the majority of the population. That presumption might well be true, but on a corporate blog, it might not reach the decision-maker.

Leveraging audio technologies for audible learners

Blogging platforms publish text and images. Video blogs publish video. Podcasts publish audio. With the popularity of the iPhone, iPod, and other music players on the market, subscribing to podcasts has become quite popular. Podcasting is a very specific approach to attracting audible learners. In the early days, podcasting required quite a bit of technology and the ability for the podcaster to mix and convert their own sound files as well as incorporate players on their blog to publish the audio.

Now, podcasting can be done simply and effortlessly. Paul Dunay converts phone interviews into podcasts for his blog, Buzz Marketing for Technology, which is aimed at business-to-business technology marketers. Paul uses a system called Veotag (www.veotag.com) with which he can easily record and then segment the podcast into chapters, making it easy to listen to. (See Figure 10-12.)

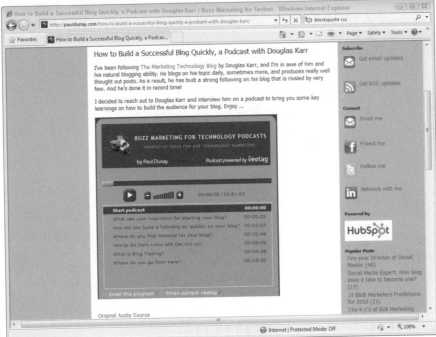

Figure 10-12:
Use pod-
casting for
audible
learners.

A product like Veotag really simplifies the process, but it's not absolutely necessary. Barbara Jones from the Stellar Thoughts blog (`http://stellartrng.com/blog/`) does interviews with Customer Relationship Management professionals using Skype and then mixes the audio by using Audacity, a free software for recording and editing,

Additional podcasting services are available, such as Podbean.com (`www.podbean.com`) and PubClip (`www.pubclip.com`), that provide simple tools for recording and publishing your podcasts by phone, online, conference calls, or even using iPhone applications. These services are highly recommended for those of you without the time or resources to learn how to mix and publish audio files.

If you're more inclined to do this yourself, using an affordable compact microphone from Blue Microphones and a copy of GarageBand (`www.apple.com/ilife/garageband`) will have you up and running in a matter of minutes.

If you decide to podcast, registering your podcast with iTunes is a must. You can find the official information about registering at

```
www.apple.com/itunes/podcasts/specs.html
```

But in general, to submit your podcast to the iTunes Store, follow these steps:

1. **Launch iTunes.**

2. **Choose iTunes Store➪Podcasts.**

3. **In the Learn More box, click Submit a Podcast. (See Figure 10-13.)**

4. **Enter your Podcast Feed URL and then click Continue.**

5. **Sign in to iTunes.**

6. **Review your Podcast.**

   You should see your artwork and information. If it's not correct, return to your podcasting application and make changes.

   A verification message is sent to your e-mail address.

   Podcasts aren't immediately published. Keep an eye on your inbox, and you'll get notified when your podcast is published.

Figure 10-13: Register your podcast with Apple iTunes.

Incorporating video for increased engagement

With the price of bandwidth and video equipment dropping, more and more blogs are turning to video to develop compelling, authentic, and sincere messages for their audiences. Video is an extremely powerful tool because it's simple to consume and provides both audio and visuals to help us retain the information.

Unpolished, noncommercialized videos provide us with a human touch that print and the Web cannot provide. Every corporate blog should have at least one video that introduces you, your staff, and your marketing message to the public.

If you don't have time to great a Flip MinoHD (www.theflip.com) to record high-definition video and mix it using iMovie (www.apple.com/ilife/imovie) or Windows Live Movie Maker (http://windowslive.com/desktop/moviemaker), opt for a video company or agency to assist you. Cantaloupe (http://cantaloupe.tv) is an agency and video hosting provider with a subscription model for companies to create video stories for their company or brand. (See Figure 10-14.) Cantaloupe even provides hosting technology that allows you to place a link in a banner over the video for your viewer to click.

The value of these videos is astonishing. Clients have been able to double and triple conversion rates simply by embedding a short video about the company, product, or service.

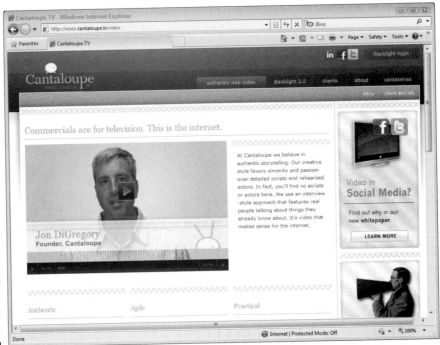

Figure 10-14:
Incorporate
video.

Rocky Walls is a videographer from TwelveStars Media (www.12stars media.blogspot.com) specializing in social media and Internet video. Rocky supplies the following advice for amateur videographers:

- ✔ **Use keywords and tags when posting your video to YouTube or other video sites.** These sites are highly indexed by search engines and videos are still rather scarce, so you have a great chance of being found.

- ✔ **Use a compelling description of your video.** Don't simply embed a video as a blog post; be sure to set expectations on what the viewer will learn after watching your video.

- ✔ **Share the video.** Everyone loves a video, so be sure to share it in e-mail, by posting the link in Facebook, and in other social media engines.

- ✔ **Make the video worth watching.** Provide something for the viewer to walk away with that they didn't have before — even if it's simply a good chuckle.

- ✔ **Make your video unique.** Don't follow a formula. This is your opportunity to apply your personality and your company's culture to your video.

Hosting options for audio and video

Like with blogging platforms, not all audio and video hosting platforms are created the same. Bandwidth for audio and video must be outstanding, or your listeners or viewers will give up and leave. Although YouTube may have the most videos and viewers online, the exposure still might not lead to conversions.

Hosting your videos on your own server might not be a good idea because the cost of bandwidth is so high. It's affordable and much more reliable to publish your media files on third-party hosting sites. Video hosting platforms have the necessary bandwidth and the distribution network, and they are optimized for viewing large, streaming videos. These platforms also permit video search — which continues to grow in popularity. Videos often have a lot less competition as well, making it easier for you to be found through video searches.

If you're a large corporation, consider using a digital asset management company, such as Widen (www.widen.com), to host only your media. (Widen also offers robust analytics, conversion capabilities, and distribution channels; see Figure 10-15.)

Mid-range solutions include Streamotor (http://www.streamotor.com) and Backlight (www.cantaloupe.tv/backlight), which are service that provide high definition and embedded advertisements directly in your video. (See Figure 10-16.)

Figure 10-15:
Consider a hosting option for your media.

Figure 10-16:
Backlight's corporate Internet video solution.

Low-cost solutions are available as well, such as Viddler's business offering at `http://b2b.viddler.com`. (See Figure 10-17.)

Beware of free video and audio hosting. Although many of these services are great for personal use, their terms of service, disclaimers, and service level agreements might prove unsuitable for your company. As an example, many video hosting sites have terms that require that you agree to their using your content or even owning it. Proceed with caution!

Another great medium for publishing content to your blog is SlideShare. SlideShare converts PowerPoint presentations into an interactive format that can be embedded easily in a blog post. (See Figure 10-18.) SlideShare also offers a lead acquisition form that you can add into any presentation.

Figure 10-17: Viddler business video offering.

To promote your presentations on your blog with SlideShare, follow these steps:

1. **Sign up for a SlideShare account at SlideShare.net.**
2. **Login and click the Upload button.**
3. **Click Browse and select Files.**
4. **Select the PowerPoint presentation you wish to upload.**

5. **Add a title, description, and tags.**

6. **Once uploaded, copy the embed code and paste it into a new blog post.**

7. **Publish the post.**

For best results on SlideShare, remove any animation from your presentation and add text to each slide that summarizes it. You can even add a lead generation form within your presentation using SlideShare's business solution at `http://slideshare.net/business`.

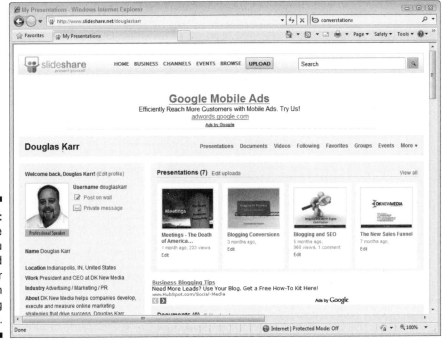

Figure 10-18:
SlideShare allows you to embed a player directly in your blog posts.

Chapter 11

Marketing and Promoting Your Blog

· ·

In This Chapter
▶ Syndicating content with RSS
▶ Interacting with the blogosphere
▶ Integrating with social media
▶ Social bookmarking
▶ Repurposing blog content in newsletters

· ·

*1*f a tree falls in the forest and there's nobody there to hear it, does it make a sound? If you write a blog post and there's no one there to read it, is it helping your company? No, unfortunately not.

Simply put, if you want to accelerate the growth of your blog beyond search and word of mouth, you must promote the blog, its content, and its value beyond your blogging platform.

Blogging platforms were developed with promotion in mind, though! For example, blogging platforms have feeds that are readable by other applications and tools using Really Simple Syndication (RSS). Syndication makes it possible to publish your blog post, but also integrate and extend the content through dozens of other distribution channels.

This is important. The prospects who might be interested in your content may never make an effort to visit your blog. However, they may be participating in Twitter, Facebook, LinkedIn, or other social networks. By syndicating your content into those networks, it allows you to bring your relevant message to them — where they want to see it!

This chapter discusses RSS syndication and a few other means of getting your blog noticed.

Using RSS to Syndicate Content

Really Simple Syndication (RSS) is a standard format for publishing content within an eXtensible Markup Language (XML) feed. XML is a data format that is easily accessed by programming languages. Whereas HyperText Markup Language (HTML) is designed for browsers to display your content properly, eXtensible Markup Language is designed to transfer data between programs and Web sites. Feeds have standards (Atom, RSS, RSS 2.0) that dictate how the content within the feed is written. This allows applications and developers to read your feed and present it, using any language on any platform.

Blogging platforms publish your content both in pages and in feeds. This allows third-party applications to access your feed, including feed readers like Google Reader (www.google.com/reader) or by other applications. Feed readers allow visitors to your site to subscribe by adding your feed to their reader. The reader then collects and keeps track of the sites they read without ever needing to visit the site!

Your feed makes your blog's content readily available to other sites, applications, feed readers, and anywhere else where the content can come in handy. Your blog's content can be published indirectly to Twitter, Facebook, your own Web site, and other applications throughout the Web.

If your company has a development team or you have the budget, the possibilities are endless for syndicating your blog content. A number of iPhone applications allow you to build a custom application from your feed. Additionally, you can integrate with virtually any platform on the market that has an API and a means for developing.

Syndicating content to your corporate home page

Search engines love fresh content, and they often return to pages that change frequently. However, many corporate home pages are static and seldom refreshed with new content. You can help your home page get indexed more often — and for a greater volume of keywords — by syndicating your content from your blog to your home page.

Flexware Innovation, a software development firm, specializes in writing applications for manufacturing firms in life sciences, automotive, and other industries. There isn't a huge demand for this niche service, so Flexware Innovation targets keywords specific to its industry to get inbound leads for its company.

Their home page (www.flexwareinnovation.com) is minimalistic (see Figure 11-1) and branded to provide visitors with a feeling that Flexware is a company on the cusp of developing these solutions, so real estate for content is scarce. By syndicating the blog content to the right sidebar, though, Flexware's content on its home page changes on a regular basis and targets terms with minimal effort. They simply write a blog post and it appears. The programming to do this uses code called "aggregators," which is described later in this chapter.

Keeping static pages fresh with syndicated excerpts

Web site pages that aren't updated often can feel more engaging and relevant to readers when they pull in syndicated content from other locations. A great example is Visit Tampa Bay.

With several events occurring at venues every day in Tampa Bay, there's no way for the visitors bureau to easily update their Web site daily to keep up. Therefore, Visit Tampa Bay uses two approaches: an events calendar and a sidebar with the latest blog posts and short descriptions. (See Figure 11-2.)

The blog posts in the left sidebar provide readers with additional content that offers the human touch, but it's also syndicated to the page to provide search engines with the food they need to keep coming back.

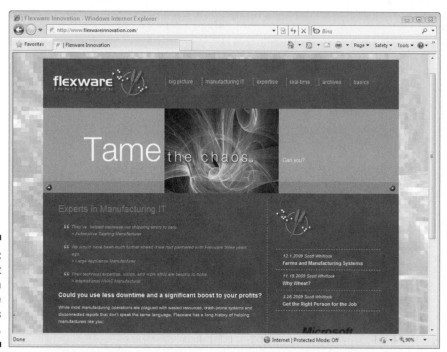

Figure 11-1:
Blog post titles on Flexware Innovation's home page.

Figure 11-2:
Visit
Tampa
Bay's
syndicated
blog on the
home page.

The feed provides such information as the blog post title, the date the blog post was published, and the content. Some feeds provide additional details, such as the author, too. When the developers integrate the feed into the home page, they can strip out images or HTML, shorten the content to a specific length, or simply post only the title. There's a lot of flexibility.

If you have great developers, it's even more compelling to strip out an image from the post and display it with a link to the post. Remember, images are worth a thousand words!

Aggregating RSS into server-side pages

Syndication is the process of making your content accessible. *Aggregation* is the opposite, it's the process of requesting that content and displaying it. *Server side* means the content is combined and presented directly from your Web server. When your browser requests the page — or a search crawler requests the page — the content is presented.

However, sometimes a Web page has content that is presented *client side*. That is, content or code (typically JavaScript or Flash) is loaded by your browser locally. Twitter widgets (http://twitter.com/goodies/widgets), for example, can be embedded in your Web page. When a user opens your page, the browser actually goes out and gets the latest Tweets, not the Web server where the page is hosted. YouTube videos are actually Flash files and they also only load when visitors open the Web page on which their code resides. (See Figure 11-3.)

Many applications offer *widgets,* which are code snippets that go out, capture, and present the code. These script tags are actually executed locally at your desktop on your browser, not at the server. Typically, these are denoted by script tags like this one:

```
<script src="http://widgets.twimg.com/j/2/widget.js"> </
            script>
```

To be easily found by search engines, content should be syndicated server side. That is, the content is presented directly to search engine crawlers. Search engine crawlers are advancing and beginning to read into Adobe Flash files and even JavaScript, but it's still not foolproof. If you wish to syndicate content and have it seen by search engines, rendering it server side is a must.

Feeds are so common that free code snippets that consume and display feeds are available for virtually every language and platform.

Figure 11-3:
An example of a client-side widget from Twitter.

Getting Engaged in the Blogosphere to Attract Attention

When you walk into a busy room, no one is aware that you are present until you have either announced yourself or begin to introduce yourself around the room. The blogosphere isn't much different, although it is a much bigger room! Announcing or introducing yourself is a key strategy within the blogosphere. Bloggers share and reciprocate, and they appreciate debate and alternative viewpoints (at least most do). Using PostRank, BlogCatalog, or Technorati, you can find other blogs of similar interest and begin commenting on those blogs.

It's easy to get engaged. Commenting on peers' blogs, promoting your blog, adding your blog in every social media profile, and joining social networks that are relevant to your business can help you to not only introduce your blog but also expand its audience.

Social media and social networks help, too. Follow your industry peers on Twitter or Facebook and try to connect on LinkedIn. If you can't connect directly on LinkedIn, join a LinkedIn Group that they belong to. Because you are unable to connect directly in LinkedIn without the other person's expressed permission, the next best tactic is to join relevant groups that they belong to. Participate in those groups and promote relevant blog posts to engage the group and lead them back to your blog.

To identify a member's groups on LinkedIn, follow these steps:

1. **If you haven't already, join LinkedIn and completely fill in your profile. Be sure to include a profile photo — people don't like to connect with blank avatars.**

2. **In the Search bar, ensure People is selected and type the name of the person you want to connect with.**

3. **If you scroll down the person's profile, you'll find groups that they've joined. In the right sidebar, you'll also find their activity. Many bloggers will join a group but may be inactive. Try to join groups where the bloggers are active.**

4. **Participate in the group by starting discussions, asking questions, or providing feedback. The group will soon notice your expertise as a peer and follow you home to your blog.**

Using a feed reader to organize and follow industry blogs

Feed readers are an effective way to subscribe to a blog without having to visit it every day. After you identify bloggers to learn from and connect with, add their feeds to your feed reader. If you don't have a feed reader, a few free ones are simple to use.

If you want a desktop application, Newsgator.com has a Mac and a PC version. Simply install the application and subscribe to the blogs feed. If you want a Web application, Google has the most well-known feed reader — Google Reader, which you can find at `www.google.com/reader`. (See Figure 11-4.)

After you add subscriptions in Google Reader, the reader organizes all the content in reverse chronological order (the latest posts are first). To navigate, simply click the "Next item" button or press "j" on your keyboard (it's a shortcut, "k" goes back one item) to proceed to the next post. Readers are an effective means of scanning or reading content from many sites in a single interface.

Figure 11-4:
Reading feed subscriptions in Google Reader.

Interacting with other blogs through guest posting and comments

Don't be shy about requesting the opportunity to do a guest post on another blog. Bloggers are always scouring for new content and many appreciate the opportunity to allow a different voice to their blog. Keep an eye on the blogs that you're reading; after you have a collection of great posts to point to, send a note to the blogger through her contact form and ask permission to post. Remember, the post isn't an opportunity to throw a sales pitch out to her audience; it's an opportunity to build credibility and cross-traffic.

A great way to sell without selling is to share a success story about a client or customer. Providing a story that is relevant to another blog's readers while promoting the success or happiness of your clients or customers is a great way to promote your brand or company without actually selling.

It's not often that a blogger reaches out to request a guest post, so be brazen and target a few bloggers. Share some posts with them that you've done so they can see the quality of your work and whether it's a fit for them.

Commenting regularly on a colleague's blog with solid content that adds to the conversation will get their attention. You may even wish to write a blog post that answers, debates, or adds to a blog post that they've written. If you meet their standards, you'll have an influential follower.

Reciprocation is a key strategy when blogging. Bloggers feel compelled to return attention. Of course, some of the selfish ones never reciprocate (don't be one!), but the majority do go out of their way to mention you. The currency of blogging is mentioning another blogger with a keyword-ridden anchor tag:

```
Today I was reading Jeff Lefevere's (he has the <a
        href="http://goodgrape.com" title="Good
        Grape">best wine blog</a>) and it reminded
        me...
```

Using `best wine blog` within the anchor tag provides Jeff some authority for that keyword term. Chances are that he'll rank a little bit higher or really lock in his rank because of the mention. Highly competitive keywords may take a few hundred more of these — but bloggers appreciate every one they receive. A great methodology is to target blogs that have a good rank, add them to your feed reader, and then read them each morning. Set a goal for yourself or your staff to comment on a few each morning. You'll be amazed at the traffic you begin to attract to your blog. After you get a mention or two — you're in!

When you comment, be sure to add to the conversation — don't simply self-promote. If you self-promote and include links to your blog, you could find yourself on a list of spammers and all your content could be blocked across many blogs. Many blogs use the same anti-spam applications, such as Akismet and SixApart AntiSpam.

Respectful dissent to attract and build readership

Nothing draws more attention than controversy. Respectfully opposing a blogger's position on an opinion article can provide you the spotlight faster than you might think. Be polite and always complimentary to the blogger's opinion, though. Just as you have an opinion based on your experience, so does the blogger with whom you disagree. This is also known as *contrarian blogging*. (Check out www.blogbloke.com/art-of-contrarian-blogging for more.)

If other readers agree with your position, or at least see your point of view, you may just win over some readers and find your blog getting some new traffic. Every opportunity to provide an alternative viewpoint with an industry blogger helps create interaction and truly demonstrates your understanding and experience in the industry.

Responding effectively to negative criticism

Marketing has changed significantly over the years, but marketing departments have not. Marketing used to simply manage the look and feel of your corporate brand, as well as execute advertising campaigns to drive sales. The new marketing department is now engaged with clients in social media, and the conversation is often one-to-one instead of one-to-many.

Your marketing team is not as formally trained in objection management as your sales professionals might be. Marketers deal directly with objections and criticisms all within the public eye. It's not a bad idea to get your marketing team to attend some sales training on how to deal with this.

Negative criticism is an incredible opportunity for your company. As more and more companies are criticized, rated, and reviewed online, consumers and prospects finally recognize that companies are not perfect. Consumers no longer demand perfection — they actually want to see what happens when your company is faced with its own imperfections, too.

Some effective means of resolving negative criticism online can actually grow sales:

✓ **Moderate user-generated content such as comments.** If the comment will damage your company or brand, don't allow it to go public; contact the person who reported the issue immediately. Do everything possible to resolve the issue offline and explain the repercussions to your company if the issue is made public.

✓ **Respond immediately and respectfully.** Always take the lead in being an advocate who cares about your customers. Even a response that you're investigating the issue provides evidence that your company cares and reacts. Resolving the problem publicly may draw a lot of attention to your company, your product, or your service. Everyone wants to work with companies who care, respond, and respect one another.

Think outside the box when you respond. Don't respond politically or by showing animosity to the person. Take the high road and you'll ultimately be recognized for it.

✓ **If the criticism is factually accurate and not an opinion, admit it immediately and respond with an offering that can help resolve the issue.** For example, if it's a complaint about a bug in your software, resolve the issue by responding that the problem has been identified, when it will be resolved, and how you'll communicate that to the customer.

You may even wish to invite them to call or e-mail you about the specifics. Once resolved, you may want to send them a gift or a hand-written thank-you note for helping you identify and correct problems within your company.

✓ **If the criticism is inaccurate or an opinion, acknowledge the person's frustration and request additional information.** Take conversations like this off-line. Keep any arguments or debates absolutely factual. If you've been misrepresented in any way, be sure to inform your audience. Many times, your customers are simply frustrated and seeking attention. If you provide them positive attention, not only will they stop flaming you online, they may actually promote you.

Integrating Your Blog into Other Social Media to Expand Your Readership

Although you may wish that all your traffic landed directly at your home page, the truth is that most does not. Aside from search engines, social media is where many people interact online nowadays. Although you might hate Twitter and think it's somewhat of a joke, you can be assured Twitter is much loved by many of your prospects, and you ignore it at your peril.

Your prospects may be frequently interacting on Twitter, Facebook, LinkedIn, YouTube, or any number of other social media channels. You want to interact with prospects where they are rather than waiting for them to come to you. If your prospects are frequently on Facebook or Twitter, they may never find you, so you need to be there for them. Lucky for you, blogging platforms offer feeds and your content can be syndicated throughout any number of platforms easily.

Thanks to Twitter's huge popularity and wide adoption, all the other platforms have followed suit and adopted the standard status update, a means of communicating a short message that is accepted through mobile text messaging, LinkedIn, Facebook, Twitter, FriendFeed, Ning, Plaxo, and virtually every new social media platform.

Using URL shorteners

A status update on Twitter is one-hundred and forty characters. Selected by the founders of Twitter, "The 140 character limit originated so tweets could be sent as mobile text messages which have a limit of 160 characters. Minus 20 characters for author attribution, that gives users just enough room." It just so happens that 140 characters is also convenient to display the title of a blog post and add a shortened Web address that readers can click to read the entire article. Twitter is perfect for "tweeting" your blog posts, and tools like URL shorteners and Twitterfeed make it even easier!

A uniform resource locator (URL) shortener is a service that converts a long Web address into a short redirected URL. Popular shorteners are TinyURL, DwarfURL, is.gd, tr.im, and bit.ly. bit.ly has become dominant because you can track how many readers click the shortened address that you distribute.

Shorteners aren't just for status updates; they're also very useful for sending Web addresses via e-mail messages. Long Web addresses often get chopped up and don't work well when sent through e-mail because different e-mail clients render messages differently. If you want to send a blog post to a friend by e-mail, shorten the address using a shortener.

To shorten a Web address with bit.ly, follow these steps (see Figure 11-5):

1. **Sign up and log in to bit.ly. By signing up, you can track your links to see how often they are clicked.**

   ```
   http://bit.ly
   ```

2. **Enter the Web address of the article you wish to distribute.**

3. **Click Shorten.**

4. **Click copy to capture your bit.ly link and paste the new link in an e-mail or your status message.**

5. **(Optional) You can also customize the link and use your own wording in the shared link, so**

```
http://bit.ly/b1Cgpt
```

can be customized by entering a custom name in the Custom Name field, such as:

```
http://bit.ly/corporateblogging
```

Most applications for automating your posts to social media status updates include automated shortening. Some blogging platforms, like WordPress, have even built URL shortening buttons directly into the latest versions of their software.

URL Shorteners work using redirects, which Google has confirmed does not pass 100 percent of search engine authority. Don't get so excited over URL shorteners that you use them every time you publish a link on the Web. They're great for tools like Twitter, Facebook, and other status updates that have character limitations, or e-mail where long URLs often get cut off — but not elsewhere.

Syndicating your blog in Twitter

You can syndicate your blog a number of ways so that new post titles and links are automatically posted to your corporate Twitter account. Perhaps the best known and original service is Twitterfeed. (See Figure 11-6.) Twitterfeed checks your feed as often as you like, finds new posts, and sends them as status updates in Twitter.

The service offers many customizations and options, such as setting the shortener service you want, setting the order to tweet the posts, and appending text before or after the Tweet. Here are a few recommendations:

- ✔ **Include only the title rather than the title and description.** When you include the title and description, the tweet will take the full 140 characters. You want to leave some room if someone wishes to retweet your post and add comments or a name.

- ✔ **Use bit.ly:** Use bit.ly as your shortener so that you can see how often the links have been clicked.

- ✔ **Add a post prefix:** If you want to distinguish these automated tweets, you can add a post prefix, such as *New blog post.*

- ✔ **Use hashtags:** Many people search Twitter for news on specific keywords. If you have specific keywords that you're targeting with your corporate blog (and you should!), add a couple using hashtags. For example, `#blogging #seo`.

Figure 11-5:
Shortening
a Web
address
with bit.ly.

Figure 11-6:
Twitterfeed
syndicates
your blog to
Twitter.

A *hashtag* allows you to tag your tweets by designating them with just one character, the pound sign (#). Because space is at a premium in a tweet, you don't want to waste it with extra characters, such as `tag:`, by surrounding the tags with brackets, or by writing your tweets in all capital letters. (Writing a tweet in all capital letters doesn't add characters, but it is considered shouting.)

You tag things by placing a # in front of whatever keywords you're using. You can find Twitter hashtags for cities, states, countries, current events, brands, sports teams, or anything else you can think of. Hashtags are a great way to create groupings and generate popularity around a particular keyword or topic.

The # symbol also carries a lot of meaning. It's basically a message to Twitterers that you're talking about this topic, and if they want to talk about it with you, they should use this hashtag in all their tweets; otherwise, you may not know they've tweeted about it (if you are not following them). It may be hard to believe you can put all that info in one little #, but you can.

Be sure to select a few overwhelmingly popular hashtags when automating your blog post titles to Twitter. They make your tweets easy to find and attract relevant traffic to your corporate blog.

Syndicating your blog in LinkedIn and Plaxo

LinkedIn dominates the business-related social media landscape. If you wish to attract customers from a specific industry or want to keep your network informed, LinkedIn is an ideal place to syndicate your blog. LinkedIn allows for syndication directly from WordPress, too. The Plaxo business network also allows for this functionality.

To syndicate your WordPress blog in LinkedIn, follow these steps:

1. **Sign up for LinkedIn and complete your profile.**

2. **Go to the LinkedIn Applications page at `www.linkedin.com/apps`.** (See Figure 11-7.)

3. **Click WordPress.**

4. **Add the application to your profile.**

5. **Add your blog's feed address in the WordPress Blog URL path.**

Add the Twitter app to synchronize your Twitter status updates to LinkedIn. It won't display an excerpt of your blog posts to your LinkedIn profile, but it will synchronize your latest Twitter status updates to your LinkedIn status updates.

Figure 11-7:
The
LinkedIn
Applications
page where
you can
integrate
WordPress.

SlideShare (www.slideshare.net/business) is a fantastic LinkedIn application that synchronizes any PowerPoint presentations that you've uploaded to SlideShare and displays them on your LinkedIn profile. SlideShare can display presentations in your blog posts, too, and has a great feature where businesses can add a form onto their presentation to collect contact information from viewers who are interested in contacting your company.

Integrating your blog into Facebook profiles and Fan Pages

Although Facebook may be free, the need to create content to attract an audience is not. This challenge is not unique to Facebook; it affects all forms of social media and social networking. Be aware that you need a strong content creation engine, but be sure your content flows from one form of social media to your other forms of social media. In other words, if you have a company blog, be sure that you synchronize it with your company's Facebook page so that when you post to your blog, the content posts for your Facebook audience to read.

People who become a fan of your Facebook Page recognize that your intent is self-promotion. Be cautious if you're posting your blog to your personal

Facebook profile — your network of friends may not be as forgiving of blatant promotion. Remember, social media is all about bringing the relevant messages to the appropriate audience at the best time.

To use Facebook to import a blog, follow these steps:

1. **Navigate to your Facebook home page.**
2. **Click Settings underneath your Wall status box.**
3. **In the Stories Posted by You section, select Blog/RSS.**
4. **In the Public URL field, enter your blog's RSS feed.**
5. **Save your settings.**

    Facebook will publish your RSS feed to your Wall without you having to interact at all. (See Figure 11-8.)

If you synchronize your blog to publish in Twitter and have Twitter synchronized with Facebook, your blog posts will publish to your Facebook Wall. Don't upset your followers by having duplicate, unnecessary posts to your Facebook Page.

Figure 11-8: Facebook adds your blog's feed to Facebook.

Your blog's feed

Promoting Your Posts through Social Bookmarking

A *bookmark* is simply a Web address that you store to view later. Bookmarking is a feature that's used in every browser. While readers browse the Internet, they often bookmark a page so that they can return to it later. Before status updates became the craze, social bookmarking sites were the tool for sharing content throughout the Internet.

Delicious is an online bookmarking system that allows you to sign up and store your bookmarks online, share them with others, and tag them with specific keywords so that you can organize and find them easier. (See Figure 11-9.) Because your bookmarks aren't stored locally with your browser, you can access them from anywhere.

Additional bookmarking sites further incorporate social interaction. These sites include

✔ **Digg (http://digg.com):** Digg offers the opportunity to share links and vote on the ones that you find compelling. Digg has been popular for quite a long time but is used by so many people that it's very rare to gain popularity and see traffic from the site.

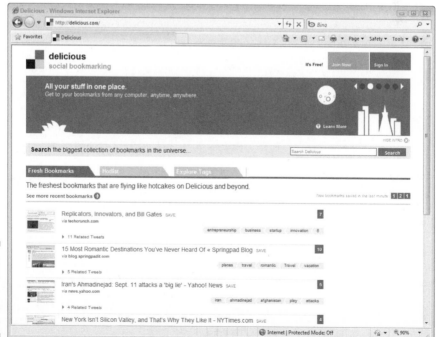

Figure 11-9: Yahoo!'s bookmarking site, Delicious.

✔ **Reddit (www.reddit.com):** Reddit is a popular vote up and vote down site for bookmarks that also allows for tagging and categorization of the bookmarks. Because the bookmarks are effectively tagged, there are opportunities to get some traffic.

✔ **StumbleUpon (www.stumbleupon.com):** StumbleUpon is perhaps the most sophisticated bookmarking engine. When you store bookmarks, the system matches your preferences with others and presents you with links to "stumble upon." As a result, it's a fantastic discovery site. Because links are tagged and categorized, you'll find that this is a great bookmarking site to gain traffic from!

Understanding social bookmarking and its impact on search and traffic

In earlier search engine algorithms, it was rumored that search engines paid close attention to bookmarking sites and increased ranking for sites that were popular or repeatedly used by users on social bookmarking sites.

As a result, many search engine optimization experts consulted with clients to promote content on social bookmarking sites. The practice was dubbed *social bookmarketing* by some in the industry. Social bookmarking sites are still popular throughout the Internet, but have lagged behind the popularity of social media applications like Facebook and Twitter.

Although social bookmarking sites have dropped in popularity, you shouldn't count them out of your efforts. Be sure to measure which paths are providing the most traffic and conversions to your blog.

You want to provide a balance of sharing other sites and promoting your own, too. Always promoting your site decreases your authority, following, and impact. Be sure to promote others within your industry before promoting yourself.

Automated posting to social bookmarking

Here are a few services and integrated plug-ins that offer the opportunity to automatically publish your posts to social bookmarking sites:

✔ **Ping.fm (http://ping.fm)** is a simple and free service that automates updating social bookmarking, social networks, and social media sites. (See Figure 11-10.)

✔ **Socializer 2.0 (http://ekstreme.com/socializer)** is a free service that allows you to submit a link to several bookmarking systems.

✔ **Auto Social (http://wp.uberdose.com/2007/11/09/auto-social-wordpress-plugin)** is a WordPress plug-in from uberdose 2.0 that automatically publishes your WordPress blog posts to Delicious.

Additionally, other services, such as OnlyWire, ShareThis, and AddThis, allow you to place a button in your blog posts that allows users to post your content to their social bookmarking and social media sites.

Guerilla marketing and social bookmarking

If you have a blog post like no other that you believe deserves to get the attention of hundreds, you may want to do a bit of guerilla marketing. That is, you may want to push and promote your site through back-end mechanisms.

With a wide network of fans and friends, you can simply ask all your connections to promote the link. Provide clear intentions to them — that you're hoping their promotion of your site will provide you with some additional attention. If they decide it's worthy, you may get enough retweets, votes on Digg, or thumbs up on StumbleUpon to push your site into the mainstream.

Be careful what you wish for! If you're site isn't made to handle tons of traffic, getting to the top of a site like TweetMeme, Digg, or Alltop can bring your Web server to a halt. Your blog post is of no use if no one can actually visit the site and read it.

Figure 11-10: Ping.fm is a popular service for updating social sites in a single interface.

If you really want to step to the dark side, several services will promote your links for money. A simple search for *"Buy Retweets"* will get you what you're looking for. When visitors arrive at your blog, your Facebook page, or your Twitter page, they'll be impressed by large numbers of subscribers, fans, or followers. As a result, buying subscribers, fans, followers, and retweets has become quite a lucrative business! It's not in the spirit of transparency, a core ethic of social media, but there's plenty of evidence that unethical behavior in social media can get you a lot of attention — and perhaps business.

The consequence, of course, is that you'll be discovered as a fraud and your authority will disappear. That's a difficult issue to rebound from — it could take years or require a total rebranding. If you decide to take this route (not recommended) and are caught — admit it, apologize, and attempt to move forward.

Combining E-Mail and Blogging for Better Marketing

Unlike a blog, an e-mail is a push technology. Your e-mail subscriber has provided you with permission to push messages into their Inbox. Blogs are also permission-based but at the convenience of the visitor or feed subscriber. The combination of e-mail and blogging is fantastic for promoting any company.

Often, you'll have a message that's timely and needs to be distributed and promoted to your network. An e-mail newsletter can ensure that the right message is delivered to the right subscriber at the right time. If your company, for example, has an event coming up, potential attendees won't be aware of the event unless they visit your blog between now and the day of the event. An e-mail with a reminder that points back to the blog post is a great way to get the word out when you need to.

Additionally, e-mail is an outstanding means of reconnecting with prospects who may have not visited your blog in a while. Multiple touches have been proven effective for increasing conversion rates for companies — e-mail may be the best option you have. An e-mail newsletter can repurpose content and drive traffic back to your blog. Your blog, in turn, can promote your e-mail subscription list and convert a one-time visitor into an ongoing subscriber who is interested in your products or services.

Many people like to have the option of using either an e-mail subscription or a feed subscription to remain in touch with your company. Usually, visitors to your site won't subscribe to a newsletter and your blog; they'll have a favorite means of keeping connected.

This provides an opportunity to add another audience to your blog without a lot of effort. Blog content makes for great e-mail content (and vice versa). Take advantage of the opportunity to publish content in both places. Some e-mail and blogging applications offer application programming interfaces (APIs), features, or plug-ins to automatically publish from one system to another.

Using advanced e-mail service features to automate content to e-mail

Swapping content between e-mail platforms and blogs doesn't have to be a chore in cut-and-paste frustration. Platforms are becoming more and more sophisticated in their ability to integrate and publish content between them. After all, the content is simply hypertext markup language (HTML).

Many e-mail clients do not support embedded objects, such as video and audio players, in blog posts but do support basic text and images. As a result, publishing your feed as a section of your e-mail newsletter, as excerpts in your e-mail newsletter, or even in its entirety is a great way to publish quality content through two channels without effort.

How to automate RSS to e-mail with MailChimp

MailChimp is a popular e-mail service provider with bloggers. MailChimp has developed a feature called RSS to E-mail that checks your feed daily, publishes new content, and automatically sends it to your subscribers. In other words, you can publish a daily e-mail without ever writing one!

To set up an RSS to e-mail job in MailChimp, follow these steps:

1. **Open or log in to a MailChimp account at `www.mailchimp.com`.**

2. **On the dashboard, click the down arrow on the Create Campaign button and then select RSS-Driven Campaign.**

3. **Enter the feed address of your blog.**

4. **Enter how frequently you want to send the e-mail (Daily, Weekly, or Monthly).**

5. **Enter the time you want to send your e-mail.**

6. **Click Next.**

7. **Select the subscriber list you want to send the campaign to. If you like, you can select a segment of the list.**

8. **Enter the required campaign information.**

9. **If you use Google Analytics, be sure to select Add Google Analytics Tracking to All URLs.**

   This will be visible in Google Analytics as referring traffic from "other" sources and can be identified as specific campaigns within Google Analytics⇨Traffic Sources⇨Campaigns.

10. **Select a design from MailChimp or you can click Templates⇨Start from Scratch to design a new template.**

11. **For additional information on merging your feed, click the RSS Merge Tags information button.**

    MailChimp provides you with a series of substitution strings for merging specific elements of your feed to your automated e-mail.

12. **Enter your plain-text message.**

    Be sure to do this because many e-mail recipients set their clients to read only the text version of e-mails. HTML e-mails typically get better response rates, but providing both an HTML and text e-mail communicates with a wider audience.

13. **Click Popup Preview to preview your e-mail.**

14. **Click Next and the campaign builder appears where you can review and change any settings on the RSS to e-mail campaign.** (See Figure 11-11.)

15. **Before clicking Start RSS Campaign, click Send Test to send an e-mail to yourself.**

    This pulls in your feed and sends an e-mail to your Inbox that you can review. Make any necessary edits.

16. **Click Start RSS Campaign.**

    If you don't publish any new content, no e-mail is sent.

If you're using Google Analytics and MailChimp, be sure to download MailChimp's Analytics 360° plug-in. It provides an overview of your e-mail campaigns and your traffic, collected through the Google Analytics and MailChimp application programming interfaces. (See Figure 11-12.)

How to automate RSS to e-mail with ExactTarget

To syndicate content from a feed to e-mail isn't just a feature of boutique e-mail service providers. If you're an enterprise corporation sending out millions of e-mails, your e-mail provider probably has similar functionality through its application programming interface (API) or through features in its application.

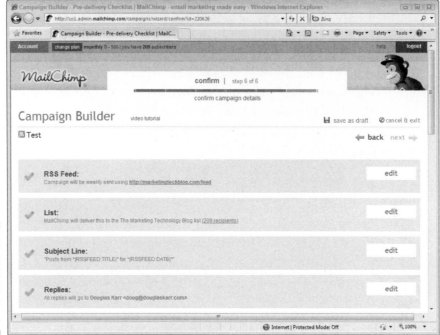

Figure 11-11:
Reviewing
an RSS
to e-mail
campaign in
MailChimp.

Figure 11-12:
MailChimp's
Analytics
360° plug-in
provides
both Google
Analytics
and e-mail
traffic
within your
WordPress
dashboard.

ExactTarget (`http://e-mail.exacttarget.com`) is an outstanding e-mail service provider serving some of the largest companies in the world, including Microsoft, Bank of America, and Papa John's. ExactTarget has a programmable script component and a user interface component for retrieving external content (called HTTPGet).

Using a feed aggregator, you can develop a robust, dynamic page on your Web site that publishes content you would like to see in an e-mail. You can then point your HTTPGet address to the external page. At the time of send, ExactTarget's engine retrieves the external content and embeds it in the e-mail where you specify!

This provides an awesome opportunity for your company to reduce the resources needed in writing a comprehensive newsletter each day or week. If you develop a template that retrieves the external blog content, you can simply leave a content area reserved for specific news or feed in your blog content and event calendar — anything you'd like.

Because blog posts can get a bit lengthy, you may want to simply publish excerpts in your e-mail rather than the entire post. You may also even wish to strip out videos and images — all possible with minimal development.

Driving e-mail readers to your blog

Although different channels, blogs, Twitter, Facebook, LinkedIn, press releases, traditional media, voice, and search engines capture attention and provide your company with inbound leads. Each medium must be leveraged for its strengths and many of them must work in tandem to provide the best benefit.

For example, your e-mail program is a fantastic, permission-based means of pushing relevant and timely messages to your subscribers. However, e-mail doesn't have the opportunity to capture search engine traffic. Blogs, on the other hand, are effective for capturing search traffic. Therefore, developing campaigns that incorporate blogging and e-mail are a fantastic way of pairing resources to increase campaign conversions.

If prospects are reading your e-mail each week and see an excerpt from a blog post they wish to read, they can click a link and land on your blog to read more. From your blog, you can have an effective call-to-action (CTA) that brings them to an effective landing page. Each link in the e-mail is tracked with campaign tracking, so you can see the traffic and conversions produced by pushing your blog posts to e-mail.

If you're a Webtrends client, the Webtrends tag builder (`http://tagbuilder.webtrends.com`) is an effective means of tagging your e-mail traffic and capturing data. Webtrends also integrates with many e-mail service providers so you can observe this traffic independent of your other referring sources.

If you're a Google Analytics client, Google also offers a tool to add campaign codes to your links. You can find it at `www.google.com/support/google analytics/bin/answer.py?hl=en&answer=55578`.

Promoting e-mail subscriptions on your blog

Understanding the value of an e-mail subscriber is a critical component to your company's online marketing strategy. If you send an e-mail once a week, have 25,000 subscribers, and acquire five hundred thousand dollars a year in new business from e-mail subscriptions, you realize that every e-mail is worth about ten thousand dollars and every subscriber is worth twenty dollars.

Growing your e-mail subscriber list is a difficult task. With the advantages of search engine optimization and blogging, you should promote your e-mail subscriptions directly on your blog. Because search engine–acquired visitors often have high bounce rates and seldom return, an e-mail subscription may be just the right medicine to keep in touch with relevant visitors.

Understanding that each subscriber is worth twenty dollars also helps you to appraise your blog. If your blog does nothing but add e-mail subscribers, you can track the subscribers acquired through the blog to set a value on your blogging program. If you acquire 2,500 new subscribers, that's another fifty thousand dollars in business. If you're writing a single blog post each day, that blog post is worth a couple hundred dollars.

Don't simply rely on a call-to-action (CTA) in your sidebar to promote subscriptions to your e-mail newsletter; promote the opportunity to subscribe within your blog posts!

How to automate RSS to e-mail with FeedBurner

FeedBurner is a feed analytics provider that has been around for a few years, is owned by Google, and has integrated Google's tools. Not surprisingly, the first feature was integrating AdSense into your feed.

Aside from providing subscriber counts, FeedBurner also provides a number of tools to optimize and publicize your feed. One way is through e-mail subscriptions. The only disadvantage of the FeedBurner e-mail is that it doesn't allow for many formatting options. If you want more, use MailChimp's RSS to E-mail feature or develop your own template through an e-mail service provider like ExactTarget.

If you don't have the option of integrating a professional outbound e-mail newsletter with your blog, FeedBurner does a nice job. Take advantage of the service. If you decide to graduate to a more robust e-mail service later, FeedBurner does allow you to export your e-mail subscribers so you may import them to another service later.

To add an e-mail subscription for your blog by using FeedBurner (see Figure 11-13), follow these steps:

1. **Register with or log in to FeedBurner at `http://feedburner.google.com`.**

2. **When your feed details are properly set, click Publicize⇨E-mail Subscriptions.**

3. **Click Activate.**

   FeedBurner provides you with sample form code to paste in your sidebar (or in a text widget in the sidebar) for acquiring subscribers. You can also download a plug-in for TypePad or Blogger.

   If you don't wish to provide a form, you can also copy a link for readers to click that you can promote.

4. **Click Save.**

   Each day that your feed updates with new posts, an e-mail is sent out via FeedBurner to your subscribers.

Figure 11-13:
Activating
e-mail
subscrip-
tions within
FeedBurner.

Part V
Measuring Success

The 5th Wave   By Rich Tennant

"I understand you've found a system to reduce the number of complaints we receive by 50 percent."

In this part . . .

This part introduces using your blog as a lead generation tool. Doing so requires you to imagine your blog as a sales funnel that directs your visitors to calls-to-action and converts sales on landing pages.

Chapter 12 discusses the sales funnel and how you can optimize conversions from search engine results pages. Differentiating where your traffic comes from is important because it impacts your strategy for attracting, retaining, and converting visitors from each group.

Chapter 13 takes you through calls-to-action — what they are and how they work. You find out how to capture your visitors' attention and measure the effectiveness of your calls-to-action campaign.

Chapter 14 discusses the calls-to-action strategy of collecting visitor information and completing conversions on landing pages.

Chapter 15 is about measuring success of calls-to-action campaigns with analytics. Proving success of a campaign is important to showing the overall value of your corporate blogging strategy.

Chapter 12

Imagining Your Blog as a Sales Funnel

In This Chapter

▶ Finding your blog

▶ Navigating your blog

▶ Converting visitors into customers

*B*logs are an extraordinary tool to use for raising awareness of your company's expertise, products, and services. However, too many companies abandon blogging when it doesn't generate the business they expect. The problem typically isn't the fault of the blog; the company simply hasn't developed an inbound marketing strategy for the blog.

A typical blog might obtain 40 percent to 60 percent of its average daily traffic of new visitors from search engines and referrals from social media Web sites. Understanding who these new visitors are, how they arrived at your blog, and what motivated them to visit is critical if you want to convert them into customers.

If you have a great corporate blog, chances are the following are true:

✔ You understand that blogging is an effective strategy for your organization, and you're committed to all that blogging has to offer.

✔ Your blog's platform is secure, flexible, and performs as needed.

✔ You established preliminary goals for your blog for acquiring traffic, customers, and industry leadership.

✔ You integrated the blog with your Web site, and you promote both throughout your company.

✔ You optimized your blog's theme and have a keyword strategy in place.

✔ Your well-written blog posts conform to best practices to ensure the reader can easily read and understand the information.

✔ Your team is seeing results in both traffic and search engine ranking by keyword.

In this chapter, you begin to visualize your blog as an inbound marketing strategy for your company to generate leads, upsell to existing clients or customers, as well as acquire new clients or customers.

Using Your Blog as a Sales Funnel

Perhaps the first misconception of a blog is that your blog starts with a home page and navigates downward to categories and eventually posts. Although you design and visualize a blog hierarchically, blogs are really quite different. Depending on how many blog posts you've written, your blog has hundreds or thousands of targeted landing pages that attract attention.

Each page independently drives traffic from search engines, social media sites, referring blogs, and referring Web sites.

A *sales funnel,* or pipeline, is a way to visualize your audience online from prospect to conversion. Not everyone becomes a customer in your business and understanding where you lost (bounced) or converted prospective customers in the path they took helps you to optimize your funnel to improve conversions. Each sale can be visualized as a series of steps:

1. Prospects read an excerpt in the search engine results page (SERP), Web site, or e-mail.

2. The prospect decides to click the referring link on that SERP, Web site, or e-mail because it's relevant to the search he made or the topic of discussion he was seeking additional information for. The link takes the reader to your blog.

3. The prospect reads your page and either bounces (leaves), continues to read, or takes action to engage with your business.

4. The prospect clicks an image or link that directs them to do something. This is a *call-to-action*. Common calls-to-action are Download buttons, Registration buttons, Add to Cart button, or other advertisements.

5. The prospect registers his information to obtain access to a download or contact with your sales team.

6. The prospect converts as a sale either on your e-commerce site or with your sales person.

When a prospect advances in each step, this is called a *conversion*. Many online marketers measure conversions by dividing the number of visitors they obtain on their site by the number of visitors who purchase. This is an overly general means of measuring conversions.

If you wish to maximize the potential of your blog, it's important to understand the steps your visitors take and where you lose them along the way. Each step in the process must be analyzed to monitor and improve the overall conversion rate of the blog.

Each step in the sales funnel loses prospects. Therefore, you want to measure what works and what doesn't work at each point in your sales funnel so that you convert more prospects and lose less business.

When a reader advances through each step in the sales funnel, that's a conversion. If a customer advances from a search engine to a purchase on your site, the conversions that happen are as follows (see Figure 12-1):

✔ The reader clicks an entry in the search engine results page and arrives at a blog post.

✔ The reader clicks a call-to-action in the sidebar after reading the relevant blog post.

✔ The reader adds the item to a shopping cart and submits.

If you wish to improve business results, you must monitor and improve conversions each step of the way. The first step is optimizing conversions from the search engine results page.

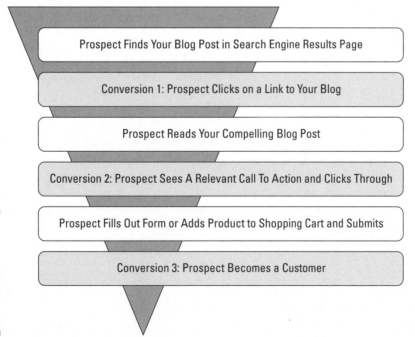

Figure 12-1: Diagram of a typical blog's sales funnel and conversions.

Prospect Finds Your Blog Post in Search Engine Results Page

Conversion 1: Prospect Clicks on a Link to Your Blog

Prospect Reads Your Compelling Blog Post

Conversion 2: Prospect Sees A Relevant Call To Action and Clicks Through

Prospect Fills Out Form or Adds Product to Shopping Cart and Submits

Conversion 3: Prospect Becomes a Customer

Optimizing conversions from the search engine results page

Search engine users use search engines to find answers. They find those answers by entering a combination of keywords and phrases, hoping that the list of results provides them with references to sites that will answer their question.

Search engines are a perfect medium for marketing your business because the search engine user is defining the relevant search at a time when they are motivated to seek out the answers to their questions. By ensuring your content is relevant and placed well on a search engine results page, you're making your business available at the right time with the perfect message.

A visitor acquired through a search engine, then, is more valuable than a visitor from, say, a banner advertisement on another Web site. Marketing is about getting the right message in front of the right prospect at the right time. By being available on a search engine, your company is present for a person when they are ready to engage.

Understanding rank and its effect on traffic

A search engine results page (SERP) provides organic search results on the left and paid search results on the right sidebar. At times, for popular terms, search engines include paid (or sponsored) search results across the top of the organic results.

This book concentrates on Google's search engine and associated tools because Google dominates the search engine market.

Organic results are search engine results based on the destination page's relevance on the topic as well as the page topic's popularity. Search engines organize pages for specific keywords but they rank them based on popularity. *Popularity* is measured by how many other relevant and authoritative sites link to the page. These links are called *backlinks*.

The organic side of a search engine results page typically gets 80 percent to 85 percent of all the clicks on the page. Other results on the page are paid search results, also known as sponsored results. While pay-per-click advertising is effective, organic results can acquire much more traffic.

Blogs are attractive because they provide a platform where you can write content frequently and present it in such a way that's optimized for search engines to find and index. This increases the likelihood that your business will be found organically in search results. Several studies on search engine results page navigation support that the top of the page gets the most results, the next result gets less, the next even less — on down the page.

In fact, being ranked as the first result on a search engine results page means you will get 50 percent to 80 percent of all the clicks on the page.

SEO Researcher (`www.seoresearcher.com`) has done extensive studies of search engine results pages and found the following:

- ✔ **Position 1:** Results in 56 percent of all clicks on a search engine results page. An additional advantage of this is that searchers spend more time (28 percent) with the first result page than they do with the other resulting pages.

- ✔ **Position 2:** Results in 13 percent of all clicks on a search engine results page with 25 percent of the time spent on the destination page.

- ✔ **Position 3:** Results in 10 percent of all clicks on a search engine results page with 15 percent of time spent on the destination page.

- ✔ **Position 4:** Results in 4 percent of all clicks on a search engine results page with 9 percent of time spent on the destination page.

Recognizing that a move in a search engine results page from position 4 to position 1 is a 1400 percent increase in traffic from the search engine provides a scale of how important rank is to building relevant traffic to your blog from a search engine. Figure 12-2 shows the importance of ranking high on a search engine. Being on the first page for your company's niche is an important factor in your overall authority in the industry; being the first result is exceptional!

Growing your business through blogging requires that you attract traffic to your blog. The most effective way of attracting relevant traffic to your business is by being found in relevant search results.

By identifying and targeting keywords in your content that have high search volumes, you can substantially improve the number of visitors and new customers to your blog and improve your corporate blogging success.

Recognizing how many keyword searches there are, knowing the keywords you are ranked for, and understanding the keywords you convert with is how you can determine how well your search engine conversion rate is. This information isn't found within your blog or fully available within your analytics, though. You have to use a combination of tools, such as the following:

- ✔ Google External Keyword Tool to identify keyword search volumes

- ✔ Google Webmasters to identify the keywords that your blog ranks for and whether searchers are clicking your links

- ✔ Your analytics software to identify the keywords that are attracting traffic and converting searchers into customers

Keyword research is the process of identifying keywords to target, their search volumes, and how your blog ranks on the search engine results pages for those keywords.

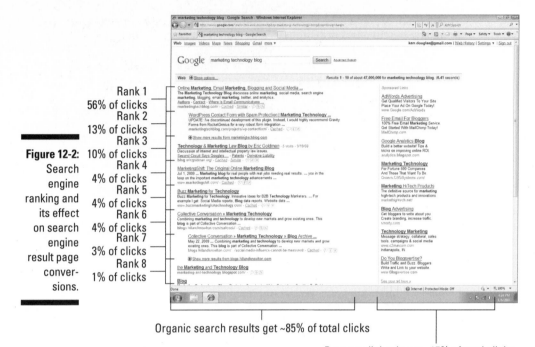

Rank 1
56% of clicks
Rank 2
13% of clicks
Rank 3
10% of clicks
Rank 4
4% of clicks
Rank 5
4% of clicks
Rank 6
4% of clicks
Rank 7
3% of clicks
Rank 8
1% of clicks

Figure 12-2: Search engine ranking and its effect on search engine result page conversions.

Organic search results get ~85% of total clicks

Pay per click ads get ~15% of total clicks

The number of keyword searches is also known as the search *volume*. Reviewing both the volumes and the ranking of your blogs on those keywords is necessary to measure your search engine conversion rate.

Not only do you want to identify your keyword ranking, but you also want to identify new keywords to target that are relevant to your business and have higher search volumes.

Google provides the External Keyword Tool to provide you with search volumes by keyword. The tool lists keywords, similar keywords and phrases, and their monthly search volumes.

To use Google's External Keyword Tool to identify search engine volumes for keywords, follow these steps:

1. **Navigate to `https://adwords.google.com/select/ KeywordToolExternal`.**

2. **Enter one keyword or phrase per line in the form.**

3. **Type the characters you see in the picture and then click Enter.**

   The search engine volumes for the keywords that you are targeting appear. (See Figure 12-3.)

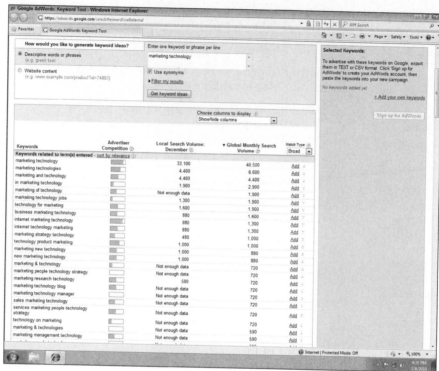

Figure 12-3:
Identifying
search
volumes for
keywords
using
Google's
External
Keyword
Tool.

Using Google Webmasters to identify search engine placement for keywords

Google Webmasters is a resource that Google has provided to monitor how Google's search engine is interacting with your site or blog. Bing has followed Google's lead, providing Bing Webmasters. Yahoo! also has Yahoo! Site Explorer.

Google Webmasters can provide a lot of information that your analytics engine can not. Analytics is only a tool for analyzing visitors to your blog. Although analytics is a critical tool, it can not provide information on anything but visitors.

Webmasters tools provide you with information on the search engine results that your blog appears in, not just visitors who click through to your blog. That's key because analyzing search engine conversions requires that you understand the potential for visits through search engines, not just the actual visits. To use Google Webmasters to identify search engine placement for keywords, follow these steps:

1. **Navigate to www.google.com/webmasters.**

2. **Log in to Google Webmasters. (See Chapter 8 for more on registering with Google Webmasters.)**

3. **Click your blog domain.**

4. **On the Top Search Queries, click More to see the full list of the keywords your blog is ranking for.**

5. **Click Position to sort the results by your rank for the specific term.**

The resulting data provides you with a clear picture of how you are ranking and what searches you are ranking on. (See Figure 12-4.) Questions to ask:

✔ **Are you ranking on terms that are relevant to your business?** If not, you need to incorporate the keywords more effectively in your content.

✔ **Are you ranking well on terms but searchers aren't clicking through?** You need to write compelling blog post titles and optimize your blog posts' descriptions in your blogging platform. Many businesses don't even realize that their blog is showing up well in search engine results but they aren't effectively converting those searchers into customers.

✔ **Are you not ranking on anything?** You can troubleshoot why your blog isn't being ranked by using the additional troubleshooting tools within Webmasters.

Figure 12-4:
Identifying your rank in Google Webmasters.

On the Top Search Queries for your blog in Google Webmasters, the left side of the page provides you with the terms you are ranking for in the last week and how well you rank. The right side of the page provides you with the terms visitors are clicking. Webmasters also retains each week so you can compare progress from week to week.

Measure your search engine conversion rate. Search engine conversion rate is the total number of searches for the keywords you appear in divided by the number of visitors acquired through those keywords.

> Search Engine Conversion Rate = Total Number of Searches / Total Number of Visitors from Search Results

Don't be surprised if your rate is extraordinarily low. You must have very high keyword ranking to increase your search engine conversion rate. By monitoring this rate each week, you can develop action plans and processes to improve the rate and the number of visitors acquired through search engines to your business.

Measuring Engagement and Conversions on Your Blog

In the early days of blogging, bloggers used to measure effectiveness of their blog with a term called *engagement*. That is, how engaged visitors were in their blog. Engagement was a difficult metric to capture, so many bloggers used comments as a key indicator of engagement.

Comments have their value on a business blog, but they don't indicate the popularity of your blog in the least when you're measuring your blog's success on the bottom line. For corporate blogs, engagement must be measured in revenue.

Not all revenue is generated directly, though. You may acquire customers directly through calls-to-action, landing pages, or e-commerce purchases on your blog, but you may also have other opportunities. Many bloggers are asked to speak publically on a given topic, for example.

Events and conferences are an ideal means of generating business for your organization. Be sure to account for revenue acquired through events and conferences when you're judging your blogs' effectiveness on your bottom line.

Understanding bounce rate and its effect on your blog

Bounce rate is the ratio (measured in a percentage) of visitors who leave after visiting any page on your blog compared to the total number of visits overall. *Exit rate* indicates the last pages that visitors — who visited either single or multiple pages — were on before they exited your site. So, bounce rate is a measurement across an entire site, regardless of the page that was landed on. Exit rate; however, is specific to the page and only that page.

If two people visit your blog on any page and one immediately leaves without visiting a second page, your site has a 50 percent bounce rate. If a page has four visitors and one leaves the blog from it, your page has a 25 percent exit rate.

Understanding the difference between the bounce rate and the exit rate is important. Exit rate is an issue specific to content in a blog post or page. A blog post with a high exit rate may be optimized for search traffic, but the content isn't compelling enough to keep or convert the customer. Make adjustments to the content of the page to ensure it is compelling and visitors either stay or convert.

You may also have pages — such as confirmation pages — designed to have high exit rates. Because exiting is the appropriate behavior for those pages, you need not worry about optimizing them.

Many organizations measure and reward based on the bounce rate of visitors. For the record, a *bounce* is a person who lands on any page on your site and leaves without viewing any additional pages. High bounce rates are not uncommon when your blog attracts a lot of search engine traffic. Bouncing is the typical behavior. Think about the last time you searched or clicked a referring link. Did you stick around, or did you find the information you were looking for, consume it, and then leave?

Most visitors bounce; this is typical behavior on the Internet. Moreover, blogs actually encourage this behavior. Because blogs provide content regularly, visitors to a blog typically don't start with your first post and read through to the final post. Instead, visitors come back on a regular basis and leave after they've read the latest posts.

Sometimes searchers enter the wrong keywords or phrases; other times, search engines index your page's keywords incorrectly. As a result, a visitor lands and leaves because she didn't find what she was looking for. You don't have total control when content is indexed incorrectly (that's why effective keyword usage is so important).

Search engines are constantly changing their algorithms and rankings, too. Unless you've written your content poorly, bounce rates may not be something you can control or place a lot of emphasis on.

Measuring trends versus instances

Bounce rates may not be a perfect metric, but they can still be very useful. You commonly see bounce rates between 80 percent and 95 percent on any given day. As an instance, a bounce rate isn't a compelling metric that requires action. As a trend, however, bounce rates can be very important. Bounce rates changing over time can point to a number of issues.

Bounce rates per page are an effective metric to review, too. Independent bounce rates per blog post can provide you with details on the characteristics of those blog posts. You can find common characteristics between blog posts with high bounce rates and those with low bounce rates.

If your search engine traffic is climbing, you can expect more bounces. If a major site refers to your blog and you receive a ton of traffic, you can expect more bounces. But if all other metrics appear constant and bounce rates are increasing, you may want to take a good look at your content and see if you're missing the mark.

Bounce rates can be measured and monitored in all modern analytics engines. *Analytics* is a back-end reporting system that provides a wealth of information and reporting on the habits and sources of visitors that come to your site.

To view bounce rates in Google Analytics, follow these steps:

1. **Navigate to `www.google.com/analytics`.**

2. **Log in to Google Analytics.**

3. **Click your blog domain.**

4. **Click Bounce Rate Report.**

5. **Choose Visitors➪Visitor Trending➪Bounce Rate. (See Figure 12-5.)**

You can employ strategies to stop visitors from bouncing from your blog. Here are a few ways to keep visitors:

- ✔ **Add a Recent Posts plug-in that lists your most recent blog posts (with links) adjacent to the content.** The visitor may read your latest posts if the titles are compelling.

- ✔ **Link to other relevant posts within your content.** If you previously wrote a post about a similar topic, mention it with a link within your post. The visitor may want to investigate the topic further. This is called *deep linking* because the link takes the reader directly to another page deep within your blog.

✔ **Add a Related Posts plug-in that lists posts related to the same topic.**
Over time, you're going to write a lot of content on your blog and you're
probably going to cover the same topics with different perspectives,
examples, or stories. Providing a list of those relevant posts provides a
visitor with options other than bouncing.

✔ **Ensure that your post title clearly matches your content.** Some blogs
and Web sites purposefully mislead people to increase the site's number
of visitors. Your business isn't paid based on the number of visitors;
your business is paid only when someone converts.

✔ **If you're providing a call-to-action that drives visitors to an external
link, add code to the link to ensure that clicking it isn't counted as a
bounce.** With Google Analytics, you can do this by adding an `onClick`
event to the anchor tag of the call-to-action:

```
<a href="http://othersite.com" title="call-to-action"
        onClick="javascript: pageTracker._
        trackPageview('/outgoing/call-to-action');"
```

When someone clicks on the call-to-action, Google Analytics tracks an additional pageview for the page found at the path `outgoing/call-to-action`. That path can be anything you would like it to be. By tracking an additional pageview, the visitor is seen as viewing a minimum of two pages. As a result, there is no bounce recorded.

✔ **Reduce page load times.** High page load times can affect bounce rates. According to Forrester and Akamai's August 2009 report, (`http://www.getelastic.com/performance/`) e-commerce sites begin to see high abandonment rates when page load times exceed two seconds. That's not a long time! You can make a number of improvements to your blog to increase its performance, but you may need to seek a professional to implement them. A few tools on the market help you troubleshoot slow page load times, including YSlow from the Yahoo! Developer Network; Firebug, a plug-in for the Firefox browser with Page Speed, a plug-in from Google; Speed Tracer for the Google Chrome browser; or an external tool, such as Pingdom.

To check your page load time with Pingdom, follow these steps:

1. **Along with your home page, select a few pages from your blog to test.**

2. **Navigate to `http://tools.pingdom.com`.**

3. **Enter the URL of the page you're testing in the Full Page Test field.**

4. **Click Test Now and allow the test to complete.**

5. **Observe the test results. (See Figure 12-6).**

   The breakdown of the results provides you with details on each object in your page and how long it took to request and display that object in the browser.

   If your page exceeds 2 seconds, you may want to invest in a professional to help improve your blog's performance. If you have excessive gadgets, widgets, videos, and other embedded tools on your site, you may want to begin disabling them.

6. **Observe the results by item.**

   You may find that some scripts or page elements are causing large delays in the page speed. Work with an infrastructure consultant or hosting provider to correct these issues.

✔ **Write great content.** Great content keeps people on your blog. Try adjusting your types of posts, lengths of posts, and the topics you cover in your posts to see what effect each variable might have. From time to time, invite guest bloggers who are successful.

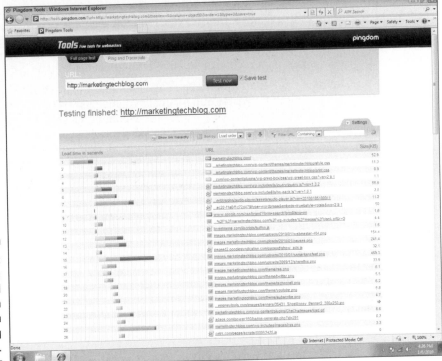

Figure 12-6:
Viewing page load times with the Pingdom monitoring service.

Comparing your analytics to industry results

Google Analytics has a beta feature that allows you to benchmark your blog against those in your own industry. This feature can be either extremely useful or extremely frustrating, depending on the results that you obtain. If other analytics users have not accurately classified their site, your results may vary greatly from the benchmark.

Benchmarks are extremely handy when analyzing seasonal trends, though. If your blog is seeing a decline in readership during the winter holidays, analyzing the benchmarks can provide supportive evidence that all industry trends are dropping during that period.

To enable benchmarks in Google Analytics, follow these steps:

1. **Log in to your Google Analytics account.**

2. **In the Visitors section, select Benchmarking (Beta).**

3. **On the Benchmarking report page, click Open Category List to expand the list of categories.**

4. Click the category you wish to compare your Web site against and then click Select Category to save your changes.

The report automatically populates the graphs with your selected category's benchmark line. (See Figure 12-7.) Industry averages are difficult to analyze and should be taken with a grain of salt. You'll find that your results will generate unique trends that often do not compare to those on the benchmarked sites. Do not be alarmed; Google has not perfected how site data is classified and how relevant it is to your blog.

Analytics systems can drive a professional nuts. If you apply two competing analytics providers to the same blog, you're guaranteed to get different counts and results. Each analytics company attempts to accurately define unique visitors, time on site, bounces, and other metrics, but the logic each one uses differs.

For this reason, it's much better to continue to monitor your blog's performance over time than at an instant. Stick with trending when analyzing your blog's performance. Pay attention to these trends:

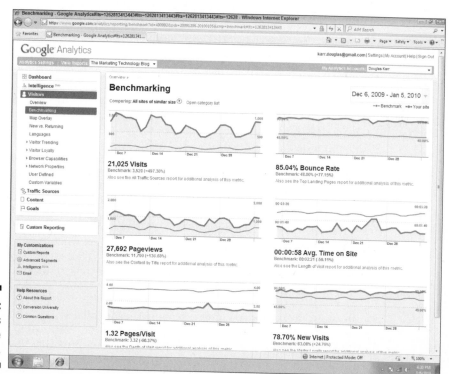

Figure 12-7:
Benchmarks
in Google
Analytics.

✔ Is the number of visitors to your blog increasing or decreasing?

✔ Is the number of visitors from search engines increasing or decreasing?

✔ What are the top referring sites that are driving traffic to your blog?

✔ What are the top blog posts on your blog?

✔ What are the top converting blog posts on your blog?

✔ What are the top converting keyword searches on your blog?

✔ If you have multiple authors, who drives the most conversions?

Each week, as you continue to analyze these results, you can monitor your blog's performance and see if it is improving or declining. Analyzing these results will provide you with insight on how you can improve your blog to increase traffic and, ultimately, conversions.

Differentiating traffic sources and business benefits

Many companies either forget or don't take into consideration that Web traffic is composed of many different audiences: investors, employees, customers, prospects, industry leaders, colleagues, and so on.

Understanding who is reaching your blog and what motivated them to read is an incredible opportunity. By understanding how and why visitors arrived, you can target content directly to those visitors. Dynamic content (content which changes and customizes based on the visitor and the information known about them), dynamic calls-to-action, and dynamic landing pages are generating a lot of buzz in online marketing because they display highly relevant content based on the audience they are speaking to.

Optimizing sales and retention strategies for direct traffic

Direct traffic to your site is generally from audiences who already have a relationship with your company, including customers. Web technologies allow you to detect how visitors are getting to your site; thus, you can dynamically change the content.

One example of how companies are using these technologies is to differentiate customers from prospects. Using a customer relationship management tool, such as Salesforce, you can develop a solution that identifies the customer from the prospect. For the customer, you may market the next Webinar or an upsell opportunity. For a prospect, you may market a whitepaper to download.

Placing upsell, training, event, and support information for direct traffic is a great way to fully leverage your blog's layout. By displaying relevant information, you're providing a path to engagement that's relevant to your visitor.

Optimizing acquisition strategies for search engine traffic

Search engine traffic is largely new visitors who are researching your products or services. Understanding how they arrived at your blog can provide you with the tools you need to provide relevant content and calls-to-action. A search engine referral not only provides you with the search engine the visitor arrived from, but also provides you with the keywords or phrases that the person used in their search.

Dynamically generating a call-to-action with messaging relevant to the search terms increases new visitor conversion rates dramatically.

Optimizing strategies for social media traffic

Referring traffic from social media could be visitors from viral campaigns, industry colleagues, your own employees, and customers. Social media sites, such as Twitter, can provide highly relevant traffic to your blog.

Dynamically changing calls-to-action and welcome messages and providing ways to engage with you further, perhaps with a subscription form, can target these visitors with relevant messaging.

An example is a new visitor from Twitter. Using the WP Greet Box plug-in, you can dynamically change messaging for someone who arrived on your blog from the Twitter Web site. Provide them with your Twitter username and a link to your page so that they can follow you. You may not get a sale today, but connecting with you will afford you the opportunity to connect with them again.

The plug-in allows you to do this from a number of sources, including search engines and social media and networking Web sites.

Chapter 13

Directing Your Readers through Calls-to-Action

In This Chapter

▶ Defining a call-to-action

▶ Designing calls-to-action

▶ Testing and measuring call-to-action performance

▶ Improving your calls-to-action click-through rate

A *call-to-action* is a general term for a page item that directs the user's attention to initiate an action. A call-to-action can be something as simple as a link on a page or, more typically, is a bold image that directs the user to click to engage with the blog further. Developing great calls-to-action can significantly impact a blog's performance on click-through rates and conversion rates.

Understanding Why You Need Calls-to-Action

Many blogs leave out calls-to-action altogether and simply rely on the reader to poke around and find ways to contact or make a purchase. At issue is that business blogs often compare themselves to the traditional blog. A traditional blog is a journal-style publication whose goal is to attract as many people as possible. It's all about the numbers. Visitors come to a traditional blog to be entertained or learn from the content and often are discouraged by too many advertisements.

Your business blog is different. The purpose of the business blog is to educate and compel visitors to connect with your company and make a purchase, to deepen their relationship with the company by buying additional products or services, or to improve their overall customer experience so they are retained as a customer.

Your blogging strategy should have three distinct steps:

1. **Find visitors.**

   Build search and promotion strategies that lead new visitors to your blog or return visitors to it.

2. **Direct visitors.**

   This is where calls-to-action are critical. You need to provide paths of engagement for your visitors to go from a blog post to becoming a customer or making a purchase.

3. **Convert visitors.**

   Provide a destination page where they complete the purchase or are entered into a process where they will be contacted by your company for the purpose of starting as a customer or increasing their engagement with your company. (Chapter 14 gives you the scoop on landing pages.)

Your visitor's intent is to investigate whether or not they wish to do business with you. Visitors aren't interrupted (unless it's really in their face) by advertisements on a business blog, they're attracted by them. Whether it's a Buy Now link, a registration, a download, a Webinar, or a subscription, these calls-to-action should be available so the visitor knows where to go next.

Not providing calls-to-action can be incredibly frustrating to a Web visitor who wishes to contact you or make a purchase – so ensure that your path to engagement through your blog is very clear and the visitor knows exactly how to proceed.

Designing Calls-to-Action That Readers Will Click

There is a science to effective call-to-action design. Aside from testing your calls-to-action and swapping them out for relevance, timeliness, and continuous improvement, a call-to-action should have specific elements that ensure that readers understand what they are to do next.

Each call-to-action should have

- ✔ **A single purpose that the visitor is aware of:** That purpose may be to sign up for a weekly newsletter, sign up for a demonstration, download a whitepaper, contact a salesperson, or even add a product to a shopping cart.

- ✔ **A benefit or list of benefits for the visitor:** You must provide visitors the reason they should take action and click-through a call-to-action. If it's a weekly newspaper, perhaps you're sharing industry best practices or the latest news. If it's a demonstration, perhaps it's to learn why your application is different. If it's a whitepaper, tell the visitor what questions are going to be answered. And if it's a product, let the visitor know what benefit she can get from the purchase.

✔ **A command:** Do not leave any subjectivity to your call to action. It's important that you let visitors know what you expect them to do and when you expect them to do it. For example, Subscribe Now, Register Now, Download Now, Add to Shopping Cart Now. If it's an offer that expires, count down the time for them, providing them with a sense of urgency.

✔ **A place to click:** The last element is the place to click. Display a graphical button or the pointer of a mouse. This element should be obvious but not overly ridiculous. Jiggling pictures and flashing colors takes the attention off your content prematurely — don't be tempted to use these.

Many sites have compelling calls-to-action but don't provide any imagery that communicates that the user is expected to click there. Visitors may think it's just an image on your page and may not realize that it's a place to actually click.

If any one of these features (see Figure 13-1) is missing from your call-to-action, you risk losing opportunities and visitor clicks. If you don't write a purpose, people won't understand what the call-to-action is for. If you don't provide benefits, they won't understand why they should connect with you. If you don't tell them what to do, they may not realize it's a call-to-action or they may put it off until later (also known as *never*).

Figure 13-1:
Viewing call-to-action elements on Lifeline Data Center's blog.

Quality content drives conversions with your audience because it builds both trust and authority. Well-designed calls-to-action provide your visitors with the path to engage once they decide that you're the right company to work with.

Finding images that draw attention to your call-to-action

Not all calls-to-action require an image. Compelling text that is hyperlinked can sometimes be just as effective. In fact, you should try to add a textual call-to-action in most of the blog posts you write. A simple example is adding a line or two at the end of a post to invite the reader to contact you for additional information.

Images, however, can be very compelling. Your visitors will remember a relevant image more so than text. To connect with your audience, providing an image with employees from your company is a great tactic. Seeing a familiar face always attracts attention (it's why many brands enlist celebrities).

Getty Images (www.gettyimages.com) and its lower-cost cousin iStock-photo (http://istockphoto.com) are two fantastic sources of photos. They both provide advanced search mechanisms to find just the right image for your calls-to-action.

As for button images, some fantastic sites offer extremely professional button templates. BittBox (www.bittbox.com) is a professional design site that educates graphic designers in the use of Illustrator and Photoshop. The blogger also supplies a plethora of freebies to choose from, all free to use commercially.

If you're at a loss as to where to find images, do not *borrow* them from other sites or a Google image search result. Putting images on your site that you don't have permission to use can cost your business thousands of dollars. Even if you find the image for use on a royalty-free site but the origin was a copyrighted site, your business could still be liable.

You're better off buying or designing the images that go into your site's blog posts.

Keeping it simple; writing call-to-action content

Copy on calls-to-action must be kept to a minimum. Avoid paragraphs at all costs and write in simple, choppy titles, bulleted points, or numbered lists. (Figure 13-2 provides some examples of highly effective calls-to-action.)

Anything more and your visitors will lose focus. The term utilized in the Web industry is *progressive disclosure.*

Progressive disclosure means that I only provide you with enough information and enough elements for you to make a single decision and move on. Many of the most effective Web sites utilize progressive disclosure. A great example is Google, who provides you with a search box, a Search button, and not much else. Only after you search are you provided with more details.

Don't try to be shy or manipulative; sometimes asking your visitors point-blank question gets the best result. Try any of the following:

✔ Already a customer? Click here to find out our latest products and features.

✔ Ready to buy? Click here to complete the order.

✔ Need more information? Our staff is here to help — just fill out a few contact details.

✔ Find out how we help! Register and download our latest case studies.

Manipulating your visitors is called *clickbait,* which is accomplished by wording your call-to-action in a way that compels the visitor to click but is dishonest in its messaging. The only goal is to get the click. If a conversion happens after that, so much the better. Although clickbaiting may work on spam sites and other sites not concerned with reputation, there's no place for it on your business blog.

Measuring Click-Through Rates on Calls-to-Action

Measurement on calls-to-action is absolutely critical. Most Web sites and Web designers design a layout, insert some great calls-to-action, and then disappear until the next design. This is a huge mistake. Rarely is the first design the one that's best optimized for conversions. Your site, your blog, your calls-to-action, and your landing pages should all undergo continuous testing and optimization.

Continuous experimentation and swapping out of calls-to-action helps you to optimize your layout and messaging, and it will increase your overall clicks and conversions. Plan this into your blogging administration schedule. Utilizing an enterprise analytics application such as Webtrends, you can even set alerts so that you are informed immediately of under-performing and over-performing posts, calls-to-action, and landing pages.

Implementing onclick events and campaign codes for tracking

If you're without optimization software, you can utilize your analytics software to capture click events manually. Monitoring and optimizing your campaigns manually requires additional resources, but is still worth the effort.

Google Analytics allows you to add pageviews with onclick events:

```
<a href="mylandingpage.html" title="My Call to Action" onclick="javascript:
        pageTracker._trackPageview('/cta/cta_name');"><img src="cta.
        jpg"></a>
```

In Google Analytics, the trackPageview event records an additional pageview when someone clicks the call-to-action. This is a simple way to track call-to-action performance because you can filter your pageviews in Google Analytics for "/cta/" and see how well your calls-to-action perform.

The downside of this approach is that you're actually skewing your Analytics statistics for pageviews, average pages viewed per visitor, and even your bounce rates. You're adding a pageview to each of those elements, so you're going to see some inflated numbers.

To avoid skewing your statistics, Google Analytics provides you the option of building multiple profiles and filtering the data that those profiles capture. To build a profile in Google Analytics:

1. **Log in to Google Analytics and click Add New Profile in the top right of your accounts list. If you don't have an account, refer to the instructions in Chapter 5 for starting a Google Analytics account.**

2. **Select the Add a Profile for an Existing Domain option (See Figure 13-2).**

3. **From the Select Domain drop-down list, select the domain that you are going to measure.**

4. **In the Profile Name text box, name your profile with the blog name followed by Campaign.**

   For instance, I named mine Marketing Technology Blog Campaigns.

5. **Select your time zone and click Finish.**

6. **After you return to the Accounts List page, click Edit on the campaign account that you created.**

7. **Click Add Filter.**

8. **Create a new filter that includes only traffic to the subdirectory "/cta/" if that's the onclick code you utilized above. (See Figure 13-3.)**

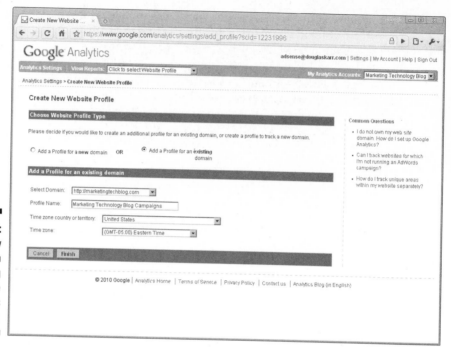

Figure 13-2:
Add a new
profile to an
existing
Google
Analytics
account.

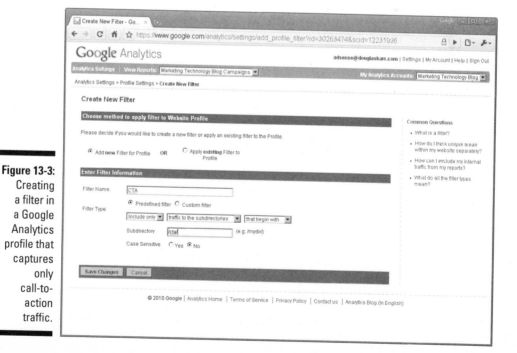

Figure 13-3:
Creating
a filter in
a Google
Analytics
profile that
captures
only
call-to-
action
traffic.

9. **Return to your main analytics profile for your domain (not this new profile) and create a filter that excludes traffic to the subdirectory "/cta/".**

The result of this is that you will have two profiles, one that measures the traffic going to your site, and one that measures only the clicks on your calls-to-action. If you want to get fancy, you can continue adding custom `track-pageview` events on your blog's footer ("/cta/start/"+page title), your landing page ("/cta/land/"+landing page title), and your confirmation page ("/cta/finish/"+landing page title+" converted").

This new campaign profile will accurately measure the campaign-related data while a visitor moves from your blog to an actual conversion.

Another methodology for tracking calls-to-action in Google Analytics is to append campaign code to your internal links. Google Analytics has a tool for you to build the campaign querystring yourself — the Google Analytics URL Builder. (See Figure 13-4.)

```
http://www.google.com/support/analytics/bin/answer.
             py?hl=en&answer=55578
```

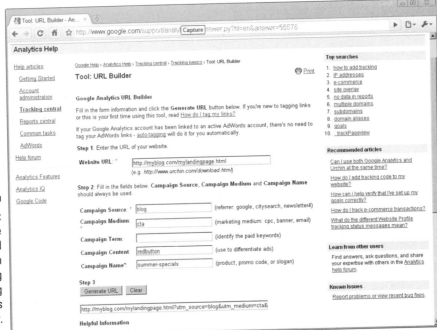

Figure 13-4: Viewing the completed campaign tracking querystring in Google's URL Builder.

A *querystring* is the section of a uniform resource locator (URL) or Web address that adds additional data and variables to pass to the page. Typically, you can identify a querystring by everything following a question mark in the Web address. Example:

```
http://www.mysite.com/mypage.html?q=query
```

To build a campaign querystring for a call-to-action in Google Analytics, take these steps:

1. **Open your browser and navigate to the Google Analytics URL builder.**

2. **Next to Website URL, enter the full Web address for the destination page, also known as the landing page.**

3. **Enter** Blog **or your blog's name in the Campaign Source text box.**

4. **Enter "cta" in the Campaign Medium text box.**

5. **Leave the Campaign Term text box blank.**

6. **In the Campaign Content text box, enter a unique name for your call-to-action that will distinguish this call-to-action from others.**

7. **Enter a unique name in the Campaign Name text box.**

8. **Click Generate URL.**

9. **Utilize this campaign Web address for your call-to-action.**

   ```
   <a href="http://myblog.com/mylandingpage.
           html?utm_source=Blog&utm_medium=cta&utm_
           content=redbutton&utm_campaign=summer-
           specials" title="My Call to Action"><img
           src="cta.jpg"></a>
   ```

If you select three unique calls-to-action to test on the same campaign, utilize the same campaign name but switch the campaign content name. This allows you to measure the overall effectiveness of your campaign, but also to see which call-to-actions perform better.

Building goals in analytics

When a visitor enters the path to engagement through your blog, he takes the following steps:

1. The visitor enters your blog.

2. The visitor clicks your call-to-action.

3. The visitor lands on your landing page.

4. The visitor fills out your form or purchases your product.

5. The visitor lands on a confirmation page.

Utilizing Google Analytics, this can be accomplished by using a feature within Google Analytics named, appropriately, Goals. In Google Analytics, Goals allow you to define the steps that you wish the person to take to monitor their progress. This allows you to clearly see where you have issues in the process so you can correct them. As an example, if very few people are clicking on your call-to-action, you'll want to test new designs and monitor the features and terminology that provides the highest click-through rates.

Follow these steps to build goals and funnels in Google Analytics:

1. **Log in to Google Analytics and Click Edit on the profile you want a goal in. If you don't have an account, refer to the instructions in Chapter 5 for starting a Google Analytics account.**

2. **In the Goals section, click "+ Add goal".**

3. **Name your Goal, ensure Active Goal is turned on, and set the Goal Position to *Set 1, Goal 1* for the page where the CTA is clicked, *Set 1, Goal 1* for the Landing Page, and *Set 1, Goal 1* for the Submission of the Landing Page.**

4. **Select *URL Destination* for the Goal Type.**

5. **Select a Match Type of Head Match**

6. **Enter the Goal URL. If you're capturing the click of the CTA, this path will be the pageview you specify in the `onclick` event, example: /** `cta/start`**.**

7. **Provide a Goal Value on the submission Goal. This amount is determined by multiplying the average value of each sale by the close rate. If you close an average of 10 out of 100 leads, that's a 10 percent close rate. If the average value of a close is $200, your Goal Value is $20.**

8. **Repeat the Steps 2 through 7 above for each of the Goals in your process: the call-to-action click, the landing page, and the submission.**

9. **Add Goal Funnel steps on the Submission Goal. (See Figure 13-5.) Using each of the `pagetrackview` events on your blog, call-to-action, landing page, and confirmation page, fill in each step of the Funnel settings.**

   Now you can actually visualize your sales funnel in Google Analytics View Reports⇨Goals⇨Overview.

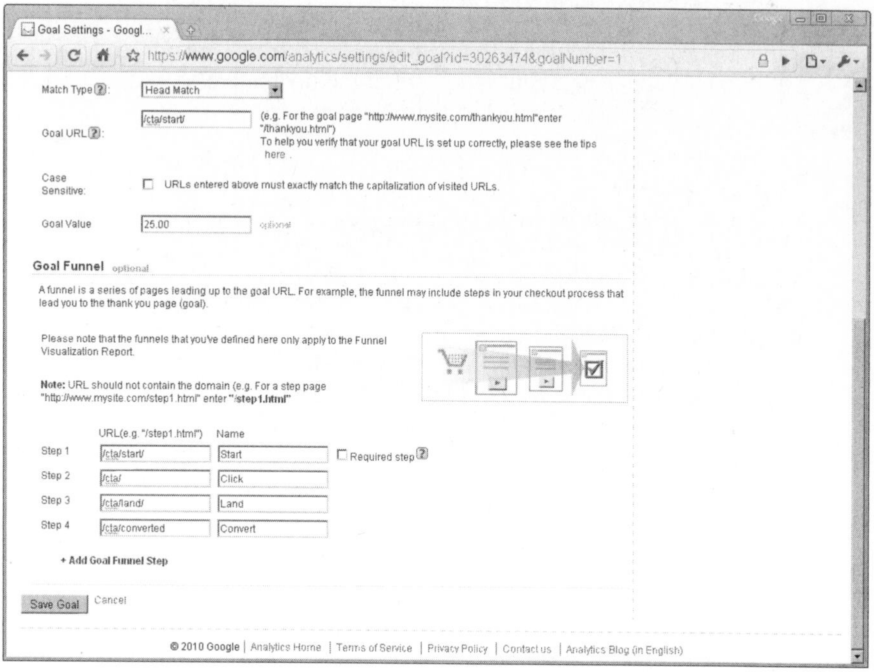

Figure 13-5:
Goal funnel
con-
figuration
in Google
Analytics.

Tracking and reporting calls-to-actions

Over time, you find that some characteristics of your campaigns work much better than others. You can refine your calls-to-action and maximize your click-through rates and conversions. Rotate each element of your calls-to-action and run each one long enough that you get enough pageviews and clicks to recognize whether or not it's working. At minimum, this should be 100 pageviews.

Follow these steps to view campaign performance in Google Analytics:

1. **Log in to Google Analytics. If you don't have an account, refer to the instructions in Chapter 5 for starting a Google Analytics account.**

2. **Navigate to Traffic Sources – Campaigns.**

3. **At the top of the data results table below the charts, select Medium in the first column drop-down filter and the Ad Content in the next drop-down filter.**

4. **Filter the data (at the bottom of the data results table) by entering "cta" in the Filter Campaign field, and then click Go.**

The resulting data set and charts provide you with a list of each of your calls-to-action and their performance.

You should always rotate and test calls-to-action to achieve the best results. Some calls-to-action will test better in specific seasons, during business cycles, when adjacent to specific blog posts, and so on. Always test, measure, and optimize your calls-to-action!

Testing and Improving Your Calls-to-Action Click-Through Rate

Testing is something that is seldom planned with a blogging strategy, but resources should be made available each time you are adjusting your offers and changing your blog's design, the calls-to-action or landing pages. Your analytics package allows you measure click-through rates on calls-to-action. Not testing is simply leaving money on the table!

A great resource for seeing the results of testing and how to improve conversion rates is Which Test Won. (www.whichtestwon.com), The blog pits two versions of a call-to-action, landing page design, or content against one another each week and then compares and contrasts the winners and losers. Anne Holland's blog provides example after example where simple layout, wording, color, and image changes have a drastic impact on conversion rates. (See Figure 13-6.)

Figure 13-6: Anne Holland's Which Test Won provides examples and advice for optimizing your pages and calls-to-action.

Understanding A/B testing versus multivariate testing

Basic testing can be accomplished using analytics and simply rotating your calls-to-action or landing page elements, monitoring the results, and making changes. Advanced testing can automate and speed up this process, providing marketers with increased conversion rates in much shorter periods of time. For advanced testing, there are formal processes and applications to measure and test features on a Web page to monitor the impact and effectiveness of each element.

Two common types of testing are

- ✔ **A/B or Split testing** is when you display two or more versions of a call-to-action or page layout and identify which one received more click-throughs and conversions.

- ✔ **Multivariate** testing typically breaks up the element into different components and randomly displays the components together. This allows you to design multiple headlines, multiple pieces of content, multiple images, and multiple buttons. The optimization software will display combinations of the elements and provide you with statistics on which combinations resulted in the highest click-through rates (CTRs) and conversions.

Multivariate testing is beyond the scope of this book and requires specialized software to execute and measure the campaigns. Professional testing solutions (such as Google Website Optimizer) and enterprise solutions (such as Webtrends Optimize) provide a robust testing interface where you can test multiple elements on a page through multivariate or split tests to see which ones yield the greatest results.

Implementing simple A/B tests with your calls-to-action

Because A/B tests are simply swapping out versions of calls-to-action, you can manually do this once every few weeks and observe activity in Google Analytics. If you're seeing a difference, utilize the version with better results, and begin to test further enhancements with the same styles that appeared to do well.

Don't be shy about calls-to-action. Test multiple calls-to-action on your page in various places:

- ✔ Within the body of your blog posts
- ✔ In multiple locations in your sidebar
- ✔ In your header
- ✔ In your footer

Varying your calls-to-action and placing different actions that serve different visitors is a great practice. Perhaps your visitor is curious but not ready to purchase — can you supply a newsletter subscription where you can keep in touch with them? Maybe your visitor is doing research — can you supply a whitepaper or case study in return for their contact information? If your visitor is ready to purchase, where can they get in direct contact or make the purchase? Feed each customer's intent with a distinctive call-to-action.

Having several calls-to-action at the same time is not uncommon. One visitor may be motivated by the contest giveaway you're having, another may be motivated by the Webinar you're planning in the next few weeks.

Analyzing results and optimizing calls-to-action

In performing A/B testing, you may wish to start with two completely separate calls-to-action, with different images, headlines, benefits, commands, and buttons. If you do this, you should see a difference in the performance of each. The next step is to vary elements on the call-to-action that received the most clicks or conversions. Build a few versions that are nearly alike with only one element switched out.

On a simple call-to-action, you can even test 27 different versions by varying the heading, the content, and the button.

Keep a spreadsheet and run each version of the call-to-action on your site until each version is viewed 1,000 times. Be sure the views are during similar periods of time so that your click-through rate isn't skewed by another factor (such as a holiday weekend that shortens the work week). Don't just measure the calls-to-action by the number of clicks, either. Be sure to associate the conversions associated with each call-to-action. It's absolutely possible to have a low click-through rate on a call-to-action but have a very high conversion rate on those same calls-to-action. You're not in the business of accumulating clicks with a corporate blog, your blog's performance must be based on conversions.

At the end of the testing, you should be able to identify the best heading, best content, and the best button as well as the combination that performs the best.

Targeting calls-to-action

Targeting is essential as well. If the visitor to your blog is a customer, why would you display calls-to-action enticing them to convert? By asking a simple polling question and saving that information in a cookie, you can then serve a dynamic call-to-action to your customer — perhaps an upsell opportunity or registration to the next customer event.

To set a cookie with JavaScript, place the following code in the header of
your blog:

```
<script type="text/javascript">
function Set_Cookie( name, value, expires, path, domain, secure ) {
   // set time, it's in milliseconds
   var today = new Date();
   today.setTime( today.getTime() );

   if ( expires ) {
   expires = expires * 1000 * 60 * 60 * 24;
   }
   var expires_date = new Date( today.getTime() + (expires) );

  document.cookie = name + "=" +escape( value ) +
   ( ( expires ) ? ";expires=" + expires_date.toGMTString() : "" ) +
   ( ( path ) ? ";path=" + path : "" ) +
   ( ( domain ) ? ";domain=" + domain : "" ) +
   ( ( secure ) ? ";secure" : "" );
   }
function Get_Cookie( check_name ) {
   name=value, not the other components
   var a_all_cookies = document.cookie.split( ';' );
   var a_temp_cookie = '';
   var cookie_name = '';
   var cookie_value = '';
   var b_cookie_found = false; // set boolean t/f default f

   for ( i = 0; i < a_all_cookies.length; i++ )
   {
      a_temp_cookie = a_all_cookies[i].split( '=' );
   cookie_name = a_temp_cookie[0].replace(/^\s+|\s+$/g, '');

   if ( cookie_name == check_name ) {
   b_cookie_found = true;

   if ( a_temp_cookie.length > 1 ) {
   cookie_value = unescape( a_temp_cookie[1].replace(/^\s+|\s+$/g, '') );
   }
   return cookie_value;
   break;
   }
   a_temp_cookie = null;
   cookie_name = '';
   }
   if ( !b_cookie_found )
   {
   return null;
   }
}
</script>
```

A simple poll in your sidebar can ask visitors if they are a customer or a new visitor. Clicking the response sets a cookie with an `onclick` event.

```
<input type="radio" name="poll" value="customer" onclick="Set_Cookie( 'type',
            'customer', '', '/', '', '' );return false"/>I'm a customer<br />
<input type="radio" name="poll" value="visitor" onclick="Set_Cookie( 'type',
            'visitor', '', '/', '', '' );return false"/>I'm a visitor
```

By obtaining whether the visitor is a customer, you can then display the appropriate call-to-action.

```
<script type="text/javascript">
if(Get_Cookie('type')=="customer") {
    var customerCTA = "<a href='/landing-page/customer.html'><img src='/call-to-
            action/customer.png' /></a>";
    document.write(customerCTA);
} else {
    var visitorCTA = "<a href='/landing-page/visitor.html'><img src='/call-to-
            action/visitor.png' /></a>";
    document.write(visitorCTA);
}
</script>
```

Personalization is a bit scary, but another great opportunity. If you have someone who registered and attended your last Webinar, perhaps the next step is to display an automated chat that routes them directly to your sales team or a call-to-action that encourages direct communication.

Dynamically Displaying Calls-to-Action to Increase Click-Through Rates

Dynamic content is a method used in the e-mail industry to increase response rates that is moving to Web sites. ExactTarget is an e-mail marketing company with a dynamic content engine, allowing clients to change the message and even images in the e-mail to increase conversion rates. It's an incredibly effective use of technology – placing a relevant offer in front of the right audience.

Dynamic content is now finding its way into Web development. An example might be to track visitors to your site and record whether or not they are a new visitor or a customer. That occurs through the use of cookies — no, not the chocolate chip kind. A *cookie* is a small text file that is saved locally on your computer by your browser.

Increasing click-through rates with relevant calls-to-action

When customers log in to your site, you can place a cookie that saves data about them; perhaps their gender, date of birth, last purchase, and account expiration date. When they return to read your blog, you can display a call-to-action specific to them — an offer for a related product or service, or even a renewal notification.

Dynamic content is also an effective use of search engine traffic. When search engine users click your link, the search engine can tell you what they searched for. If a user who searches for a Dyson vacuum cleaner finds your blog post about the Dyson, for example, display a call-to-action that advertises your latest selection of Dyson vacuum cleaners.

Integrating third-party ad serving systems for your e-commerce blog

Building the code to display content dynamically into your corporate blog can be a complex task and requires development resources, You can associate offers and calls-to-action with search engine keywords, specific browsers, dates and date ranges, day of the week, even the screen resolution your visitor is running. If you capture data about visitors in polls, surveys, registration data, or purchases, you can even dynamically display offers that way.

Third-party ad serving engines can also help. iGoDigital (www.igodigital.com) can target specific products to specific readers of your blog on a variety of data elements. (See Figure 13-7.) Ad service engines can be expensive and typically charge by the number of impressions that your advertisement gets.

An *impression* is a count of the times your advertisement is served to visitors.

Some third-party ad serving engines can also serve calls-to-action based on your activities on other sites. These days, your data is being captured everywhere — by search engines, ad servers, social media sites, and even the software you utilize. That data can be accessed and leveraged to display relevant calls-to-action.

If your company serves business to business (B2B) customers and has an outbound sales team, there are even ways of capturing the companies who are visiting your site. For example, DemandBase (www.demandbase.com) allows you to track the visitors to your site and provides you with the company information based on the Internet Protocol (IP) address they arrived from.

Figure 13-7:
iGoDigital is
an ad server
for the
e-commerce
industry.

Understanding Where Readers Click on a Web Page

Chances are good your blog is written in English. English-speaking countries typically view pages top to bottom and left to right. You'll find that blogs are typically designed with the sidebar is on the right; it's not a coincidence.

Laying out your blog's content to impact retention and conversion

The overall design of your corporate blog can have a significant impact on your readership and conversion rates. Investing in a design that's professional and uses best practices is worthwhile.

Putting the compelling content to the left of your page and the sidebar to the right tells people where to look for what's important.

Putting a call-to-action above the content draws their attention to the call-to-action first, and then your content. Utilize this to your advantage. It could be a quick catch if the visitor is simply browsing and wants additional information.

Placing calls-to-action, either text or images, in-line with your content can draw high click-throughs but may also increase the number of visitors who bounce because of the interruption. A common tactic with publishing sites is trying to get more clicks to make more money not nurture a lead. Use caution when deploying this technique.

Calls-to-action in your sidebar should be laid out in line with your blog posts to the left, putting them into the visitor's field of vision. The blog post should answer the question that the visitor had when they arrived, and the call-to-action should lead them down a path of engagement to becoming a customer.

Although higher on the page is better, don't be afraid to put additional calls-to-action lower on the page or in the footer. (Old school marketers will scream about staying *above-the-fold,* a term that was coined with newspapers for what is printed above and below the fold of the newspaper.)

Luckily, it's easier to scroll down a Web site than to unfold a newspaper. Some e-commerce sites and landing pages that place the actual purchase button at the very base of the page have very high conversion rates. The trick is to test, test, test.

Implementing heat-maps to monitor where readers click

Heat-maps are a tool that provides a visual or graphical representation of where visitors are clicking on your site. These are great tools that provide instantaneous feedback to you on where and how people click on a page. Google Analytics has a Site Overlay tool (see Figure 13-8) that displays either clicks or conversions on your site. The site overlay tool is found in Google Analytics⇨Content⇨Site Overlay This is a great visual method for displaying the activity that's happening on your site as well as where your revenue is coming from.

More robust solutions are available, such as CrazyEgg. CrazyEgg provides a color-coded heat-map (see Figure 13-9) where the click coordinates are captured and areas with high concentrations of clicks are colored red and low concentrations are blue.

You have to actually have something compelling to click on for heatmaps to provide feedback. If you don't have a compelling call-to-action at the base of your page, it may not be the location but the actual design of the call-to-action.

Figure 13-8:
Overlaying
click
statistics
on your blog
in Google
Analytics.

Figure 13-9:
Viewing a
heatmap in
CrazyEgg to
find where
activity is
occurring
on your
blog.

Figuring out what elements are important

Keep notes on each of your campaigns in a spreadsheet, including the campaign name, run dates, call-to-action used, colors, buttons, title, message, and so on. The three metrics you want to measure with respect to calls-to-action are the number of pageviews, the number of clicks, and the number of conversions associated with each specific call-to-action.

This helps you test different headlines, different benefits, different commands and different buttons independently and leads you to design combinations that result in the most traffic and conversions. You may even want to implement a path of multiple landing pages that ask different questions so that you can prequalify visitors and supply the right interaction.

Test and measure your calls-to-action for the click-throughs they receive and the conversions. Having a large volume of click-throughs versus conversions may be a message that your landing page needs some work. You were able to get them that far, so continue optimizing.

It's okay for you to move backward. If you push a new call-to-action live and aren't seeing any results, pull it and rework the offer. Don't waste time; maximize every visit!

Chapter 14

Leading Your Readers through Landing Pages

In This Chapter

▶ Understanding landing pages

▶ Designing landing pages that convert visitors into customers

▶ Testing and measuring landing page performance

A *landing page* is a destination where you want to lead your readers. The landing page could be a subscription form for a newsletter, a contact form, a request form for your sales department, a registration form for a Webinar or an event, a submission form to a poll or survey, or even a shopping cart page where visitors complete their purchase.

Landing pages are an extremely important element when designing a blog, a Web site, or an e-commerce application. The landing page is the finish line in the journey your visitors take.

For corporate blogging, the landing page is critical because a blog is a publishing engine. Blogs and blogging platforms weren't designed to optimize conversions, they were built to automate and efficiently publish content to the Web.

As a result, the use of calls-to-action and landing pages has been an effective means of building an inbound marketing strategy for a company. The visitor finds the content, reads the content, decides to do business, clicks a compelling, well-designed call-to-action, and converts through an effective landing page.

Designing a Landing Page That Closes the Conversion

As a destination, landing pages must be optimized to attract visitors, capture their information, and lead them to conversion. All the elements of a landing page are critical — the layout, the use of images and video, the design and length of forms, and the conversion point.

A *conversion* is a step in the process that visitors take to engage with you further. Search engine conversions occur when users click a search engine result to arrive at your blog. *Call-to-action conversions* happen when a reader clicks a call-to-action.

A *landing page conversion* occurs when someone completes the step you want them to on the landing page. Typically, the landing page conversion occurs when the visitor submits details via some kind of form by clicking a button or image that represents a button.

Be sure to test, measure and optimize your landing page, just as you do for calls-to-action, as described in Chapter 13. Most companies simply leave up and running a landing page that was designed with their site or blog. By testing, your company can significantly improve your conversion rates.

James Paden is a conversion optimization expert with Vibrant Solutions. James scoured the Internet and did a blog post on some amazing case studies for companies who tested, measured, and optimized their landing pages. In some cases, companies more than doubled their signups or sales. You can find those studies in this Web article:

```
http://marketingtechblog.com/blogging/the-power-of-
              conversion-optimization
```

Many companies have experienced Web designers who have impressive backgrounds in user experience and design, but come up short when it actually comes to conversions. Don't trust your conversion optimization to gut instinct and experience. Using analytics (discussed in Chapter 15), test and optimize your landing pages.

Designing the path from a call-to-action to a landing page

Your blog provided the authority and trust that led a visitor to click your call-to-action. The call-to-action had a simple message that provided insight into the benefits of doing business with your organization. Chapter 9 discusses how to design and implement calls-to-action.

If your blog has more than one call-to-action, you should have accompanying landing pages. If you attempt to cut some corners and build a universal landing page to capture every call-to-action, you won't get the results you hope for.

The goal of the call-to-action is to capture the attention of the visitor and provide them with a path to engagement onto a landing page via the content you write — and ultimately *converting* them from a reader into a customer. To optimize this path, your readers should feel the progression is natural. The calls-to-action should be relevant to the content and compelling. The landing page should be targeted, well-written, and effective.

Checking out the elements of an effective landing page strategy

The five basic elements of an effective landing page strategy are

- ✔ **Design:** Typically, the design uses a visual element (such as a logo or header) that incorporates the same design that the related call-to-action has. Maintaining the integrity of the design is important so that the user recognizes that they arrived at the correct destination.

- ✔ **Message:** Providing a compelling message that entices the reader into completing the form is essential to increasing the conversions. When you write the message, ask yourself, "Why would I click?" If your answer to that question is rich content, folks will click.

- ✔ **Form:** Form design is typically where visitors will make the decision to proceed forward or abandon the process. A form that requests too much information can drive visitors away and a form that doesn't request enough information may leave your sales team without the necessary information they need. Your form may also have a couple of questions that prequalify the prospect, such as how soon they would like to make a purchase or how large their budget is. Strike a careful balance when designing an online form.

- ✔ **Offer:** The offer is the value proposition that you are offering to the visitor. It's the motivating factor for them to actually submit the form. Your offer may be to simply educate them, or it might be to actually reward them. One of Compendium Blogware's most active offerings is a fifty-dollar gift card.

- ✔ **Action:** The action is most likely a form submission. If your form is a purchase, it's the button that completes the sale. If your form is for a Webinar registration, it's the button that submits the registration information.

Knowing your landing page goals and tactics

The landing page strategy has to accomplish three goals for the visitor to fully convert:

- ✔ Provide additional insight into the benefits that you've teased the visitor with an accompanying call-to-action. If you view your landing page and it has navigation, information, or any other element that is not relevant to the precise benefit that you are proposing, you haven't met the goal.

- ✔ Provide a form to capture the conversion or the necessary information to provide your sales team to sell your product or service. On an e-commerce blog, this may simply be the shopping cart page where the person enters credit card information to make the purchase.

- ✔ Provide confirmation after the form is submitted that the visitor has completed the transaction and set expectations on what will happen next. Will someone be in touch? Will the order be shipped? Is there an alternative e-mail or phone number to supply prospects with in the event they need to speak to someone from your company immediately?

A common tactic for increasing landing page conversions is to minimize the number of elements and the number of actions that a visitor has to make. This doesn't necessarily mean that you should minimize the actual landing page, though. Many landing pages with very high conversion rates are actually quite long. Some multi-page processes also work to simplify the conversion process.

Simplicity is key. Your landing page should be enough to acquire the conversion and qualify your lead but never more. After you create a baseline for measuring your conversion rates, try adjusting the elements and adding things like video, audio, images, and customer quotes and then measure the responses against how your standard form performed.

Laying out your landing page

People read from top to bottom left to right, and elements of a page should be laid out the same (see Figure 14-1). The whitespace techniques (described in Chapter 9) that you use for blogging are also effective for landing page design.

- ✔ Leave a moderate space around images so text is not running into them.

- ✔ Keep your paragraphs short.

- ✔ Use bulleted or numbered lists.

✔ Use headings and subheadings to break up the page.

✔ Bold terms that you wish to stand out to the visitor who's reading the page.

While you may want to defy the odds and layout your page differently, start with a best practice approach and then test against it. You may feel that a very different page acquires more customers, but test and measure against the standard to find out.

Figure 14-1:
A standard landing page layout that uses best practices.

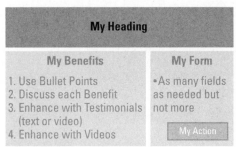

Let visitors know what to expect when they submit their form. If you're going to have a sales representative reach out, then let them know. If they are going to receive a package, let them know how to track it. If they are going to receive a download or a whitepaper, let them know that the directions will be provided to them in an e-mail.

Oh, and be sure to thank them! Courtesy is important when it comes to working with prospects on the Internet.

Narrowing the Focus with Your Landing Page's Content

An effective landing page is designed without extraneous navigation, alternative navigation, alternative product links to click, or widgets and gadgets that dissuade or distract the visitor from what you want them to do. The only action that a prospect should take on an effective landing page is completing the conversion.

Two elements to keep on your landing page are your phone number and a link to a contact form (see Figure 14-2). In the event someone has difficulties with your landing page or it doesn't provide the exact information they require, these are appropriate back-ups. Publishing your e-mail address on a landing page may also be an option, but publish it as an image instead of text — that way the spammers of the world can't harvest it from your page.

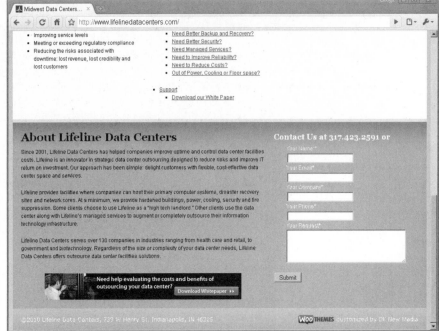

Figure 14-2:
Lifeline Data
Center's
blog design
has a footer
with a
contact
form on
every page.

A contact form is something that you'll want to keep obvious on all pages. The contact form may be your greatest means of converting visitors to customers on a blog.

A common design pattern seen on the Web now is a footer. Large footers can provide you with enough room to have a contact form on every page.

Understanding how much information is enough

The central theme of your landing page is to convert your visitor. As such, all information available on a landing page should be targeted toward only that benefit.

Many companies try to fill their landing pages with every product, service, feature, or functionality. They are attempting to cover all the bases. This is a mistake. A landing page isn't a selling brochure. The person landed there because they followed a specific path of engagement. They may have done a very specific search, landed on a very specific blog post, clicked a relevant call-to-action, and now wish to do business with you — all because they were able to follow the specific path you developed.

Providing different options and alternatives to the discrete path is distracting, and may even allow your prospective customer to disqualify themselves based on too much information. It's fairly common for companies to err on the side of huge, complex Web sites with tons of information about their products and services. This is an approach that is frustrating for readers.

The typical visitor to your blog has a question. Providing the answer builds credibility with your reader. Providing an option for your reader to connect with your company to get the answer through a conversion is a great way to grow your business online.

Trading information for benefits to capture inbound marketing leads

Your blog is an incredible social media platform for connecting with visitors online. When you provide tips, tricks, best practices, industry news, and customer success stories via your blog, you're providing a free service to your audience without asking them for any compensation or expectation.

A common mistake of blogs is to post a download page and provide incredibly robust and detailed product, pricing, and other information without any requirement of the visitor to register with your company. Your blog is free — providing further content should require your visitor to give a bit of their information.

Trade content for data. Offering a trade for visitor information is a strategy that works well. Set an expectation with your visitors that, if they provide you with some personal contact information, you'll provide them with the additional content they're seeking. In a company with an inside sales team, this is the contact information the team needs to reach out and connect with prospective customers.

Providing contact info is nothing new to the Internet. Visitors understand that in the online world they have to give to get. It's important that you set accurate expectations of the content you're making available and then meet those expectations. If you don't, your visitors may feel ripped off and you could have a public relations problem on your hands.

Providing downloads for registration

If you're a software company and can build or provide demonstrations, add-ins, or plug-ins for your application, providing a registration form is a great way of capturing details on your application usage and finding new leads for your sales team.

You don't have to have a complex solution developed for delivering these downloads. A simple form, using a third party form designer like Formstack (www.Formstack.com), can simplify your effort. Simply add an auto-response e-mail to the form that has a specific link to download the necessary files.

Providing whitepapers for registration

Whitepaper is a keyword that is often used in searches when businesses are evaluating industries and vendors on the Internet. If your visitors are comparing vendors, evaluating products or exploring companies, they may be searching for relevant whitepapers.

If, for example, you're an IT management firm, you may want to publish a series of whitepapers on outsourcing your IT; whitepapers on security; whitepapers on industry solutions; and whitepapers on evaluating an IT vendor. When prospects search for information on these topics, they'll find your whitepapers — making you the expert and increasing the chances that you'll be their next vendor.

Having a complete list of industry whitepapers available for download (through a landing page) can get your company found (see Figure 14-3). Be sure to write a blog post each time you publish a whitepaper and describe the purpose, the industry, and where visitors can register and download the whitepaper from (the landing page).

Whitepapers educate the visitor. Perhaps your visitor is simply doing some research for their company to acquire statistics and information on your industry. Providing a robust, informative whitepaper, gives you an edge on your competition.

You can also tailor a whitepaper to your company's strengths. If your competitive advantage is providing a great return on investment (ROI), focus on how important ROI is. If your advantage is your product design, focus on how easy your product is to use and how the industry has awarded you.

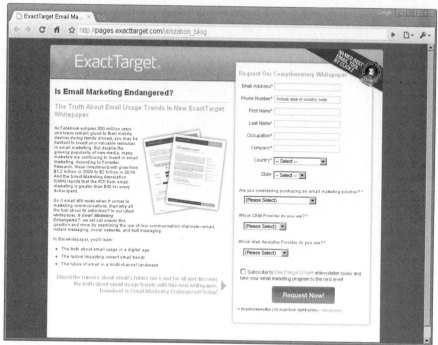

Figure 14-3:
Exact
Target's
landing
page on
e-mail
marketing's
future.

Writing an effective whitepaper takes a bit more effort than writing a blog post. Like a blog post, each whitepaper should have a very specific goal. A whitepaper is much more comprehensive than a blog post, though. Your whitepaper should have the following components:

- **Introduction:** Explain the issue, introduce your company, and say why you're an authority on the topic.

- **Overview:** Provide the reader with an expectation of the whitepaper's content and any opinions you're going to discuss.

- **Supporting information:** Provide as much detailed information, with supporting data, about the issue and the arguments to support your opinion if you've provided one.

- **Why it matters:** Visitors download whitepapers because they want to educate themselves or make an educated evaluation. Provide the details on why this whitepaper matters to their business.

- **Conclusion:** Reinforce the premise of your argument or the lessons learned from your whitepaper. Provide additional information on who to contact and any resources cited within the document.

Sometimes working within the industry, companies tend to overcomplicate their whitepapers by using industry-specific terminology and acronyms. Have a customer or prospective buyer read your whitepaper and provide you with feedback. Is it compelling? Would they want to do business with you after reading it? If the answer is yes, put it on the landing page and get some leads.

After your whitepaper is written, it may be a good idea to work with a designer to optimize the figures and brand the whitepaper with your company. If the whitepaper is distributed, it should be both professional and credited to your company.

Providing case studies for registration

Although whitepapers are about educating prospects, *case studies* provide distinct examples of customer success through the use of your products or services. Your case study should have the following elements:

- ✔ **Title:** Provide a title that is results-driven. Using numerical results adds that extra punch that compels prospective customers to engage with your company. An example might be *Managed search engine marketing services result in a 70% drop in cost per lead.*

- ✔ **Overview:** Your overview should be a discreet summary of the problem and the solution you provided.

- ✔ **Problem:** Provide a detailed explanation of the problem.

- ✔ **Solution:** Define how your product or services solved the problem.

Within your case study, use facts, figures, and quotes directly from the client (with a photo or business logo of them) to fully detail the problem and solution. Be sure to provide a closing paragraph that incorporates details on how the reader can contact your company for additional details or wishes to make a purchase.

Providing Webinars

Webinars provide a safe means for attendees to engage with your company without strong-arm sales techniques. Webinars are much less expensive than purchasing booth space at conferences or paying for travel expenses, so prospects often attend Webinars. The combination of audio and a presentation make the Webinar easily consumable as well.

Here are a few tips for creating effective Webinars:

- ✔ **Select a controversial, timely, or compelling topic.** A great topic gets attention.

- ✔ **Promote.** Discuss the Webinar on your blog and invite people via LinkedIn, Facebook, and other social event systems.

✔ **Start and end your presentation on time.** Some attendees will show up late so make the first couple minutes a discussion about the Webinar's purpose, or take the opportunity to do a small audience poll that you can discuss later during the Webinar.

✔ **Use a moderator.** The moderator runs the show, introduces you, and captures any questions or comments throughout the Webinar. As the speaker, you don't want to have to worry about all the details; you want to entertain and educate the attendees.

✔ **Offer follow-up.** Your closing slide should always provide how the attendee can engage with your company, but you may wish to offer your attendees a distinct offer, discount, or download, too.

Your presentation should be very simple to follow: one idea per slide, not too many slides, stay on target, and lots of examples. Telling stories is the most effective method to make your point (in blog posts, too!).

Presentations make fantastic blog posts. With one idea per slide, and ten or so slides, you've got a dozen blog posts: a post to advertise the Webinar; ten content posts (one idea per slide); and a post that wraps up and pulls it all together.

Capturing the Right Amount of Info on Your Landing Page

Asking for too much information can kill your conversion rates, but the right number of fields can improve conversion rates and provide a sense of whether visitors are good prospects. Strike a careful balance between what you want to know and what you need to know. Remember, you can always ask for more information later — but asking for too much information at first can frustrate your visitor who then will abandon the process.

If you're developing the form yourself, be sure to use JavaScript validation techniques that make your form simple to use. If you require a phone number in a specific format, use code to produce that format automatically when the person enters the information. There's nothing as frustrating as fixing formats and required fields repeatedly to resubmit a form. Make it simple and obvious.

Requesting the right amount of information

Only ask for enough information to contact the prospect or make a conversion. If your landing page is a subscription form, ask for enough information to get the subscription started, but nothing more. You can always ask your prospects for more information later. Asking for it all up front is a great way to intimidate your readers and scare them away.

Don't ask for more than you need. Think about what you're using the information for and the minimum amount needed for the purpose of tracking and prequalifying your prospects.

Prequalification is a technique that's used on forms to measure the intent and urgency of the visitor. Some visitors will happen across your blog casually and may complete your registration process simply to attend a Webinar, download a whitepaper, or view case studies. If you have a busy sales team, you don't want to waste their time making appointment after appointment with visitors who are never going to purchase.

Other visitors are truly researching for their next purchase and have both intent and the budget to make the purchase. Asking a couple questions on your form can help you filter and prioritize the leads that are ready to do business with your company. Ask such questions as:

- Do you have budget set aside for this?
- How soon are you going to make a decision?
- Would you like a demonstration?
- Would you like our sales team to contact you?

These questions provide you with information about the prospect. Those that have budget, those making an immediate decision, those wanting a demo or sales to contact them are prequalified leads. The questions help your lead qualification team sort your leads and prepare for a sales call.

Landing page forms are a perfect opportunity to ask your prospects whether they wish to subscribe to your e-mail announcements or newsletter. E-mail is a proven method for putting you in touch with a prospect multiple times and keeping your business in mind when the prospect is ready to make a purchase. A simple check box on your subscription form that opts prospects in is all that is needed (see Figure 14-4). Default the check box to Yes and be sure to pass an identifier to your e-mail system that the lead came from the blog.

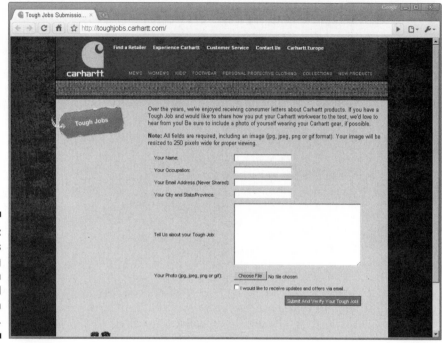

Figure 14-4:
Carharrt's
landing
page with
an e-mail
subscription
opt-in.

Your form's abandonment rate will skyrocket if you ask for too much information at first. If you require a lot of information, break it up into multiple steps and provide the visitor with feedback on what step they're at.

As long as you break up the steps into short forms and provide the user with feedback, you should be able to sustain a higher conversion rate. If you're using steps, be sure visitors know what step they're on and how many steps are in the process (*Step 1 of 4,* for example).

Abandonment is the measure of how many visitors landed on your page versus actually completing the form. You will want to monitor this with your analytics package. Adjust your form fields and messaging and test, test, test. Using landing page optimization software, such as Optimize, can provide you with multivariate and split testing, which we discuss in Chapter 13.

Integrating your landing pages with your CRM

Most customer relationship management (CRM) systems offer the opportunity to capture leads from Web forms. Contact your customer relationship management provider for documentation. Salesforce, for example, a well-known CRM platform, includes a method called Web to Lead with their enterprise offering.

Developing your landing page form to post directly to your CRM system takes some proficiency and isn't the job for a beginner. Mapping fields is the process by which you program your form to submit and capture specific form fields in specific record fields in your CRM system. You map form fields to a field within Salesforce to capture your landing page conversions. You can even map the prequalification questions (if you have any) and set your sales team's processes in motion. Contact your CRM vendor for additional details because this will differ with each system.

Doing this provides your company with a clear picture of how your customers acquired through the blog compare to those acquired through other means. Measure their value and their retention. You might find that your blog attracts a lot of leads, but they aren't high value or retaining well. Therefore, you can change your offer and your message accordingly.

Using third-party form solutions to capture information

Designing and implementing forms that capture data is not an easy process. It requires a Web server, development resources, and a secure database. If your company doesn't have the budget or resources to do this, some fantastic third-party tools on the market allow you to build forms and integrate them seamlessly.

Formstack (www.formstack.com) is a subscription-based application that can help you manage your data, send auto responders, and submit form submissions securely to all the people that need the data (see Figure 14-5). The Formstack application provides you with code or HTML to embed in the landing page, or you can even use the end form *as* the landing page.

Follow these steps to build a registration form with Formstack:

1. **After you log in to Formstack, click Create a New Form (see Figure 14-6).**

2. **Name your form.**

3. **Select a pre-built contact form and then click Next Step.**

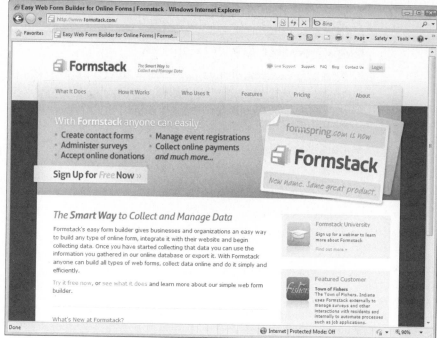

Figure 14-5:
Formstack provides a form builder for contact forms, event registration, purchasing, downloads, and other uses.

Figure 14-6:
Creating a form with Formstack.

4. **Click Add Field on the bottom toolbar and then select Short Answer.**

5. **Check the Required option and label the field** *Company Name.*

6. **Click Save.**

7. **Move the Company Name field below the Name fields by grabbing the far right direction icon and dragging the field up (see Figure 14-7).**

8. **Unless your company requires it, delete the Address and Home Phone section by clicking the red X on each.**

9. **Click Work Phone and enable the Required field.**

10. **Click Save.**

11. **Click Next Step**

12. **Select a style for your form.**

13. **Click Next Step.**

Your form is ready to use! Formstack supplies you with a link or code that you can copy and paste into your landing page (see Figure 14-8).

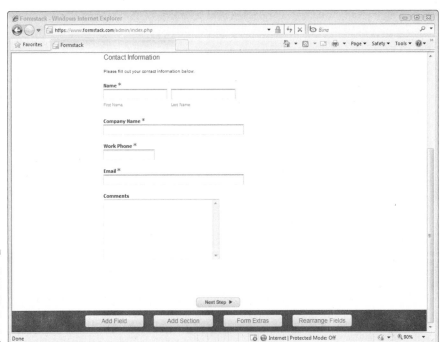

Figure 14-7:
Adding and adjusting fields in Formstack.

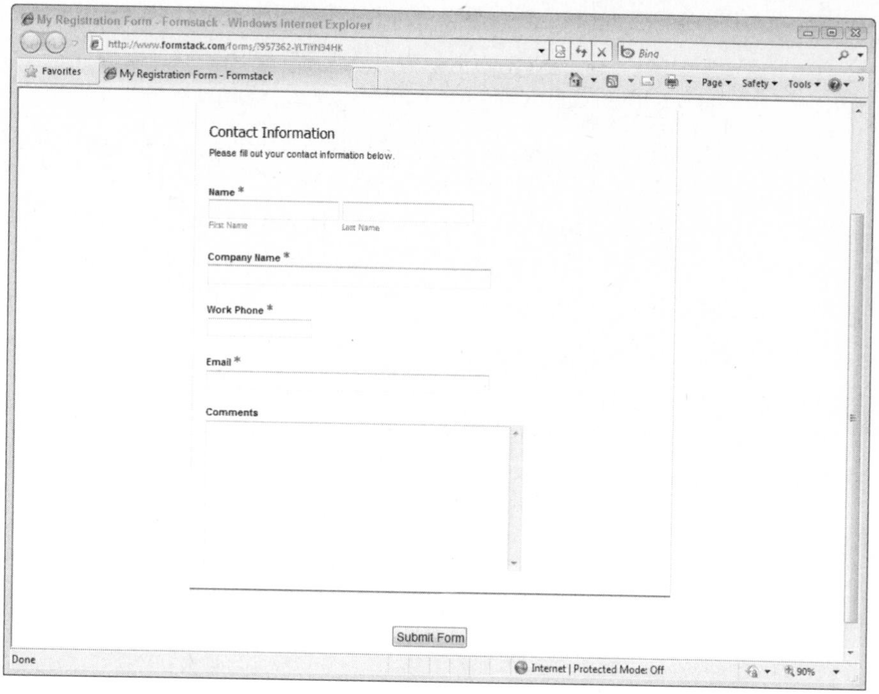

Figure 14-8:
A simple contact form completed using Formstack.

Formstack can integrate with CampaignMonitor, Email Center Pro, ExactTarget, FreshBooks, Google Apps, Highrise, MailChimp, Salesforce.com, and TypePad. If you want your data saved to any of these applications, select the option on your form entries. Formstack also has a host of other integration tools.

If you're using a WordPress blog, Gravity Forms (www.gravityforms.com) is a plug-in with extensive capabilities that stores the data in your WordPress database.

While implementing your landing page strategy, be sure to allow it enough time to gather visitors (in the hundreds or thousands) so that you can accurately validate the findings of testing different versions. You can attempt wholesale design changes on your landing pages from time to time, but try to keep your process logical.

Test different layouts, headings, images, colors, buttons, and prices. Always keep the design congruent with your call-to-actions and overall branding of your company.

Chapter 15

Measuring Success with Analytics

In This Chapter

▶ Understanding standard analytics metrics

▶ Setting analytics goals

▶ Setting the value of a blog post

▶ Monitoring shortened links

▶ Monitoring feeds and RSS subscribers

*A*side from your blogging platform, your analytics application is important when building a successful corporate blogging strategy. Analytics provide you insight into your visitors; specifically, how they are getting to your blog, what they are reading on your blog, and what actions they are taking while they visit your blog.

There are several analytics platforms on the market to choose from, including the following:

- **Alterian Webjourney** (www.alterian.com/products/web-analytics): Enterprise-level analytics application

- **Clicky** (www.getclicky.com): Optimized for small blogs with real-time statistics

- **CoreMetrics** (www.coremetrics.com): Enterprise-level analytics application

- **Google Analytics** (www.google.com/analytics): Free analytics application from Google

- **Omniture** (www.omniture.com): Enterprise-level analytics application

- **Webtrends** (www.webtrends.com): Enterprise-level analytics application

- **Yahoo** (http://web.analytics.yahoo.com): Small business-level analytics application

By recording and observing your blogs' visitors, you will have insight into how to improve your blog to increase overall visitor volume and conversions.

It's important to note that the majority of companies never fully leverage analytics. Most companies keep an eye on statistics but never actually take action based on the results. This is an enormous opportunity for your business to learn how to improve its marketing efforts.

This chapter covers the important things you need to know about your analytics software, the best metrics to track, and the ways to interpret the information your software gives you.

Implementing an Analytics Solution That Works

The key to improving your blogging will always come down to how you measure success. As you dive into blogging, your analytics application or applications will provide you with the insight you need to adjust your strategy or continue steamrolling ahead with sales, fame, and fortune.

To get this insight, many companies prefer to use freebie analytics applications, such as Google Analytics. Google Analytics does a fine job, but it has a rather steep learning curve for the average user, has some fairly confusing metrics, and doesn't measure some significant metrics.

Also, companies often fail to include their feed's consumption in their analysis. Google Analytics does not track feed metrics, so you need to sign up for an account with FeedBurner, also owned by Google. Unfortunately, there's no integration between the two to provide you with all the readership and subscriber data in a single spot.

You'll also need to be able to closely monitor your blog's effect on Web site traffic, e-commerce traffic, conversions, and overall business revenue. Most of those features won't come standard with an analytics package, either, so you might want to invest in a great analytics package with the support and education you need or put aside some budget to invest in an analytics consultant to come help you get set up.

Analytics applications were never designed for blogs. Most analytics programs were developed when people arrived at your site through your home page and then navigated through the site. As e-commerce went mainstream, analytics adjusted and added tracking data for shopping carts. As search engines became more prominent for driving traffic, analytics applications adjusted and started to track search data down to the keyword. Blogs, however, work in a different way than the average Web site. Blogs publish content in multiple places — on the home page, in category pages, in tag pages, in author pages, and on the single posts page. On any given blog, there are several ways that visitors can navigate and find your content.

Analytics applications were typically server-side installed packages that tracked through your server. However, SaaS analytics providers have become prominent now in the market. There's no application to install or maintain — you simply paste some code in the footer of your page, and you're up and running.

Analytics applications aren't there to tell you every detail on every visitor; instead, they capture as much information as possible to provide you with enough information to make decisions. In most instances, the trend is more important than the actual counts. How many visits you had today isn't as important as how many more visitors you had today compared with yesterday, last week, last month, and this time last year.

 Analytics applications like Google Analytics don't capture every visitor to your blog. Analytics works by saving data in *cookies,* which are stored files that your browser can access, and then relaying that data through code executed via JavaScript. The data passed is actually from your visitors' browser directly to your analytics provider, not through your server.

If you have visitors that block cookies, clear cookies, or disable JavaScript in their browser, you're probably not tracking them. As a result, if you run ten different analytics packages on your blog, no two will report data the same way.

Translating Statistics to Improve Your Strategy

Analytics allows you to monitor every element of your blogging strategy so you can decipher the results and take action to make improvements. Analytics applications have evolved over the years, too. Although many analytics applications simply monitor the basics — the number of visitors, the most popular pages, the volume of bounces, and pageviews — modern analytics vendors are providing integrated social media measurement, such as e-mail tracking, real-time statistics, robust integration platforms, alert systems, and much, much more.

Analytics allow bloggers and platforms to evolve. Based on readership and conversion rates, platforms can dynamically change related posts, calls-to-action, and landing pages.

Which metrics should you track? The following sections describe the available metrics in most analytics applications and how to use them to improve your blogging.

Tracking visits and visitors

At the root of all blog analysis is whether you have a growing or shrinking audience. Understanding your visitors, whether they are new or returning, and how to adjust your strategy to impact this is key to expanding your audience, and ultimately your business online. Here are a few metrics to track regarding visits and visitors:

- **Visits:** A visit is any detected visit to your blog. Total visits is a great way to see how your blog is performing over periods of time. To increase the number of visits without increasing your audience, you may experiment with writing more posts per week or even per day. If you post once a week, your visitors will visit once a week, but if you post once a day, visitors will return more often. As well, you'll have more pages indexed by search engines — increasing your opportunity to be found and visited.

  By posting content throughout the day, those who follow or subscribe to your blog will return more often. You may increase the number of visits and decrease the time needed to actually convert a customer.

- **New Visits:** A *new visit* is a visit made to your blog that was never detected before. This could be a visit from someone who typed your Web address, clicked a search engine result, or clicked a link on another site.

  Analyzing how new visits are getting to your blog is a great way to increase your traffic. For example, if links from social media sites, such as Twitter, are providing you with a lot of new visits, you may want to promote your blog more on Twitter.

- **Returning Visits:** *Returning visits* are visits made from visitors who have been to your blog at least once before. Your returning visitors are important because they are your reader base. They may be industry experts, customers, prospects who haven't decided to purchase, or your own employees. Growing your base is a great way to grow authority in your industry.

  Some companies that are always after new visits don't ignore returning visitors because they may be fans who will echo the company's posts across the Web. If a majority of your visits are returning visitors, you may wish to poll them to see whether they are already customers. If they are, writing to that audience could be a great retention strategy for keeping them as customers.

- **Visitor:** Someone who visits your blog. If they visit your blog three times in a day, they are counted as one visitor with three visits to your blog.

  Maximize visits by writing compelling, relevant blog posts more often. Don't go too far, though. If you begin writing too often, your audience may not be able to keep up and readership may actually decline.

✔ **Unique Visitor:** If a visitor visits your blog several times from the same browser, they will be counted only one time as a unique visitor. Unique visitor counts are often exaggerated because people clear cookies or visit from multiple computers.

Observe the overall trend on unique visitors and watch whether they're increasing. The new visitors who are unique are your prospects!

This metric can differ depending on the application, however. See the section, "Observing trends and opportunities in reporting data," later in this chapter.

✔ **Loyalty:** Visitor *loyalty* is the number of times within a measured period that visitors return to your blog. You'll probably find while you gain search engine traffic that the number of visitors who visit only one time is very, very high. That's common.

Keep an eye on visitor loyalty. If visitors are returning only two or three times, you may have to increase the quality of your writing and put some very compelling offers out to attract them to convert.

Your subscriber count on your feed and the subscriber count on an e-mail delivering your content are very effective metrics for loyalty as well. Feedburner can supply you with subscriber counts on your feed. Your e-mail service provider will have list counts.

✔ **Recency:** Recency measures how frequently your visitors return to your blog. As with loyalty, keep an eye on this. This provides feedback regarding the desire of visitors to return to your blog over time.

Writing great content may keep them coming back within one to three days. If you see that recency is closer to seven days, then you may want to try to write more often to get people returning or write great posts once a week or so to meet their expectations.

Tracing site references and visitor traffic

Understanding how people are finding and getting to your blog is critical to determine which sources you should be investing the most time and effort in. Don't just keep an eye on the number of visits from these sources, be sure to monitor conversions as well. A site like Digg can send you hundreds of thousands of visitors — but if none make a single purchase, it's not a source worth developing. Here are a few metrics to track to trace your site references:

✔ **Referring Site:** A referring site is any site outside of a search engine where a visitor clicks a link that sends them to your site. Keep an eye on referring sites, sometimes they may be people clicking comments that you submitted to other blogs.

Writing a compelling comment on another blog that has huge volumes of traffic is a great way to find new readers. Referring sites may also provide you with some great opportunities to sponsor or advertise. If you see great traffic and conversions coming from an industry blog, you may look into sponsoring some posts or advertising on their blog.

✔ **Search Engine Traffic:** Search engines are the one source of traffic that you can definitely affect. You can't make other sites link to you, but a comprehensive search engine strategy can skyrocket your traffic.

Pay close attention to the keywords that are driving traffic and conversions to your blog and continue to build strategies around them. Using different combinations of keywords and synonymous phrases can expand and attract more long-tail searches that drive business to your blog.

Note: You discover a lot about keyword targeting and optimizing your blog for search engines throughout Part III.

✔ **Direct Traffic:** Direct traffic is traffic from people who have saved your blog as their browser home page, clicked links from software other than browsers, or typed in your Web address.

You can increase the volume of direct traffic to your blog by promoting your blog aggressively. Promote your blog in all your distributed marketing materials, billing materials, business cards, e-mail signatures, and signage. You can even use a service like Skinit (www.skinit.com) to build a custom skin for your laptop that promotes your business — include your blog URL.

✔ **Keywords:** *Keywords* are the combinations of words used in searches that have brought visitors to your site from a search engine results page (SERP). Keywords are important for gaining exposure and visits from search engines. Keywords will also provide you with feedback on whether you are being found for the terms that are relevant to your business.

If you review your analytics and find keywords that aren't relevant, ensure your blog theme is optimized well and that you are using relevant keywords effectively in post titles, meta descriptions, headings, subheadings, page titles, blog titles, alternative text tags for images, title tags on anchor text, and content.

✔ **Campaigns:** *Campaigns* are typically custom codes added to Web addresses that indicate to the analytics application that someone arrived to your site from a specific link distributed for a campaign. Some sites and applications, such as Twitter, FeedBurner, and MailChimp, will automatically add campaign codes so that you can track people clicking from Twitter, your feed, or your e-mails.

Use campaign codes in e-mail and really simple syndication (RSS) feeds so you understand where visitors are coming from and how well they convert on your blog. Attach the necessary code to each one of your calls-to-action to track campaigns in your analytics campaign tracking, too, so you can monitor the performance of your campaign independently.

Measuring pageviews and bounce rates

The behavior your visitors take once they reach your site is important. Ultimately, your goal is to design a blog and write content compelling enough that visitors spend more time on your site to find additional information. Once they find value, the chances of them engaging with your company increases. Here are some metrics to track to measure pageviews and bounce rates:

✔ **Pageviews:** If a visitor clicks and reads three pages on your blog, that's three pageviews. Many companies view pageviews as an important element that indicates a visitor's overall interest in your blog. A blog, however, is typically attracting someone who is interested in that single post — so you may not see high pageviews.

To increase advertising revenues, some major blogs break up blog posts into two or more pages. This increases the number of pageviews, makes it easier to display more advertisements, and feigns the actual interest visitors have. The real question for you is whether there is a correlation between pageviews and conversions. If conversions go up with pageviews, then you may want to try to impact pageviews.

On blogs, often providing links to related blog posts can increase pageviews as well. If you're writing on a topic often, providing links can draw visitors' attention to those posts and keep them on your blog. If you can keep them around longer, they may convert better.

✔ **Pages per Visit/Depth of Visit:** The number of blog pages each visitor reads in a single session is known as the Pages per Visit. Depth of Visit tells you what percentages of your visitors read the provided ranges of pages. As with *pageviews* and the other metrics, keep an eye on your analytics and determine whether there is a correlation between conversions and pages per visit.

✔ **Bounce Rate:** A *bounce* is recorded when a visitor arrives at your blog, doesn't visit any other page on your blog, and leaves. That's a single page per visit.

It seems every company is possessed with reduction of bounce rates. As with pageviews, the real question is whether bounce rates correlate to your conversions. If you have a single blog post that is promoted highly on a social bookmarking engine, like StumbleUpon, you could see huge volumes of visits and your bounce rate skyrocket. That's not necessarily indicative of a problem.

High volumes of search engine traffic with keywords that aren't relevant to your business can also cause high bounce rates. Of course, irrelevant traffic can still draw attention to your blog and eventual conversions. You may find your time better spent concentrating on improving your conversion rate than trying to decrease your bounce rate.

Related posts can also help with bounce rates. Because related posts are typically filtered through tags or keywords, a visitor landing on your blog searching for a specific keyword may not find it in the immediate post they've landed on — but may find it in other related posts.

✔ **Time on Site/Length of Visit:** The amount of time a visitor spends on your site is very important because it provides you with how long you have to grab the visitor's attention. It's very common for visitors to browse by clicking a link, scanning the page, and clicking off the page immediately.

With very low times on site, you may want to work on breaking up your posts with subheadings, bullet points, lists, and bold terms to capture the reader's attention and help him dig in further.

Evaluating overall performance

The behavior of the visitor on your site provides you with information regarding which elements are important, which elements aren't necessary or need to be optimized. Tracking this helps you continuously improve your ongoing blogging strategy. Here are some metrics to track in this category:

✔ **Site Overlay:** Google Analytics offers a site overlay that overlays statistics on each of the links on your blog to provide you with feedback on which links are getting clicked the most. On a static Web site, this is more critical than on a blog because a blog's content may be changing every day (each time you publish a post).

Viewing the positions of your calls-to-action with the site overlay is an effective way of viewing their performance with regard to their placement on the page, though. You may find that your topmost call-to-action performs the best — so combining your best performing call-to-action with the best positioning on the page can increase overall conversions.

✔ **Content by Title:** Understanding which blog posts draw the most attention and conversions will help you decide what topics you want to focus your blog's attention on. It will also give you insight into which blog post titles work better than others. You may find that countdown titles perform the best; for example, *Five ways to increase sales results*.

✔ **Site Search:** At times, visitors will search your blog for additional information. Every blogging application has an internal search function. (In Google Analytics, for example, it's called Site Search.) To view what people are searching on, though, you may have to turn on this functionality.

To turn on Site Search in Google Analytics, follow these steps:

1. **Log in to Google Analytics.**

2. **Click Edit on the profile you wish to enable Site Search on.**

3. **Click Edit on the Main Website Profile Information panel.**

4. **Click Do Track Site Search.**

    Your blogging application uses a querystring to capture searches. Search for your blog and you'll find that the Web address looks something like `http://www.marketingtechblog. com?q=search+phrase`.

    In the above example, the query parameter (q) needs to be entered into the Query Parameter field so that searches are properly captured.

    Searches are a great opportunity for you to identify additional topics to write about. If visitors arrive at your blog looking for information and search for that information, it must be important. Chances are they were unable to find the information elsewhere.

5. **Click Save Changes. (See Figure 15-1.)**

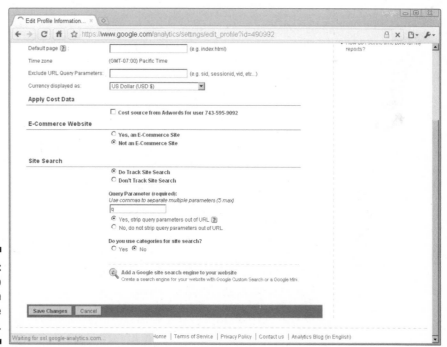

Figure 15-1:
Setting up
Site Search
in Google
Analytics.

✔ **Event Tracking:** Google Analytics allows you to capture other events on your site, such as viewing a video. If you embed a video in your blog from a site, say Backlight, you'll automatically see how many times the video was displayed, started, and completed.

You can also use event tracking to capture how many times your calls-to-action (CTA) have been clicked or your forms submitted. The code for the click of a call-to-action is:

```
<a href="mylandingpage.html" onClick="pageTracker._trackEvent('Campaign',
        'CTA Clicked', 'My Campaign Name');"><img src="myctaimage.
        jpg"></a>
```

Unfortunately, there's no way of relating events to goal tracking in Google Analytics. If you wish to use goals and set up a funnel, you need to follow the instructions in Chapter 13 on setting up goals and funnels in Google Analytics.

✔ **Conversions:** Ultimately, a conversion occurs when a reader turns into a customer. Sometimes, however, registering a conversion isn't possible in Google Analytics, especially if the purchase occurs offline. Nevertheless, in the online realm, a conversion can refer to any specific action you wish a visitor to take.

You might classify a click on a search engine results page (SERP) as the first conversion a searcher takes, then a click on a call-to-action the second, and a submission via a registration form the third. Monitoring conversions is an essential part of your overall blogging strategy.

You need not limit conversions to just sidebars and calls-to-action; you can add links directly in your blog posts that drive conversions. Experimentation, testing, and monitoring the results is essential to maximize conversions on your corporate blog.

✔ **Benchmarking:** Within Google Analytics, there is an option to share your statistics by industry to compare your blog to other industry sites and blogs. At issue is that you'll typically find large disparities between the benchmark charts and your statistics. Every blog varies greatly, so there really is no benchmark to measure yourself against. The best means of benchmarking your blog is against itself.

Assessing visitors' language and platform needs

Knowing the languages and platforms your visitors are using helps you optimize your blog for your readers. You want to make sure you're reaching your audience on their terms, not just on your own. Here are some metrics to track in this category:

✔ **Languages:** The Internet doesn't have language boundaries, and automated translation services are becoming more commonplace. If your company reaches, or can reach, international clients, then you may wish to enlist a translation service to translate your blog into the target language of your visitors. Beware of automated translators; they still do a very poor job of translating. Additionally, you may want to hire bloggers or use a translation service.

✔ **Browser Capabilities:** Many screens are getting wider and wider today with very high resolutions. Taking advantage of this screen real estate may be something you do when designing your blog's theme. Many Web designers design for the poorest resolutions. By doing so, you may actually hurt your traffic with those with the highest resolutions. Understanding your target market is essential when designing your blog layout.

✔ **Mobile Devices:** If your blog sees a lot of traffic from mobile devices (or even if it's doesn't), you should optimize your layout for those devices. If you're running WordPress, there's an exceptionally good plug-in called the WordPress Mobile Edition from Crowd Favorite.

```
http://crowdfavorite.com/wordpress
```

The WordPress Mobile Edition will optimize your theme for both iPhone and iPad Safari browsers as well as other device browsers. With the launch of tablet computers and smart phones, browser resolutions on these devices are much different from desktop and laptop computers. You should optimize the design and readability of your blog for these devices.

Translating Traffic Sources to Opportunities

Understanding where your blog's traffic is coming from is critical when determining how to grow that traffic. While you review your analytics for your traffic sources, you can work to increase that traffic.

Traffic breaks down into the following segments:

✔ **Traffic from search engines:** By far, this source offers the greatest conversion opportunities for your blog. Optimizing your blogging platform, researching, using keywords effectively, writing content, and promoting your blog to accumulate backlinks can increase the volume of relevant traffic to your blog significantly. Many blogs see 40 percent to 60 percent of their traffic coming directly from search engines.

✔ **Traffic from referring sites:** Sites that link and drive traffic to your corporate blog are important, not simply because of the traffic they drive but also because of the backlinks that search engines index. Referring sites should be reviewed regularly. Referring sites aren't just other blogs and Web sites that are pointing to your blog, they are also social media sites (Facebook, LinkedIn, and others), social bookmarking sites (StumbleUpon, Digg, Delicious), and other social media, such as Twitter.

✔ **Direct traffic:** This refers to traffic from users who are entering your blog's Web address directly into a Web address field in a Web browser. You may not believe that you have a lot of impact over this traffic, but you do. Printing your Web address on all company stationary, business cards, marketing materials and even clothing can increase your direct traffic. If you speak publically or give presentations, put your Web address on your last slide or announce it for the audience.

✔ **Other traffic:** You might not believe there can be other types of traffic, but there are. Typically, other traffic arrives through people clicking links in documents, e-mail newsletters, and e-mail signatures. Such visitors don't count as direct traffic because they did click somewhere — analytics just can't tell where unless you take advantage of campaign tracking. This traffic can increase by embedding links in your hypertext markup language e-mails, putting hyperlinks in documents and portable document files (PDFs).

Viewing traffic sources

Keeping a close eye on your referring sources is the first step in determining how to increase overall traffic to your blog. You will want to put the most effort in those sources that produce the most relevant traffic over time.

Many companies look only at the quantity of referring traffic. You do not need traffic, you need business. Be sure not to reverse engineer your conversion information. Instead of looking at what referral source drives the most traffic, look at what referral source drives the most conversions. Increasing traffic on sources that drive conversions should increase the quantity of conversions.

Follow these steps to view traffic sources in Google Analytics:

1. **Log in to Google Analytics.**

2. **Click View Reports on the Web site profile for your blog.**

3. **Click Traffic Sources from the left navigation panel. (See Figure 15-2.)**

   This overview provides you with the traffic sources metrics. If you want, you can select Direct Traffic, Referring Sites, and Search Engines to drill down for more specific information.

Calculating social media as a referral source

The majority of free analytics engines, including Google Analytics, lump traffic from social media in with any other referring site traffic. Unfortunately, that makes it difficult for you to determine how social media is impacting your overall site's traffic. Social media can impact your efforts significantly when leveraged, though.

Because you can't rely on other social media users tagging your links with campaign and source codes, your only option is to filter your list of referring sites to identify the traffic that's impacting it. To filter referring sites in Google Analytics, follow these steps:

1. **Log in to Google Analytics.**

2. **Click View Reports on the Web site profile for your blog.**

3. **Choose Traffic Sources⇨Referring Sites from the left navigation pane.**

4. **In the base of the results table, filter the results using the Filter Source/Medium field. Select *containing* as the type of filter and enter the site you would like to view; for example, *stumbleupon*.**

5. **Click Apply. (See Figure 15-3.)**

To filter referring sites in Webtrends OnDemand, follow these steps:

1. **Log in to Webtrends.**

2. **Select your profile from your Account Dashboard.**

3. **Select Referring Site from your list of reports.**

4. **Add *stumbleupon* in the search box in the top right (not case-sensitive) and press the Enter key.**

   The resulting data compares your visits from StumbleUpon to the preceding period. (See Figure 15-4.) You can select different date ranges if you'd like.

Figure 15-3:
Filtering traffic from Stumble Upon in Google Analytics.

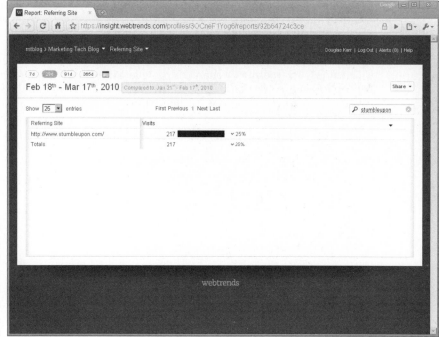

Figure 15-4:
Filtering
traffic from
Stumble
Upon in
Webtrends.

Observing Trends and Opportunities in Reporting Data

If you have the luxury of adding multiple analytics applications to your blog, you'll find that the same metrics will differ on each. Each analytics program measures each metric its own way. For example, the Unique Visitor metric causes much confusion. The logical definition of a unique visitor is one person visiting your blog over the duration of time you're viewing.

However, a unique visitor is actually measured with respect to a browser. If you open two different browsers on two computers and your iPhone, that's five unique visitors on your blog. The Google Analytics *cookie,* the small text file-saving information in your browser, expires after two years. As a result, if you're measuring unique visitors over two years, your unique visitors count is exaggerated. Many visitors clear their cookies if they run into issues, causing them to appear as a unique visitor more than one time.

Read more about Google Analytics cookies and expiration times at

`http://code.google.com/apis/analytics/docs/concepts/gaConceptsCookies.html`

This is just one example. Some visitors also block JavaScript from running, which stops any tracking by analytics providers like Google. Some mobile browsers don't even execute the scripts that capture visits. As a result, the number of actual visitors to your blog may be higher than you are actually measuring.

You might find yourself getting dizzy after trying to account for each metric in analytics and apply it to visitors. No analytics platform definitively captures every event that occurs on your blog, but the good news is that the margin of error from day to day is fairly consistent. As a result, you're much better off observing and acting on the trends from your analytics, not microanalyzing day to day changes.

Keep an eye on the highs and lows within your analytics. For instance, if a post is publicized by another blog or site with a major following, you'll find a substantial increase in traffic. (See Figure 15-5.)

You'll want to observe trends from week to week, month to month, and year to year to fully analyze what kind of impact your blogging efforts are making. If you don't, then trends like lower readership and conversions around the holidays may send everyone in your company scrambling.

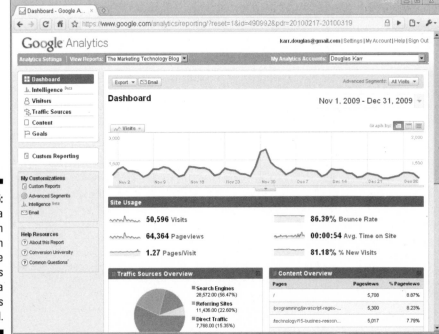

Figure 15-5:
Viewing a spike in traffic in Google Analytics after a post is mentioned.

Understanding how your traffic differs from day to day, week to week, and month to month is important and beneficial. For example, if Monday generally garners the most visits to your blog, then take advantage of that traffic and make announcements when you can expect the largest audience.

Setting Goals in Analytics to Measure Conversions

In blogging terms, a *goal* is where you wish to ultimately lead your visitors. For your blog, this could be a contact page, a download, a form submission, a registration, or a purchase. In the process of a conversion on your blog, you can have the first goal be a call-to-action, the next be a form submission, and the last be a confirmation of the form submission. (Sometimes, forms are abandoned if errors arise.)

Goals allow you to view trends across your selected date ranges. (See Figure 15-6.) Refer to Chapter 13 for additional information on how to set up the Goals feature. Setting up and monitoring goals will make it easier to visualize whether your blog is driving conversions.

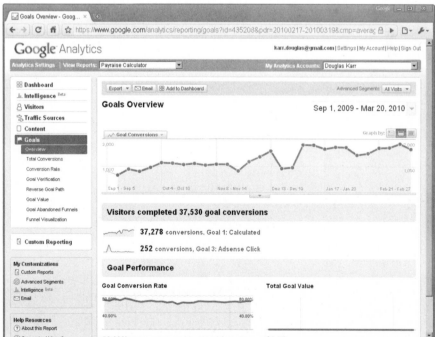

Figure 15-6: Viewing goals in Google Analytics.

Capturing click events in Google Analytics

The easiest means of visualizing and segmenting your goals within Google Analytics is to capture clicks as actual pageviews. In other words, when someone clicks on a link, such as a call-to-action, you record a pageview that is unique to that call-to-action. The page physically doesn't exist, but you create a virtual page upon which you can then base a goal. (Fore more on setting up goals, see Chapter 13.) Although this works well for tracking goals, it skews your pageviews, pageviews per visitor, and bounce rates.

If you want to avoid skewing your analytics in your blog's profile, you can add another profile to the existing domain in Google Analytics that is only used to measure your call-to-action performance. To add pageviews for a second Google Analytics account, follow these steps:

1. **Login to Google Analytics and click Add New Profile.**

2. **Select Add a Profile for an Existing Domain and call the profile Call-to-Action Performance.**

3. **Click Finish and record the account code (UA-*XXXXXX-X*) you are provided within the embed script.**

4. **Within your footer of your blog and landing pages, find the existing Google Analytics script and insert a second tracking section with the proper UA code for your additional goal-tracking profile.**

   Your tracking section should look like this:

   ```
   <script type="text/javascript">
   var pageTracker = _gat._getTracker("UA-AAAAAA-A");
   pageTracker._initData();
   pageTracker._trackPageview();
   var goalTracker = _gat._getTracker("UA-BBBBBB-B");
   goalTracker._initData();
   goalTracker._trackPageview();
   </script>
   ```

5. **Within your blog's template, on your call-to-action, add the necessary JavaScript to capture the click event.**

   Be sure to add this virtual page name to the step field in the Goal setup section of Google Analytics. (See Chapter 13.) The code you add should look like this:

   ```
   <a href="mylandingpage.html" onclick="javascript: goalTracker._
             trackPageview('/goal/this-cta-clicked');"><img src="mycta.
             jpg"></a>
   ```

   You can also add this code to links and images within your blog posts by viewing the hypertext markup language (HTML) code and adding the `onlick` event directly.

6. **Within your landing page, on your form, add another event to capture the submission and completion of the conversion event.**

   Your event should look like this:

   ```
   <form onsubmit="javascript: goalTracker._trackPageview('/goal/this-form-
           submitted');" />
   ```

   Be sure to add this as the final Web address in your Goal setup within Google Analytics.

7. **Now one profile accurately measures all your traffic and another profile captures your conversion traffic on your blog.**

Developing custom reports for conversion tracking

Setting goals in your analytics allows you to track specific conversions by defining your funnel from the first click until the goal is accomplished. However, goals are not integrated into the reporting within Google Analytics by default. You must develop custom reports that combine goals with the additional metrics.

One custom report to develop is a comparison of goals to keywords. This report allows you to recognize the topics that drive the most business through your blog.

To build a custom report in Google Analytics that displays keywords versus goals, follow these steps:

1. **Log in to Google Analytics.**

2. **Click Custom Reporting⇨Manage Custom Reports.**

3. **Click Create New Custom Report.**

4. **In the Title text box, enter** Keywords and Goals **and then click Apply.**

5. **In the Metric section on the left sidebar, drag Goal 1 Completions to the first Metric box below the chart. If you have additional goals set up, add them in the additional metric boxes.**

6. **In the Dimensions section, navigate to Dimensions⇨Traffic Sources⇨ Keywords to the Dimensions box.**

7. **Click Create Report.**

   The resulting report provides you a breakdown of conversions by the keyword that led the visitor to your blog.

If your blog has multiple authors, you may also want to develop a profile to track authors and conversions. Using the same technique for tracking goals in a profile, you can also track an author in her own profile.

If you're using a WordPress blog, you can add the following code in the footer to set up such a profile:

```
<?php if (have_posts()) : while (have_posts()) : the_post(); ?>
var authorTracker = _gat._getTracker("UA-CCCCCC-C");
authorTracker._trackPageview("/by-author/<? echo the_author_meta('display_
            name'); ?>");
<?php endwhile; else: ?>
<?php endif; ?>
```

If you wish to combine both goals *and* authors, you will need to add pageviews with multiple `pageview` events to the `onclick` events for the calls-to-action and landing pages. Example:

```
<a href="mylandingpage.html" onclick="javascript: goalTracker._trackPageview('/
        goal/this-cta-clicked'); authorTracker._trackPageview('/goal/this-
        cta-clicked');"><img src="mycta.jpg"></a>
```

These additional pageviews will skew your total statistics with respect to views and bounce rates.

Determining the Value of a Blog Post for Your Company

One of the most common concerns with corporate blogging is finding the resources to blog regularly. Because blogging takes time and momentum to achieve any degree of success, you may be tempted to throw in the towel or move blogging down the list of marketing priorities.

Remember that each published blog post is an opportunity to attract traffic and convert a visitor into a customer. As you publish posts, your odds of acquiring business through your blog improve. One way to justify the resources it takes to blog is to put a value on each blog post that you've written.

As you continue writing, building traffic, and increasing the number of conversions, you continue to add to that value. A typical marketing campaign expires, but a blog post can drive traffic forever. This is precisely why your company must be dedicated to the strategy and continue to stick with it. Companies that give up do so prematurely and before they recognize the incredible benefits that blogging brings.

Measuring lead-to-close ratios with sales

To determine the value of your blog, you must first be able to measure the revenue that is produced by prospects finding your blog, clicking on a call-to-action and submitting their information (or making their purchase) from a landing page.

If your company has a sales team, you're going to capture leads through the use of your landing page. Companies that have a lot of inbound leads typically have a qualification team that might call the prospect to see if they are ready to make a purchase of your product or service. If the lead is ready, they become a "qualified lead" and are sent off to your sales team.

If a conversion from a landing page isn't a true sale, you'll want to keep track of the ratio of leads that actually close a sale. This is typically accomplished through use of customer relationship management (CRM) software such as Salesforce.com, your lead qualification team, and some simple math.

Here are some metrics that you'll want to monitor:

- **Lead-to-close ratio:** If you get a single customer for every ten leads, then your lead-to-close ratio is 10 percent. Now you can roll those numbers back through your site. If you can get ten conversions for every 1,000 visitors — then you know that it takes 1,000 visitors to get a single customer. Understanding this helps you set expectations for growing your traffic so that you can increase sales.

- **Total cost of blogging:** Calculate the total budget with the wages spent to blog, the hosting or platform costs, optimization, maintenance, and any consultation or design expenses you incur. Then calculate your overall cost per lead. For example, one blog post per weekday, with your staff making an average of $25 per hour, and a post taking one hour to write, equates to $125 per week. Additionally, you may have spent $10,000 to get the blog set up in the first year.

- **Blog promotional budget:** Understanding your overall budget also assists you in determining a promotional budget for your blog. Just as you invest time and money on other campaigns, you should also invest in your blog. The additional funding could go to reward bloggers who are driving the most traffic and conversions, it could go to reader contests that help grow your audience, or it could go to external promotion sources that drive traffic to your blog. Your budget should accommodate all three.

- **Customer service savings:** At the end of each year, you should get these costs and benefits down on paper. If your blog is serving your customers, you may wish to analyze the reduction in calls per customer and overall savings to your customer savings team in with your blogging budget. You will probably even see some improvements in customer retention — a byproduct of opening this communication channel with your customers.

✔ **Average deal size** or **Average customer value:** As you continue to target audiences and write your content, you must be aware of whether you're reaching the right target. Small deal sizes can be an indicator that you're not speaking the same language or providing the level of sophistication in your content that you should to attract higher value customers. Divide your total new business revenue by your quantity of closes to find your average customer value. Compare deals from your blog with other deals you've acquired. Average customer value is important to monitor whether the value of each close is increasing or decreasing over time.

✔ **Return on blogging investment (ROBI):** Now that you fully understand the costs and revenue associated with your blogging program, you can calculate your ROBI. ROBI is simply a ratio of the revenue produced divided by the marketing investment made over a specific period.

ROBI increases as you acquire more leads and larger deal sizes — and the costs of your program reduce naturally over time. ROBI is a calculation of Total Revenue / Total Investment x 100%. For example, if a blogging program generates $20,000 and costs $10,000, there's a 200 percent return on blogging investment.

You need to figure out what the right investment is for blogging to make sense for your company and then push to exceed those goals over time.

Measuring leads coming from your blog

As your blog builds in authority with search engines and you are recognized as an industry expert, your cost per lead through the blog will continue to drop. To keep track of this, you'll want to measure and compare the following two metrics to your other sales and marketing efforts:

✔ **Cost per lead:** Compared to other media, you'll find that blogging is a very affordable inbound marketing strategy — but it takes time to begin seeing the results. The cost per lead for blogging will decrease over time while your readership and authority grows and the ownership costs of the blog decline.

✔ **Revenue per lead:** To calculate the revenue per lead, divide your total new business revenue by your quantity of leads. Compare that number with your revenue per lead from blogging. This helps you further understand how important blogging will be to your overall sales and marketing strategy. Over time, you may find that the revenue per lead from your blog is substantially higher than that of your inbound marketing team or external sales team.

When you are accurately tracking each of the previous metrics, you will be able identify how blogging is impacting your business and plan resources accordingly. You may even want to begin shifting budget to your corporate blogging strategy as it begins to drive more business than other marketing efforts. Additional budget can supply you with additional content from third-party sources, contests and giveaways on your blog, automation and integration, and rewards for your bloggers.

Measuring conversions from blog to landing pages

In addition to the metrics described in the previous sections, you want to monitor the following conversion metrics:

- **Search conversion rate:** What is the total number of searches for the keywords that will attract visitors to your business? You can obtain this information through Google's keyword tool. Look within your analytics package and calculate how many visitors arrived through those searches. These are conversions from a performed search via a search engine results page (SERP) to your blog. Achieving high ranking for keywords, writing compelling post titles, and meta descriptions will help improve these conversion rates.

- **Promotion conversion rate:** If you're spending time promoting your blog through pay-per-click, social media, and other sites, you want a clear picture of the audience size for those sites versus the actual number of clicks that are acquiring visits to your site. This helps you tweak your off-site promotion efforts to increase click-through rates (CTR).

- **Blog conversion rate:** This ratio compares the total number of conversions on your blog's landing pages to the total number of visitors to your blog. Monitoring this metric helps you understand what impact the quality and quantity of your content has on your overall inbound marketing strategy.

- **Close ratio:** This is the number of leads compared to the number of closes that your business acquired through the blog. Your close ratio is going to help you determine whether or not your blog is reaching the appropriate target audience. You may need to adjust your keywords if you are not reaching the right audience.

- **Program conversion rate:** This is the total number of customers acquired compared to the total audience that you've reached. Don't limit your measurement to only people who subscribe to your feed or physically visit your blog through a browser — take the audiences in your social networks, e-mail subscriptions, and total searches into consideration. Once fully integrated and optimized, your blog extends well beyond your domain.

Your conversion rate may look pretty small, but it's still worth under-standing. It should show you how a new promotional medium can help your business. If you know that exposure to 250,000 people in social media is driving 50 leads per week to your business, then it may be worth it to engage in a new social media site that is gaining popularity.

Tying it all together — estimating the sales value of your blog and each post

If you can publish two blog posts a week and your blog leads to $5,000 in sales, each blog post is effectively worth $50. How does that adjust the priorities of blogging in comparison to your other marketing efforts? Many companies find that their return on blogging can exceed hundreds of dollars per post.

Still don't have time to post? You'll probably change your mind when you begin to see the revenues and costs associated with blogging over a year.

Now you can calculate how much *not* posting is costing your business in new revenue. Calculate your total revenue per posts after a year of blogging by dividing the total revenue acquired through your blog by the total number of posts on your blog.

If your company is getting additional opportunities to speak at industry events because of your blog's authority, don't shortchange your blogging program by not accounting for those leads and the associated revenue. Account for that business within your return on blogging investment (ROBI).

Monitoring Shortened Links with Third-Party Applications

There are Internet services that allow you to reduce the length of Web addresses. These services are known as *URL shorteners*. *URL* is an acro-nym for Uniform Resource Locator, the technical name for a Web address. TinyURL was one of the first URL shorteners, and many have followed. These days, bit.ly is the most popular URL shortener, owing its popularity to the fact that it tracks the number of times a shortened Web address is clicked.

You might be wondering how URL shorteners impact analytics. Because URL shorteners are simply redirect pages, your analytics application will still cap-ture the referring site rather than the URL shortener domain. For example, a bit.ly link on Twitter that drives traffic to your blog will still show up with Twitter as the referring source.

Not all URL shorteners are built the same. bit.ly uses a 301 redirect and also supplies analytics on the number of visitors who used the shortened link. If you want to use another service, or even develop your own for your company blog, be sure to use a service or code that uses 301 redirects. Although they don't pass all search engine authority, 301 redirects are the best for search engine optimization.

Setting up backtweets to alert your company of mentions

Companies must respond to mentions on social media. Those who do not are assailed online and lose credibility with their customers and prospects. Consumers and prospects expect that companies will respond proactively to defend their brand and to support their clients. To monitor these communications, it's imperative that you listen for the mentions of your company.

Products such as Radian6, Trackur, and ScoutLabs allow you to closely monitor your brands online. Simple tools such as Google Alerts and Backtweets send e-mail alerts whenever your company's domain is mentioned. Backtweets alerts you when your domain is mentioned in Twitter, even if your Web address has been shortened using a third-party URL shortener.

Setting up these alerts is imperative for managing your brand online and taking opportunities to connect with new networks of audiences. When you respond publicly to a tweet about your blog or company, you are also responding to the audience of that Twitter member. Provide a path to your blog, your contact form, or a landing page to bring the conversation home.

Monitoring shortened links more effectively with bit.ly

Of the URL shorteners on the market bit.ly (http://bit.ly) is unique because it tracks clicks. bit.ly also has extensive integration into other third-party tools and an application programming interface for integrating it into your own tools.

bit.ly gets unique user-level data and aggregated link data, which allows you to see real-time data on how your link is distributed and linked to across the Web. (See Figure 15-7.)

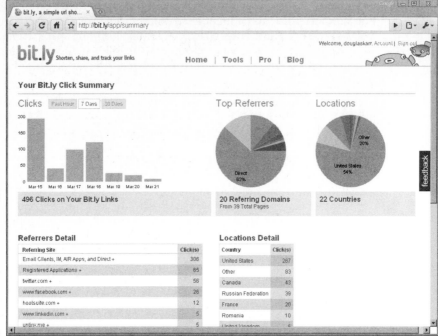

Figure 15-7:
Viewing
reporting
data in
bit.ly for
shortened
Web
addresses.

Measuring Your Feed's Consumption and Number of RSS Subscribers

Monitoring how many people are visiting your blog's feed is not possible by default in modern blogging platforms nor is it a feature in analytics applications.

Measuring consumption of your feed isn't an easy task. Feed analytics applications must try to estimate the number of times the feed was requested by each source and your reach on a daily basis. Not only feed readers request your feed. If you've syndicated your feed throughout social networks and other social applications, each of those requests adds up, too.

There are also several different standards of feeds, including Atom, Really Simple Syndication (RSS) 1.0, and Really Simple Syndication (RSS) 2.0. In the past, these multiple standards offered quite a challenge for developers to keep track of. However, Google's FeedBurner allows you to monitor your feed consumption and publishes your feed in multiple standards.

Setting up your blog and its feeds on FeedBurner

Ideally, you want to keep track of the number of daily subscriptions your feed gets as well as its *reach* — an estimate of the number of daily readers. One application has come forward to take on the challenge of measuring the number of subscriptions and the daily reach your feed has — Google FeedBurner (`http://feedburner.google.com`). (See Figure 15-8.)

FeedBurner approximates the number of requests for your feed and the reach of your feed in a 24-hour period. Total number of subscribers incorporates the total number of requests for your feed, including automated methodologies.

Observing your feed subscribers is an important metric and a number which you will look to grow over time with your blog. Your feed's subscribers are your most ardent supporters and hard-core readers. Many times, these are industry leaders with influence who echo and amplify your blog's message. Writing consistent, compelling blog posts on a daily basis allows your business to grow and provides you with a core network of dedicated readers.

You can take advantage of this community by targeting them. If you're on a WordPress blog, you can search for and install the PostPost plug-in, which allows you to customize your feed with distinct messaging for this group.

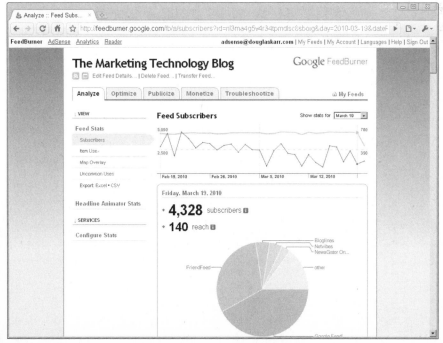

Figure 15-8: Viewing reporting data in Google FeedBurner.

To add FeedBurner to your blog, follow these steps:

1. **Sign up for an account on FeedBurner.**

2. **Enter your blog's feed address in the Burn a Feed Right Now field.**

   If you don't know your blog's feed address, try adding *feed* after your blog's Web address, like this:

   ```
   http://blog.yourcompany.com/feed
   ```

   If you're not aware of your blog's feed address, you can look for a link on your home page, view the hypertext markup language (HTML) source of your page, or contact your platform's support department.

3. **Enter a title for your feed.**

   A default title populates from your feed's information.

4. **Enter a unique name for your feed.**

   This will be the text immediately following the FeedBurner address that uniquely identifies your feed. Try to keep it short and easy to remember!

5. **Click Next.**

   FeedBurner provides you with your new feed address.

Modifying your blog's theme to integrate FeedBurner

You're not done after you *burn* your feed! You want to enter that feed address into the header file throughout your blog. Browsers automatically detect feed addresses through a specific chunk of code within the code of your page; it's not visible in the actual page. The code looks similar to the following:

```
<link rel="alternate" type="application/rss+xml" title="RSS 2.0" href="http://
          marketingtechblog.com/feed" />
```

When you update the feed address with your FeedBurner address, applications that automatically detect your feed through your domain find the FeedBurner address and you'll capture the necessary feed analytics. Be sure to update all template references to your Really Simple Syndication (RSS) feed with your new FeedBurner address.

You may have to wait a few hours to begin noticing changes. As well, FeedBurner doesn't always request a new copy of your feed immediately. To save on resources, FeedBurner stores a *cached* version (copy) of your feed. As a result, you may not see blog posts you've recently published display immediately in your blog's feed.

Part VI
The Part of Tens

"No, we're here to introduce Google Bloggers.
Bloggers. Not loggers..."

In this part . . .

This part provides ten ways to promote your blog, ten ways to grow your audience, and ten ways to re-ignite old content. You'll find some simple bullets to improve your blog, grow readership and build on the content you've already written. These aren't meant to be one-time efforts, so you should turn to this part of the book every month or so.

Reviewing and deploying the steps in this part of the book will continue to improve the results that you are getting from your blog. Remember, blogging is not a matter of simply pushing content out to the Web — it's a long-term marketing strategy that requires ongoing effort. Writing compelling content is the basis of any great blog and the business it attracts — but if you want get great business results and reduce the time it takes to get them, you need to leverage blogging for all its features and benefits.

Chapter 16

Ten Ways to Promote Your Blog

In This Chapter

▶ Targeting networks and leading people to your blog

▶ Syncicating your feed in other communities

*I*f your company is investing resources into a corporate blogging strategy, getting your blog found outside the search engines can jumpstart your blog's return on investment. Sitting and waiting for your great content to be discovered isn't going to help you. Promotion is a necessary requirement in a corporate blogging strategy to help your blog accelerate growth and, ultimately, impact your business positively.

Publishing Posts on Your Home Page

One way to ensure your prospects know about your blog is to publish excerpts and articles on your company's home page. In Chapter 11, we provide resources on how to syndicate your blog's content on other pages. Be sure your home page is one of them. Adding a blog to your home page is a brilliant strategy to connect with consumers, build authority in your industry, drive traffic from search engines and social media, and ultimately, drive more business.

Premier agency and consulting firm, Kristian Andersen + Associates (`http://kaplusa.com`), incorporated its latest blog posts on its home page using a toggle to display or turn off the preview of the latest posts. The most recent posts can be seen by toggling the KA+A Blog section, as shown in Figure 16-1.

Promoting your corporate blog on your Web site will not only provide a human touch for your visitors, it can also provide some search engine goodness for your corporate site. By publishing your blog's feed, the search engines will constantly re-index your Web site and see changes occurring. That means they'll index your site often, which can help your overall site with search engine placement, not just your blog.

Figure 16-1: Kristian Andersen + Associates promotes their blog in a toggled divider on their home page.

Don't use a JavaScript or Flash aggregator. You won't fully realize the benefits of search engines because those both load client-side and the search engines may not see the content.

Don't stop on your home page! If you have category sections on your site, you can also publish category level feeds that are specific to those category pages. By providing relevant, frequently changed, and compelling content on your category pages, you can drive their search engine traffic significantly.

Publishing Your Blog's Link in E-Mail Signatures

Your blog is your personal voice, and e-mail is a personal communication medium. Writing and responding to e-mails each day is an opportunity to promote your blog to the network of people you communicate with.

Be sure to post a link to your blog. You can simply write that it's your blog or you can sum up the goals and vision of your blog by writing a small blurb expressing why your recipients should check out the blog.

If you're using e-mails formatted in hypertext markup language (HTML), you can add a campaign query string formatted for your analytics application. If you're using Google Analytics, that link might look like this:

```
http://marketingtechblog.com/?utm_source=email&utm_
         medium=signature&utm_campaign=blog
```

This allows you to view how much traffic your blog is getting directly from your e-mail signature. You may want to try publishing a link to your corporate blog and each of your posts. The majority of blogs have a unique Web address that points directly to posts, similar to the address shown in Figure 16-2.

If you incorporate FeedBurner, as discussed in Chapter 15, FeedBurner supplies a dynamic footer image to place in your signatures that pulls and circulates your latest blog posts on a rotation. You can find out more about using FeedBurner by going to www.feedburner.com/fb/a/publishers/headlineanimator and www.google.com/support/feedburner/bin/topic.py?topic=13244.

Figure 16-2:
Viewing a unique author page on the Marketing Technology Blog.

Promoting Your Blog in Business Cards

Business cards are an accepted means of marketing your business — take advantage of this and promote your blog on them. Put your blog address on your business card and a note on why the person should read it. Folks may throw your card away as soon as they get back to their desk and add you to their customer relationship management tool and LinkedIn, but they may also subscribe to your blog.

Publishing Posts to Twitter

Twitter has exploded in popularity. It's simple to use and the information is easily digestible in small chunks of 140 characters. It's a permission-based medium as well, meaning that you must follow people in order for them to market to you.

Your company can have an effective presence and participation in social media by joining Twitter and adding to the conversations about your industry, your business, and your products and services. Combining those conversations with your blog is an effective way of grabbing attention and leading prospects to your blog where you can try to convert them to customers.

In Chapter 11, we provide examples of how to syndicate your blog to services like Twitter using Twitterfeed. If you're publishing content from your blog to e-mail, several e-mail service providers have incorporated tools to retweet articles to Twitter.

Follow industry leaders, prospective clients, vendors, and customers when you find them on Twitter. These connections extend your network and anything noteworthy you publish is promoted throughout their networks and yours. If you have ground-breaking news, don't be shy about asking connections to promote you as well. Just don't do it so much that you irritate them. Be sure to return the favor every chance you get.

For additional tips, pick up *Twitter Marketing For Dummies* (Wiley). Author Kyle Lacy has many tips on how to leverage Twitter effectively for your business.

Publishing Your Blog in Facebook

In Chapter 11, we also share how to publish your blog to Facebook. Facebook has Fan Pages that you can incorporate on your blog, converting traffic to and from the social network.

As well as adding your blog's feed to your corporate Facebook Page (see Figure 16-3), encourage your bloggers to add their blog to their personal profiles to reach a much wider network. This is a bit like word of mouth marketing — people are much more likely to make a purchase from companies within our network of friends and colleagues.

Like Twitter, leveraging feeds throughout Facebook is a great corporate blogging strategy. Be sure to participate and respond to comments within Facebook when they arise, though. Followers and readers in social networks will quickly ignore your presence if they feel it's only automated.

For additional tips, pick up *Facebook Marketing For Dummies* (Wiley). Authors Paul Dunay and Richard Krueger have many tips on how to leverage Facebook effectively for your business.

Find industry leaders, customers, and vendors on Facebook and become fans of their pages as well. Cross-promotion of businesses is an effective way to promote within social networks like Facebook.

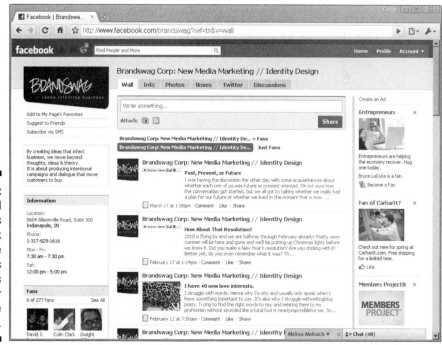

Figure 16-3:
Brand swag's Facebook Page syndicates excerpts from their corporate blog.

Facebook has also added a social plug-in called the Like button. Integrating the Like button on your blog offers another opportunity — to publish your blog posts on other peoples' walls. Users who appreciate your content can then click the Like button. See `http://developers.facebook.com/docs/reference/plugins/like`.

For additional information on how to integrate the Like button in WordPress, detailed information is available at `www.marketingtechblog.com/wordpress/facebook-link-and-wordpress-integration`.

Publishing Your Blog in LinkedIn

LinkedIn may be the easiest and most relevant tool for businesses to market their events, personnel, and latest blog posts. LinkedIn is an incredible tool intended to help you find people or companies to do business with. By having a blog presence there (see Figure 16-4), you're not just providing your resume; you're also providing your voice and expertise.

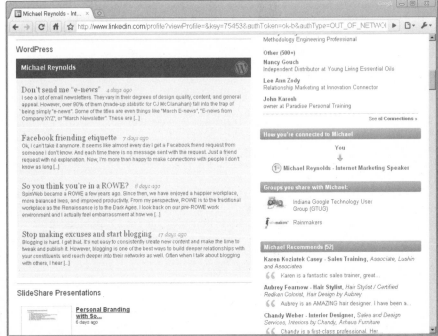

Figure 16-4:
Michael Reynolds publishes his blog on LinkedIn by using WordPress.

LinkedIn also promotes network updates that are customized to your network. Status updates can also be integrated with Twitter or Ping.fm so that your latest blog posts are published in those updates. You should set up both syndication and status updates to fully leverage this network.

Unlike Twitter and Facebook, LinkedIn doesn't really promote conversation — only internal messaging. That means that you need not spend time monitoring LinkedIn for conversations, those messages will come to you.

See Chapter 11 for more about syndicating your blog on LinkedIn.

Publishing Posts in Company Publications

Every publication your company publishes, either online or in print, should reference your blog. Educating your customers about your blog can significantly reduce the number of customer service calls your company receives. In recent years, it's become commonplace to publish your Web site address — don't forget to publish your blog as well.

Whether it's an invoice, an envelope, a visitor badge, or a prospectus, your customers, investors, prospects, and the media should be informed that you publish a blog.

Promoting Your Blog in Other Blogs' Comments

When writing content on your blog, search for and identify other blogs with perspectives on the same topic. Not only should you mention the blogs within your blog post, visit their blog and in a comment, provide a synopsis of the post that you just wrote, state why it's applicable to their post, and insert a link back to your post.

When you write fantastic comments on other blogs that are relevant to your business, you'll be surprised at the attention that your blog receives in return. Blogging was one of the original social mediums to provide a means to publish content, have people react to that content, and communicate with one another.

Although search engines don't weigh comments heavily, bloggers and visitors pay closer attention. When the opportunity arises for you to thank a blogger for a great post, add some detail to that post that may be valuable to their readers or provide a different opinion of their post. Comments are the perfect forum to do this. Bloggers appreciate comments and love responding to them.

Some blogging platforms don't actually allow you to enter links in comments. In that case, refer to your blog post by title and put it in quotes. This allows the blogger or readers of the blog to search for your post.

Even if you vehemently disagree with a blogger, don't make the mistake of being disrespectful. Your comments are a record on the Internet and controversial comments will always come back to haunt you. Defend your position logically and unemotionally.

Avoid responding to attacks on you posted on other blogs. If someone talks negatively about your company, bring the conversation back home to your site where you have advocates, can moderate, and can better control the conversation. Countless companies have made the mistake of responding to attacks on blogs in detail. This only gives that blog the spotlight and perhaps greater search engine ranking on searches for your company.

If you must respond to a comment, simply point the person to your blog or ask them to talk about it offline. Any public response should drive the attention and the traffic to your blog where you can better control the conversation.

Another tactic is to simply ask your company's advocates and fans to respond for you. If a blog post is spreading mistruths about your company, the best response may not be from your company at all, but from a customer who is an avid fan of your business.

Publishing and Distributing Your Corporate Blog in Print

Your blog is a collection of case studies, industry information, frequently asked questions, and countless other pieces of content that are valuable. Using that content in user guides, whitepapers, case studies, and books is an incredible way of repurposing the content to further promote your blog.

When Walker Information, a customer intelligence company, held its regional conference, it surprised its customers with a Blog Book — a collection of the most impactful blog posts that the company had published online.

The book was inexpensive to print and provided a gift to attendees that they could see and touch. They could write notes, earmark pages, and keep it on their desk for information and references.

Be on the lookout for other industry sites, social media sites, and tools you can use to publish your blog. Some companies, such as Connective Mobile, even offer a mobile text messaging club to instantly alert their readers when there are new blog posts. If you're the kind of company that posts big news, specials, discounts, or coupons via your blog, having a text club can drive a lot of traffic to your storefront.

Submitting Your Blog for Awards and Recognition

Guerilla marketing is alive and well in the blogging industry. A great way of attracting traffic to your site is to get your blog onto a list of top blogs for a given industry. When someone makes a list of best blogs, they often promote that list, and the blogs on that list get exposure.

When you catch wind of an industry award, blogging award, social media award, or list that you're eligible for, attack the opportunity with everything you have. Invite customers to vote for you. Pass the voting links on social media sites, Twitter, LinkedIn, and Facebook. Write blog posts and send them to everyone you know. Ask for their support.

Winning an award or getting ranked on an industry "best of" list can drive relevant traffic to your blog. Technorati and PostRank both rank blogs based on their popularity. Technorati allows users to "favorite" their blogs. PostRank allows users to "follow" blogs. Continue to promote links so people will favorite you on Technorati or add your feed on PostRank.

When bloggers find they're on a list of top industry blogs, they typically publish the list on their blog. If your blog is on that list as well, they're going to mention your blog, too. Not only are you accumulating links from relevant sites, which improves your search authority, you're also going to be visited by the audiences on other relevant blogs. Making rank on industry lists is an effective way to promote your blog and get a lot of attention!

When you are awarded, be sure to promote the award in a blog post and elsewhere on your blog — perhaps in a sidebar, as shown in Figure 16-5. Letting new visitors see how your blog has been recognized in the industry shows that your blog is trusted and has authority.

Recognition from third-party sites provides your readers with a sense that you are an authority in your industry, in your region, or across social media.

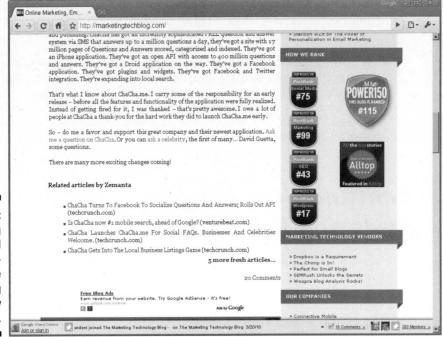

Figure 16-5:
Blogging
awards and
recogni-
tion on the
Marketing
Technology
Blog.

Chapter 17

Ten Ways to Grow Your Audience

In This Chapter

▶ Marketing to target readers for your blog

▶ Luring new visitors to your blog with incentives

▶ Using viral tools to get the word out on your blog

*W*hile your blog's profitability shifts from a plan to a reality, you begin to recognize how many new visitors you need for your blog to sustain growth in your business. If you need additional qualified leads or purchases from your blog, you can predict how many new visitors you'll require to get those leads or purchases.

A number of strategies to drive new visitors to your blog are available to you. When you launch your blog, budget some money for applying resources across multiple strategies. Trying each strategy and measuring the impact of those results helps you fine-tune your blogging strategy to grow your traffic.

The following sections describe eleven strategies, not ten. Consider that last one a bonus!

The goal isn't more eyeballs, it's more business! Beware of the get-rich-quick methodologies of growing your blog audience. A lot of get-rich bloggers out there have tons of advice on building readership, but they're not trying to grow a sustainable business — they're actually counting on your one-time purchase of their get-rich-quick information.

There is momentum in large numbers, however. When people scour the Internet looking for resources they can trust, the first thing they look for are resources that already have a large following. After all, if your blog has thousands of readers, you must be a reliable source of information. You can take advantage of this by proactively promoting your numbers.

Coming out of the gate and promoting your blog as the best, the industry leading, or the favorite blog may be a declaration that's worthwhile. It's also impossible to disprove. Online marketers John Chow (http://www.john chow.com) and Jeremy Shoemoney (http://www.shoemoney.com) have an incredible following on the Internet from promoting their blogs as the top resources for making money online. Along with their bold statements, they've crafted great personas of wealth and influence online. You can argue whether John and Jeremy are the best resources, but their influence in the industry is clear and they both are now very successful. By promoting their blogs this way, they continue to grow their following because readers believe it. Be bold when promoting your blog!

Is this deceptive? If you don't believe in your company, your products, and services, this would be deceptive. Hopefully, that's not the case! Do not be deceptive in promoting your blog, but don't shy away from bold statements that promote your blog.

Buying Visitors with Pay-Per-Click

When you view a search engine results page, sometimes the organic search results aren't even visible unless you scroll down the page. Google, for example, has paid search results on top of the page and in the right sidebar. With a local search, a map is displayed with regional results. Figure 17-1 shows you what I mean. Now, where did those organic search results go?

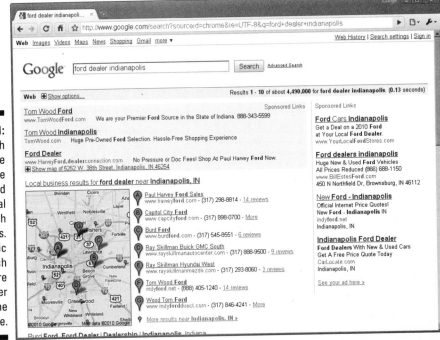

Figure 17-1:
A search engine results page with paid and local search results. Organic search results are further down the page.

If you discover that you can't beat the paid search placement, why not join 'em? Paid search placement may actually be an appropriate solution for highly competitive organic search terms. The advantage of paid search results is that you can absolutely measure your return on investment because you understand what each click costs and how many conversions you achieve. The disadvantage is that paid search, or pay-per-click (PPC) advertising, can clean out your budget without results if you don't know what you're doing.

Pay-per-click advertising agencies, such as Imavex, Hanapin Marketing, and EverEffect, can manage your account for you and determine where the ads run, keywords to avoid, when the ads run, and optimize your advertising message and landing page. In many cases, these agencies can turn pay-per-click campaigns that generate zero leads into one with several leads with very inexpensive acquisition costs.

Targeting your paid search keywords, in addition to the terms *blog, news, training, professionals, experts, articles,* and *advice,* can lead relevant, timely visitors directly to your blog. You want to keep a very close eye on your blog's growth versus conversions when executing paid search campaigns.

In many cases, you won't see a great return on investment, but it will jump-start your readership.

Paying for Blog Reviews

You can find organizations online where you can pay people to write about your blog in their own blogs. Pay Per Post (see Figure 17-2) is one such marketplace. Advertisers can sign up and search for bloggers to write about them. Pricing is based on the blogger's ranking and overall authority. If you use a service like this, you work with bloggers who have the largest and highest-ranking blogs (relevant to your audience) who have a good following of their own.

You may also wish to target bloggers directly. Believe it or not, although industry publication blogs get a ton of exposure and traffic, they typically don't make the blogger a lot of money. Offering a sponsorship to a blog in return for a single post or series of posts is a great way for the blogger to make some additional income.

Always ensure that the blogger discloses that the post was sponsored or the company is a client. New federal communications laws in the United States actually demand it.

Figure 17-2:
Pay Per Post is a marketplace for advertisers to find bloggers.

Regardless of the service you decide to use, be prepared for positive and negative reviews! Bloggers are an interesting group — just because you're greasing their palm doesn't mean that they won't be honest about your blog, your company, your products, or your services.

If you're overly concerned that a blogger might write something negative about your company, request to see the post and approve it prior to it being published. This will allow you to fix the problem. It's also great to respond to a blogger's opinion or advice and let them know that the problems they saw were resolved.

Rest assured that there's nothing unethical about reviewing a paid post before it's published. It's your responsibility to ensure you have the right to review a paid post before it goes live. Let your blogger know up front that you would like to have a right to refuse the post. If your paid post can do damage to your brand, then pay the bill and decline the post. Let the blogger know that you had to decline it because it could hurt your business. No ethical blogger should *want* to hurt another business.

Commenting on Other Industry Blogs

By following and interacting with other industry blogs, you can see how others are blogging, and even promote your own blog. Start by finding industry blogs through Technorati, PostRank or BlogCatalog, and then target the blogs with high ranking and large followings. You can also use Google Blog Search (http://blogsearch.google.com) and type relevant keywords to see who ranks highest.

After you find blogs with products and services that are complementary to your company, interact with those blogs by writing compelling comments that add to the conversation. A comment on a highly trafficked blog may bring direct visits from curious readers of the comments. You may also capture the attention of the blogger. Typically, bloggers write about other bloggers who are in the same industry and produce quality content.

Adding additional links within the content of a comment or writing content with no value that simply tries to push visitors to your blog is comment spam. You could actually drive traffic away from your business by spamming comments on other blogs. You'll get blocked and, chances are, you'll get called out for it and lose credibility in your industry.

Trading Posts and Guest-Blogging

Leverage existing networks by offering to write guest posts for blogs that have audiences similar to the readers you have or want to have. Blogging is time-consuming, so bloggers love to get a break once in a while. You might also want to do a trade of posts, where you offer a guest post on your blog in return for a guest post on theirs.

The ability to tap into each others' audiences is a great opportunity. The conventional wisdom might be that this poaches audiences. That isn't the case at all. If your blog is relevant to the other blog, you both will benefit from new readers. People don't mind reading more great content!

Guest blogging is not guaranteed, though. Many bloggers are suspicious nowadays that you'll simply spam their readers. Bloggers get deluged with offers every day. Rather than simply asking for the opportunity, propose an actual topic to write on. You may even want to supply an excerpt or point to some of the blog posts you've written.

Promoting Other Blogs

Promoting other industry blogs and bloggers on your blog will draw those bloggers' attention, which can be very helpful to you. Through the use of Google Alerts, many bloggers track any mention of their blog and monitor their reputation by seeking out those posts and responding to them. Be liberal in your promotion of others! Bloggers appreciate getting promoted and often return the favor.

This view is shortsighted and doesn't take the goal into consideration. Your blog is there to build credibility and authority with your readers. When you find an incredible resource via a blog, the blog you found it on becomes more valuable to you! Some blogs, like Chips Quips (www.chipsquips.com) do nothing except collect great resources for readers!

You're not actually giving away anything by promoting a great resource to your readers. In fact, you'll build credibility with them quicker. Many bloggers never link to other sites for fear that their audience will follow the link and not come back.

Driving Traffic from Social Media

Social media is a broad definition that refers to all the interactive sites where people have the opportunity to publish, network, share, and discuss topics of interest. Blogs are a social medium, but sites such as Twitter, Facebook and LinkedIn are the common target of social media discussions. Social media is a fantastic way to extend the reach of your blog.

Twitter can be a highly valuable social media tool. Here are some ideas for incorporating Twitter:

✔ Automatically post your blog posts to Twitter using Twitterfeed.

✔ Automatically post your blog posts to Facebook by enabling your blog's feed integration with your Facebook profile or Facebook Page. Additionally, as discussed in Chapter 16, you can integrate the Facebook Like button so that anyone who likes your posts can publish the link to their wall.

✔ If you're already publishing your posts to Twitter, you can automatically post these Twitter updates to Facebook using the Facebook Twitter integration (http://www.facebook.com/twitter).

✔ If you belong to any Ning social networks, integrate your Twitter account with the network (`http://blog.ning.com/2010/01/ integrate-twitter-with-your-ning-network.html`). Your Ning administrator may need to turn Twitter integration on as an option within the network's administrative settings.

✔ Use tools like Tweetmeme so that readers can automatically retweet your blog posts.

You don't need to stop at Twitter, though. Here are some other social media options to consider:

✔ Try a tool like ShareThis. ShareThis integrates with your blog and allows people to share the link through a multitude of social media services or by e-mail. ShareThis also provides statistics on how your blog post was shared.

✔ Automatically post your blog posts to LinkedIn by enabling the integration in LinkedIn settings.

✔ If you have posts that are timely, such as coupons or discounts, try starting a mobile text club. Connective Mobile has a text club WordPress plug-in that automatically posts text messages to the club.

✔ ChaCha.me and FormSpring.me are a new wave of social question and answer services. Unlike Twitter or Facebook, these applications allow your users to publically ask you questions that you can respond to. Both services offer widgets you can publish on your blog that solicit questions from your audience. This is a great way to connect with your audience and, perhaps, write about some common questions that you hadn't thought of.

ChaCha.me offers several integrations to publish the responses directly to Twitter, Tumblr, Facebook, or WordPress.

✔ Ping.fm posts your post title and link from your RSS feed to all major social media sites and mobile devices. Instead of integrating each social media site to your blog, you can integrate with Ping.fm and then use Ping.fm's service to automate the updates everywhere else.

Link Baiting Traffic to Your Blog

Link baiting is the use of highly remarkable post titles to address attention to a specific audience. If your company makes air cleaning systems, a title for a blog post named "Improving Air Quality for Your Children" could be made more dramatic with a title such as "How the Air in Your Home is Hurting Your Children."

People will click on that headline because it's so controversial and attention-grabbing. Link baiting is a common practice and can draw a lot of attention and traffic to your blog. Figure 17-3 provides an example from The Marketing Technology Blog.

Many bloggers write false story headings about search topics that are trending as well, resulting in high bounce rates, abandonment by subscribers, and raising the ire of other bloggers in the industry. You should never write false headings or try to manipulate your readers with link bait.

For post titles, humor or controversy tends to drive the most traffic. Trending news is also an effective means of link-baiting because you can use keywords that are gaining a lot of attention publically and put them to use in your post titles. If you're using WordPress, install the ChaCha Answers plug-in and you can identify trends on ChaCha, Twitter, and Google from your WordPress dashboard.

Link baiting takes some talent. If it's done well, you can really get a lot of attention. Some of that attention may not be relevant, though, so don't be surprised if your spike in traffic doesn't lead to a spike in conversions. If it's not done effectively and people are visiting your blog and don't find a relevant story, you could upset them. Using trending topics incorrectly could lead to increased traffic, but will also lead to higher bounce rates — this isn't going to help your overall corporate blogging strategy or drive business.

Figure 17-3:
Meetings - The Death of American Productivity is a link bait post title.

Holding Promotions and Giveaways

Create a buzz to increase your audience engagement and recruit new followers with promotions and giveaways on your blog. Giving away money, prizes, gift cards, or books, as shown in Figure 17-4, will attract a lot of people. A giveaway doesn't even have to be to your readers: If you provide gifts for those who blog about your company, product, or service, you'll not only get some traffic from those blogs, you'll also get some search engine authority.

Promotions and giveaways are also good for converting frequent visitors that have never interacted with you. Sometimes all you need is a little incentive to have someone click the purchase button, submit the form, or sign up for a newsletter.

Giveaways don't actually have to cost you anything. Sometimes you can partner with vendors or industry coalitions and organizations to provide you with some gifts.

Figure 17-4:
Lydias Uniforms' blog runs promotions on the sidebar to attract traffic.

Giving away a series of gifts (for instance, a month of giveaways) is sometimes more effective than doing one big giveaway. Each day, pick a visitor who commented, promoted your blog in social media, or wrote about your product and service — and you send them something inexpensive but thoughtful. As they begin to tell their network about their winnings, you'll see more opportunists take advantage. Keep in mind that this can draw traffic but not necessarily conversions.

Steeply discount or giveaway your own product! If you have a great product or service, why not promote your business by giving it away on your blog? It will draw attention and will be especially relevant.

Offering E-books, Whitepapers, and Case Studies

Providing gifts and promotional items on your blog is an effective technique to grow your audience — but the traffic you attain may be opportunists rather than potential customers. Do not underestimate the power of well-written publications to draw relevant visitors.

E-books, whitepapers, and case studies are often publicized and promoted across industry blogs and Web sites. Underlying in each is the opportunity for you to promote your products or services. Take advantage of this opportunity.

Combine the promotion of your blog, e-books, whitepapers, and case-studies along with training, Webinars, and conference events to maximize the impact. Cross-promoting all of them will grow your audience, grow attendance and, as a result, grow your inbound leads to your business.

Syndicating Your Blog Everywhere

The more places your content can be found, the more people are exposed to it, and the more new readers you find on your blog. *Aggregation blogs* throughout the Internet pull from blogs and push aggregate content.

As long as these aggregation sites are fully providing credit and backlinks to your site, you may want to join them. Test and measure the traffic that is coming from them. LinkedIn and Facebook are fantastic social networks that offer applications to syndicate your full blog posts directly into their platforms, extending your blog beyond your site.

Don't forget to syndicate your blog across your own Web pages, internal publications, and even vendor and partner sites! The more places your posts are, the more opportunity to attract new readers to your blog.

You can even create a custom iPhone application to publish your blog in an application that is easily readable and customized to your brand. iSites (`http://isites.us`), shown in Figure 17-5, allows you to create a personal iPhone application using your blog's feed. The cost of the service is inexpensive, only $99 per year!

Make sure that you are keeping up with each of the locations you are syndicating your blog to. For instance, if your blog content can be found on your Facebook page, make sure that you are answering questions and listening to feedback and comments that are made on Facebook about your blog.

Figure 17-5: iSites allows you to build an iPhone application with your blog's feed.

Integrating Word-of-Mouth Widgets in Your Blog

Word-of-mouth marketing is a marketing technique in which your customers, readers, and followers spread the word on your behalf. Word-of-mouth marketing is one of the most trusted and effective means of marketing because it doesn't come from the company but from your network of friends and colleagues.

Widgets allow you to aggregate, publish, and share your blog content with a variety of different potential visitors. Widgets for blog promotion can draw traffic and allow for additional communication. Here are some useful widgets:

- ✔ Facebook Fan Pages (www.facebook.com/facebook-widgets) are a great way to cross-promote your traffic on Facebook.

- ✔ Facebook Like buttons (http://developers.facebook.com/docs/reference/plugins/like) allow your blog's visitors to publish a link to your post within their Facebook Wall, extending the reach of your blog into your readers' networks. The widget also keeps count of friends you know who click the button.

- ✔ Tweetmeme has a Retweet Button widget (http://tweetmeme.com/about/retweet_button) you can add to your blog that allows Twitter users to publish the link directly to Twitter. Tweetmeme keeps track of how many clicks Web pages are getting and ranks them on their site. It's an effective means of measuring your blog's reach across Twitter.

- ✔ Google Friend Connect (www.google.com/friendconnect) offers a community widget that can be embedded in your sidebar or footer that promotes your content through a network of followers.

- ✔ BlogCatalog (www.blogcatalog.com/widgets) offers a series of widgets to connect with relevant followers through the BlogCatalog system. These are typically bloggers, too!

Running these widgets is a great way to get your blog's readership off the ground or get some increase in traffic, but you'll want to pay close attention to how they impact your bounce rates and conversions. If people are coming to your blog and then leaving by way of these widgets, you may want to remove them.

Chapter 18

Ten Ways to Reignite Old Content

In This Chapter

▶ Optimizing previously written content

▶ Modifying material to improve search placement

▶ Promoting old content in new networks

Most companies look at a blog and only envision their latest posts being read and driving sales. This is a huge misconception about blogs. Although a blog is optimized to display the latest content first, there's no reason why every post in your blog couldn't be working hard for you long after it's been written.

Most companies don't ever think about returning to old posts to tweak content, but it's an incredibly powerful method for acquiring search engine traffic. Your old posts are like undiscovered treasure. You just need to unbury it and reap the benefits!

Search engines *do* discriminate on content by its age. Content is only old if it's never been changed, though. Change a few elements on a five year-old blog post and you've got fresh content again! And you have a number of ways to do this.

Promoting Old Content in New Blog Posts

As search engines analyze your blog, they're not just looking at the content, they're analyzing the structure and formatting of the page and also taking the site's hierarchy into consideration. Important elements are the home page, navigation, and the internal links promoted throughout the page.

When you write your post, think about referencing other relevant posts within the body of your content. Not only does it provide additional content to support the post you're writing, it also provides a *deep link* internal to your blog. Deep linking is a methodology often used by search engine optimization professionals to increase the impact of other pages within the site.

The first step of promoting old content is to identify whether the content is even found within search results. The easiest method for doing this is to use an online service like SEMRush. SEMRush captures the top 40 million searches on the Internet and the associated results. If your blog post is buried on page two or beyond, you have a great opportunity to increase the ranking of that page for the keywords it's already indexed for.

Another means of doing this is to add a plug-in (such as the WordPress Related Posts plug-in from Fairyfish.net) that lists other relevant posts associated with the same content that you've just written. (See Figure 18-1.) These plug-ins analyze the categories and tags associated with your content and find additional content that has overlap.

When you write blog posts, consider the content you are writing about. Do you have an old blog post you can refer to? Use a few of those links within (or following) your content.

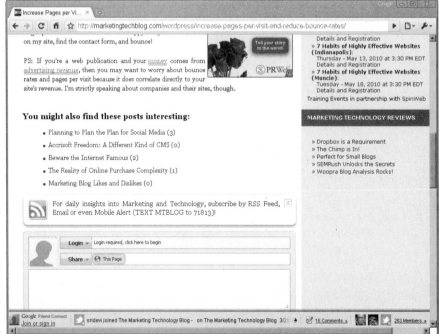

Figure 18-1:
Displaying additional relevant posts after each new post.

Many sites take an excerpt of the first few sentences or paragraph of your post and republish it. By including a deep link within the first sentence or two, these other sites may not only grab the link to your post, they may also grab a deep link that's inserted.

Promoting Old Content in Other Blogs' Comments

When you read industry blogs and respond via comments, don't hesitate to include a link to posts that you've written on the same topic. Some blogs won't allow those links, and others may exclude your comment as a possible spam attack. Keep track of the blogs that never publish your comments and don't bother doing it there again — you don't want to annoy the blogger.

Although there's not a lot of search engine authority, if any, passed through a link in a blog comment, it can still revive your content. (Chapters 8 and 9 have more information on search engine optimization.) If nothing else, the readers who are doing some comprehensive research will wind up on those posts. Don't be surprised to see some new comments, or some new promotion of those older links. This can revive the content and improve its ranking because it's already ranking for some relative keywords.

Reviving Old Content with New Comments

Comments are a fantastic gift for a blog. Not only do they provide support or feedback for the posts that you've written, they also change the content of the page, so search engines will come back and re-index the page with the latest remarks. This is another good reason to stay vigilant on moderating comments — you want to ensure the comments add value to your page.

You'll find that it's no coincidence that old blog posts with lots of comments wind up in the top rankings of search engines. This is because their content is consistently changing. There's no evidence that search engines take comments specifically into consideration, but you will find that the additional content helps.

This content is called user-generated content (UGC) and is the best kind of content because it doesn't cost your business anything. Solicit feedback in each of your blog posts for comments. Encourage your readers to write and be sure to respond to them.

You might also want to install plug-ins that display the blog posts with the most discussions. PostRank Labs has a Top Posts Widget (`http://labs.postrank.com/top_posts`) where the ranking is based on the most referred-to blog posts off-site. These plug-ins put a list in your sidebar or beneath each of your posts. Lorelle lists a number of WordPress plugins for leveraging comments in WordPress at `http://lorelle.wordpress.com/2007/02/26/wordpress-plugins-for-comments`.

Another great advancement in blogging is the use of *universal commenting systems*. Universal commenting systems track comments across all blogs by user and allow people to read and follow that user's comments in a single location. The most widely used commenting systems are Intense Debate (`www.intensedebate.com`), Echo (`www.js-kit.com`), and Disqus (`www.disqus.com`).

If you decide to implement any one of these systems, always ensure that your site's comments are fully imported and synchronized with the system. If you have a lot of comments, this could even turn into a manual import process. It's essential that you synchronize, though, to ensure your comments are both stored locally and displayed for search engines to see.

A couple of commenting systems have gone out of business, so always ensure that you own and store your content in the event the system is unavailable or discontinued.

Modifying Post Titles

Updating your page title is the single biggest change you can incorporate for search engine optimization. By updating page and post titles, you can take a great blog post that's not getting any traffic, and push it up in the rankings significantly with this minor edit.

Using a tool like paid service like SEOPivot (`www.seopivot.com`) or simply by using Google Webmasters⇨*Your site on the Web*⇨Search queries, you can see which of your blog posts have potential to rank better for specific keywords if the content in them was better optimized. Download a list of the blog posts where you are not ranking well and make edits to the post title and/or the page title.

Although most blogging applications treat the page title and post title the same, there's a difference between them. If your platform allows you to, you may want to modify a page title rather than the post title. The All in One SEO Pack plug-in for WordPress (`http://wordpress.org/extend/plugins/all-in-one-seo-pack`) allows you to do exactly that. If you're on a different blogging platform that doesn't allow it, simply update your post title instead.

Modifying Meta Descriptions

Meta descriptions are another overlooked but critical component of your blog. *Meta tags* are HTML tags within the head section of your blog that are not visible to the visitor but are visible to search engines. A *meta description tag* is a tag with approximately 160 characters of text to describe the page. If a meta description is included in the page, a search engine will crawl the information and typically display that information on the search engine results page (SERP).

If you do not or cannot update the meta descriptions of a blog post, the search engine will just grab some text from the page — typically the first few sentences of the content. Many times, you'll find that the search engine really pulls some wacky stuff, though, such as content half-way down your sidebar.

If you have the time, modifying meta descriptions is worth the effort on *every* blog post because it allows you to put some compelling content in the SERP to drive someone to click through on the result. If you don't, however, using a tool like SEOPivot (www.seopivot.com) to identify posts with opportunities to rank better is another alternative.

Modifying Content with Keyword Enhancements

Keywords, keywords, keywords. Search engines today are fairly dumb. You must repeatedly tell them the keywords you should be indexed for; otherwise, they won't do it.

Keywords usage in domains, post titles, post slugs, headings, subheadings, and content is going to make a huge difference in where your content is found. If you truly want to have an impact on your blog's quality, proper usage of keywords ensures that your content is indexed correctly for the keywords you want it to be found for. Images or video related to keyword topics work well also.

New corporate and enterprise blogging platform provider, Compendium (www.compendium.com), has focused its user interface on keyword optimization. Within the content editor, Compendium has incorporated a keyword strength indicator (see Figure 18-2) that turns from red to green when you mention your keywords enough. If you overdo it, it returns to red.

If you want to capture search engine traffic for specific keywords, then you need to write content for those keywords. Compendium has a proprietary engine that automatically categorizes your content by keywords you've used within the blog post. The software also tracks how many times you've written about each keyword.

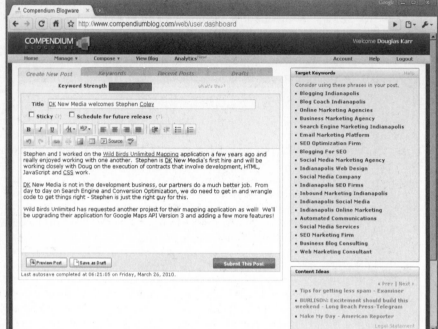

Figure 18-2:
Compen-
dium's
Keyword
Strength
indicator.

If you have old content that you're not getting any traffic on, don't give up on it. If it's useful content, optimize the content for specific keywords that have good search volumes.

For WordPress, Scribe (`www.scribeseo.com`) offers a service to professional bloggers that will provide feedback on the construction of your title, meta description, and post content through a simple interface.

Removing Dates from Blog Posts

Because blogs are timely, people tend to put dates all over them — in the permalink construction and on the interface. The problem is readers prefer new content over old content. Here are a couple ways you can avoid dating your posts:

✔ **Remove explicit dates from your theme design.** If you'd like to include a date, add it without the year. There's no reason to expire your content for a reader. A blog post about a product you developed two years ago may still be relevant.

✔ **When you design your blog, modify your permalinks so that they don't include the date and time.** To do this with WordPress, use the WordPress Permalinks Migration plug-in. This plug-in automatically adds a 301 code, redirects both users and search engines, and lets the search engine know that the page has been relocated. Keep in mind that you might lose some search engine authority when redirecting to new pages.

If your blog is already up and running, changing permalinks can have a disastrous impact on your search engine optimization. Do not change them unless you have the ability to redirect readers properly from the old Web address to the new Web address.

Submitting Excerpts to Social Networks

Unfortunately, your blog isn't as important to other people as it is to you. For some people, LinkedIn is where they like to research and communicate with one another. For others, it's Facebook or Twitter. Others appreciate a feed reader or even a daily e-mail.

Through the use of syndication, it's possible for you to reach others where they want to be reached. Even though you may already have your content syndicated throughout these social media sites, don't be shy about reviving older blog posts that are still relevant. Select your most popular posts and publish them out to Twitter, Facebook, and LinkedIn periodically to revive them.

Tagging Content and Building Tag Clouds

Tagging is the act of assigning keywords and phrases to a blog post so that it's easily found based on that keyword or phrase. Understanding which keywords are going to draw the most traffic allows you to proactively use search terms as keywords. Each time you write a blog post, tag it with those keywords.

Tags are a great element on your blog for reviving old content. If a visitor arrives and is only interested in specific topics, they may either click on a category on your blog or they may try clicking on a tag. Blogging platforms like WordPress incorporate tagging and even *tag clouds*, collections of tags organized and displayed by popularity that allow a visitor to filter the content on the blog to that single tag.

To add a tag cloud in your WordPress blog's theme is simple; they've developed their own function you can call:

```
<?php wp_tag_cloud( $args ); ?>
```

Zemanta (www.zemanta.com) provides additional content and references for all major blogging platforms. While you write your post, Zemanta scours its resources and brings back suggestions based on the content you're writing. They provide photos, articles, and tags. The plug-in is effective at identifying the words and phrases you should be tagging your blog post with. If you're not sure what words to tag your posts with, Zemanta makes it very easy. (See Figure 18-3.)

Promoting Internal Search on Your Blog

When your blog becomes widely used, more and more readers will use your internal search to find articles and information they're interested in. Monitoring the internal searches can provide you with ideas on what to write about but it can also help you promote the posts that are most searched for.

When you know the terms, you can hand-select the articles for those posts and promote them in your sidebar as the Most Searched For blog posts. By putting links to these posts on your home page, you effectively tell the search engine how important they are.

Along with displaying links to other relevant posts, promote your search form throughout your blog. You may even wish to place it at the end of each blog post with a nice note, "Didn't find what you were looking for?" to prompt the user to search deeper into your blog.

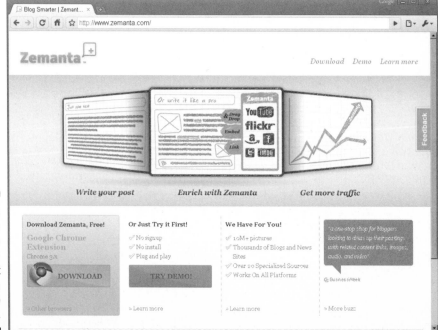

Figure 18-3:
Zemanta
can
enhance
the content
in your blog
and help
promote it.

Index

• A •

A/B testing, 309–310
ABC News, SaaS solutions, 101
above-the-fold, layout issues, 315
accreditation, blog posts, 42–43
actions, landing page element, 321
Address Fix, geographic location tool, 192
AddThis, social bookmarking, 269
administrative section, 18
Adobe, AIR technology, 109
aggregation blogs, aggregate content, 386
aggregation, server-side page syndication, 254–255
Akamai, content management service, 189
Akismet, spam-blocking, 240–241
Alerding Castor Hewitt blog, 79–80
alerts
  Backtweets, 361.
  Text Messaging plug-in, 118
algorithms, search engine, 165
aliases, provider subdomain alternative, 81
alignments, image, 220
All in One SEO Pack plug-in
  canonical URLs, 175
  keyword meta descriptions, 185
  page titles, 206
  post titles, 206, 392
alt tag, images, 215
Alterian Webjourney, 337
alternative text, alt tag, 215
Amazon S3, 95, 189
analytics
  A/B testing, 309
  abandonment measurement, 331
  average customer value, 358
  average deal size, 358
  backtweets, 361
  benchmarking, 346
  blog conversion rate, 359
  blogging tools, 28–29
  bounce rates, 343–344
  campaigns, 342

Click application, 115–116
click event captures, 354–355
close ratio, 359
content by title, 344
conversion tracking reports, 355–356
conversions, 346
cookies, 339
cost per lead, 358
customer service savings, 357
data reporting trends, 351–353
depth of visit, 343
direct traffic, 342
event tracking, 346
goal setting, 353–356
Google Webmasters, 59–60
implementation process, 338–339
keyword research tools, 180–184
keywords, 342
landing page conversions, 359–360
language needs, 346–347
lead-to-close ratio, 357
length of visit, 344
loyalty, 341
mobile devices, 347
multivariate testing, 309
new visits, 340
pages per visit, 343
pageviews, 343
performance evaluation, 344–346
platform needs, 346–347
post evaluations, 356–360
program conversion rate, 359
promotion conversion rate, 359
promotional budget, 357
recency, 341
referring site, 341–342
return on blogging investment (ROBI), 358
returning visits, 340
revenue per lead, 358
RSS subscribers, 362–364
sales value, 360
search conversion rate, 359

analytics *(continued)*
  search engine traffic, 342
  server-side applications, 339
  site overlay, 344
  site references, 341–342
  site search, 344–345
  social media as referral source, 349–351
  synonymous keywords, 212–213
  team member tracking, 156–159
  time on site, 344
  total budget, 357
  traffic sources, 347–351
  unique visitors, 341
  URL shorteners, 360–362
  visitor tracking, 340–341
  visitors, 57, 340
  Webtrends plug-in, 110
Andersen, Kristian, KA+A blog, 367–368
Android Phones, 108
application programming interface (API)
  blog functionality enhancement, 21
  embedded content, 118–119
Arnold, Jon, Tuitive Group CEO, 40
Arrington, Michael, blog reviews, 94–95
Ask, 187–188
Asynchronous JavaScript and XML (AJAX),
    widgets, 116
Atom, feed standard, 362
Audacity, recording/editing software, 244
audible, learning type, 243
audience questions, API, 21
audio
  blogging benefit, 35
  content incorporation, 243–245
  hosting services, 247–250
authenticity, corporate identity, 77–79
author pages, 75
Author plug-in, user profiles, 121–122
authority building
  backlinking, 128
  blogging benefit, 34
  level of expertise, 64
  vendor/partner promotion, 238–239
Authority Labs, rank monitoring tool, 191
authors
  analytics, 156–159
  post element, 16
Auto Social, social bookmarking, 268

average customer value, analytics, 358
average deal size, analytics, 358
awards, blog promotion method, 375–376
awareness building, 34

• *B* •

backgrounds, theme building, 106
Backlight, 117, 247–248
backlinking
  reciprocal posts, 41–42
  search engine optimization, 128, 186
  sales effects, 282–285
Backtweets, e-mail alerts, 361
backups
  content protection, 133
  content strategies, 147–148
  team members, 37
Bailey, Kevin, Slingshot SEO
    co-founder, 228
bbPress forums, WordPress integration, 92
benchmarking, analytics, 292–294, 346
best practices, knowledge base, 67
Bing
  headline titles, 201
  local search registration, 193
  manual registration, 188
  site search, 187–188
Bing Webmaster Central, site analysis, 188
Bing Webmasters, 59, 88
biographies, identity element, 79–80
bit.ly, URL shortener, 261–263, 360–362
BittBox, button images, 300
`blockquote` tag, 42–43, 236
blocks, Google Analytics, 292–294
Blog Book, blog promotion, 374–375
blog consultants, 96
blog conversion rate, analytics, 359
blog design, 37–39, 75, 96
blog reviews, Pay Per Post, 379–380
Blog World & New Media Expo, 151
BlogBloke, 152, 207
BlogCatalog, 230–231, 388
Blogger
  cascading style sheets (CSS) support, 76
  hosted software solutions, 97–98
  personal/publication blogs, 92
  subdomain provider, 81

blogging platforms
  application programming interface (API), 118–119
  Blogger, 92
  budget considerations, 93–96
  canonical URLs, 173–175
  Compendium, 92
  exporting contents, 131–132
  Expression Engine, 92
  "free" software pitfalls, 93
  hosted solutions, 96–98
  infrastructure guidelines, 94–95
  Movable Type, 92
  moving between domains, 85–88
  SaaS solutions, 96, 100–102
  self-hosted solutions, 96, 98–100
  sitemap building, 170–171
  templating engines, 102–108
  TypePad, 92
  TypePad Business, 92
  Vox, 92
  WordPress, 92
  WordPress Multi-User, 92
  WordPress VIP, 92
  Wordpress.com, 92
blogging strategies, 35–36
blogosphere, 40, 256–260
BlogRank, guest blogger search, 230, 232
blogs
  Alerding Castor Hewitt, 79–80
  back-end elements, 18
  BlogBloke, 152
  bounce rate effects, 288
  Buzz Marketing for Technology, 243–244
  Chips Quips, 382
  comment as promotion, 373–374
  communications tool, 10–11
  content layouts, 314–315
  copyblogger, 152
  corporate versus personal, 13–16
  e-mail integration, 270–276
  engagement measurement, 287–295
  Facebook integration, 265–266
  Fairytale Brownies, 83
  front-end elements, 16–18
  funneling sales, 280–287
  Gadgets, Google, and SEO, 37–38
  guest posting, 258–259
  HP Community, 11

  humanizing, 14–15
  inbound marketing, 12–13
  KA+A, 367–368
  Kyle Lacy, 114–115
  Lifeline Data Center, 299
  LinkedIn syndication, 264–265
  Lydia's Uniforms, 237
  The Marketing Technology Blog, 95, 151, 228–229
  message and response control, 10–11
  performance testing, 115–116
  Plaxo syndication, 264–265
  ProBlogger, 152
  public relations representative, 10
  publishing articles via the Web, 9
  rank monitoring, 190–191
  search engine marketing platform, 11–12
  search engine registration, 187–191
  site search, 187–188
  Social Media Explorer, 152
  social media integration, 260–266
  Stellar Thoughts, 244
  Sun Microsystems, 51–53
  Tampa Bay, 62–63
  Terms of Service, 138–139
  third-party ad serving systems, 313–314
  Tough Jobs, 68
  TwelveStars Media, 247
  Twitter incorporation, 382–383
  Twitter syndication, 262–264
  Visit Tampa Bay, 253–254
  Walker Information, 76–78
  versus Web sites, 10–13
  Which Test Won, 308
  word-of-mouth widgets, 388
blogs, public relations representative, 10
Blue Microphones, audio recording, 244
body contents, 16–17
boldface terms
  keyword emphasis, 177–178
  search engine optimization, 186
bookmarks, 267–270
bots, search engines, 167
bounce rate
  analytics, 343–344
  page views, 20
  trends versus instances, 289–292
  visitor engagement, 288

Brachhold, Arne, Google XML Sitemaps, 170

brand marketing, corporate versus personal blogs, 13–14

brand recognition, blogging benefit, 35

browsers, 116, 347

BuddyPress, WordPress social network, 92

bulleted lists, contents, 221

business cards, 370

business to business (B2B), 313

BusinessWeek, blog reviews, 94–95

Buzz Marketing for Technology, 243–244

• *C* •

caching, 116

Calacanis, Jason, blog reviews, 94–95

calls-to-action (CTAs)
  sales lead element, 23
  A/B tests, 309–310
  blog element tracking, 317
  bounce stopping strategy, 290–291
  campaign performance viewing, 307–308
  clickbait, 301
  click-through rate improvements, 308–312
  click-through rate measurement, 301–308
  content layouts, 314–315
  content writing, 300–301
  conversion tactics, 61
  desirable traits, 298–300
  dynamic contents, 312–314
  images, 300
  landing page design, 320–321
  onclick events, 302–305
  optimization methods, 310
  progressive disclosure, 301
  reasons for, 297–298
  results analyzation, 310
  sidebar element, 16
  targeting, 310–312
  testimonial guidelines, 69

campaign codes, `onclick` events, 302–305

CampaignMonitor, Formstack, 335

campaigns, analytics, 342

canonical name record (CNAME), 81

canonical URLs, post pages, 173–175

Cantaloupe, 117, 246

Cantaloupe TV, video blogging, 35

CAPTCHA forms, 241

Carhartt, Tough Jobs blog, 68

Cascading Style Sheets (CSS), 76, 102–103

case studies
  landing page registration, 328
  online/offline publishing, 23
  promotional method, 386

categories, sidebar element, 16

ChaCha.me, 21, 383

challenge questions, 241

Children's Online Privacy Protection Act (COPPA), 137

Chips Quips blog, reader resources, 382

Chow, John, online marketer, 377–378

Clark, Brian, Copyblogger, 152, 199

click events, Google Analytic captures, 354–355

clickbait, visitor manipulation, 301

click-through rates
  dynamic contents, 312–314
  improvement methods, 308–312
  measurement methods, 301–308

Clicky, analytics application, 115–116, 337

client support, blogging use, 11

close ratio, analytics, 359

cloud services, blog host alternative, 95

cloud-based servers, hosting platform, 26

CNAME records, redirects, 88

Coca-Cola, SaaS solutions, 101

code of ethics, corporate blogger, 40–43

commenting system, post element, 16

comments
  blog promotion method, 373–374
  blogosphere interaction method, 258–259
  CAPTCHA forms, 241
  challenge questions, 241
  content freshening methods, 239–242
  e-mail verification, 241
  employee encouragement, 242
  industry blog posts, 381
  measure of engagement, 240
  moderated, 240–241
  negative, 241
  negative criticism response, 259–260
  old content reignition method, 391
  reciprocal posts, 41–42
  respectful dissent, 259
  search engine optimization, 186

third-party services, 241–242
universal commenting systems, 392
user generated content (UGC), 242
visitor engagement, 61
communications
    blogging benefit, 35
    blogging use, 10–11
    customer relationship management
        (CRM), 65–69
    humanizing your blog, 14–15
company mentions, Backtweets, 361
company news, content idea, 47
company publications, blogs, 373
Compendium
    blog scheduling, 149–150
    blogging platform, 93
    cascading style sheets (CSS) support, 76
    corporate blogging platform, 26
    corporate blogs, 92–93
    Keyword Strength indicator, 393–394
    SaaS solutions, 100–102
    Web to Post, 68
Compendium Blogware
    automating customer testimonials,
        237–238
    canonical URLs, 175
    sitemap building, 170
    Web to Post, 237–238
competitors, 15, 194–195
conclusion, whitepaper component, 327
conferences
    customer communications activity, 66
    educational opportunities, 151
    team member motivation/reward, 160
confirmation pages, exit rates, 288
Connective Mobile, 118, 383
contact forms, 23, 319, 323–324
contact information, 17, 23, 325
content by title, analytics, 344
content placement, keyword emphasis, 177
content words, 177
contents
    accreditation, 42–43
    aggregation blogs, 386
    application programming interface (API),
        118–119
    audio incorporation, 243–245
    audio/video hosting services, 247–250

automated e-mail, 271
backup strategies, 133, 147–148
blog importance, 35–36
blogging benefit 31
body page, 16–17
bounce stopping strategy, 291
bulleted lists, 221
calls-to-action guidelines, 300–301
comment freshening methods, 239–242
copyright infringement, 134
customer focus, 40
customer testimonials, 148
development elements, 39–43
development process, 46–47
diagrams, 214–220
disclaimers, 135–137
exporting between platforms, 131–132
formatting for comprehension, 220–222
formatting images, 216–220
FTC guidelines, 129, 136–137
geographic search optimization, 186–187
ghostblogging, 123–126
Google Alerts, 134–135
guest bloggers, 148
hacker protections, 133
headlines, 199
high converting, 222–223
images, 214–220
industry bloggers, 128–129
industry news, 148
keyword enhancements, 393–394
keyword recognition, 24–25
landing pages, 323–329
layouts, 314–315
link baiting, 200
local search optimization, 186–187
moving between domains, 86–88
new blog posts, 389–391
online/offline publishing, 23
ordered lists, 221
ownership issues, 130, 147
page title formatting, 204–205
page title keywords, 206–207
paragraph sizing, 221–222
podcasting, 243–245
poor performance handling, 159
post element, 16
post titles, 198–209

contents *(continued)*
PowerPoint presentations, 148
privacy laws, 137–138
professional writers, 124–126
publication schedule development, 37–39
purchasing guidelines, 126–127
really simple syndication (RSS), 252–255
repeating topics, 207–209
return on investment (ROI) strategies, 33–35
runtime monitoring, 133–134
sales driving importance, 16
search engine keyword indexing, 209–213
search engine optimization, 27–28, 64–65, 186
search engine rankings, 105
search engine results page, 201–104
sitemap priorities, 171–173
sizing images, 216–220
speeches, 148
syndication integration, 119–121
tag clouds, 395–396
timelines, 147
topic planning, 147
user-generated content (UGC), 391–392
vacation planning, 148–151
video incorporation, 245–247
voice ownership, 44–45
weekend planning, 148–151
whitepapers, 148
contests, customer reviews, 195
contrarian blogging, respectful dissent, 259
conversions
analytic goal setting, 353–356
analytics, 346
calls to action, 61
client acquisition process, 57
engagement terms, 222–223
goal setting element, 50
Google Webmaster analytics, 59–60
landing page analytics, 359–360
landing page design, 61, 320–323
link tactics, 60
measurement methods, 287–295
post tactics, 61
sales funnel progression, 280–281
search engine results, 281–282
tracking reports, 355–356

traffic source viewing, 58
visitor types, 57
cookies
analytic data saving element, 339
calls-to-action targeting, 310–312
dynamic contents, 312–313
copyblogger, content production, 152
copyrights
Creative Commons, 138
footer element, 17
infringement, 134
CoreMetrics, analytics platform, 337
corporate bloggers
benefits, 22–24, 31–35
identity integration, 74–80
industry expectations, 40–43
leadership determinations, 44–45
manifesto writing, 43
versus personal blogging, 13–16
publishing goals, 25
reciprocal posts, 41–42
return on investment (ROI), 33–35
strategy adjustments, 28–29
team member recruiting, 25–26
Corporate Blogging Tips, 151
corporate identity
authenticity recognition, 77–79
author pages, 75
biographies, 79–80
blog integration, 74–80
portraits, 79–80
themes, 76–77
corporate vision, blogging benefit, 35
cost per blogging lead, return on investment (ROI) evaluation, 54
cost per click (CPC), keyword competitiveness monitoring, 179
cost per lead, analytics, 358
coupons, promotion tool, 195
CrazyEgg, color-coded heat-map, 315–316
Creative Commons, 138
crisis management, blogging benefit, 35
cross-selling, 66
Crowd Favorite, WordPress Mobile Edition plug-in, 347
crowdsourcing, design requests, 75
CSS Tricks, block quote examples, 236

customer conversion, blogging use, 23–24
customer relationship management (CRM)
  blogging activities, 66–67
  communications software, 65
  knowledge base, 67
  landing page integration, 332
customer reviews, promotion tool, 194–195
customer service, 51, 142–143, 357
customer support, 66
customer testimonials, 148, 235–238
customers, 15, 40
Cutts, Matt, Gadgets, Google, and SEO blog,
  37–38

• D •

dates, 16, 394–395
De Valk, Joost, canonical URL plug-in, 175
Dearringer, Jeremy, Slingshot SEO
  co-founder, 228–229
deep linking, 186, 289, 390
Delicious, online bookmarking system, 267
DemandBase, B2B visitor tracking, 313
depth of visit, analytics, 343
descriptions, images, 220
design, landing page element, 321
diagrams, content enhancements, 214–220
Digg, bookmarking site, 267
direct traffic
  analytics, 342
  sales/retention strategies, 294–295
  traffic source analytics, 348
  visitor type, 57
disclaimers, 17, 135–137
discounts, promotion tool, 195
Disqus, universal commenting system,
  241, 392
domain names, 176, 178, 187–188
domainers, expiring domain acquisitions, 81
domains
  canonical name record (CNAME), 81
  content ownership issues, 130
  domainer acquisitions, 81
  existing domain benefits, 84
  moving between services, 85–88
  name impact, 82–83
  search engine authority, 82–88
  selection methods, 82–83

subdomain providers, 81
subdomain structure, 88–90
traffic history, 81
Whois service, 135
downloads, landing page registration, 326
Dreamstime, stock images, 220
Dunay, Paul, Buzz Marketing for
  Technology blog, 243–244
duplicate content, 173–175
DwarfURL, URL shortener service, 261
dynamic contents, calls-to-action, 312–314

• E •

e-books, 23, 386
EC2, content management service, 189
Echo, universal commenting system,
  241, 392
e-commerce, product information, 22
editors, back-end element, 18
edublogs, WordPress MU, 93
e-mail
  automated RSS feeds, 271–276
  blog subscription promotion, 275
  blogging integration, 270–276
  comment verification, 241
  content automation, 271
  driving readers to your blog, 274–275
  guest blogger targeting, 232–233
  MailChimp, 119
  opt-in communications, 10
  signatures, 368–369
e-mail address, landing page, 323
e-mail alerts, Backtweets, 361
Email Center Pro, Formstack, 335
embedded contents, 118–119
embedded keywords, meta tagging, 166
employee spotlights, blogging benefit, 35
employees
  content focus, 40
  encouraging comments, 242
  social media guidelines, 154
  target audience source, 15
engagement terms, 222–223
engagement, measurement methods,
  287–285
European Union (EU), 137–138
event promotion, blogging benefit, 35

event tracking, analytics, 346
event-specific blogs, target audience, 51
EverEffect, pay-per-click advertising
  agency, 379
ExactTarget
  e-mail solution, 100–102
  Formstack integration, 335
  RSS to e-mail, 272–274
Excel, rank monitoring tool, 190–191
excerpts, social network submissions, 395
exit rate, visitor engagement, 288
experts, guest blogger, 234–235
Expression Engine, 76, 92
extensible markup language (XML),
  sitemaps, 167, 170–171
External Keyword Tool, search engine
  volume identification, 284–285

• F •

Facebook
  blog integration, 265–266
  blog publishing, 370–372
  employee guidelines, 154
  Like button, 372
  Twitter integration, 382
Facebook Fan Pages, 388
Facebook Like buttons, 388
Fairley, Jeremy, Tampa Bay blog, 62–63
Fairyfish.net, WordPress Related Posts
  plug-in, 390
Fairytale Brownies, 83
Fall, Jason, Social Media Explorer blog, 152
Federal Trade Commission (FTC), 129,
  136–137, 153
feed readers,120–121, 257
FeedBurner, 132, 275–276, 369
Financial Services Modernization Act, 137
Firebug plug-in, 291
Firefox, 216–217, 291
Fiskin, Rand, SEOmoz article, 190
Flash, widget identification, 113
Flexware Innovation, 252–253
Flickr, stock images, 220
Flip MinoHD, videos, 246
focus, content development element, 40
fonts, theme building, 107
footers, 17, 324

forms, 321, 330–336
FormSpring, question/answer service, 383
Formstack, 103, 326, 332–335
Forrester, SaaS solutions, 101
forums, 10, 92
FreeFoto.com, stock images, 220
frequency, search engine
  methodology, 165
Frequently Asked Questions (FAQs), 51, 67
FreshBooks, Formstack integration, 335

• G •

Gadgets, Google, and SEO blog, 37–38
gadgets, versus widgets, 108
gaming the system, search engine
  optimization (SEO), 197
GarageBand, audio, 244
General Electric, SaaS solutions, 101
geocoding, map location adjustments, 194
geographic searches, 186–187
geographics, 34, 191–195
Getty Images, stock photos, 300
ghostblogging, 123–126
giveaways, audience building, 385–386
glossary, knowledge base component, 67
Glover, Megan, Compendium Marketing
  Director, 144
goals
  analytics, 353–356
  authority building, 64
  conversions, 50, 57–61
  defining, 49–50
  landing page, 322
  objectives, 50, 62–63
  return on investment (ROI), 50, 52–57
  search engine keyword ranking, 64–65
  target audience, 50–52
  team member expectations, 145–146
  team member vision, 155
Godin, Seth, blog reviews, 94–95
Godley, John, Redirection plug-in, 87
Google
  External Keyword Tool, 284–285
  feed readers, 257
  gadgets, 108–109
  headline titles, 202
  keyword research, 182–184

local search registration, 193
manual registration, 188
Page Speed plug-in, 291
ranking algorithms, 95
search engine methodologies, 165
site search, 187–188
Google AdWords Keyword Tool, 183–184
Google AdWords, search traffic, 54–56
Google Alerts, 134–135, 361
Google Analytics
  analytics platform, 337
  author tracking, 157–159
  benchmarks, 292–294, 346
  bounce rate viewing, 289–290
  call-to-action tracking, 290–291
  campaign code, 275, 304–305
  campaign performance viewing, 307–308
  click event captures, 354–355
  conversion tracking reports, 355–356
  conversions, 346
  cookie expiration times, 352
  event tracking, 346
  filters, 302–303
  goal building, 305–307
  goal viewing, 353
  keyword research, 181–182
  limitations, 28
  multiple subdomain tracking, 210–211
  `onclick` events, 302–304
  profiles, 302–304
  pros/cons, 338
  referring site filters, 349–350
  sales funnel building, 305–307
  screen resolution tracking, 107
  Site Overlay tool, 315–316
  Site Search, 344–345
  `trackPageview` event, 302–304
  traffic source viewing, 58
  viewing traffic sources, 348–349
  visitor statistics, 23–24
Google Analytics URL Builder, 304–305
Google Apps, Formstack integration, 335
Google Blog Search, 229–230, 381
Google Chrome, Speed Tracer, 291
Google FeedBurner, 363–364
Google Friend Connect, 388
Google Local Business Center, 193–195
Google Maps, 191–195

Google Reader, 120–121, 257
Google Trends, 184, 200
Google Webmasters. *See also* Webmasters
  keyword placement identification,
    285–287
  Page Not Found error tracking, 88
  resubmitting sitemaps, 88
  site analysis, 188
  sitemap verification, 172–174
  visitor tracking, 59–60
Google Website Optimizer, 309
Google XML Sitemaps, WordPress plug-in,
  170–171
Graham-Leach-Bliley Act (GLBA), 137
Gravity Forms plug-in
  automating customer testimonials,
    238–239
  form builder, 335
guerilla marketing, 269–270
guest bloggers
  backup contents, 148
  blogosphere interaction method, 258–259
  e-mail targeting, 232–233
  expert solicitations, 234–235
  industry blogger searches, 227–233
  momentum sustaining tactic, 227–229
  permissions, 233–234
  post trading, 233–234, 381
Guides Concerning the Use of
  Endorsements and Testimonials in
  Advertising 136

• H •

hackers, content protections, 133
Hanapin Marketing, 379
hashtags, tweets, 262, 264
headers, front-end element, 16–17
heading tags, 104–105, 176
headline titles, 201–204
headlines, 199. *See also* post titles
Health Insurance Portability and
  Accountability Act (HIPPA), 137
healthcare industry, patient rights, 153
Healthcare Insurance Portability and
  Accounting Act, blog restrictions, 39
heat-maps, 315–316
height, image formatting, 218–219

Highrise, Formstack integration, 335
Holland, Anne, Which Test Won blog, 308
home page, 104, 252–253, 367–368
hosted solutions, 97–98
hosting platforms, 26
HP Community blog, 11
htaccess file, redirects, 87
human resources, team members, 143
humanization, testimonial guidelines, 69
Hypertext Markup Language (HTML)
   content placement, 177
   meta tags, 393
   page title versus post title, 204–205
   search engine component, 104–105

• I •

IBM, Social Computing Guidelines, 43
IGoDigital, ad serving engine, 313–314
image alt tags, 177–178
images, 214–220, 300
Imavex, advertising agency, 379
iMovie, videos, 246
impressions, visitor counts, 313
inbound marketing, 12–13, 31, 84
incoming links, 41–42
indexes, content keywords, 209–213
industry articles, publishing, 23
industry bloggers, 128–129, 229–234
industry blogs, 51, 257, 381
industry experts, guest blogger, 234–235
industry news, 66, 148
industry professionals, 15
information captures, 329–335
instances, versus trends, 289–292
integration blogs, target audience, 51
intellectual property, 155
Intense Debate, 241, 392
internal links, 177, 304–305
internal searches, content reignition, 396
Internet Information Services (IIS), 87
introduction, whitepaper component, 327
iPhones, 108
iPods, 108
is.gd, URL shortener service, 261
iSites, iPhone application building, 387
iStockphoto, 300
iTunes Store, podcast registration, 244–245

• J •

JavaScript, 113, 310–312
Jones, Barbara, Stellar Thoughts blog, 244
JournalSpace, content sabotage, 130
JS-Kit Echo, commenting system, 103, 241

• K •

KA+A blog, home page post, 367–368
Kahlow, Aaron, Online Marketing
   Summit, 74
Kawasaki, Guy, blog reviews, 94–95
keyword competitiveness, 179–180
keyword density, 167
Keyword Discovery, 184
Keyword Spy, keyword research tool, 184
keyword stuffing, 167, 210
keywords
   alternative text, 215
   analytics, 342
   content element, 24–25
   content enhancements, 393–394
   keyword stuffing, 210
   meta descriptions, 185
   meta tagging, 166
   page title, 206–207
   placement identification, 285–287
   post title, 206–207
   research tools, 180–184
   sales effects, 284–285
   search engine emphasis, 176–179
   search engine goals, 64–65
   search engine indexing, 209–213
   search engine optimization, 27–28
   search traffic evaluation, 54–57
   synonymous keyword terms, 212–213
   Tag Cloud widget, 19–20
   tag clouds, 395–396
   target audience identifying, 50–51
   testimonial guidelines, 69
   trending topics, 184, 200
   visitor tracking, 59–60
kinesthetic, learning type, 243
KML files, geographic locations, 192–193
knowledge base, 31, 35, 67
Konfabulator, widgets developer, 108
Kyle Lacy blog, 114–115

• L •

landing pages
  case studies, 328
  contents, 323–329
  conversion analytics, 359–360
  conversion tactics, 61
  customer relationship management
    (CRM) integration, 332
  design guidelines, 320–323
  footers, 324
  goals, 322
  information captures, 329–335
  information for benefits tradeoffs, 325
  information guidelines, 324–325
  layouts, 322–323
  reader destination types, 319
  registration downloads, 326
  registration whitepapers, 326–328
  third-party forms, 332–335
  Webinars, 328–329
languages, analytics, 346–347
layouts, 314–315, 322–323
leadership, 44–45, 142
leadership blogs, target audience, 51
leads, analytics, 358
lead-to-close ratio, analytics, 357
length of visit, analytics, 344
Lifeline Data Center blog, 78–79, 299
Like button, Facebook, 372
link baiting, 184, 200, 383–384
LinkedIn
  blog publishing, 372–373
  blog syndication, 264–265
  employee guidelines, 154
  member's group identification, 256
  social media integration, 383
links
  backlinking, 128, 186, 282–285
  bounce stopping strategy, 289
  conversion tactics, 60
  customer testimonials, 236
  deep linking, 186, 289, 390
  e-mail signatures, 368–369
  incoming, 41–42
  link baiting, 200, 383–384
  reciprocal posts, 41–42
  Related Post plug-in, 20–21

  third-party applications, 360–362
  unfound, 189
Linux, htaccess file, 87
lists, contents, 221
local searches, 186–187, 193
logos, header element, 16
long-tail keywords, 180
Lorelle, WordPress plug-ins, 392
Los Angles Times, SaaS solutions, 101
loyalty, analytics, 341
Lydia's Uniforms blog, 237

• M •

MailChimp, 103, 119, 271–273, 333
MailChimps Analytics, 360, 119
mailing address, 23, 194
manifesto, blogging guidelines, 43
maps, 191–195
marketing blogs, target audience, 51
marketing department, 45, 142
marketing leads, blogging use, 11
marketing platforms, 11–12
Marketing Technology blog, 95, 151,
    228–229
MediaTemple, cloud services, 95
message, landing page element, 321
meta data, search engines, 166
meta descriptions, 176, 185–186, 393
meta keywords, 176
meta tags, 166, 393
micro formats, map services, 193
microphones, Blue Microphones, 244
mobile CSS, theme building, 108
mobile devices, 108, 347
moderated comments, 240–241
morgueFile, stock images, 220
Most Recent Search Phrases Report, 55
motivations, team members, 159–161
Movable Type, 92
multimedia, 243–250
multivariate versus A/B testing, 309

• N •

names, testimonial guidelines, 69
navigation menu, header element, 16
Navigator.com, feed readers, 257

negative criticism, response, 259–260
new blog posts, 389–391
new visits, analytics, 340
news releases, 66
newsletters, online publishing, 23
Ning social networks, Twitter, 383
Notepad, robots.txt file, 168–169
notes, blog element tracking, 317

• O •

objectibes, post title writing, 198
objectives, 50–62–63
offers, 195, 321
old contents, reignition, 391–392
Omniture, analytics platform, 337
onclick events, calls-to-action, 302–305
online marketing, 10
OnlyWite, social bookmarking, 269
open forums, blogging benefit, 35
ordered lists, contents, 221
organic results, 282
overview, 327–328
owners, content planning, 147

• P •

padding, image space, 219
Paden, James, conversion optimization
    expert, 320
page load times, 291
Page Speed plug-in, 291
page title tags, 104
page titles, 176–178, 204–207
page views, 20
page-load times, 115–116
pages per visit, analytics, 343
pageviews, 57, 302–304, 343
Paint, resizing images, 218–219
Panopta, blog monitoring, 133
paragraphs, sizing, 221–222
partners, authority building, 238–239
partnership blogs, target audience, 51
pay per click (PPC), 179, 378–379
Pay Per Post, blog reviews, 379–380
PDAs, 108
performance evaluation, 344–346
permissions, 69, 233–238

personal blogs, versus corporate blogs,
    13–16
personal facts, 69
philanthropy blogs, 51
phone numbers, 323–324
photographs, 69
photos, customer testimonials, 236
PHP, redirects, 87
phrases, synonymous terms, 212–213
PicApp, stock images, 220
Ping.fm, 268–269, 383
pingdom, 116, 133, 291–292
pings, search engine contacts, 166–168
platforms, 26–27, 50, 346–347
Plaxo, blog syndication, 264–265
plug-ins
    blog functionality enhancement, 20–21
    performance testing, 115–116
    WordPress installation, 110–113
Podbean.com, 244
podcasts, 243–245
portraits, corporate identity element,
    79–80
post pages, canonical URLs, 173–175
post prefix, Twitter syndication, 262
post slugs, keyword emphasis, 176
post titles. *See also* headlines
    bounce stopping strategy, 290
    headline writing, 199
    keyword emphasis, 177–178
    keywords, 206–207
    link baiting, 200
    modifying, 392
    page title formatting, 204–205
    versus page titles, 204–205
    search engine optimization, 186
    search engine results page (SERP),
        201–204
    writing objectives, 198
PostPost plug-in, 121–122
PostRank, 128, 230–231, 375
PostRank Labs, Top Posts Widget, 392
posts
    analytic evaluations, 356–360
    blockquotes, 42–43
    content ideas, 47
    conversion tactics, 61
    customer testimonials, 235–238

formatting for comprehension, 220–222
front-end element, 16–17
guest posting, 258–259
home page publishing, 367–368
industry blogs, 381
negative criticism response, 259–260
reciprocal, 41–42
Related Post plug-in, 20–21
removing dates, 394–395
respectful dissent, 259
search engine authority building, 84–85
search engine ranking modifications, 186
social bookmarking promotion, 267–270
sticky posts, 79
trackbacks, 41
trading between blogs, 233–234, 381
pound sign (#) character, 262, 264
PowerPoint presentations, 148, 249–250
prequalification, information captures, 330
press releases, 35, 47
print media, 374–375
privacy laws, content protection, 137–138
problems, case study, 328
ProBlogger, 152
problogservice, ghostwriting service, 125
product information, 34–35
professional writers, 124–126
program conversion rate, 359
progressive disclosure, calls-to-action, 301
promotional budget, analytics, 357
promotions
    audience building, 385–386
    awards submissions, 375–376
    blog subscriptions, 275
    business cards, 370
    company publications, 373
    conversion rate, 359
    customer communications activity, 66
    e-mail signatures, 370
    Facebook publishing, 370–372
    internal searches, 396
    LinkedIn publishing, 372–373
    other blog's comments, 373–374, 382
    print media, 374–375
    recognition submissions, 375–376
    social bookmarking, 267–270
    Twitter posts, 370
prospects, target audience, 15, 16

PubClip, podcasting services, 244
public relations blogs, 51
public relations department, 10, 44–45, 142
public speaking, booking engagements, 22
publication date, post element, 16
publication schedules, 37–39

• *Q* •

questions, application programming
    interface (API), 21
quote characters, testimonials, 236

• *R* •

Radian6, 28–29, 361
Radious Digital Content Services, 126–127
raffles, customer reviews, 195
Raven Tools, keyword research tool, 184
real estate sales, 22
Really Simple Syndication (RSS). *See also*
    syndication
  analytics, 362–364
  content integration, 119–121
  e-mail integration, 271–272
  feed standards, 362
  front-end element, 17
  home page contents, 252–253
  PostPost plug-in, 121–122
  redirects, 88
  server-side pages, 254–255
  static pages, 252–254
Recent Posts plug-in, 289
reciprocal posts, 41–42
recognition awards, 375–376
Reddit, bookmarking site, 268
Redirection plug-in, redirects, 87
redirects, 86–88, 261–263
referring site, 341–342, 348–350
referring traffic, visitor type, 57
regional searches, map services, 191–195
registration downloads, 326
registration forms, 319
registration whitepapers, 326–328
registrations, search engines, 187–191
Related or Most Commented Posts, 122
Related Post, 20–21, 290
relevance, search engine methodology, 165

repetition, keyword emphasis, 177

request forms, landing page type, 319

resolutions, screen width/audience matching, 107

respectful dissent, readership building, 259

return on blogging investment (ROBI), 358

return on investment (ROI)

  blogging strategies, 33–35

  cost per blogging lead evaluation, 54

  formulas, 52–54

  goal setting element, 50

  search traffic evaluation, 54–57

returning visits, analytics, 340

Retweet Button, 388

revenue per lead, analytics, 358

reviews, Pay Per Post, 379–380

rewards, team members, 159–161

`robots.txt` file, search engines, 167–169

Rowse, Darren, ProBlogger blog, 152

• S •

Safe Harbor, 137

sales department, team members, 142

sales funnel, 280–285

sales leads, 23, 357–358

sales value, analytics, 360

Salesforce, 100–102, 335

Schwartz, Jonathan, Sun Microsystems CEO, 51

Scoble, Robert, Microsoft blogger, 37

ScoutLabs, social media monitoring, 361

screen widths, theme building, 107

Scribe, feedback service, 394

search conversion rate, analytics, 359

search engine authority, 82–88, 128

search engine optimization (SEO)

  backlinking, 186

  comment additions, 186

  contents, 64–65, 186

  deep linking, 186

  gaming the system, 197

  HTML component rankings, 104–105

  meta descriptions, 186

  post titles, 186

  subdomains, 89

  subheadings, 186

  synonymous terms, 186

search engine results page (SERP)

  advertising placement, 54

  conversions, 281–282

  mapping searches, 192

  organic results, 282

  post titles, 201–204

  subdomains, 89

search engine traffic, 57, 295, 342

search engines

  canonical URLs, 173–175

  contact pings, 166–168

  content keyword indexing, 209–213

  content keywords, 24–25

  customer reviews, 194–195

  duplicate content, 173–175

  frequency methodology, 165

  HTML component rankings, 104–105

  keyword competitiveness, 179–180

  keyword density, 167

  keyword emphasis, 176–179

  keyword ranking goals, 64–65

  keyword research, 27–28, 180–184

  keyword stuffing, 167

  long-tail keywords, 180

  marketing platform, 11–12

  meta data, 166

  meta tagging, 166

  optimized content, 27–28

  organic search results, 32–33

  popularity methodology, 165

  post modifications, 186

  rank monitoring, 190–191

  recency methodology, 165

  registration process, 187–191

  relevance methodology, 165

  results page, 201–204

  `robots.txt` file, 167, 168–169

  sitemaps, 166–168, 170–173

  social bookmarking impact, 268

  synonymous terms, 212–213

  target audience identifying, 50–51

  traffic source analytics, 347

  visitor tracking, 59–60

search fields, front-end element, 17

search traffic, 54–57, 282–285

self-hosted solutions, 98–100

Semper Fi Designs, 175

SEMRush, 184, 203, 212, 390

SEO Book, keyword research tool, 184
SEO Browser, page testing, 105–106, 177
SEO Post Link plug-in, 206
SEO Researcher, 282–283
SEOmoz, 176, 180
SEOPivot, post title modifications, 392
serif fonts, theme building, 108
server-side packages, 339
server-side pages, 254–255
shareholders, target audience source, 15
ShareThis, social bookmarking, 269, 383
Shoemoney, Jeremy, online marketer,
    377–378
shopping carts, landing page type, 319
showcase, blogging benefit, 31
sidebars, 16–17, 19–20, 112–113, 314–315
signatures, e-mail, 368–369
Site Explorer. *See* Yahoo! Site Explorer
Site Overlay tool, click statistics, 315–316
site overlay, 344
site references, 341–342
site search, 344–345
sitemaps, 88, 166–168, 170–174
SlideShare, 152, 249–250, 265
Slingshot SEO, 228
SOBCon, educational opportunity, 151
social bookmarking, 267–270
Social Computing Guidelines, 43
social media
  backtweets, 361
  blog integration, 260–266
  blogging use, 10
  employee guidelines, 154
  referral source, 349–351
  target audience building, 382–383
  URL shorteners, 261–262
Social Media Explorer blog, 152
social media traffic, 295
social networks, 22, 395
Socializer 2.0, social bookmarking, 268
Software as a Service (SaaS), 100–102
solutions, case study element, 328
South by Southwest, 151
spam, 41, 240–241
"Spec" work, blog designer issues, 75
specials, customer communications, 66
speeches, backup contents, 148
Speed Tracer, page load time, 291

split, versus multivariate testing, 309
splogs, 132
spreadsheets, 190–191, 317
SpyFu, 212
Squarespace, 87–88
static pages, 253–254
Stellar Thoughts blog, 244
sticky posts, profile displays, 79
Stock.XCHNG, stock images, 220
stockholders, information platform, 22, 34
stories, testimonial guidelines, 69
Streamotor, video hosting service, 247
StumbleUpon, 268, 350–351
subdomains, domain structure, 88–90
subfolders, versus subdomains, 90
subheadings, 177, 186
submission forms, landing page type, 319
subscription forms, 319, 330–331
Sun Microsystems, blog example, 51–53
supplemental blogging, 123
supporting information, whitepaper, 327
syndication. *See also* really simple
    syndication (RSS)
  content integration, 119–121
  Facebook integration, 265–266
  LinkedIn, 264–265
  Plaxo, 264–265
  promotional method, 386–387
  Twitter, 262–264
synonymous terms, 186, 212–213

● *T* ●

Tag Cloud, keywords widgets, 19–20
tag clouds, 395–396
tags
  alt, 215
  blockquotes, 42–43
  HTML component rankings, 104–105
  meta descriptions, 393
  widget identification, 113
Tampa Bay blog, 62–63
target audience. *See also* visitors
  blog reviews, 379–380
  blogging benefit, 35
  comment posts, 381
  defining, 50–52
  giveaways, 385–386

target audience *(continued)*
  goal setting element, 50
  link baiting, 383–384
  multiple blog benefits, 51
  pay-per-click, 378–379
  promotions, 385–386
  screen width guidelines, 107
  social media traffic, 382–383
  sources, 15
  specialty blogs, 51
  visitor statistic analytics, 23–24
team members
  analytics, 156–159
  autonomy balancing, 155–156
  backups, 37
  content planning, 146–150
  content versus traffic/conversions, 156
  customer service, 142–143
  desirable traits, 142–143
  education programs, 151–152
  expectations, 145–146, 155–156
  goal setting, 155
  human resources, 143
  individualism issues, 155–156
  intellectual property guidelines, 155
  leadership, 142
  marketing department, 142
  marketing strategy, 144
  motivations/rewards, 159–161
  policy development, 153–155
  poor performance handling, 159
  public relations, 142
  recruiting, 25–26
  recruitment, 143–144
  sales department, 142
  selection guidelines, 37
  social media guidelines, 154
technology consultants, 22
Technorati128–129, 232–233, 375
templates, 102–108
Terms of Service, 17, 130, 138–139
testimonials, 67–69, 148
text alerts, Text Messaging plug-in, 118
text editors, robots.txt file, 168–169
Text Messaging, Connective Mobile, 118
text, background guidelines, 106
Theis, Doug, Lifeline Data Centers, 78

themes
  audience/width matching, 107
  corporate identity, 76–77
  FeedBurner modifications, 364
  fonts, 107
  mobile devices, 108
  serif fonts, 108
  text backgrounds, 106
  white space, 108
third-party
  ad serving systems, 313–314
  blogging, 123
  forms, 332–335
  keyword tools, 184
  services, comments, 241–242
time on site, analytics, 344
timelines, content planning, 147
TinyURL, URL shortener, 261, 360
titles, 16, 262, 328
title tags, search engine rankings, 104
Top Posts widget, blog posts, 392
topics, 147, 207–209
total budget, analytics, 357
Tough Jobs blog, 68
tr.im, URL shortener service, 261
trackbacks, blog posts, 41
tracking reports, conversions, 355–356
trackPageview event, 302–304
Trackur, social media monitoring, 361
traffic sources, analytics, 347–351
trending topics, 184, 200
trends, versus instances, 289–292
Tweetmeme, 383, 388
tweets, hashtags, 262, 264
TwelveStars Media blog, videos, 247
Twitter
  Backtweets, 361
  blog incorporation, 382–383
  blog syndication, 262–264
  communications tool, 10
  employee guidelines, 154
  Facebook Twitter integration, 382
  hashtags, 262, 264
  Ning social network integration, 383
  promotion posts, 370
  URL shorteners, 261–262
  WP Greet Box plug-in, 295

Twitter Trends, 200
Twitterfeed, blog syndication, 262–264
TypePad
  cascading style sheets (CSS) support, 76
  Formstack integration, 335
  hosted software solutions, 97–98
  personal/publication blogs, 92
  sitemap building, 170
  subdomain provider, 81
TypePad AntiSpam, 240–241
TypePad Business, 26, 92, 101–102

• *U* •

U.S. Department of Commerce, Safe
    Harbor, 137
Uniform Resource Locator (URL), 176,
    261–262
unique visitors, analytics, 341
United States, privacy laws, 137–138
universal commenting systems, 392
Unix, htaccess file, 87
unmoderated comments, avoidance
    reasons, 240
upselling, 35, 66
Uptrends, blog monitoring, 133
URL shorteners, 261–262, 360–362
USA Today, SaaS solutions, 101
user generated content (UGC), 242,
    391–392
user interface, blog elements, 16–18
user-agents, robots.txt file, 168–169

• *V* •

vacations, content planning, 148–151
vendors, authority building, 238–239
Veotag, podcasting, 243–244
Viddler, video hosting, 249
videos
  Backlight, 117
  blogging benefit, 35
  content enhancements, 214
  content incorporation, 245–247
  hosting services, 247–250
  testimonial guidelines, 69
vision statement, goal setting, 155

Visit Tampa Bay blog, 253–254
visit, versus pageviews, 57
visitor engagement, 61
visitor statistics, 23–24
visitors. *See also* target audience
  abandonment measurement, 331
  analytic application types, 57
  bounce rate, 20, 288–291
  clickbait, 301
  exit rate, 288
  Google Webmaster analytics, 59–60
  heat-maps, 315–316
  impressions, 313
  information captures, 329–335
  language needs, 346–347
  learning types, 243
  platform needs, 346–347
  tracking, 340–341
visits, analytics, 340
visual, learning type, 243
Vocus, public relations firm, 234
voice, 31, 44–45, 235–238
Vox, personal/publication blogs, 92

• *W* •

Walker Information blog, 36, 76–78,
    374–375
Walls, Rocky, TwelveStars Media, 247
Web 2.0 Summit, 151
Web pages, 189–190
Web presence, corporate identity, 74–75
Web sites
  Address Fix, 192
  Akismet, 241
  All in One SEO Pack plug-in, 392
  Alterian Webjourney, 337
  Author plug-in, 121–122
  Authority Labs, 191
  Auto Social, 268
  Backlight, 247
  bit.ly, 361
  BittBox, 300
  block quote examples, 236
  Blog World & New Media Expo, 151
  BlogBloke, 207
  BlogCatalog, 230–231, 388
  Blogger, 97

Web sites *(continued)*
BlogRank, 230, 232
versus blogs, 10–13
Cantaloupe, 117, 246
ChaCha.me, 21
Clicky, 115, 337
Compendium, 393
Compendium Blogware, 18, 93, 170
Connective Mobile, 118
contrarian blogging, 259
CoreMetrics, 337
Corporate Blogging Tips, 151
Creative Commons, 138
Crowd Favorite, 347
CrowdSPRING, 75
CSS Tricks, 236
De Valk, Joost, 175
DemandBase, 313
Digg, 267
Disqus, 392
Dreamstime, 220
Echo, 392
edublogs, 93
ExactTarget, 100, 274
Facebook, 382
Facebook Fan Pages, 388
Facebook Like button, 372, 388
Fairyfish.net, 390
Federal Trade Commission, 129, 153
Feedburner, 132, 276
Flexware Innovation, 252
Flickr, 220
Flip MinoHD, 246
Formstack, 326, 332
FreeFoto.com, 220
GarageBand, 244
geographic micro formats, 193
Getty Images, 300
Google Analytics, 24, 275, 289, 337
Google Blog Search, 229, 381
Google FeedBurner, 363
Google Friend Connect, 388
Google Reader, 120, 257
Google Webmasters, 172, 285
Google XML Sitemaps, 170
Gravity Forms, 335
healthcare industry requirements, 153

IBM's Social Computing Guidelines, 43
IGoDigital, 313–314
iMovie, 246
Intense Debate, 392
iSites, 387
iStockphoto, 300
iTunes Store, 244
Jeremy Shoemoney, 377
John Chow, 377
kaplusa.com, 367
Keyword Discovery, 184
Keyword Spy, 184
Lifeline Data Centers, 78–79
Lorelle, 392
MailChimp, 119, 271
morgueFile, 220
99designs, 75
Omniture, 337
online marketing brochures, 10
Online Marketing Summit, 74
PicApp, 220
Ping.fm, 268
Pingdom, 116, 133, 291
Podbean.com, 244
PostPost plug-in, 122
PostRank, 128, 230, 392
problogservice, 125
PubClip, 244
Radian6, 29
Radious Digital Content Services, 126
Raven Tools, 184
Reddit, 268
Related or Most Commented Posts, 122
Retweet Button widget, 388
Safe Harbor, 137
Salesforce, 100
Scribe, 394
SEMRush, 184, 203, 212
SEO Book, 184
SEO Browser, 105, 177
SEO Post Link, 206
SEO Researcher, 282
SEOmoz, 180, 190
SEOPivot, 392
Sitemap protocol, 170
SlideShare, 152, 249, 265
Slingshot SEO, 228

SOBCon, 151
Socializer 2.0, 268
South by Southwest, 151
splogs, 132
SpyFu, 212
Stock.XCHNG, 220
Streamotor, 247
StumbleUpon, 268
Technorati, 128, 232–233
Tweetmeme, 388
Twitter widgets, 254
TypePad, 97, 170
TypePad AntiSpam, 241
TypePad Business, 101
Veotag, 243
Viddler, 249
Vocus, 234
Web 2.0 Summit, 151
Web Robots Pages, 168
Webtracker, 184
Webtrends, 115, 274, 337
Whois service, 135
Widen, 247
Windows Live Movie Maker, 246
WordCamp, 151
WordPress, 97, 170
WordPress Widgets Administration, 19
Wordze, 184
Yahoo!, 154, 337
Zemanta, 395
Web to Post, Compendium Blogware, 68,
    237–238
Webinars, 66, 228–229
Webmasters. *See also* Bing Webmasters;
    Google Webmasters
  keyword research tool, 180–181
  non-appearance in search results, 190
  rank monitoring, 190–191
  timed out pages, 189
  unfound links, 189
  unreachable pages, 189–190
Webmetrics, blog monitoring, 133
Webtracker, keyword research tool, 184
Webtrends
  analytics platform, 110, 337
  author analytics, 157
  keyword research, 182–183

Most Recent Search Phrases Report, 55
multiple blogs example, 34
Offsite Links report, 115
Radian6 integration, 28–29
real-time analytics, 28
tag builder, 274
Web analytics, 22
Webtrends OnDemand, 350–351
Webtrends Optimize, 309
weekends, content planning, 148–151
Which Test Won blog, 308
whitepapers
  backup contents, 148
  landing page registration, 326–328
  online/offline publishing, 23
  promotional method, 386
  writing guidelines, 327
whitespace, 108, 214, 221
Whois service, domain search, 135
why it matters, whitepaper
    component, 327
Widen, hosting service, 247–248
widgets
  Asynchronous JavaScript and XML
    (AJAX), 116
  blog functionality enhancement, 19–20
  BlogCatalog, 388
  distraction avoidance, 113–115
  Facebook Fan Pages, 388
  Facebook Like buttons, 388
  Flash identification, 113
  versus gadgets, 108
  Google Friend Connect, 388
  JavaScript identification, 113
  performance testing, 115–116
  Related Post plug-in, 20–21
  Retweet Button, 388
  server-side page syndication, 254–255
  sidebar element, 19–20
  Tag Cloud, 19–20
  Tweetmeme, 388
  word-of-mouth, 388
  WordPress installation, 112–113
width, image formatting, 218–219
Windows, gadgets, 108
Windows Live Movie Maker, 246
Windows Live Writer, 238

WordCamp, 151
word-of-mouth widgets, 388
WordPress
  All in One SEO Pack, 175, 206, 392
  application programming interface (API)
    addition, 21
  Author plug-in, 121–122
  author tracking, 157–159
  Auto Social plug-in, 268
  bbPress forums, 92
  blog scheduling, 149–150
  BuddyPress social network, 92
  canonical URL plug-in, 175
  cascading style sheets (CSS) support, 76
  comment notification, 241
  exporting/importing contents, 131–132
  extensible markup language remote
    procedure call (XML-RPC), 238
  Google Analytics, 157–159
  Google XML Sitemaps, 170–171
  Gravity Forms, 238–239, 335
  hosted software solutions, 97–98
  incoming link checking, 41–42
  keyword meta descriptions, 185
  Like button integration, 372
  Linkedin blog syndication, 264–265
  MailChimp integration, 119
  moving between domains, 86–88
  page title formatting, 207
  personal/publication/corporate blogs, 92
  plug-in installation, 110–113
  PostPost plug-in, 121–122
  Redirection plug-in, 87
  Related or Most Commented Posts, 122
  Related Post plug-in, 20–21
  SEO Post Link plug-in, 206
  sitemap content priorities, 171–172
  subdomain provider, 81
  Tag Cloud widget, 19–20
  tag clouds, 395–396
  Text Messaging plug-in, 118
  versions, 92–93
  Webtrends plug-in, 110
  WordPress Mobile Edition plug-in, 347
WordPress Multi-User (MU), 92–93
WordPress VIP, 26–27, 92
Wordpress.com, 92
WordPress.org, 92, 98–100
Wordze, keyword research tool, 184
WP Greet Box plug-in, 295

Yahoo!
  analytics platform, 337
  blogging policy example, 154
  Delicious bookmarking system, 267
  local search registration, 193
  manual registration, 188
  site search, 187–188
  widgets, 108
Yahoo! Developer Network, 291
Yahoo! Maps, 191–195
Yahoo! Site Explorer
  keyword research tool, 180
  Page Not Found error tracking, 88
  site analysis, 188
  visitor tracking, 59
YSlow, page load time, 291

• **Z** •

Zawodney, Jeremy, blogging policy, 154
Zemanta, content enhancements, 395–396